Part One of

THE CANADIANS 1867-1967

Toronto   Macmillan of Canada
New York   St. Martin's Press

Edited by

J. M. S. CARELESS and R. CRAIG BROWN

Part One of

THE CANADIANS 1867–1967

This volume is Part One of "The Canadians 1867-1967", first published in 1967 by The Macmillan Company of Canada Limited, Toronto, & St. Martin's Press, New York.

First printed February 1968

Reprinted September 1968

Printed in Canada by the T. H. Best Printing Company Limited
for The Macmillan Company of Canada Limited,
70 Bond Street, Toronto, Ontario

Contents

Illustrations

in the text

(Selected cartoons from the John T. Saywell Collection)

Introduction

Frugal and diligent, parochial and isolated, loyal to empires secular or holy, the people of British North America before 1867 seemed almost to live in a middle ages of their own. They were subjects of a distant imperial Queen-Protector. Their life in the main was rural; the church and family were powerful forces moulding it. Their settlements were small amid a vast wilderness, and they had known invasion and threat of attack from far more powerful American neighbours. Separate colonies had grown in diversity; in discord, above all, between French and English-speaking elements that could only be quietened, not resolved, by never-easy compromise.

Yet compromise became a means to unity for these colonials. Impelled by threat and dissension, they had come by the

1860s to look beyond a mere *modus vivendi* to wider, bolder opportunity, and to one transcontinental nation-state in a future which only they could make. They must reach for it across an empty expanse of prairie and mountain to an ocean so remote that men still journeyed there from eastern North America by rounding Cape Horn. Their new union must bear the birth-mark, lauded or deplored, of the conquest of French by British in 1760, and its citizens must always face the problems of living with the mighty continental power of the United States beside them. Their hope was bold; but the omens were by no means all propitious.

On July 1, 1867, these men of different regions, two languages and cultures, and sharp religious divisions, began their union, a broad confederation under the name of Canada. It was in the keeping of a score of leading colonial politicians, solid worthies in their black frock-coats, who yet had force and fervour in no way hampered by the guise of Victorian respectability. These politicians, in the soberly ordered language of the mid nineteenth century, had drafted terms for a new national entity, one that was already growing and changing as the words were proclaimed law. The federal Canadian authority that was to supply peace, order, and good government and express vital agreement between descendants of two nations, French and British, thrust out over the continent with almost incredible speed. It was like a fresh sail spread on a good wind, bearing the Canadians' Confederation from harbours on the St. Lawrence and Atlantic to Arctic and Pacific waters: to great northern barrens, the sweep of western grassland, and soaring coastal ranges.

The course for the Canadian union continued west and north for years to follow; but gradually long-established conditions seemed to dissolve. Old patterns changed and new emerged: the permanent protecting British Empire subsided and disappeared. The power of Washington and New York replaced it, to aid or involve Canada. Meanwhile railways pierced the western mountain barriers, and the prairies yielded classic riches of grain, then oil. Science and technology, immigration, industry, and dominating cities transformed the ways of an older, simpler, rural society, while the granite vastness of the Precambrian Shield, once the inhospitable core of the ancient Canadian wilderness, offered wealth from deep-cut mines, thick forests, and the reservoirs of countless lakes and streams. The canoes of an earlier Canada were gone; bush planes now anchored by the overgrown portage. And the complex modern country that had emerged faced problems and potentialities scarcely conceivable to the colonial Canadians of a hundred years before.

THE AUTHORS

Donald Creighton, Professor and former Chairman of the Department of History at the University of Toronto, opens the volume with an account of Canada in the 1860s, when Confederation was being shaped. George F. G. Stanley, Dean of Arts and Head of the History Department at Royal Military College, then continues with the 1870s; and W. S. MacNutt, Professor of History at the University of New Brunswick, takes up the 1880s. The 1890s are dealt with by John T. Saywell, Dean of Arts and Science and Professor of History at York University, while the first decade of the new century is treated by H. Blair Neatby, Professor of History at Carleton University.

The years surrounding the First World War are the concern of Roger Graham, Professor of History at the University of Saskatchewan. The 1920s fall to W. L. Morton, formerly Head of History at the University of Manitoba and now Master of Champlain College at Trent University. Kenneth McNaught, Professor of History at the University of Toronto, examines the 1930s. Colonel C. P. Stacey, former Director of the Historical Section of the Canadian General Staff and now Professor of History at the University of Toronto, describes the 1940s, the decade of the Second World War. William Kilbourn, Professor and Chairman of the Humanities Division at York University, deals with the

1950s. And finally Laurier LaPierre, Director of the Institute of French Canadian Studies at McGill University, provides an estimate of the 1960s, with particular reference to French Canada, whose development has assumed such critical significance in this latest decade.

These are the contributors and their chapters which comprise the volume. But one other name must be mentioned. Gordon C. Trent of Toronto originally suggested a centennial work of broad character and scope, and so inspired the present project. The end result of this widely collaborative effort is a history which does not seek to sum up Canadian activities and achievements since Confederation so much as to present their range, variety, and significance. It does so in the belief that whatever failures or shortcomings there may be, the experience of Canadians living and endeavouring together within their union for a century deserves to be remembered and appraised.

J. M. S. Careless
R. Craig Brown

Part One of

THE CANADIANS 1867-1967

1. The 1860s

DONALD CREIGHTON

The 1860s was the decade of the great decision – the decision to found a transcontinental British American nation. It was a greater decision than any that British North America had ever taken before, greater than any it would ever take again: and it was reached only after many hesitations and misgivings and a large amount of anxious argument. The great decision was in fact preceded by the great debate about the future of British America. The debate had its climax in the prolonged and vehement controversy over the plan for a federal union drawn up at the Quebec Conference; but its origins went back to the fears, uncertainties, and questionings that had been inspired by the opening of the American Civil War. The decade as a whole saw the working out of a long process of self-realization and self-determination. British North Americans were far more concerned than they had ever been before about their probable destiny in the New World; and this concern was prompted by an awareness both of their own internal development and of the vastly changed circumstances in which they lived. Two decades before, in the years immediately following the rebellions of 1837, the backwardness and frustration of British America had been obvious. Then the provinces had been small, relatively poor, widely scattered colonial communities, dependent both economically and politically upon Great Britain and limited by the narrow, parochial outlook of the colonial mind. They had come a long way since then. They were more aware than they had been of the promises and perils of the external world, and more curious about the place they might accept in it. They were conscious also of a new sense of maturity.

In 1861, some 3,230,000 British Americans faced what was to be the most critical decade in their history. Measured by the enormous extent of their territorial inheritance they seemed a very small people; and they were distributed unevenly at great intervals across the continent. The vast majority–approximately 2,500,000–lived in the Province of Canada, British America's empire province, the most populous, prosperous, dynamic, and aggressive of the lot. The Canadians outnumbered all other British Americans by three to one: they reduced the populations of the remaining provinces to very small proportions. The two largest–Nova Scotia with 325,000 people and New Brunswick with 250,000–seemed tiny communities in comparison; and the others were even smaller. Newfoundland, where persistent efforts had been made to limit the number of inhabitants for the benefit of visiting fishermen, had considerably fewer than 150,000 settlers; and Prince Edward Island, with a population of about 80,000, was smaller than the largest of the Canadian towns, Montreal. In the North-west and on the Pacific coast, where settlement had occupied only a tiny fraction of the vast and empty wilderness, the disparities were even more startling. The little company of whites and half-breeds at the junction of the Red and Assiniboine rivers numbered fewer than 10,000; and the population of the two small colonies on the Pacific coast, British Columbia and Vancouver Island, did not greatly exceed that total.

The two founding peoples of British America were the French who had remained in Canada after the Conquest and the English-speaking North Americans who had come up from the Thirteen Colonies before, during, and after the American Revolution. These first settlers had been outnumbered, though not submerged, by the huge, successive waves of immigrants which had kept flooding in from the British Isles ever since 1820. English and Scots had come in large and not unequal numbers; but the massive 'famine' migrations of the 1840s had left the Irish the largest of the three British groups. There were a few Germans and a good many Gaelic-speaking Scots; but British North America was, on the whole, a community of two languages, rather than a babel of many strange tongues. The French-speaking Canadians and the Acadians of the Maritime Provinces were remarkably homogeneous peoples; but the English-speaking communities, settled by Celts and Saxons, Protestants and Roman Catholics, Britishers and North Americans, were mixtures of incredible complexity and diversity.

It was a rural rather than an urban population. In 1861, Montreal was a city of 90,000 people, Toronto only half that size; and the Maritime towns, including the provincial capitals, were still smaller. Most British Americans lived in small villages or the open countryside, and farmed, fished, built ships, milled flour, or worked in lumber camps for a living. The provinces concentrated upon the production of a few basic staple products for export to more industrialized nations; and ever since the decline of the fur trade, early in the nineteenth century, the principal export staples had been wheat, flour, fish, timber, and lumber. In the past, ocean, lake, and river had been the chief avenues of transport; and wind- and water-power had driven the ships, moved the timber rafts, and worked the grist-mills and the sawmills. But now this old state of affairs was perceptibly changing.

The steam-engine, the railway, and the new machinery were diversifying the character, increasing the production, and hastening the transport of Canadian industry.

The industrial revolution first entered British America on the wheels of the new transport. Nova Scotia and New Brunswick each built short, provincially owned railways; Canada preferred to subsidize commercial companies, of which the most ambitious was the Grand Trunk Railway, an enormous system that ran all the way from Portland in the State of Maine to Sarnia on Lake Huron. Steamships were beginning to supplant sailing vessels on the Great Lakes, the St. Lawrence River, and in the passenger traffic between the Maritime Provinces, though neither Nova Scotians nor New Brunswickers ever succeeded in adapting their skills in wooden-ship building to the construction of the iron, steam-driven vessel of the future. Steam was also rapidly overtaking water-power as the main motive force in the saw-milling industry, and to a much lesser extent in flour-milling. Grist-mills and sawmills, which were linked so closely to the old staple trades, still accounted for over forty per cent of British American manufacturing in the 1860s; but the larger provinces, and particularly Canada, had already ventured into newer types of production – agricultural implements, tools, machines, and a variety of consumer goods – that would have been unheard of a generation earlier.

Yet, despite the advent of the new industrialism, British America still tended to think instinctively in terms of the old commercial age in which it had grown up. In the eyes of both Canadians and Maritimers, British America was a staple-producing economy whose prosperity depended upon the export of a few bulky, primary commodities, on highly preferential terms, to more mature industrialized nations. Great Britain's old Colonial system, with its tariff preferences and shipping monopolies, had given the northern provinces a very privileged place in imperial markets; and when, in 1846, the British adoption of free trade brought an end to these historic advantages, the first instinctive move of the British American merchants was to seek a comparable preferential treatment in the United States. The Reciprocity Treaty of 1854, which established free trade between the provinces and the United States in all major natural products, realized this aim successfully; and to many Canadians and Maritimers the Reciprocity Treaty came to seem the main basis of the prosperity which, with one great interruption, was to last for the next dozen years.

Yet the old commercial strategy did not dominate British American thinking and planning in quite the same way as it had done a generation before. The northern provinces were becoming far more conscious of themselves as a group of British colonies, far more interested in collective partnerships for a variety of purposes, and far more alive to the importance of their enormous territorial inheritance on the North American continent. In the past, British Americans had been inclined to consider that common membership in the British Empire was their most significant bond of union; but now, within the last few years, the idea of a British American nation and the ambitious hope of its westward expansion across the continent had awakened the interest of both Maritimers and Canadians. The discovery of gold on the Fraser River had dramatically revealed the great potential importance of the British inheritance on the Pacific slope; the westward drive of American settlement had brought up the portentous question of the future government of the chartered and licensed territories of the Hudson's Bay Company. More than a third of the North American continent lay waiting for occupation and development in the British American north-west; and for the first time the technology of modern industrialism had made its exploitation possible, even by the present generation of British Americans. Railways could make a united, transcontinental nation. The first stage in this giant enterprise–the Intercolonial Railway linking the Maritime Provinces with the St. Lawrence valley –was a practicable project which could be undertaken immediately. The next stage–the railway to the Pacific–was still for many people a dream for the future, though no longer for the far-distant future.

No province felt these importunate urges towards expansion more strongly than the Province of Canada; and no province was less fitted politically to carry them out. In form, Canada was a united province, with a single legislature; in fact, it was an unacknowledged federal system based on the unworkable principle of dualism. Canada East, which was largely French-speaking, and Canada West, which was overwhelmingly English-speaking, had been given equal representation in the provincial legislature; and the division of cabinet posts, the organization of government departments, and the appropriation of government expenditures were decided in general upon the same basis of sectional equality. Dualism ensured an almost chronic state of sectional rivalries and disputes: it also meant small, precarious majorities in parliament, short-lived governments, frequent elections, and a permanent condition of governmental instability. The Province of Canada could hardly govern itself within its existing limits; it was not capable, with its unreformed constitution, of any large expansion whatever.

The decade of the 1850s had been spent in vain attempts to escape from the maddening frustrations of dualism. Broadly speaking, the plans of reform fell into two main categories – the proposals, like George Brown's 'Representation by Population', which would have made the union a real legislative union, and those, on the other hand, which would deepen and formalize the division between the two sections of the Province. Soon it became clear that drastic solutions in either of these two directions were politically impossible. 'Rep. by Pop.', which would have placed French Canada in a hopeless minority in the united legislature, could never be voluntarily accepted by Canada East; and Canada West, which was convinced that it had suffered most from the injustices of dualism, could never quite bring itself to endorse such a desperate remedy as the dissolution of the union. Upper Canadians and Lower Canadians obviously did not enjoy living too closely together; but on the other hand they were not in the least attracted by the prospect of living completely apart. Federalism was the only system that seemed to combine the advantages of both union and separation; and by the end of the 1850s many Canadians were coming reluctantly to the conclusion that the 'federal principle' was probably the only effective remedy for provincial ills. In 1858, the Conservative government, with George E. Cartier and John A. Macdonald as joint leaders, proposed a federation of the whole of British America. In the following year, a convention of the 'Clear Grit' Reformers of Canada West, in which George Brown played a dominating role, adopted a plan for the federal union of the two Canadas. By the end of the decade, projects for two new unions, one national, one provincial, had been presented to the Canadian people.

II

Yet, when the decade of the 1860s opened, it seemed, strangely enough, as if both projects were dead and the great debate over the future of British America had temporarily fallen silent. The Conservative plan for a British American federation had been viewed mainly with indifference or hostility by the other provinces and with disfavour by the British government. The Reform scheme for a small federal union of the two Canadas had never won general acceptance among the party leaders and had foundered among the jealousies and quarrels of Grit politics. The ambitious plans for western settlement and railway building, with which the union schemes had always been associated, seemed also to dwindle into a temporary eclipse. The agitation for the annexation of the North-west, which had aroused such a furor in Canada West only a few years before, faded away into virtual silence; and the project of the Intercolonial Railway, for which plans had been made and re-made repeatedly during the 1850s, had apparently been completely abandoned.

It seemed as if the provinces had temporarily talked themselves out on the subject of political union. But they remained irrepressibly concerned about their future. They could never quite rid themselves of the intimate conviction that this future was to be a collective future; and in 1861, when they least expected it, this belief was confirmed with decisive force and passion. In 1861, the American Civil War broke out; and during the four long years of its duration, the war was to be a potent factor in all British American calculations. It was, in the first place, a spectacle, a thrilling and terrible spectacle for which Maritimers and Canadians occupied front-row seats. It was exciting, but it was something else as well. It was dangerous. British America might possibly become involved, either directly in the conflict itself, or indirectly through one of its unknown but fearful consequences. The thought of involvement was an irrepressible apprehension. At times it almost disappeared in a growing sense of security; at other times it grew suddenly into an expectation of immediate crisis. But it was always there, and it had been lodged in British American hearts and minds, for the duration, at the very beginning of the struggle.

On the 8th of November, not much more than six months after the opening of the war, Captain Charles Wilkes, of the U.S.S. *San Jacinto,* stopped by force the British mail packet *Trent* and took from her two diplomatic agents who were on their way to Europe in the hope of enlisting support for the Southern Confederacy. Neither Great Britain nor the United States wanted to make a war out of this incident. Great Britain had ceased to play the role of a colonial power in North America with any enthusiasm or conviction; and the last thing she desired was a desperate struggle in the new continent for colonies that most Englishmen now regarded as liabilities rather than assets. For the United States, a second war, which would have led almost certainly to the independence of the South, would have been an unrelieved disaster. But England was determined to obtain reparation for Wilkes's affront to her prestige; and the

United States, where the excited populace seemed ready and eager to take on all comers in mortal combat, was unwilling to make too humiliating an apology. For nearly two months the outcome of the dangerous issue rested in suspense. Maritimers and Canadians, who realized that their provinces would inevitably be the first objects of American attack, braced themselves for a terrible encounter.

A remarkable demonstration of British and British American solidarity followed. The imperial government hurriedly dispatched transports bearing a force of nearly 14,000 men – the largest troop movement across the Atlantic since the War of 1812. The provincial governments called up their volunteers and tried to energize their militia units, long enfeebled by neglect and disuse. It was a moment of acute danger and anxiety; but it was also a moment of illumination in which the northern provinces suddenly comprehended their true character and their proper destiny. They realized that they wanted an independent existence in North America. They realized that they wanted to be linked with Great Britain and to remain separate from the United States.

Late in December 1861 the United States restored the captured envoys, though without an apology, and the *Trent* crisis was suddenly over. It had brought British America a moment of self-knowledge rare in its history; but it had by no means clarified or settled the ways and means by which its collective future might be realized. And once the crisis ended, the sense of urgency immediately slackened. The American Civil War was still big with menace; but in 1862-3, when the fortunes of the Confederacy were at their flood-tide, its perils might well seem extremely remote. The South might win its independence – the outcome which most British Americans would have decidedly preferred. Even if it failed, it seemed certain that the conflict was going to be a very long one.

In these circumstances, the creative urge of 1858-9 did not return; the ambitious national planning of these years was not resumed. The provinces seemed to slump back into their accustomed state of provincialism and colonial dependence.

They did little to improve the militia forces whose inadequacy had been so clearly revealed in the crisis of 1861; and to the intense exasperation of the British, the Canadian Militia Bill of 1862, the one serious attempt at military reform that followed the *Trent* affair, was defeated in the Canadian legislature. For years Great Britain had been attempting to transfer some of her North American obligations to the shoulders of colonies that were now so largely self-governing; but British America was still in no hurry to assume the responsibilities of maturity. The provinces still shied away from the burden of their own defence; they were not even doing very much to promote their own internal development. Western expansion, intercolonial railways, and interprovincial trade could only be realized effectively through British American political union. But in 1862 and 1863, Maritimers and Canadians were thinking rather of co-operative effort without political union, or, at any rate, with no more political union than they already enjoyed within the easy and flexible framework of the British Empire. In the Maritime Provinces only a handful of people were giving any thought to political reorganization in British America. In Canada, the principal authors of the plans of 1858-9 had been swept from the political scene. George Brown, who had been defeated in the election of 1861, was temporarily out of politics; and in May 1862, George E. Cartier and John A. Macdonald resigned office after the defeat of their Militia Bill.

The Canadian initiative had been abandoned, and the men who assumed power after the defeat of the Cartier-Macdonald government were not likely to take it up again. These men–John Sandfield Macdonald, Luther Holton, W. P. Howland, L. V. Sicotte, and A. A. Dorion–had no definite policies and few clear political ideas. Apart from the business of staying in power, they had no real purpose in government. Their solutions for the major Canadian problems were essentially negative and temporizing. They proposed to make the unreformed Canadian union work acceptably to both sections of the Province by what was called the 'double majority'–a principle which was supposed to require that government measures should have a legislative majority in the section or sections to which they were intended to apply. The three other principal Canadian projects–defence, western expansion, and the intercolonial railway–would, the ministers declared, be pushed forward cautiously, within the limits imposed by their professed desire for retrenchment and the monotonously repeated deficits of the past few years.

Even this modest program was singularly barren of results. In the actual circumstances of Canadian politics, the 'double majority' could hardly be more than a pious hope; and when the test came, Sandfield Macdonald permitted legislation applying to one section of the Province to be imposed by a majority of the members of the other section in exactly the same way as his predecessors had done. He made some progress with defence, though here he was probably moved less by his own wishes than by the constant urgings of the Governor General, Lord Monck. As for the twin projects of eastern communications and western expansion, they hardly advanced at all. The only way in which Canada could come to grips with the problem of the North-west was by buying out the territorial rights of the Hudson's Bay Company, or by challenging the validity of its charter in the courts; and both these courses were far too heroic for the impoverished Canadian government to take. It even failed in the end to honour an agreement with Nova Scotia and New Brunswick to divide the cost of the construction of the Intercolonial Railway. The British government, which had consented to guarantee the necessary loan, had imposed extremely onerous conditions for the sinking-fund that it required; and the Canadians, pushing their objections to these requirements to the limit, had in the end repudiated the agreement. Canada had not thrown over the whole idea of the Intercolonial; it had simply rejected a particular scheme for the construction. But at the moment the angry Nova Scotians and New Brunswickers were in no mood to notice this distinction.

By the autumn of 1863, two important facts had become

clearly evident: the first was that the attempt to promote western expansion and intercolonial communications without political union had failed; the second was that the hope of continuing the Canadian union without radical constitutional changes had been proved false. The realization of these two truths was the point at which the movement for political union had its beginning in both Canada and the Maritime Provinces. The two advances followed each other fairly rapidly; but it was New Brunswick and Nova Scotia that made the first move. The long-term sense of frustration and dissatisfaction was less acute in the Maritime Provinces than in Canada in the autumn of 1863; but the momentary feeling of injury and disillusionment was keener. In Nova Scotia and New Brunswick, the Canadian repudiation of the Intercolonial agreement of 1862 was regarded as a shocking, an outrageous, blow. 'Canadian perfidy' became the text of numerous angry sermons in which Maritime newspaper editors warned their readers that co-operation with Canada was impossible, that all thought of political union with Canada must be given up, and that henceforth the Maritime Provinces must draw close together and 'go it alone'.

III

It was out of this sense of angry and determined Maritime feeling of solidarity that the movement for a legislative union of the Atlantic provinces began to get under way. Its chief advocate was Arthur Hamilton Gordon, the Lieutenant-Governor of New Brunswick, a young man with very positive opinions on a wide variety of subjects and a strong desire to take a vigorous lead in the political reorganization of British North America. A general union of the northern provinces was, he believed, essential to their preservation independently of the United States; but he had come to the conclusion that such a union would not be feasible until the Intercolonial Railway was built, and the Canadian repudiation of the agreement of 1862 seemed to postpone that prerequisite indefinitely. In the meantime, he considered a smaller union, a legislative union of the Maritime Provinces, could be usefully undertaken, principally for its own sake, but also as a first step to a united British America. He was convinced that provinces as small and underpopulated as Nova Scotia, New Brunswick, and Prince Edward Island were simply overgrown municipalities, that their public affairs were parochial and petty, and that there were far too few men of ability and devotion to administer them. To govern such tiny provinces separately, with the elaborate organization of a provincial parliament in each, was simply to invite expense, inefficiency, corruption, and low buffoonery. The remedy was to unite the three provinces in a single province of some real consequence and genuine dignity.

Gordon's campaign for Maritime union had a certain limited success. He was able to persuade his own Premier, Samuel Leonard Tilley, as well as Charles Tupper, the Premier of Nova Scotia, that his scheme was desirable and might be practicable; but he had little real success with the politicians of Prince Edward Island, though for a time he fondly assumed that they were favourable too. This provincial separatism, the inward-looking parochialism that was such a dominant feature of colonial British America, confronted him everywhere; and nowhere were its manifestations more absurdly exaggerated than in the smallest of all the provinces, Prince Edward Island. During the winter and spring of 1864, all three provincial legislatures–Newfoundland was never included in the planning for Maritime union–passed resolutions empowering their executive governments to nominate delegates to a conference at which Maritime legislative union would be formally considered. But the highly unfriendly and critical reception which the little Island parliament gave to this resolution made the success of the projected Conference look very unlikely from the beginning. Even in Nova Scotia and New Brunswick, very few people seemed enthusiastic about Maritime union; a good many appeared indifferent or actively opposed to it. June 1864 came, and the very date and place of the conference had not been decided. It is quite possible that it would never have been held at all, if it had not been for a revolutionary change which in the meantime had taken place in Canada.

In the year that had elapsed since the general election of June 1863, affairs in the Province of Canada had gone from bad to worse. John Sandfield Macdonald had failed to improve his position in Parliament in the general election; and in March 1864, after vain attempts to secure further support from among the moderate Conservatives of Canada East, his cabinet resigned. A new Conservative government, led by Sir Etienne Taché and John A. Macdonald, took office. Its supporters in the Assembly were distributed in a fashion the opposite of that of the previous administration, for it was weaker in Canada West than in Canada East; but its following as a whole was no greater than that of its predecessor, if as great, and it remained in power by the narrowest and most precarious of margins. George Brown, who had returned to provincial politics in 1863, but in a much less partisan mood than he had ever shown before, had been pressing for the appointment of a parliamentary committee to examine the various possibilities of constitutional reform. The Assembly finally yielded to his persuasions, the committee was established, and on the 14th of June, Brown presented its report. On the very same day, the Taché-Macdonald government was defeated by two votes on a want-of-confidence motion.

The coincidence of the government's defeat and the presentation of the committee's report impressed George Brown deeply. He decided that he would try to take advantage of the first to realize the objects of the second. He let it be known through supporters of the defeated administration that he thought the crisis ought to be utilized to settle for ever the constitutional difficulties between the two sections of the Province, and that he was willing to give his support to this or any other government that would take up this question earnestly and vigorously with a view to its final settlement. The Conservative leaders responded at once to this invitation. A series of conferences between them and

Brown was held, and eight days later, on the 22nd of June, John A. Macdonald and George Cartier announced the formation of a Coalition ministry – a Coalition ministry that would have overwhelming support from both sections of the Province in the Assembly. Its program was constitutional reform through what was called 'the adoption of the federal principle', applied either to British America as a whole, or to the Province of Canada alone. The new government announced that it would first attempt, by sending special missions to the Maritime Provinces and England, to carry out the larger British North America federation. In other words, the two previous plans – the Conservative scheme of 1858 for a general British America federal union and the Reform scheme of 1859 for a federation of the two Canadas – had been combined in the Coalition's program; but the Conservative plan had been given priority.

The Maritime governments, which up to that moment had made literally no preparations for their own proposed meeting on constitutional changes, were electrified to receive dispatches from the Canadian Coalition, politely requesting permission to send delegates to the Conference on Maritime Union. The Maritimers replied that of course the Canadians would be welcome, though in an unofficial capacity, and they then quickly decided that the meeting would be held in Charlottetown, Prince Edward Island, beginning on the first of September, 1864. These three astounding circumstances – the formation of the Coalition government in Canada, the publication of its proposal of a general British American federation, and the announcement of definite arrangements for the approaching constitutional conference at Charlottetown – seemed in combination to constitute the greatest breakthrough in British American political history. Together they roused Maritimers and Canadians to a high state of speculation, planning, and argument. The government of Canada set out boldly and at once on an exhilarating career of constitution-making on a national scale. Speakers, newspaper editors, and pamphleteers began to argue the merits of federalism for British America. British Americans everywhere were busily reflecting upon the potential implications of their federal union. They became more aware of each other's existence, more interested in each other's activities, more excited than they had ever been before by the prospect of a great transcontinental nation in which they would all be united. The great debate on the future of British North America had begun.

The year 1864 was the year of the 'coming together' of the British Americans. They had never visited each other, entertained each other, talked, argued, feasted, and danced with each other so often and for such long periods before. Early in August, three weeks before the delegates were to gather at Charlottetown for the conference on union, the first of these interprovincial expeditions–an unofficial party of Canadian politicians and journalists under the leadership of that convinced Unionist, Thomas D'Arcy McGee–set out for a tour of the Maritime Provinces. Travel between Montreal and Halifax and Saint John was far from an easy and expeditious matter in those days. D'Arcy McGee's party went by the Grand Trunk Railway from Montreal to Portland, Maine; and then, in an overcrowded and extremely uncomfortable vessel, from Portland to Saint John, New Brunswick. They travelled by steamer up the St. John River to Fredericton; they crossed the Bay of Fundy by steamer, and at Windsor took the Nova Scotia government railway train to Halifax. Everywhere the Maritimers turned out in thousands to greet the Canadian visitors and everywhere they were offered frequent and lavish entertainments.

Only a fortnight after D'Arcy McGee's touring Canadians had said good-bye to Halifax, the official Canadian delegation to the Charlottetown Conference started down the St. Lawrence to Prince Edward Island in the government steamer *Queen Victoria*. The Charlottetown Conference, the first of the conferences that built Canadian Confederation, was a highly mobile, peripatetic gathering; the delegates spent about half their time in travelling around the Maritime Provinces, just as the unofficial Canadian visitors had done only a few weeks before. But the real work of the Conference was completed in Charlottetown in the first week of September. The only official item on the agenda was Maritime union; but the Maritimers courteously postponed consideration of their own project and the Canadians were given the opportunity of presenting their plan of a general federation first. For three days, the principal Canadian leaders–Cartier, Macdonald, Brown, and Galt–described and analysed in detail the scheme they had drawn up in cabinet meetings that summer. On the 7th of September, after another day of general discussion, the Maritime delegates reached a momentous decision. A British American federal union was desirable, they declared, and they were prepared to waive their own smaller project in order that this more ambitious plan could be fully examined and discussed. A few days later, at Halifax, the next stop in their travels, the delegates decided that a second conference would be held at Quebec on the 10th of October and that there a general federal union would be the official subject of discussion.

The *Queen Victoria*, bearing the jubilant Canadians back to Canada, did not reach Quebec until the 19th of September, and only a fortnight later it was steaming down the Gulf of St. Lawrence to pick up the Maritime delegates and transport them to the Canadian capital for the second and the most crucial of the conferences on union. There were twenty-one Maritime delegates to Quebec; and with them came five of their wives and nine young and marriageable daughters. By the evening of Sunday, the 9th of October, they had all reached Quebec and were comfortably established in the St. Louis Hotel, where the Canadian government, determined to equal or better Maritime hospitality, had put them up at its own expense.

IV

At eleven o'clock the next morning, Monday, the 10th of October, the Quebec Conference held its first session in that severely plain structure, the Canadian legislative building, which stood at the very edge of the rock of Quebec. The

Canadian federal plan, which Macdonald, Cartier, Galt, and Brown had sketched at Charlottetown, was the basis of the discussions; and it was laid before the Maritime delegates at Quebec in a series of resolutions, which were moved by various members of the Canadian cabinet, and which the Conference then debated and passed, sometimes with amendments. Each province, however large or small its delegation, had one vote, with two for Canada in view of the two sections into which it was divided. If they had so wished, the Maritime Provinces could have outvoted Canada two to one on any of the fundamentals of the Canadian plan; and the fact that they did not, and that the Canadian plan was accepted with only minor alterations, testifies to the basic similarity of political beliefs with which all British Americans approached the problem of a federal union.

They realized, in the first place, that the union would have to be federal. The absence of municipal institutions in the Maritime Provinces, and Lower Canada's insistence on a measure of autonomy in its own local affairs, made a single sovereign parliament for the whole of British America impossible. A federal union would have to be accepted, the delegates realized; but at the same time they regarded it with serious doubts and apprehensions. Federalism was alien to the political tradition and experience of Great Britain and British America. In the United States, where, alone among English-speaking nations, the federal principle had been tried, it had been deeply discredited by more than three years of bloody civil war. The 'federal principle' of government was a divisive principle which could be employed only in small quantities and within strict limits in British America. It must be purged of those centrifugal weaknesses that had brought on the Civil War in the United States; and it must be adapted to the British political traditions of monarchical institutions, parliamentary sovereignty, and responsible government.

In his opening speech to the Conference, John A. Macdonald told the delegates that the constitution they were framing for a united British America, must, in the words of

Governor Simcoe, be an 'image and transcript' of the British constitution. The fundamental principle of the Canadian plan was parliamentary government under the British Crown. The lower house of the new federal bicameral legislature was to be called the 'House of Commons' in conscious imitation of the Mother of Parliaments; and the upper house, though it was eventually named Senate, resembled the American Senate much less than it did a House of Lords composed of life peers. It was true that the essence of parliamentary institutions was the sovereignty of parliament, and that this could not be secured in British America if legislative power was to be divided between two levels of government and the resulting division set down in a written and binding constitution. The federal legislature of the future could not be an absolutely faithful 'image and transcript' of the Parliament at Westminster; but if it lacked sovereignty in theory, it could be given powers and controls which would approximate it in practice. The provinces of the future must under no circumstances be copies of the aggressive and powerful states that had broken up the American union. They must be subordinate, not co-ordinate, governments, simple, inexpensive, quasi-municipal in character, and concerned only with a relatively small number of local affairs.

It was easy for the delegates at the Quebec Conference to reach these conclusions, for these conclusions were the natural result of their entire political experience. Unlike the successfully revolting Thirteen Colonies, the northern provinces had never claimed or acquired sovereign powers. They wanted British protection and recognized British imperial sovereignty. There was thus no solid constitutional basis for the assertion of provincial rights at the Conference. There was no recognition of provincial sovereignty in the Canadian plan; instead the plan laid down strict limits to provincial legislative powers and provided the Dominion government with powerful controls over provincial legislation. In the United States, the equal sovereignty of the contracting states had been honoured in the provision that each, whether small or large in population, was to have equal representation in the federal Senate. In British America, this alien precedent was consciously and deliberately rejected. The Canadian plan provided for an upper house based on the quite different principle of regional representation, with Canada East and Canada West as the first two regions, and the Maritime Provinces together forming the third.

In the crucial matter of the division of legislative power, the Quebec Conference also deliberately refused to follow the American example. In the constitution of the United States, all powers not specifically granted to the federal government were reserved to the states and the people. The Canadians regarded this as a mistaken and dangerous principle which they must completely reverse. In the Canadian plan, residuary powers were granted, not to the provinces, but to the federal government; and this distribution, though opposed by a small number of individual delegates, was accepted by a unanimous vote of all provincial delegations.

On the 27th of October, the delegates left Quebec for a tour of the Province of Canada – a tour in which the Maritimers received the same kind of hearty welcome that they had given the travelling Canadians during the summer. Early in November they were all scattering to their homes; and at about the same time the Quebec Resolutions, the fruit of their labours, were published in most newspapers throughout the provinces. By the time the delegates were back among their constituents, the British American electorate knew exactly what had been done at Quebec; and from that moment Confederation and the future of British North America became a subject that everybody could debate with knowledge as well as interest. The murmur of discussion and argument could be heard everywhere; but its pitch and volume varied considerably from province to province and region to region. The debate was perhaps least animated, though for very different reasons, in Canada West, and in Newfoundland and Prince Edward Island, than it was elsewhere.

In Canada West, which might have looked on the Quebec

scheme as virtually its own, there was little significant opposition. In Newfoundland and Prince Edward Island there was so much that, despite the efforts of a handful of devoted Unionists and the support of a few influential newspapers, the chances of a favourable reception, or even of a serious discussion, were very slight from the beginning. Opinion in Canada East was rather more evenly divided. There the influence of Cartier's *Bleus*, the dominant political party in the section, ensured widespread and general support for the scheme; but at the same time a British American union seemed to many to mean an uncertain future for French Canada, and the Seventy-two Resolutions obviously provided for a highly centralized federation. The *Rouges*, though politically a small minority, did their best to promote and exploit this vague, general apprehension over the prospect of the survival of the French-Canadian individuality in a British American nation. They had some success in their novel role as the conservative defenders of the historic identity of French Canada; but on the whole the discussion of the Quebec scheme in Canada East continued on a reasoning and unexcited level. It never approached the vehemence of the argument that rapidly developed in Nova Scotia and New Brunswick.

There the Quebec Resolutions were attacked from two different, and, indeed, completely contradictory, points of view. The plan was criticized in the first place precisely because it provided for a federal rather than a unitary system of government–because it was based on the 'federal principle' whose fatally divisive character had obviously wrecked the United States. In the second place, it was criticized, and with equal trenchancy, as a too strongly centralized federal union–a federal union that concentrated power in the federal parliament, where the larger provinces would be dominant, and left the local legislatures only insignificant duties and very little revenue with which to carry them out. The first criticism was, of course, an expression of British America's characteristic preference for legislative unity and parliamentary sovereignty–of the belief in strength as the essence of the great transcontinental nation of the future. The second and contradictory criticism was prompted by two other characteristic British American habits of mind—the widespread and deep-rooted sense of provincial exclusiveness and the inherited colonial feeling that membership within the unconfining framework of the British Empire already supplied all the unity that the northern colonies needed or desired. It was Joseph Howe, an early imperial federationist out of tune with his own age, who gave most eloquent expression to this older idea of British and American union. In his view, the Atlantic provinces were more naturally members of a great maritime British Empire, based on sea power and ocean commerce and linked with metropolitan London, than of a North American continental union governed from backwoods Ottawa.

It was in New Brunswick, however, that the two contradictory criticisms of the Quebec scheme united to achieve their greatest political success. Soon after his return from Quebec, the premier of the province, Samuel Leonard Tilley, had been persuaded, or forced, to announce publicly that the Seventy-two Resolutions would not be presented to the provincial legislature until after the next general election. The next general election did not need to be held for another six months; but Tilley, who was under considerable pressure from his Lieutenant-Governor, Arthur Hamilton Gordon, decided, against his better judgement, to risk his doubtful chances in an immediate winter contest. His government, old and tired, with a somewhat unsavoury reputation, was vulnerable politically; but even Tilley himself may not have anticipated the extent of the disaster that now overtook it. The elections, beginning on the 28th of February, were spread over a period of about a fortnight. But as early as the 4th of March it was known that Tilley and all his principal Unionist friends had been defeated and that the next government in New Brunswick would be opposed to Confederation.

That week-end early in March 1865 was the blackest hour in the long struggle for Confederation. A British American union would certainly be able to get along for a while–and perhaps for a long while–without either Newfoundland or Prince Edward Island; but New Brunswick, which supplied the necessary link between Canada and Nova Scotia, was absolutely essential to any union that was worthy of the name. Without New Brunswick, Confederation simply could not be. Without New Brunswick, the movement towards union could make no further progress. Tilley's defeat fortified the strong resistance in Prince Edward Island and Newfoundland; and in Nova Scotia, where the division of opinion was more keen, it gave the Anti-Confederates new hope and confidence. The passage of the Quebec Resolutions, which was to have been completed in all the provinces during the session of 1865, must now be held up indefinitely. Within another year, the Coalition government in Canada would probably have to abandon the longer project of Confederation and take up its second alternative of a federal union of the Canadas. If that ever happened, the hope of British American union was gone for a generation. And how could the second-best alternative be avoided, unless the Anti-Confederate government in New Brunswick was overthrown, and quickly?

V

Up to this point the movement for British American federation had been prompted largely by domestic interests rather than by external pressures. Maritimers and Canadians were, of course, always aware of the wider imperial context of their public affairs and of the serious effects which the American Civil War might have upon their relations with the United States; but so far any influences from outside upon the movement for union had been general and indirect, rather than particular and immediate. Then, in the autumn of 1864, this relative immunity from external pressure ended. As the Civil War went on, and as the fortunes of the Confederacy grew more desperate, there was an increasing likelihood that the South might attempt to distract the

North, to throw it off balance, by raids or surprises from British North America. The affair of the *Chesapeake*, which had alarmed Halifax in December 1863, was a foretaste of what might happen; and now nearly a year later, after the campaigns of the summer of 1864, the Confederacy was close to the end of its tether. On the 19th of October a score of commissioned Confederate soldiers, operating secretly from a base in Canada East, made a small, ineffectual raid on the town of St. Albans, in Vermont.

The St. Albans raid was of no military benefit whatever to the cause of the Southern Confederacy; but it roused the Northern Americans to a state of fury against the Province of Canada. The Americans were aware that by this time public opinion in British America had become largely pro-Southern in sympathy; and they were convinced that in failing to stop the raid on St. Albans the Canadians had been guilty of a glaring violation of their neutrality. Relations between the republic and the northern provinces, which had never recovered completely from the effects of the *Trent* crisis, now deteriorated with frightening rapidity. Northern politicians, generals, and newspapers threatened savage reprisals against Canada. The United States served notice to Great Britain that it no longer considered itself bound by the Rush-Bagot agreement, which limited naval armaments on the Great Lakes. The American Congress angrily began to discuss the early termination of the Reciprocity Treaty with British North America.

Canada was badly alarmed. So also was Great Britain. The British were already aware that in the United States they too were angrily accused of pro-Southern sympathies and unneutral actions; and the St. Albans raid and its consequences simply brought home to them more vividly the enormity of the potential danger they faced in North America. Everybody knew in the winter of 1864-5 that the American Civil War, after nearly four long years of carnage, was coming inevitably to an end. What if the triumphant Union were now to seek revenge for the injuries it claimed to have suffered at the hands of an unneutral British Empire? What if the Americans should attempt to exact a recompense on the St. Lawrence for their losses on the Potomac? To Lord Palmerston, the British Prime Minister, it was inconceivable that in such an event British America should be left to its fate; but, though most of the British governing class grudgingly accepted this obligation, they did their best to reduce its scope and weight. As W. E. Gladstone, Chancellor of the Exchequer, argued, it was quite possible to 'shift the centre of responsibility' in defence and to compel the colonies to accept a much larger part of the burden of their own protection. Lieut.-Colonel Jervois was sent over to plan a new defence system for Canada; and the British government earnestly pressed the Canadian government to consider the matter seriously and to assume the major responsibility in a new arrangement.

But the settlement of the defence question by itself was not enough. As Gladstone and Edward Cardwell, the Colonial Secretary, began to realize very quickly, the problem of the future of British America was political as well as military. If Canada was to become a principal in its own defence, if it was to take over the control of the Hudson's Bay Company's territories and thus assume the guardianship of a third of the North American continent, it must cease to be an ordinary colonial dependency of the Crown. If British North America as a whole was to become the residuary legatee for British properties and commitments in the northern part of the new world, then obviously it must, in Gladstone's words, be brought closer to 'a national sentiment and position' than it had ever been before. For its own imperial reasons, the British government welcomed Confederation. In Confederation lay the best chance of its own orderly and dignified withdrawal from its North American responsibilities. And as early as December 1864 the Colonial Office had given its cordial approval to the Quebec scheme.

But now Canada desperately needed stronger support. The combination of defeat in New Brunswick and danger from the United States seriously alarmed the Canadian government; and England was the only power to which the Province could appeal in its extremity. The news of the Anti-Confederate victory in New Brunswick was a shattering blow; but the Coalition cabinet put on a bold front against adversity. On Monday, the 6th of March, Macdonald announced in the Canadian Assembly that the Ministers did not regard the reverse in New Brunswick as a reason for any change in their program, but simply as a spur to 'prompt and vigorous action' in carrying it out. The 'prompt and vigorous action' that the government proposed was a special mission of senior ministers to London – a mission that would try to obtain stronger British support for Confederation and for defence against the United States. In the spring, Macdonald, Cartier, Brown, and Galt – the 'big four' of the Canadian Coalition – crossed the Atlantic for talks with the British ministers.

They had a fair measure of success. Galt's elaborate and extremely expensive defence plans were, of course, rejected by Whig-Liberal politicians who were determined to do no more for Canada than they absolutely had to. But England and Canada exchanged pledges to defend British America with all their forces in the event of a war with the United States; and the British commitment, though the London newspapers did their best to belittle its significance, reassured the worried and apprehensive Canadians. They were also encouraged by the British government's promise to use all its influence with the Maritime Provinces in favour of Confederation. There were obvious limits to what Great Britain could do. She could rely only on moral authority to give weight to her earnest exhortations. But the Colonial Secretary's reasoned dispatches, reprinted through the Atlantic provinces, might win over Maritime voters; and Maritime lieutenant-governors, instructed to do all in their power to forward the Quebec scheme, might be able to influence the course of provincial politics.

The pressure of danger from the United States and of persuasion from England made together a heavy impact upon British America; but it was not this combined external force which, in the main, overcame the resistance of the

Anti-Confederate government in New Brunswick and thus cleared the road for the advance of the Union movement. Influences from outside were strong; but they were not so serious as the inward weaknesses and differences of opinion that divided and enfeebled the Anti-Confederate forces throughout the Atlantic provinces and from the start brought dissension and trouble to the new government at Fredericton. The fact was that the majority of the Anti-Confederates were not opposed in principle to the idea of British American union: they simply disliked the Quebec scheme; and it was this completely negative feeling that alone held the heterogeneous elements of the Anti-Unionist party together. Of the two leaders of the new New Brunswick government, one, R. D. Wilmot, opposed the Quebec scheme because it was not a legislative union, and the other, Albert J. Smith, attacked it because it was a too highly centralized federation. If the Anti-Confederates could not discover a viable alternative to Confederation, they were very likely to split apart over the very issue that had united them.

Yet where were viable alternatives to be found? The only obvious substitutes for union with Canada were a continued and possibly closer association with Great Britain or a closer commercial and railway connection with the United States. Joseph Howe's plan for colonial representation in the imperial House of Commons was an expression of the first idea; Wilmot and Smith, with their scheme for the 'western extension' of the provincial railway to the American border, were in effect basing their hopes upon the second alternative. But, in the circumstances of the time, both policies were hopelessly unrealistic. The prevailing anti-colonial sentiment in the United Kingdom made Howe's vain hopes impossible of achievement; and the animosity with which wartime United States regarded British America sealed the fate of New Brunswick's designs for closer economic relations with the republic. Smith could not induce any group of capitalists to build 'western extension' as a commercial enterprise, and the province was too poor and debt-ridden to undertake it as a public work. The American abrogation of the

Reciprocity Treaty was an even more crushing reverse; and when it became clear that the United States would not listen to any proposals for the prolongation of the Treaty in any form, the only New Brunswick alternative to Confederation had obviously reached a dead end.

By the autumn of 1865, the divisions inside the Smith-Wilmot government and its growing unpopularity with the New Brunswick electorate were both becoming manifest. Early in November the New Brunswick Confederates won an important by-election in the County of York; and the York by-election encouraged and strengthened the Unionist cause over all British America. It reunited the Canadian Coalition cabinet, which had been on the verge of a split over the course it would pursue if a general union proved to be unrealizable; and, more important still, it proved to be the first sign of the rapid decline and fall of the Anti-Confederate government in Fredericton. By this time, R. D. Wilmot had accepted the Quebec scheme as the only practicable form of British American union; and this was a conflict, at the very heart of the Fredericton government, that Lieutenant-Governor Arthur Hamilton Gordon was able to exploit with telling force. He persuaded the wavering and undecided Smith, as a price of his remaining in office, to make a half-hearted public avowal of belief in some form of union; and when Smith, who seemed ready to betray both sides in his determination to remain in power, repeatedly postponed doing anything to carry out his pledge, Lieutenant-Governor Gordon brusquely forced a decision upon him. In April 1866 Albert Smith and his Anti-Unionist colleagues angrily resigned; a new Confederate government, with Wilmot as one of its leaders, took office; and in another six weeks a second New Brunswick general election ended in a Unionist victory even more decisive than the defeat of the previous year.

The resignation of the Smith cabinet and its subsequent defeat at the polls ensured the success of Confederation in both New Brunswick and Nova Scotia. The crisis in Fredericton could hardly have come at a more fortunate time for the Confederates. A year before, the American Civil War had come to an end, and the Union Army, long dreaded in British America, had been quietly disbanded. But the Fenian organizations, now greatly enlarged with veterans of the Civil War, had concocted their crazy scheme of striking a blow for Irish freedom by invading British America; and the first of the abortive Fenian raids miscarried on the borders of New Brunswick only a few days after the Smith government had resigned. The Fenians publicly announced that they had come to prevent Confederation and to sever the connection between the provinces and Great Britain; and for many people this declaration placed an indelible stigma of disloyalty on the Anti-Confederate cause. The vain Fenian raid of April clinched Tilley's victory at the polls in May and June. It also noticeably strengthened Charles Tupper's position at Halifax; and in April, at the height of the Fenian excitement, the Nova Scotian legislature passed a resolution authorizing its delegates to continue the negotiations for British American union in London.

By June of 1866, Confederation had become a virtual certainty. Nothing–neither American threats, British persuasions, nor Canadian argument–could overcome the obstinate resistance of Newfoundland and Prince Edward Island; but if the islands had rejected union, the continental colonies had accepted it as the only way in which the survival of a separate British North America could be ensured. By this time the Anti-Confederate cause had been proved bankrupt: its leaders had failed to provide viable alternatives to Confederation or develop successful policies for a future of provincial isolation. Their failure had left them irresolute and purposeless; and this inward deterioration was the main cause of their movement's defeat. Many Anti-Confederates, however much they disliked the Quebec scheme, had always assumed, at bottom, that union was the ultimate destiny of British North America. Now, in the troubled and dangerous times of 1865-6, it began to look as if union was not merely desirable for the future, but necessary in the present.

It was too late for the British Parliament to unite the

three provinces by imperial legislation during the session of 1866; but delegates from Canada, Nova Scotia, and New Brunswick met in London in the late autumn in good time before the re-opening of Parliament in February of 1867. The London Conference, which made some significant but no fundamental changes in the Quebec scheme, completed its final review of the new constitution before the end of December. The British North America Act, based on the London Resolutions, passed the imperial Parliament in February and March with only trifling amendments; and on the 1st of July, the three provinces were united to 'form and be one Dominion under the name of Canada'.

VI

The members of the first Dominion cabinet took office on the 1st of July; and on the 6th of November 1867 the first Parliament of Canada listened to the Governor General read the first speech from the throne. The machinery of government had begun to turn; but the task of integrating the new union and of promoting its welfare had barely begun, and the business of nation-building on a continental scale had got only as far as its first preliminary stage. The three provinces that united on the 1st of July formed only a part–though a very important part–of what the Fathers of Confederation hoped and believed the Dominion of Canada would one day become. In the east, the two islands, Newfoundland and Prince Edward Island, remained obstinately aloof; and in Nova Scotia Joseph Howe was leading a popular and determined agitation for the repeal of the Union. In the west, the Hudson's Bay Company still retained its feeble hold on the vast domain of its chartered territory; and on the Pacific slope, the future of Vancouver Island and British Columbia, those two remote outposts of British power in North America, remained uncertain. In both west and east there was much to be done; and if a rough balance was to be maintained in national expansion the work in both directions must be carried forward simultaneously.

In the east there were provinces still to be won over; there was also serious resistance to be met in one province already a part of the Dominion. In Nova Scotia the Anti-Confederates, taking advantage of their first chance to show the strength of their popular support, made virtually a clean sweep of both the provincial and federal general elections; and in 1868 another Nova Scotian delegation, headed by Howe, left to beg the imperial Parliament to release their province from Confederation. Outwardly the Anti-Confederate cause seemed powerful, as it had done in New Brunswick three years before; but once again there was no real alternative to Confederation for which the Anti-Unionists could work with resolution and, if necessary, by radical methods; and all about them was the resistance of existing commitments and established authorities, new and old. In the words of Sir John Macdonald, the Dominion refused even to admit that repeal of the Union was 'a matter for discussion'. In Great Britain, Disraeli's government, which had sponsored the British North America Act, declined to undo its own handiwork at the request of one discontented province; and in the late autumn of the year when the Liberals, led by Gladstone, formed a new administration, this decision was confirmed, even though John Bright, who had shown some sympathy for the Nova Scotians, was a member of the new cabinet. Obviously constitutional methods had completely failed; and the defeated Anti-Confederates could not agree on the course they must now pursue. Howe, old, tired, and disillusioned, was ready for any honourable capitulation; and, on its part, the Dominion government was prepared to offer Nova Scotia substantially better financial terms in Confederation.

In the autumn of 1868, when Macdonald was making his first conciliatory approaches to Howe, the Dominion government also took its first definite step towards the acquisition of the North-west. The Canadians were now prepared to recognize, what they had always previously declined to admit, that the Hudson's Bay Company held proprietary rights which would only be surrendered for adequate compensation; and Sir George Cartier and William McDougall, an early Reform advocate of Western expansion, were sent over to London to negotiate realistically for the cession of the territory. The terms of transfer–a cash payment by Canada of £300,000 and the retention by the Hudson's Bay Company of one-twentieth of the fertile belt–was ratified by the Canadian Parliament, which also passed a statute setting up a temporary provisional government for the Northwest Territories. Parties of engineers and workmen were already busy cutting roads that would link Lake Superior with Red River; and in the summer of 1869 a group of surveyors went west to begin the enormous enterprise of the survey which would open up the Canadian North-west for settlement. Late in September, William McDougall, the first Lieutenant-Governor, set out with a small staff for his new domain. The transfer of the territory was to take place on the 1st of December.

The resistance that Confederation met in the Red River settlement and the gravity with which the Dominion government regarded it can be fully understood only in the broad context of North American power politics. The tension with which the decade had opened, between the United States on the one hand and Great Britain and British America on the other, had never been really relaxed; and until the destined continental limits of the new nation had been reached, there was always the dangerous possibility that one or other of the still detached parts of British America might fall into the control of the republic. The United States had never recognized and accepted the new Dominion; she and Great Britain had never reached a settlement of the issues outstanding from the American Civil War. The criminally unneutral conduct during the struggle with which Great Britain was charged had now become the basis of fantastic claims for reparations, and the new American President, General U. S. Grant, and his Secretary of State, Hamilton Fish, were hoping and urging that a penitent England would 'withdraw' from the North American continent and that all or most of her possessions would fall into the hands of the United States. Behind them a small army of interested

Americans – governors, senators, congressmen, members of state legislatures, railway promoters, newspapermen, State Department special agents, and American consuls – were steadily working towards the same end.

The United States would not, of course, adopt an official policy of intervention; but American citizens might exploit the gaps and weaknesses in the partly built structure of Confederation so successfully that in the end official intervention would become inevitable. The strange, remote settlement at Red River was a potential centre of resistance to Canadian nationalism. The unrest in Nova Scotia and the detachment of Newfoundland and Prince Edward Island could be used to weaken the Canadian union and prevent its expansion. In the summer of 1868 Senator Benjamin F. Butler led a congressional party on a visit to Nova Scotia and Prince Edward Island. A year later, Senator Alexander Ramsay of Minnesota, a state that took an eager interest in the fate of the British American North-west, succeeded in having an American consul, Oscar Malmros, appointed to the little outpost at Red River. Obviously Malmros's only important duty was to watch over and encourage tactfully the anti-Canadian feelings of Fort Garry. Butler's purpose was to emphasize and reward Prince Edward Island's separatist tendencies by offering to it alone the generous reciprocal trade agreement for which all Canada had been vainly hoping ever since the abrogation of the Reciprocity Treaty in 1866. The Butler mission and the new consul were two fingers of investigation hopefully probing for a weakness in the perfunctory defences of the new Dominion.

It was not Malmros who inspired and directed the resistance at Red River in 1869-70. This was the work of the Métis, the French half-breeds, led by Louis Riel and supported and advised by the French-speaking priests Lestanc, Ritchot, and Dugas. The Métis, a semi-nomadic people, with a rough military organization derived from buffalo hunts, were the strongest political force at Red River. They saw in Confederation and the coming of mass immigration the inevitable extinction of their own free, wild way of life. With

Louis Riel as their political theorist and revolutionary leader, they prepared to resist; and they were aided by the French-speaking priests, who, through a combination of religious bigotry and devotion to their half-savage charges, were prepared to use any means to delay the advent of the hated English-speaking Protestants from Ontario. It was Louis Riel's Métis who stopped Lieutenant-Governor McDougall and his party at the international border, occupied Fort Garry, and imposed a so-called 'provisional government' on the little community. Such a protest by force was bound to perturb the government of a state that was little more than two years old; but for Macdonald's cabinet more than half of the importance of the Red River rising derived from its place in the complex of North American power politics. The publication in 1869 of Butler's report of his mission to Prince Edward Island had prompted the Canadian government to make another serious effort to persuade the Island to enter Confederation. Now the prominence of Americans in the inner counsels of the new 'provisional government' and the excited interest of the press and people of Minnesota and the American north-west were more than enough to make Macdonald suspect that Riel might be only too ready to appeal for support to the United States. As the last year of the decade closed, the Canadian government was selecting and briefing the emissaries who were to go to Red River in the hope of satisfying the settlement's grievances and ending its resistance. The vast transcontinental design lay incomplete. If British Americans had made the great decision, it had yet to be fulfilled.

2. The 1870s

GEORGE F. G. STANLEY

As 1870 opened, Canadian eyes were on the troubles at the Red River settlement, which had delayed the transfer of the great North-west from the Hudson's Bay Company to the new Dominion. Forces of resistance ruled at Red River, where Louis Riel, youthful, idealistic, and vigorous, had organized the Métis National Committee to prevent William McDougall, Canada's governor designate, from entering the colony, had arrested a party of Canadian settlers who sought to back up the installation of Canadian authority by armed force, and had proclaimed a provisional government with headquarters at Fort Garry. In response the Macdonald government in Ottawa, having refused to accept title to the troubled North-west on December 1, 1869, as originally planned, took belated steps to explain Canada's intention to the inhabitants of Red River. Bishop Taché of St. Boniface was summoned back from Rome, where he had been attending the Vatican Council. Two distinguished French Canadians were dispatched to the colony to allay the suspicions of the Métis, and Donald A. Smith, an official of the Hudson's Bay Company, was also sent out as a special commissioner to investigate the situation at Fort Garry. There Smith attended two large public meetings at which he put forward the Canadian case. He was sufficiently impressive that the Red River settlers resolved to draw up a list of rights and send delegates to Ottawa to confer with Sir John Macdonald and the members of the Canadian government.

All would undoubtedly have gone well had not the Canadians in Red River resolved to try another show of force. They had resented the imprisonment of sixty-five of their number in December and, goaded by several escapees, they organized a small armed force at Portage la Prairie. The Portage party planned to join another group from the lower parishes. The ostensible purpose of their demonstration was to compel Riel to release his prisoners. Again the whole movement fell flat for lack of adequate support, and when it became generally known that Riel had, in fact, already given the prisoners their release, the Portage Canadians turned around and set off for home. The Métis, however, had been alarmed by the threat of attack, and as the Canadians were passing Fort Garry–their action in returning so close to the fort was an unnecessary provocation–the Métis horsemen rounded them up and herded them into the cells recently vacated by the previous prisoners. Determined to make an example of one of the troublemakers, Riel picked upon Thomas Scott, a belligerent Irish Canadian from Ontario, whose conduct in prison was both violent and insulting. Scott was tried by a Métis court-martial and executed by a firing-squad on March 4.

Scott's execution aroused the racial and religious animosities of the Orangemen of Ontario, who demanded the immediate despatch of a punitive expedition to the west and the arrest of the delegates of the provisional government, then on their way to Ottawa. Despite the Orange agitation and the efforts of Ontario Liberals to make political capital out of it, the Macdonald government received Riel's emissaries and concluded a mutually satisfactory agreement with them. This was embodied in an act passed by the Canadian Parliament in May. Known as the Manitoba Act, it provided for the entry of the Red River settlement into the Canadian Confederation as a province. The transfer of the territories of the Hudson's Bay Company to Canada then took place, and on July 15 the Red River settlement became the fifth province of Canada, under the name of Manitoba.

These political developments had removed all urgency for the dispatch of a military force. However, Macdonald went ahead with the proposed military expedition, if only to satisfy the demands of his Ontario constituents and to afford protection to the new lieutenant-governor, A. G. Archibald, when he should reach Fort Garry. The troops arrived in Red River before Archibald, and Louis Riel fled to the United States. At the last moment he had been warned by a friendly Hudson's Bay Company man that the Ontario militia was determined to avenge Scott. All along Riel had protested his loyalty to the Crown: subsequently he was able to give proof of that loyalty when the Métis rallied under his leadership to resist a threatened Fenian invasion of Manitoba in October 1871. But for the present it was thought better that he remain out of sight. In later years Riel himself ran for Parliament and was elected several times, but, always fearing for his life, he never took his seat. Finally, in 1875 he was exiled for five years.

At the same time that Canada acquired Manitoba as a province it also acquired the remainder of the Hudson's Bay Company territories. This vast, unorganized region was administered, during the eighteen-seventies, by a governor and council appointed by Ottawa. Territorial administration continued, with the later introduction of elected members, until the formation of the provinces of Saskatchewan and Alberta in 1905.

Once the North-west became firmly part of Canada, the next step in Macdonald's great design for a transcontinental union was to open negotiations with the British colony on the Pacific coast. As long as the prairies remained under Company rule, there could be no effective union between the eastern and western parts of British North America. However, by 1866 the question of the future of British Columbia was becoming urgent. The economic situation of the colony was precarious and men were talking of either union with Canada or annexation to the United States. The latter was by no means impossible. After all, who were the Canadians? A people living far to the east, over the Rocky Mountains. Only a small number of them had reached the west coast and they had not made any great impact on the political life of the colony. As far as the colonial governor and his officials were concerned, they wanted union neither with Canada nor with the United States. Confederation or annexation was bound to mean the introduction of responsible government and the end of their specially privileged position. They hoped that things would remain as they were.

In spite of the opposition of the pro-American element and of the little group who controlled the government there were forces at work in favour of union with Canada. Led by James Trimble and Amor de Cosmos, the latter a Nova Scotian whose original name was William Smith, a Confederation League was formed in 1868 to publicize the advantages of Confederation. This body organized a series of public meetings throughout the colony of British Columbia, the most important of which was held at Yale on September 14. This 'Yale Convention' adopted various resolutions prepared by de Cosmos, a leading proponent of responsible government for British Columbia and incorporation of the colony in Canada. Governor Seymour sent these resolutions to the Colonial Secretary, but attached a letter to them belittling their importance. However, in 1869 Seymour died, and the way was clear for the appointment of a man sympathetic to the union idea. Macdonald himself favoured Anthony Musgrave, the Lieutenant-Governor of Newfoundland, who had already proved his devotion to the Confederate cause by his efforts to bring about the union of Newfoundland with Canada. Musgrave accepted the appointment when it was offered by the Colonial Office, and persuaded his Legislative Council to suggest the kind of union terms that might be acceptable to them. The next step was to appoint delegates to go to Ottawa. It was all done very quickly; and when Canada accepted the British Columbian proposals, the Legislative Council of the colony passed an address to the Crown asking for admittance to Canada as a province. The Canadian Parliament adopted a similar resolution and the union was given legal status by an imperial Order-in-Council dated May 16, 1871. A little over a month later, on July 20, 1871, the Canadian union was augmented by the addition of its sixth province, British Columbia.

The terms under which the west-coast province became part of Canada included not only the assumption by the federal government of the debt of the pre-Confederate colony, a favourable subsidy, and fully responsible government, but also the promise of a transcontinental railway to be started within two years and completed within ten. The railway stipulation was, in fact, the most important clause in the agreement between Canada and British Columbia. The ten-year limit was to be the guarantee of Canada's intentions to honour its agreement with its new Pacific province.

Newfoundland's delegates had also returned from the Quebec Conference of 1864 enthusiastic about the idea of British North American union. But they had found their colleagues considerably less so. The government leader, Frederick Carter, felt it advisable to postpone public discussion of the issue, particularly when he saw Tilley thrown out of office in New Brunswick on the same issue and Tupper reluctant to broach the matter in his Nova Scotian legislature. There was no use talking about Confederation in Newfoundland when the other Maritime colonies showed no desire to have any part of it. When the reverse experienced by the Confederates in the Maritimes proved to be only temporary, however, Lieutenant-Governor

Musgrave prompted Carter to re-open the question in 1869. Possible terms of union with Canada were discussed in the legislature and a delegation headed by Carter was appointed to go to Ottawa.

Before going to the Canadian capital, Carter gave a positive undertaking to submit any agreement reached in Ottawa to the people of the colony. Accordingly, in November 1869, a general election was fought in Newfoundland almost exclusively on the federation issue. Despite the support of the Lieutenant-Governor in St. John's and the Colonial Secretary in London, the people of the island voted against the Confederates. Carter was thrown out of office and the Anti-Confederate Charles Bennett left no doubt in anyone's mind that union with Canada was dead as far as Newfoundland was concerned. The Lieutenant-Governor wondered if perhaps the imperial government might not coerce the colony into union with the mainland; but the Canadian Prime Minister, Sir John Macdonald, would have nothing to do with coercion. In any event, he was, at the time, much more concerned about the future of Prince Edward Island than about that of Newfoundland. Britain's 'oldest colony', with its appendage, Labrador, therefore remained outside the Canadian Confederation until 1949.

The Prince Edward Islanders had shown far less partiality for union at the Quebec Conference than had the Newfoundlanders. Almost invariably they had been the men who presented the most embarrassing problems and who raised the most controversial issues. Nevertheless, the Island delegates had accepted the Quebec scheme and when they returned to Charlottetown felt obliged to stand by it. But there was no such obligation on the part of the members of the provincial legislature. And with hostility to the Quebec Resolutions apparent throughout the whole of the Island there was little doubt that Confederation would have a rough time of it. In the legislature the supporters of union were outnumbered and out-argued, and an address to the Queen was adopted praying Her Majesty 'not to give her Royal Assent or sanction to any Act or Measure . . . that would have the effect of uniting Prince Edward Island in a Federal Union with Canada . . .' Subsequently the Colonial Office endeavoured to convince the Island government that it should modify its attitude, but without success. The Islanders were adamant in their opposition to the wishes of Great Britain and Canada alike.

Then in 1869 came the news that General Benjamin Butler of Massachusetts, an advocate of the annexation of British North America to the United States, was on his way to Charlottetown to discuss the possibility of American trade concessions in return for special privileges for American fishermen in Island waters. The Canadians were so alarmed at the implications of Butler's mission (particularly after they read his report) that Macdonald felt it advisable to forget about Newfoundland and bend his efforts towards winning the Prince Edward Islanders away from the wily Americans. The astonishing thing is that the Islanders were able, in 1869, to resist the combined efforts of London and Ottawa to induce them to renew negotiations for the union of the Island and Canada. Some of the members of the legislature might be disposed to take a second look at union; but the people themselves remained coldly aloof. Clearly, unless some crisis arose, Prince Edward Island would not voluntarily unite its future with that of Canada.

Then the crisis came. The Islanders, who in 1866 had not wanted to pay for the building of an intercolonial railway for the benefit of Nova Scotia and New Brunswick, decided in 1871 to embark upon an ambitious program of railway construction on their own. Rather too ambitious. Some of the members wondered if they might not find themselves saddled with a debt higher than anything that union with Canada would involve. However, the supporters of the line talked optimistically and convincingly about the prosperity it would bring, the new industries, the additional population, the American tourists. But the opponents of the line were right. The line did cost more than expected and the Islanders did find the provincial debt mounting by leaps and bounds. So strained were the finances of the colony and so embarrassed the banks that had underwritten the railway that both feared a financial collapse. The way out of the difficulty seemed to be Confederation. The bankers urged it as well as some of the politicians. With great reluctance the premier, Robert Haythorne, appointed a delegation to go to Ottawa in February 1873. The Canadians, led by Macdonald, did not take advantage of the Islanders' journey to Canossa. They offered fair and generous terms and these were accepted. In the general election that followed, Haythorne was defeated; but Confederation was not an issue. The new government of J. C. Pope was pro-Confederate, and after further negotiations on matters of detail, Prince Edward Island agreed to enter the Canadian union.

The terms included the assumption of the Island debt by Canada and the advance of $800,000 to buy out the absentee landowners. The federal authorities also agreed to take over the railway guarantee and to establish and maintain 'efficient steam service for the conveyance of mails and passengers . . . between the Island and the mainland of the Dominion, winter and summer, thus placing the Island in continuous communication with the Intercolonial Railway and the railway system of Canada.' In May 1873, the Island legislature unanimously adopted a resolution in favour of Confederation with Canada on the terms outlined above. In Ottawa, at the same time, a similar address was adopted. On June 26, an imperial Order-in-Council authorized the formal union of Prince Edward Island and Canada effective 'from and after the first of July, 1873'.

'I greatly desire to complete the work of Confederation before I make my final bow to the Canadian audience,' Macdonald had once written. Now, within the short space of six years after the four original provinces had come together in 1867, that work was virtually completed. Only Newfoundland still remained outside. Canada was a country extending 'from sea to sea and from the river to the uttermost ends of the earth', a country of seven provinces and a vast region known as the North-West Territories. Before the decade of the eighteen-seventies had even reached a half-way mark,

Canadians had become proprietors of half a continent. It was a great and mighty achievement. Just how great only a few of them as yet appreciated. Perhaps time would help them to understand.

II

The union of 1867 had, in large measure, been the response of British North America to the threat of absorption by the United States. This threat had not taken the form of open warfare since 1812, but war still remained a possibility. The Fenians had come near it, with their unsuccessful raids upon Canadian territory in 1866 and their equally unsuccessful raids upon Quebec and Manitoba in 1870 and 1871. If these raids had not had official backing of Washington, there were still many Americans who believed in the doctrine of 'Manifest Destiny'. William Seward, President Lincoln's Secretary of State, and Charles Sumner, the Republican leader of the Senate, both adhered to Benjamin Franklin's view that the division of North America was 'unnatural'. In July 1866, before Confederation had been achieved, General N. P. Banks of Massachusetts introduced into the American Congress a bill providing for 'the admission of the States of Nova Scotia, New Brunswick, Canada East and Canada West and for the organization of the Territories of Selkirk, Saskatchewan and Columbia'. It was the answer of American continentalists to the national union movement north of the United States' frontier. The continentalists did not want to see a British-sponsored union; and Congress was persuaded to pass a joint resolution to the effect that the United States should view the Canadian Confederation 'with extreme solicitude', on the grounds that it contravened the Monroe Doctrine.

If Canadian-American relations had been bad prior to Confederation, after 1867 they grew steadily worse. Seward's purchase of Alaska was frankly designed to strengthen American influence in British Columbia and to assist the annexationists in that colony. It was, said Seward, 'a visible step in the occupation of the whole North American continent'. Minnesotan interest in the Hudson's Bay Company territories was well known to and encouraged by official circles in the United States' capital. In June 1869, two years after Confederation, Secretary of State Hamilton Fish approached the British ambassador with the suggestion that Great Britain should cede Canada to the United States in payment of the damages inflicted by the *Alabama* and her sister ships, built in British shipyards during the Civil War. Several times Fish returned to the same proposal, urging in 1870 that the time was ripe to remove all sources of friction between Washington and London by turning over Canada to the American republic. Edward Thorton, the ambassador, might have returned a strong reply to this preposterous proposal; instead he merely remarked that Great Britain would not initiate such a cession without Canadian consent, although the British government might be 'willing and even desirous' of doing so. That a British official should speak so mildly, and so cautiously refrain from pressing the Canadian demands upon the United States for compensation for the Fenian damages, seemed to suggest that Great Britain was no longer a pillar on which Canadians might lean. The proposed withdrawal of the British troops from their Canadian stations gave credibility to this idea, unpalatable as it might appear to Sir John A. Macdonald and to most Canadians at that time.

Most of the heat between Canada and the United States arose from the friction generated by the abrogation of the Reciprocity Treaty of 1854. On January 15, 1865, three months before Lincoln's assassination, the American Secretary of State gave formal notice that the treaty would terminate in one year's time. There is no doubt that Canada had profited more from the treaty than the United States, particularly while the Americans were busy fighting a civil war; but the treaty was not a one-sided affair. It had given the Americans a privilege of which they were very jealous, that of fishing in the waters of the British North American colonies. After 1866 this privilege was denied them. At first the

British colonials were disposed to exercise the right to exclude their rivals in a conciliatory manner, asking only the payment of a licence fee; but when the Americans abused this privilege and neglected to take out the required licences, the Canadian authorities resolved to enforce the letter of the law. The energetic federal Minister of Marine and Fisheries from New Brunswick, Peter Mitchell, fitted out several cruisers to protect the rights of Canada, and arrests of American interlopers became frequent—so frequent that even Macdonald became alarmed at the possible consequences.

The situation rapidly developed into a crisis. In December 1870, President Grant denounced the 'harsh treatment' meted out to American fishermen by the Canadians and threatened retaliation. Great Britain, deeply concerned over the implications of the German victories in the Franco-Prussian War in Europe, became alarmed at a prospective breach with the United States over a few colonial codfish. After all, did they not have their own problems with the Americans over those *Alabama* claims? Accordingly the suggestion was advanced that a joint high commission be established by Great Britain and the United States to discuss and settle all outstanding controversies between the two countries. Sumner wanted to make it contingent upon the United States' obtaining in advance an undertaking that the British flag would be withdrawn from all North America; but Hamilton Fish did not wish to kill the commission before it was born and Sumner's proposed ultimatum was ignored.

When the names of the British commissioners were announced both Canadians and Americans were surprised to see included among them that of the Canadian Prime Minister, Sir John Macdonald. It was the first time a colonial politician had received such a distinction. But the British recognition of Macdonald did not involve the recognition of any special Canadian right to be represented. Macdonald was not a Canadian commissioner; he was a British commissioner on the same terms as his colleagues. And the other members of the commission did not let him forget it.

The joint high commission held its sittings between February 27 and May 8, 1870. During these ten weeks Macdonald frequently found himself at odds with the other members of the British team. Canadian claims against the United States or Canadian demands for substantial trade concessions in return for the granting of fishing privileges to the Americans were ignored, not only by the Americans, but, what was more irritating to Macdonald, by the British. The latter were anxious, dreadfully anxious, for an accommodation with the Americans and were prepared to give them almost everything they wanted if only war could be avoided; why wouldn't the Canadians be willing to accept a money payment for their miserable fish? What could Macdonald do? He knew that Canadian claims were going to be sacrificed in the interest of appeasement. Should he agree with his British colleagues and be a party to an agreement of which he could not, at heart, approve; or should he withdraw from the commission and imperil any chances of an Anglo-American accord? He protested; he threatened the rejection of the draft treaty by the Canadian Parliament; but in the end he signed.

By the Treaty of Washington the Americans obtained from Canada the fishing privileges they wanted in return for a cash payment, the amount of which was to be subsequently agreed upon. They also obtained the free navigation of the St. Lawrence River. From Great Britain they obtained satisfaction for the *Alabama* claims. The British in return obtained a relaxation of tension between Great Britain and the United States. Canada seemed to get nothing, except the privilege to navigate freely on several obscure Alaskan rivers and a tentative promise from the British that they would pay the Fenian claims which the Americans ignored. But, in reality, the provision for Canadian ratification of the fishery articles of the treaty signified American acceptance of an emerging Canadian nation on her northern border.

In Ottawa it was Macdonald's task to see the unpopular treaty through the Canadian Parliament. The British government's offer to pay the Fenian claims would be of some help; but Macdonald felt the Canadian sacrifices were worth more than that and insisted upon a British loan to help finance the new railway to British Columbia. Finally the British agreed to guarantee a loan of £2,500,000. Macdonald fulfilled his share of the bargain by cajoling and arguing the members of his own party into supporting the Washington Treaty and voting for its ratification by the Canadian Parliament. In May 1872, one year after the treaty was signed, the ratification was complete. The Canadians had not succeeded in making the fisheries a lever to restore reciprocal free trade with the United States, but they could console themselves with the thought that the British loan would strengthen the bonds of Canadian unity and make the Pacific railway something more than a scheme on the drafting board.

Even though Macdonald had failed signally to obtain any trade concessions, much less a renewal of the Reciprocity Treaty, while in Washington, there were those Canadians who felt that the effort should not be abandoned. Alexander Mackenzie's Liberals felt that a truly free-trade party might stand a better chance of success if they could deal with the Americans. In 1873 they won power, following charges of glaring scandal in negotiations for the Pacific railway which effectively discredited the Macdonald Conservative government. The Liberals had the opportunity now to approach the Americans, particularly with reports reaching George Brown, former Liberal leader and still a power in the party, that Washington might consider a trade agreement in return for the fisheries, rather than the cash payment that had orginally been proposed. Filled with self-confidence—had he not always been an advocate of reciprocity and an ardent supporter of the North during the Civil War?—George Brown left his Toronto *Globe* office and hurried to Washington. But Hamilton Fish was no more interested in reciprocity in 1874 than he had been in 1871. Brown was annoyed to discover that he was looked upon as a kind of political beggar coming to pick the crumbs from the great man's table. But he choked down his resentment and continued his negotiations. A draft treaty was finally drawn up. But Fish would not sign it until he had the opinion of the

Senate. That opinion came – one year later. It was unfavourable. Not that the Americans were hostile to Brown; rather they were completely apathetic. Reciprocity, as the Canadians defined it, was not for them.

Brown's failure was a disappointment both to him and to Mackenzie. The Liberals had counted heavily upon a trade agreement with the United States as the answer to the severe economic depression into which the country had sunk in 1873. Without reciprocity, the Liberals had virtually no economic policy to offer the people of Canada other than retrenchment and careful administration. The impact of depression weakened the bonds of a scarcely formed new nation-state, causing a resurgence of provincial or sectional feelings and disillusionment with the nation-building dreams of Confederation. The Atlantic provinces chafed restlessly in a union that many Maritimers felt had benefited central Canada at their expense. British Columbia grew increasingly impatient over the Mackenzie government's failure to proceed fast enough with a Pacific railway – especially when Edward Blake, a brilliant orator and Mackenzie's strongest rival within the Liberal party – denounced the extravagance of a railway to the west at such a time.

Blake was loosely associated with a little group of eager young national idealists known as the 'Canada First' movement. They, like him, looked for measures to advance Canada's development as a nation, and applauded his ringing speech at Aurora, Ontario, in 1874, when he spoke eloquently of 'four million Britons who are not free'. But, again like Blake, they were not sure if the answer lay in an imperial federation giving the leading self-governing colonies a voice in the British Parliament or in enlarging Canada's own national status in the world. Blake and the 'Canada Firsters' assuredly did not seek to break with Britain. But more conservative Liberals like Mackenzie and Brown feared the trend of their ideas – and particularly their association with Goldwin Smith, the free-trade British liberal and former Oxford professor, who had settled in Toronto and first advocated outright independence for Canada and subse-

THE POLITICAL GIANT-KILLER; OR, "CANADA FIRST."

From *A Caricature History of Canadian Politics* by J. W. Bengough, Toronto, 1886, vol. 1.

quently annexation of Canada to the United States.

But the young nationalists did not take over the Liberal party. When Blake returned from dissent to membership in Mackenzie's government, 'Canada First' lost its zealous drive, and Goldwin Smith was left a powerful but isolated figure denouncing the emptiness and partisan vehemence of Canadian politics. The Mackenzie régime had other difficulties with its supporters. It was weak in Quebec, where the French-Canadian *Rouge* Liberals who had opposed Confederation were still rather lukewarm towards it. And *Rouge*-ism, which had long sought to curtail church influence in secular affairs, if not outright separation of church and state, was under heavy attack for its anti-clerical or 'irreligious' views from the growing spirit of Catholic ultramontanism in French Canada.

For the present, ultramontanism was in the ascendant. It had crushed the Institut Canadien, intellectual centre of *Rouge*-ism. The Guibord case of 1875, when ultramontane forces succeeded in preventing the burial of an Institut member in consecrated Catholic ground, marked the final collapse of the old *Rouge* organization. Fortunately for the Liberal party a young French-Canadian politician, Wilfrid Laurier (a lesser minister in Mackenzie's cabinet in 1877-8), began laying a new basis for liberalism in Quebec by asserting that it was not associated with the anti-Catholic, anti-religious European form so much opposed by the Church, but really derived from British roots that had long been linked with religious and Christian causes.

But whatever Laurier might do for the Canadian Liberal party in the future, he could do little now. The Mackenzie regime's problems continued in Quebec and all across Canada – as did the unremitting depression. Meanwhile Sir John Macdonald watched and waited. Although he did not like the attempt by George Brown to regain American reciprocity as an answer to Canada's problems, he kept his silence during 1874. But in 1875 there was no need for him to reserve judgment any longer. He knew what the answer was to the depression and the ills it had brought to Canada: the 'National Policy', a modified protectionism that would remedy the trade depression, foster a national economy, prevent Canada from becoming the dumping-ground for American goods, and encourage home industry. Macdonald correctly gauged the strength of the growing opinion in favour of protection and the resentment with which Canadians had viewed the uninterested, uncooperative attitude of the government at Washington. Thus, when Mackenzie appealed to the electorate in 1878, he found Canadians ready to vote for the National Policy and for the man who had proposed it. The fact is that the people of Canada were weary of the uncertainties and the hesitations of the Liberal regime. They wanted positive, dynamic political leadership. And from Macdonald they believed they would get it.

The return of Macdonald to power in 1878 and the Tilley tariff of 1879 were followed by good times. The economic revival was to be of short duration, but Canadians did not know that as they welcomed the New Year in 1880. They believed that they had discovered the touchstone of prosperity. There would be no more starving of Canadians into an annexation they did not want; no more running, cap in hand, to Washington for trade concessions they would not get. A good dose of nationalism was the answer to Canada's economic ills. Henceforth Canada would chart her own course, political and economic, in the years that lay ahead.

III

Bonds of steel as well as of sentiment were needed to hold the new Confederation together. Without railways there would be and could be no Canada. For years prior to the union of 1867, men had talked about uniting the Maritime colonies with those on the St. Lawrence. The first proposal, in 1836, was to build a railway line between the New Brunswick port of St. Andrews and the city of Quebec. It came to nothing when the United States queried the location of the boundary line. The railway builders would have to wait until Webster and Ashburton had decided where the frontier actually lay. Even so, St. Andrews was much too close to the United States, and subsequent proposals were based upon the idea of Halifax rather than St. Andrews being the eastern terminus of any railway line. During the eighteen-fifties and -sixties the Grand Trunk had built a series of railway lines in Canada, linking the major cities of the upper provinces with Chicago in the west and with Rivière du Loup and Portland in the east. And in the Maritimes two new lines were built, including a line from Halifax to Truro and another from Saint John to Shediac.

Meanwhile routes for the proposed intercolonial railway between the Maritimes and Canada were surveyed. Three possibilities offered themselves: the Frontier route by way of the St. John River, the Central route, and the Bay of Chaleur route. The Canadian engineer Sandford Fleming was asked to select the most suitable route, and in 1865 he recommended the last–the north shore or Bay of Chaleur route. Fleming believed that this would provide the greatest financial return for the money expended, if only because it would pass through rich lumber country and would touch at the various fishing villages along the coast. Even more significant was the fact that it was a long way from the American frontier and could be reached by ships from Great Britain carrying troops in the event of war. At the Quebec Conference in 1864 and at London in 1866 the construction of a railway between Truro and Rivière du Loup had been stated by the Maritime delegates to be a *sine qua non* of any union. And so it was asserted in the British North America Act of 1807, section 145, 'it shall be the duty of the Government and Parliament of Canada to provide for the commencement within six months after the Union, of a railway, connecting the River St. Lawrence with the City of Halifax in Nova Scotia, and for the construction thereof without intermission, and the completion thereof with all practicable speed.'

It took nine years thereafter to build the Intercolonial. It was not an achievement of private enterprise but a government work, built with money raised by the Canadian taxpayers and by British loans backed by an imperial guarantee of four per cent on three-quarters of the total amount. The road was intended to be a political as well as an economic bond pulling the interior and coastal regions together; it was never intended to be a purely commercial venture. Responsibility for the administration of the line was given to four commissioners appointed by Ottawa, and the engineer who superintended the work was the Canadian who had chosen the route, Sandford Fleming. The line was opened in 1876. Other lines already built in the Maritimes were taken over and in 1879 the section between Rivière du Loup and Quebec, built by the Grand Trunk, was turned over to the Intercolonial. Arrangements were made for running privileges on the Grand Trunk line between Quebec and Montreal. Thus the Intercolonial was able, eventually, to operate its trains from the two great seaports of Canada, Montreal and Halifax.

Equally essential was a railway to the west. Sandford Fleming had talked about the advantages of a line to the Pacific in 1858, when Allan Macdonnell of Toronto obtained a charter for his North West Transportation, Navigation and Railway Company. But neither Macdonnell's company nor Fleming's dream was realized at that time. In 1863, Edward Watkin of the Grand Trunk, who had his eyes on the acquisition of the Hudson's Bay Company territories, made tentative plans for the building of a telegraph line across the prairies from Fort Langley in British Columbia to Fort William; but when the Canadian government refused its financial backing unless a road was built also, the telegraph project too was set aside for the time being. There were vague references in the list of 'rights' that Riel's delegates took to Ottawa in 1870 about 'uninterrupted railroad communication between Winnipeg and Saint Paul, and also steam communication between Winnipeg and Lake Superior', but no formal demand was put forward during the negotiations and nothing appeared in the Manitoba Act. The British Columbians, however, left no doubt in anyone's mind that, like the Maritimers, they too wanted their railway and were prepared to make it the price of their entry into Confederation.

When Macdonald came to consider the problem of the Pacific railway he resolved upon a policy quite different from that followed in building the Intercolonial. The Maritime line was bearing heavily upon the financial resources of the federal government, and Macdonald wanted the new railway built by a private company. Two possibilities offered themselves: the Canada Pacific, headed by Sir Hugh Allan of Montreal, the founder of the Allan Steamship Line, and the Interoceanic, headed by David Macpherson, a Toronto financier. Macdonald would have liked both syndicates to come together and pool their resources. But Macpherson did not trust Allan, whom he believed to be backed by a number of leading American railroad financiers such as G. W. McMullen and Jay Cooke, who were also interested in the Northern Pacific, a rival American transcontinental line; Allan would never consent to Macpherson's demand that he, Macpherson, should appoint the majority of the board of directors. Allan glibly denied his American associations and eventually received the promise of the charter for the Pacific railway from Macdonald. The Prime Minister, owing to his long political and personal friendship with Macpherson, was unwilling to expose himself to the charge of favouritism that a grant of the charter to the Toronto financier would bring.

At this point Allan's American friends took over. They had put up the money that Allan needed and were determined that they were not going to be excluded from the control they intended to exercise over the Canada Pacific. One of them, G. W. McMullen, went to Macdonald and threatened to reveal to the public the fact that Allan had contributed substantially to the Conservative campaign fund during the election of 1872 and especially that he had assisted Sir George Cartier, albeit unsuccessfully. McMullen's threat was political blackmail. But he and his associates were unscrupulous men and ruthless. And McMullen carried out his threat. The files of Allan's solicitor in Montreal were rifled and the necessary incriminating documents were stolen. These were then turned over to the Liberal party. On April 2, 1872, Seth Huntington, the Liberal member for Shefford, rose in his place in the House of Commons and charged the government with having accepted a bribe from

Sir Hugh Allan in return for the railway charter. Macdonald was sustained by a majority vote in the House; but the charges were too serious to be pushed aside in this fashion, and he himself proposed the appointment of a royal commission to take evidence on oath and report to Parliament.

The debate over what became known in our history as the 'Pacific Scandal' made a tremendous impact upon the people of Canada. Macdonald defended himself well in Parliament. Some authorities say that he gave the best speech of his career with its dramatic gesture, 'These hands are clean!' But the Liberal disclosures shocked the none-too-tender consciences of the people and shook the loyalty of some of Macdonald's supporters. Finally, on November 5, 1873, Macdonald resigned, and Mackenzie took office. McMullen had paid back Allan; but in doing so he had discredited Macdonald, whom Lord Dufferin, the Governor General, regarded as 'by far the ablest man in Canada'.

The defeat of Macdonald meant the end of Allan's contract and the end of the Canada Pacific. It almost meant the end of the railway scheme itself. The Liberals, when in opposition, had made it clear that while they welcomed British Columbia into Confederation they were strongly opposed to the railway concessions promised by Macdonald. Now they were in power, they were anxious to modify the terms to which Macdonald had agreed. British Columbians protested. In fact they had already protested to Macdonald during the summer of 1873, prior to his resignation, that he was not living up to the terms of his agreement, by failing to start the railway within the two-year limit. When they heard that Mackenzie in his nomination speech at Sarnia in November of the same year had declared that there would be an entirely new railway policy instead of the 'insane' thing Macdonald had devised, they stormed the legislative buildings of Victoria, denouncing the Liberal Prime Minister's words as a breach of solemn contract.

Mackenzie was a stubborn Scot. He had made up his mind and he was not going to allow it to be changed by a few noisy British Columbians. He sent James Edgar, the young, per-

WHITHER ARE WE DRIFTING?

From *A Caricature History of Canadian Politics* by J. W. Bengough, Toronto, 1886, vol. 1.

sonable Liberal whip, to Victoria to talk with the provincial premier, George Walkem, to suggest to him that the ten-year time limit was wholly absurd. After all, the Pacific line was at least five times as long as the Intercolonial, and the Intercolonial was not yet finished after seven years. How could the longer line be built in ten? Mackenzie's may have been a thoroughly rational approach but it was not a politic one. The British Columbians wanted 'the bond and nothing but the bond'. They would tolerate no compromise. Throwing politics to the winds, Mackenzie refused to listen to the British Columbian demands. He would go ahead with his own plans and build the Pacific railway as a public work, building sections of the line as the country's means warranted and settlement demanded, and using existing waterways and American lines to fill the intervals.

So incensed were the people of British Columbia at Mackenzie's attitude that they appealed to the Colonial Secretary. Walkem hurried to London to convince Lord Carnarvon that the Canadians had dishonoured their agreement and that something should be done about it. Carnarvon felt that Walkem's views were not without some justification and urged Mackenzie to speed up the surveys and make larger financial appropriations for the railway. At the same time he recognized that the ten-year time limit was probably too short and recommended that it be extended to 1890. Armed with Carnarvon's proposals – they were in his eyes an ultimatum – Walkem returned to Victoria where 'Carnarvon or Separation' became the battle cry of the west-coast province. Either Mackenzie would live up to the Carnarvon terms or British Columbia would leave Confederation.

The Conservatives rather enjoyed Mackenzie's discomfiture. They prodded the government and encouraged their friends and supporters in British Columbia to do likewise. Tupper denounced Mackenzie's effort to build the line as a public work and demanded that it be turned over to a private company. Mackenzie would probably have agreed. But where was the company? These were the dark days of depression and no one had come forward to take the place of the Canada Pacific. Tempers grew shorter and words sharper as the weeks passed and Mackenzie sought some way out of the horrible mess in which he was caught. But there was no easy way out and Lord Dufferin wrote to the premier of British Columbia suggesting that if the Canadian government did not make a bona fide start on that portion of the railway to be built in British Columbia by 1878, then there should be a general conference in London with the representatives of Canada and British Columbia and the Colonial Secretary.

But the proposed conference was never held. In 1878 Mackenzie went to the people and they rejected him. They wanted Macdonald back again. They wanted the man who had said 'Until this great work is completed our Dominion is little more than a "Geographical Expression". We have as much interest in British Columbia as in Australia, and no more. The railway once finished, we become one great united country with a large interprovincial trade and a common interest.' And with the return of Macdonald came the return of brighter days.

For two years Macdonald carried on much as Mackenzie had done as far as the railway was concerned. He had made a bad choice once when he had given the railway charter to Sir Hugh Allan. He could not afford to make another such blunder. Which of the prospective syndicates should he choose? There was the Grand Trunk, the Canada Company, the Canada Central Railway, and firms in England and France, all of which were said to be interested. But Macdonald wanted a Canadian firm, and in the end the charter went to a body called the Canadian Pacific Railway Company headed by George Stephen, the president of the Bank of Montreal. Stephen was backed largely by Canadian capital, although there was a small amount of foreign capital from Great Britain, France, and the United States. On October 21, 1880, Charles Tupper, Macdonald's Minister of Railways and Canals, and George Stephen penned their signatures to the contract that was to build the first Canadian transcontinental railway.

Mackenzie's administration had occupied five years of the eighteen-seventies, from 1873 to 1878. They were dull years; years of frugality, of depression, and of restlessness in the provinces, in New Brunswick over the separate-school issue, in Manitoba over the natural resources issue, in British Columbia over the railway issue. With all his integrity Mackenzie was never a popular figure; perhaps because he lacked imagination; perhaps because he lacked the qualities of leadership. When Canada needed boldness he gave it caution; when it demanded large constructive measures he gave it small practical necessities. Canada did receive during his regime the Royal Military College of Canada, the North West Mounted Police, the western Indian treaties, the Supreme Court of Canada, and the secret ballot–all of them good and necessary measures, but none of the stature that would inspire the admiration of foreign observers or the pride of Canadians. Goldwin Smith's jibe, 'Mr. Mackenzie was a stonemason; he is a stonemason still,' was unkind; but it had an element of truth in it.

IV

The Canada that had been formed in 1867 was not the outcome of a grass-roots movement. It was not the product of a strong sense of nationalistic idealism. It was, instead, the practical answer of practical politicians to the problems of the eighteen-sixties. It was the achievement of the few, rather than of the many; the work of governments, rather than of peoples.

There were not really very many people in the new federation–not, at least, by European or American standards. The first federal census, published in 1871, gave the population of Canada as 3,492,878, to which could be added 102,358 Indians to bring it up to three and a half million people. Canadians were distributed among the several provinces in much the same proportion as they are today, with about eighty per cent concentrated in Ontario and Quebec. There were very few people of racial origins other than British or French, with the latter numbering about thirty per cent, much as they do at the present time.

During the next ten years the population of Canada increased by 831,932 to a total of 4,324,810. Part of this increase was due to the incorporation of Prince Edward Island in the federal union; but if we subtract the 108,891 people this province added to the Canadian population, the increase was 723,041, or about twenty per cent. This was a net increase only; for the number of births during the decade was estimated at 799,000, and the number of immigrants at 342,000, making a total of 1,141,000. Obviously there was, during the same period, a drain of about 400,000 people to the United States. This exodus may be attributed largely to the demand for labour in the mill towns of New England, and partly to the opening for settlement of the American west, where there were no trees and no large stumps to remove, and where lands were readily accessible to the railways.

From time to time during the eighteen-seventies efforts were made to persuade expatriates to return to Canada. Other efforts were made to divert Canadian emigrants towards Manitoba. But neither of these attempts was really successful in stemming the human flow to the United States. Only a strong national patriotism could have achieved this; and in the first decade after Confederation, national patriotism had not taken firm root in the minds of Canadians in the various parts of Canada. Everywhere there was the same cry, both in French and in English: the young people were not content to remain on the farm but were seeking the more exciting life of the cities and the better-paying jobs in the American factories.

The typical Canadian of the period was a countryman, living on a farm, in the bush, or in some fishing village along the Atlantic coast. In the whole of Canada there were not more than nine cities with populations over 10,000. Montreal, Quebec, and Toronto were the largest with 115,000, 59,699, and 59,000 respectively. Then followed Saint John with 41,325, and Halifax and Hamilton in the twenty thousands. Ottawa had 24,141 people; London 18,000, and Kingston 12,407. Others ranged from Charlottetown with 8,807 to Winnipeg with 241. As the population grew between 1871 and 1881, so too did the proportions of countrymen and city-dwellers change. Whereas in 1871 eighty per cent of all Canadians were classified as rural, by 1881 this figure had declined to seventy-four per cent. There was already a strong trend towards urbanization, which has gone on unchecked to the present.

The very earliest farms in Canada had been self-sufficient subsistence units. During the nineteenth century, under the impact of the prosperity which Canadians enjoyed under the Reciprocity Treaty, there was a change from self-sufficiency to emphasis upon a single cash crop, wheat in particular. However, after Confederation wheat growing tended to give way to greater diversification in farm production. The invention in Sweden of the de Laval centrifugal cream separator, replacing the old method of skimming cream by hand, gave an impetus to dairying. Regional specialties began to appear – fruit in Niagara, cheese in the Ingersoll and Belleville districts of Ontario, and garden truck in the vicinity of the large cities. Changes of this nature necessitated greater knowledge on the part of the farmer, and agricultural schools were started. The first of these had been opened in 1859 at Ste. Anne de la Pocatière. Others were founded at L'Assomption in Quebec in 1867 and at Guelph in 1874.

Improved mechanical aids to farming also became a familiar sight on Canadian farms. The average farmer of the eighteen-seventies required a wheel cultivator with long shovel-shaped teeth to tear up the soil, a set of harrows, a horse-drawn seeder, a 'buckeye' mower, and a hay rake. The reaper was the common harvesting implement until the twine binder came into use in the eighteen-eighties. Threshing was done largely on a contract basis, if only because of the expense involved in buying a threshing machine. Some farmers still used horse-power for threshing but by the end of the seventies the steam thresher was the common machine on all farms in Canada.

Because Canada was still in 1870 a land of countrymen, barter was a familiar method of exchanging goods in the rural areas. In every village the general store was always the main feature, after the church. Usually located in the centre of a village or town, the general store often had a porch or verandah to which a man might descend from his horse or his buggy without getting directly to the ground. In the back was the warehouse, where the bulky barrels and heavy goods were stored. Along the side walls were the rows of shelves displaying their stock of hardware, dry goods, harness, and foodstuffs. At one end, near the door, would be the post office, for the proprietor often doubled as postmaster and storekeeper. In the main body of the store would be the stove around which men would gather to talk about the wild feuds of the Black Donnellys in Biddulph Township, Macdonald's role in the 'Pacific Scandal', Louis Riel's appearance in the House of Commons in Ottawa, or the great fire in Saint John. The general store was the centre for gossip, political argument, or a quiet game of checkers.

In spite of the hardships of the great depression of 1873, there were many improvements in living conditions during the years that followed. In the Maritimes and in the upper provinces, the expansion of the railways made personal travel and the transportation of goods easier and cheaper. The completion of the Intercolonial in 1876 ended the isolation in which both Canada and the Maritimes had previously existed during the long winter months when the St. Lawrence was closed by ice. The adoption of trawl-line fishing brought improved catches for the Lunenburg fishermen, and during the eighteen-seventies Halifax grew as the entrepôt for the large fish-export firms that drew their supplies from as far away as Gaspé. In Cape Breton the demand for coal for the railways and steamships acted as a stimulus to mining on the island, and Sydney became an important coaling-station for vessels en route to Montreal. There were active sugar refineries in both Nova Scotia and New Brunswick at this time; but generally speaking, manufacturing in the Maritimes was held back by too little capital and too severe competition from both the United States and the Upper Canadian provinces. Perhaps the outstanding general feature of the economic life of the Maritimes during the years of the seventies was the gradual shift of business from the schooners to the railways.

In the St. Lawrence valley there was the same emphasis upon railway and steamship transportation, both of which combined to make Montreal into a great metropolis. Other factors contributed to this development; such as the insistence from 1871 upon proper qualifications for ships' officers, and the expansion of the system of lighthouses and buoys by the federal marine department. The discovery of petroleum in Ontario during the late fifties had provided lighthouse-keepers with a mineral oil that was a vast improvement over the animal oil previously used for signal lights; and although the Ontario oil industry went into a decline during the eighteen-seventies, increased oil production in the United States provided a cheap and easily acquired substitute for the Canadian product.

The lumber industry remained an important economic activity during the seventies, particularly in Ontario, where great timber rafts still floated from the upper reaches of the Ottawa, and down the St. Lawrence from Kingston to Quebec, where they were loaded on ships bound for Europe. But there were also new industries that were attracting attention: for instance, the silver mine at Silver Islet in Lake Superior, which produced over three millions of dollars' worth of the precious metal between 1868 and 1884; and the asbestos mine opened at Quebec in 1878. The demand for iron and steel grew, especially with increased railway construction, and this demand led to a revival of iron-mining in Canada. In the field of farm machinery, Canadian companies like the Massey company, which had been originally established near Newcastle, and the Harris company, at Beamsville, both expanded their production in spite of American competition. The Massey works had won the highest award at the Paris Exposition in 1867 for their mower and reaper. They took out the first Canadian patent for a self-binder and in 1878 introduced a new harvester. In the same year they moved to Toronto to take over the Toronto Reaper and Mower Company. Meanwhile, the Harris company moved to Brantford in 1872, whence it found its way to Manitoba, even prior to the building of the transcontinental railway, to open a distributing agency in Winnipeg in 1879.

By the eighteen-seventies Canada was well beyond its pioneer days, except, perhaps, in Manitoba and the North-West Territories. The brick house had increasingly replaced the frame house and in some places the stone house, particularly in Ontario. Picturesque eclecticism dominated the architecture of all public buildings. Every city had its 'villas' and its 'mansions' on well-treed lots behind ironwork fences. Most of them were not much different in size and shape from the farmhouses to be seen in the country, but they were more pretentious and more elaborately trimmed with gingerbread. Inside a visitor would recognize the fringed sofas, the embroidered stools, the fire-screens, the whatnots, and the easel with the portrait or landscape on it. There would be the marble fireplaces with the gold-framed mirrors over the mantelpiece, the heavy draperies, and the mahogany furniture with the machine-carved ornaments. The lighting might be by gas; more frequently it was by kerosene-oil lamps. On the tables would be found stereographs by Louis Vallé, W. J. Topley, or James Esson; or, if the houses were in the Maritimes, by J. S. Climo or James Notman, a younger brother of the more famous William of Toronto and Montreal. Outside, the streets were still seas of mud after heavy rainstorms; but there were improvements there too. Scarcely any town worth the name did not possess gas lighting by the seventies. In 1876 Alexander Graham Bell succeeded for the first time in transmitting speech over a telephone wire. On August 3, in Wallis Ellis's general store in Mount Pleasant, Ontario, he received a telephone call from his uncle a few miles away in Brantford. A new era was on the way. During the seventies the well-off Canadian took the waters at the Grand Hotel, Caledonia Springs, married within his own circle, paid an occasional visit to 'the old country', invested his money in gilt-edged bonds. But as often as not he would haggle over ten cents with the local grocer, for he was usually not more than one generation removed from the farm.

Life in the eighteen-seventies was not all a matter of pushing the plough or driving in a carriage or cab to the office. There may not have been as much time for play as there is today; but there was still plenty of play. Some people found their relaxation in the bottle, for many Canadians were hard drinkers, if we can believe the reports of contemporary visitors or judge from the number of temperance societies and the passing of the Canada Temperance Act in 1878. Dancing, too, was popular, whether it was carried on in the ball room, in the barn, or in the local community hall. Regattas and canoe races on the lakes and rivers were popular in the summer as well as political picnics and excursions of all kinds; and in the winter there was tobogganing, skating, carrioling, and curling. This last sport was introduced into Quebec during the last years of the eighteenth century by Scottish officers of the British garrisons. It is probably the game that has retained its popularity in Canada longer than any other. And this in spite of the fact that a large segment of the population, the French Canadians, always had difficulty in understanding what amusement there could be in hurling large pieces of granite over the ice to the cries of 'Soop! Soop!'

Curling enjoyed considerable popularity during the years we are discussing. At the last great open-air bonspiel at Burlington in 1875 there were no fewer than 360 curlers present; and, according to the *Annual Report* of the Ontario Curling Association, 'The Bay presented a most lively and festive appearance. Crowds of spectators, including many of the fair sex, on foot and in sleighs, covered the Bay during the contest.' In the following year, 1876, the first bonspiel was held in Winnipeg, with the prize, a barrel of oatmeal, being presented by the winning team to the Winnipeg General Hospital. During this period the Toronto Red Jackets, who played together between 1868 and 1878, dominated the Canadian curling world.

There were, of course, other sports. Cricket was played in many centres and was stimulated by tours of Canada by visiting British teams. One such tour took place in 1872. Lacrosse was popular, as was also soccer football, which seems to have become an almost universal game. Christenings, weddings, and funerals were then, as now, occasions for social gatherings; charivaris were still the noisy and sometimes riotous affairs of earlier years; meetings of the 'national' societies, such as the St. Andrew's Society, the St. George's Society, and the St. Patrick's Society, were well attended; so too were the parades of the militia, the firemen, the St. Jean Baptiste Society and the Orangemen. Both in the towns and in the country there were horse races to be seen and bets to be placed, although the more sophisticated and well-to-do in Toronto went to see the steeplechase at the Toronto Hunt Club, where they could display the latest fashions in bustles and top hats. For the countrymen in particular, there were the provincial ploughing-matches. These began in the early years of the nineteenth century and have maintained public interest ever since, although it is probably a declining interest with the increase in urbanization.

Declining, too, is the excitement that once attended Canadian elections. In the nineteenth century they were always occasions of jollity, often of fisticuffs, and sometimes of fatalities. The prohibition of alcohol on election days and the introduction of the ballot have done much to rob elections of the violence and glamour of our grandfathers' day. It was the early seventies that witnessed the first use of the secret ballot in Canada. It was introduced into Nova Scotia in 1870, British Columbia in 1873, Ontario in 1874, Quebec in 1875, and New Brunswick in 1876. The Parliament of Canada adopted the ballot for federal purposes in 1874, although it was not put to use until the election which returned Sir John Macdonald to power in 1878.

Canadian society in the eighteen-seventies was not only predominantly rural in character, it was also basically conservative. Unlike the United States, Canada was not the product of a revolution, of a defiance of established authority; it was, on the contrary, the achievement of the Establishment—of government, church, army, and traditional loyalties. Even in the west, where the frontier influence might be expected to be strong, law and order were maintained by a para-military body, the North West Mounted Police. There were no vigilantes on the Canadian prairies. And in British

Columbia the presence of the Royal Engineers had checked any early lawlessness in the gold-mining camps.

Because they were conservative, because they had not willed the new federal union, the people who lived in the provinces that became Canada were not, in the eighteen-seventies, really Canadians at heart. They were Nova Scotians, New Brunswickers, Islanders, French Canadians, Westerners, British Columbians, and Ontarians. Confederation was still, as Macdonald put it, 'in the gristle'; it had not hardened into bone. It was still too early to expect a Maritimer to feel a deep bond of kinship with an Upper Canadian whom he knew only by distant report. How could a French Canadian feel a sense of identity with the Anglo-Saxon Protestant Ontarian, from whom he was separated by language, law, and culture? When French Canadians became nationalists–as they did to defeat Sir George Cartier in Montreal in the election of 1873–it was nationalist in the narrower French-Canadian sense, not in the broader supra-racial sense. And the Ontarian, when he thought himself wildly nationalist – as he did when he listened to 'Canada First' voices like William Foster or the *Nation* – was really demonstrating only his Upper Canadian nationalism. 'Canada First' was too prone to identify Canada with Ontario and the British supremacy. In British Columbia there were comparatively few ties, economic or family, with the remote region called 'eastern' Canada.

The grey stone Victorian Gothic structure in Ottawa, which had been opened in 1867 and housed the Parliament of Canada, was the symbol of the new nation that some of the Fathers of Confederation had talked about in 1864. But in the critical years of the seventies, it was still only a symbol of the future. Canada was as yet only a federation of provinces. Nevertheless, as the eighteen-seventies ended, times were improving. Macdonald the nation-builder was back in Ottawa, and many Canadian people looked hopefully ahead, trusting that the next decade might achieve for them the strong transcontinental union the politicians had talked of building when Confederation had first set forth its outlines.

3. The 1880s

W. S. MACNUTT

No decade in Canadian history has opened more hopefully. Providence seemed to be smiling upon the great national enterprise that Canada had become, and the idea of nationality, daring by reason of its novelty a dozen years before, was being trumpeted throughout the land. Blandly and self-confidently Macdonald and his Conservative ministers enjoyed the tide of good fortune that was allegedly the consequence of their policies. The C.P.R. was building, and Canada was becoming all of one piece. Only the dourest Grit in opposition or the gloomiest of pessimists could deny that the experiment of 1867 seemed to be successful. Pessimism, such as that of Goldwin Smith, was possible only on the philosophical plane. The national prosperity and the rapidly increasing rate of immigration that prevailed at the opening of 1881 were ample proof of the righteousness of nationality and of the measures of economic nationalism that Macdonald had introduced. The tone of life was buoyant.

Canadianism had become a living force, though it was encompassed in a more universal loyalty. Disraeli's period of power in Britain had ended in 1880, but the imperialist sentiments he had fostered were affecting the habits of thought of the British at home and overseas. Being British was tantamount to being successful, and the world had been forced to admit the paramount position of the island race and its numerous offshoots on all the continents. To the Canadians being British especially meant the ability to look the Americans in the face on something better than equal terms. America was still adolescent but the British Empire was established and supreme. All its citizens could acquire an increased sense of self-importance by reason of its triumphs in peace and war.

The new sense of imperial unity that became so noticeable in the eighties was the more novel because of the old and well-founded Canadian conviction that Britain had little enthusiasm and regard for her overseas possessions. But the disruption of the historic balance of power in Europe caused by Bismarck's triumphs, culminating in the defeat of France in 1870 and the establishment of the German Empire, had made the British people more aware of their world heritage. Canadians were being flattered by a new and respectful regard for their country expressed in British newspapers. The strengthening of the historic ties with the Mother Country, that often had visibly been weakened, was more than superficially reflected by the presence at Rideau Hall in Ottawa of Lord Lorne, the son-in-law of the Queen. Sensing the imponderable and highly symbolic possibilities in the appointment of a new governor general, Disraeli in 1878 had won the consent of Queen Victoria to the dispatch of her fourth daughter, the Princess Louise, to Ottawa. 'Her Canadian Majesty', the consort of Lorne, who was the chief scion of the great Campbell clan and the heir to the dukedom of Argyll, might presume to represent an aspiration to imperial unity as dazzling as the Crown of India, so recently presented to Her Royal Mother.

Initially the appointment of Lorne appeared to achieve the results hoped for. The public felt complimented and the Scots of Canada, never an element to allow pride of place to others, were exuberant. To the empire-minded men of the time Canada appeared a field for statecraft, and the office of governor general, though nominally a sinecure, was a post from which real influence could be exercised. To Disraeli Canada had been 'one of our great vice-royalties', and the panoply of imperial power throughout the world presented no sharp contradiction to Canadians whose great ambition was a nation extending from sea to sea. The mother-image of the Queen, the embodiment of all the virtues cherished by Victorian moralists, was a real factor in sustaining this view of Canada's place in the world that was challenged only by the querulous and the academic. On the Ottawa scene the vice-regal court, which became more notable by reason of the presence of royalty, seemed to represent a North American version of British world power.

Yet, though Canadians were impressed by visitations of royalty and vice-royalty, the consequences were impermanent. The outpourings of imperial sentiment on occasions of state, the genuine affection for the person of the Queen, the triumphal arches bearing the inscription of 'Lorne and Louise' that appeared on the streets of every community of consequence during the season of summer travel, could make but a transient impression on the North American quality of the people that was emerging. A Canadian vice-royalty, it was pointed out very firmly, could never be the equivalent of that at Delhi. Public functionaries solemnly performed their duties on occasions of state in the best British tradition. The most bucolic of politicians rivalled one another in professions of loyalty to the Crown and to British institutions. Yet, so far as civil affairs were concerned, this was almost the only heritage of the Old World that really counted. Though accepting 'the court' and the whole superstructure of vice-regal state, Canadians were almost unanimous in declaring that theirs was a country in which social distinction did not count. Only in Quebec City was the acceptance of an aristocracy openly defended in the press. Everywhere else opinion was tempered by a considerable degree of levelling egalitarianism. A little of this drew inspiration from radical opinion in Britain, much more from the hostile and sneering tone of a portion of the American press that liked to remind its readers of the dangers of monarchic institutions in the Western Hemisphere. Canadian journalists, ambitious for notoriety and eager to shock their readers, liked to reproduce racy items of gossip from British and American sources that had the effect of mildly discrediting monarchy. The bolder condemned 'court tomfoolery'. The Toronto *Telegram,* then allegedly a paper of annexationist sympathies, could declare that Canadians had become a nation of toadies.

British institutions were in favour but the British pattern of society was alien to the Canadian soil. Politicians could accept knighthood, but unknightly deportment was more in favour with the public. Prejudices against pretensions to social superiority were easy to evoke so that the idea of an aristocracy beyond the portals of Rideau Hall was really unacceptable. The Governor General had to learn to be unshaken when expatriate Scots failed to remove their caps in his presence. Independence of demeanour was a popular Canadian affectation. Independence could be asserted not only against the class system of Britain but against unwarranted intrusions from south of the border. Americans who too roundly applauded the Canadians for similarity to themselves were frequently reminded that there was a great deal about the United States, too, that Canadians did not like. American ignorance of Canada could be just as irritating as that of the British, and was less excusable. In March 1881, when the Chicago *Tribune* reported that 'Lady Tilley, one of the Court ladies at Rideau Hall, gave a grand ball last week, and no wine was served, an unusual innovation at the table of an English nobleman,' the nation laughed in contempt as well as in amusement.

The ideas of the Canada Firsters constituted a kind of vanguard of opinion that all were obliged to follow to one degree or another. Macdonald could not gainsay the feeling that prevailed throughout the country on the necessity of keeping Canada's particular interests before the attention of the imperial authorities. At London Sir Alexander T. Galt, just appointed as Canadian High Commissioner, harassed the Foreign Office by aggressive demands for a virtually independent role in commercial negotiations with foreign states. Political independence was a goal kept before the public by those who clamoured for complete freedom from Britain. Enraged opponents retorted that independence was wanted only as a prelude to annexation. The more moderate would not deny that political independence was a reasonable objective, insisting that it did not imply separation from the Mother Country. The only objection to independence, said the *Illustrated News* of Montreal on March 7, 1881, was that the people were satisfied with things as they were, a statement that, in the light of events for years to come, might be considered a fair one.

Great satisfaction was derived from the Proclamation of the Imperial Privy Council of 1880 which annexed Britain's Arctic territories to the Dominion and added the Eskimos to the Canadian population. There were ill-humoured reflections in the newspapers on how the United States in 1867 had, in spite of geography and the doctrine of natural frontiers, filched Alaska. American schemes for establishing a protectorate over Panama, voiced by Secretary of State Blaine, aroused protests from the people of the Maritime Provinces who, with a ton of shipping afloat for every individual in the population, boasted of the third, or perhaps fourth, greatest merchant navy in the world. This high level of self-estimation that was in the wind acquired a note of shrillness with the remark of Nicholas Flood Davin, a newly arrived Irish journalist, who wrote for the *Canadian Monthly* that 'three or four of our statesmen' could have become

Prime Minister of Britain. Almost every newspaper in the country carried the quotation, but comment was guarded.

Much of this confidence represented only the beginning of adolescence, but the years of the early eighties were producing evidence of the commencement of a real national life. On the material side the Conservative policy of knitting the country together by tariffs and railways seemed to be working wondrously. A frequent remark of foreign visitors at the time was that Canadians seemed totally absorbed in the business of becoming rich. Especially on the English-speaking side there had been general lamentation on the absence of cultural advancement. But the work of the Royal Canadian Academy of Art, established in 1880, was being supplemented by that of many local art societies. The Royal Society of Canada came into existence in 1881. In spite of the parochial jealousies of artists, savants, and journalists, both of these organizations were spurred into activity by the Governor General. The Royal Society was compelled to face a curtain of hostility and indifference drawn by the press of the country that professed fears for the egalitarian character of Canadian society. It would be, said the Toronto *Globe*, 'a mutual admiration society of nincompoops'. Yet both performed in a fair way the task of making Canadians more conscious of one another. The literary *élan* of French Canada had been sparked by the award of the Prix Montajou to its leading poet, Louis Fréchette, by the French Academy in 1880. In this realm French Canada's leaders had no doubt about their own superiority. How could a people such as the English Canadians, with their roots barely fixed in the soil, acquire a respectable degree of literary and philosophical achievement? The French Canadians successfully demanded ten of the forty seats in the Royal Society. Their poets, moralists, and philosophers continued to be preoccupied with the pathos of their past. Young English Canadians of literary enthusiasms were fired by the fame that accrued to the young New Brunswicker, Charles G. D. Roberts, who published *Orion* in the same year. The first distinctive school of English-Canadian poetry was in the making.

From a print in the Public Archives of Canada.

II

The prosperity of the early eighties softened the discontent that had, in some parts of the country, accompanied the early years of Confederation. In the Maritime Provinces the union was now being accepted with some grace. The oceanic economy of the great days of wood, wind, and water was enjoying its last decade of real importance. But the little secondary industries that depended almost exclusively on local markets were succumbing to the competition of the new manufacturing giants of Montreal and Toronto. The Intercolonial Railway, completed in 1876, served as a unifying force primarily for the manufacturing industries of central Canada. The traffic was largely one-way, for Maritime goods of appreciable value and quality were not wanted in Montreal. The merchants of Saint John and Halifax, schooled in the lore of an international traffic, were discovering that, owing to the high levels to which Macdonald had raised the tariff in 1879, goods from abroad could not be imported at salable prices. More and more their activities were becoming tributary to those of Montreal. Along the route of the Intercolonial the National Policy had conjured up some small manufacturing industries. Many Nova Scotians, rejoicing in the notion that the coal of Pictou and Cape Breton would make their province the Black Country of the Dominion, were certain that great prosperity would come. But the buoyancy of the country at large was not generally reflected in the demeanour of the people of the three provinces. At Confederation Maritimers had been told that they would exercise an influence of approximately one-third in the life of the new nation, that they could derive a preponderant advantage from an endemic hostility between Quebec and Ontario. Notions of this kind had been thoroughly dissipated and the general humour was one of regretful resignation. On Dominion Day flags still flew at half-mast in the Annapolis Valley and the idea of secession, though dormant, was not far removed from practical politics. The *Chronicle* of Halifax sustained memories of the great coercion of 1867. On the fourteenth anniversary of union with Canada it declared that not one honest heart in the province would rejoice upon the event.

Within the structure of Confederation Quebec rested easily. The safeguards guaranteed to her in the B.N.A. Act seemed to serve their purpose. French Canadians were so busy with their own political quarrels that they seldom bothered to complain of domination by 'les Anglais'. At Ottawa nothing of great consequence could be done contrary to the wishes of the Quebec bloc of ministers, and one of Macdonald's great concerns, in the course of the infighting during the parliamentary session, was to keep his large number of Quebec supporters in line. A common complaint among English-speaking Canadians was that Quebec's dominating place in Confederation was well-nigh intolerable. This was modified by the expectation that it could not last for long, and that as the English-speaking provinces were filled by new immigrants Quebec would lose what was virtually a right of veto in the conduct of Canadian affairs.

The factories of Montreal were annually increasing their production. Port activities enjoyed similar expansion as the export trade gained the benefits of the aggressive work of Canada's Grand Trunk Railway, which by this time was moving into Chicago and tapping much of the traffic of the northern mid-west of the United States. New textile mills were opening in Sherbrooke and other centres of the Eastern Townships. In the great river valleys of the province, where the primeval forests had long been hewn down for square timber, the pulp-and-paper industry was commencing to thrive on the new growth. Making every effort to keep its people at home, rather than allow them to emigrate to the United States, the French Catholic church was organizing colonies wherever fertile land could be had, sometimes making bad choices of areas that were barely marginal. Owing to its systematic formation of new communities of French Canadians, the Eastern Townships were rapidly losing their character as an English-speaking land. The fastening of the parish-school system of education on this Protestant countryside resulted in the withdrawal of the original Anglo-American stock in large numbers.

Amid Gallic fury Quebec continued to endure its Holy War. There were many nuances of opinion, but fundamentally the question was whether or not those who called themselves liberal in the European sense of the expression, who were willing to separate the religious and the profane, who would allow the State a large share in the direction of human affairs, could be regarded as trustworthy Catholics. The conservative, ultra-Catholic, ultramontane *castors* held hard to the Syllabus of Errors of Pius IX, turning their backs on the science and progress of the nineteenth century. The integral Catholic state was their grand aspiration. Liberal Catholics and Catholic Liberals (there was a difference) believed that Church and State could march side by side, but that each could be largely free of the other. 'Muzzling the clergy' was the avowed aim of Liberal *Rouge* extremists. Montreal opposed Quebec, and Laval University endeavoured to prevent the establishment of infant colleges that were to be the seedlings of a new university in the larger city. Even the hierarchy of the Church was divided as the aged Bishop Bourget of Montreal, the grand protagonist of the *castors,* with his fervent disciple, Bishop Laflèche of Three Rivers, endeavoured to restore French Canada to 'its true principles'. The question could not, of course, be confined to theological circles. Young Wilfrid Laurier, who prided himself on being a Liberal after the English fashion, found the going difficult in his great effort to free his party from the innuendo of being Freemason and un-Catholic. The clergy persisted in regarding the *bleu* of Conservatism as their favourite colour. 'Le ciel est bleu, l'enfer est rouge' was still enunciated from Quebec pulpits at election time, and the Liberals, beneath the weight of this great prejudice, continued to labour at a disadvantage.

Ontario was asserting its role as the strong backbone of Confederation. In the making of national policy and in the winning of national elections her influence was becoming more and more pronounced. Proud of her prosperity and favoured by the new tariff, Ontario was developing a sense of community, a consciousness of being the great heartland of Canada to which all other elements must be ancillary. Oliver Mowat, the Liberal premier, was the foremost champion of what were beginning to be called provincial rights and he thought of his province as 'our country', a glaring contradiction to the concept of Confederation that was in the ascendancy under the Macdonald Conservatives at Ottawa. Ontario was the province in which peaches were given to the pigs. Local pride became more notable as the industry of the cities became more productive. Toronto was becoming famous for its indulgence in congratulating itself upon its brand-new industries, its eighty churches, and its educational institutions. Its rivals ringing it about accused it of greedy monopoly. At Hamilton, already known as the 'Ambitious City', it was frequently boasted that the opulent county of Wentworth could always challenge Toronto either in industry or in the arts.

Assimilation of the elements making up the population was proceeding more rapidly in Ontario than in the other provinces. At Berlin German-speaking crowds still sang 'The Watch on the Rhine', but boasts of loyalty to the British Crown were as frequent here as elsewhere. Newly arrived English and Scottish immigrants, taking to the manufacturing towns between Toronto and Sarnia, quietly became absorbed in the mixture of Loyalist gentility and brash Yankeeism that had made up the old frontier. In Toronto there was a large Irish community with an archbishop who was sometimes called a Fenian and who was endowed, it was said, with a marvellous capacity to organize the Irish vote at election time. Occasionally he challenged the dicta of the Minister of Education on the content of the school curriculum. The summer of 1882 saw a great controversy on the issue of whether or not Scott's *Marmion* was a subject of study fit for the children of the province.

The exuberance that prevailed on the purely provincial scene in Ontario was given increased emphasis by the success of the contest over Dominion and provincial powers that

Mowat waged with Macdonald. The great Conservative chieftain, largely by the judicious exercise of Ottawa's powers of patronage, had been able to keep the smaller provinces in accord with the policies of the federal government. But Ontario proved her bigness by an ability to fight Ottawa. Mowat and his Grits never flagged in their legal battle against Macdonald's wide interpretation of Ottawa's powers as defined by the British North America Act. A sustained action at law, with a comic-opera setting, over the powers of licensing taverns and tavern-keepers, was finally won by Mowat in 1884. In the same year there came Mowat's victory on the Rivers and Streams Act that gave to the provinces the right to control navigation on provincial rivers. The law-lords at Westminster, cogitating upon problems of Canadian jurisdictions, were leaning more and more heavily on the Property and Civil Rights clause of Section 93, and the Dominion government was emerging in a thoroughly weakened condition. Sensing the tide of provincial self-righteousness that developed in the wake of these decisions, Macdonald, thinking above all things of keeping his majority in Parliament, would no longer employ the power of disallowance which, ever since Confederation, he had used to chasten provincial governments. Mowat was the first of a long line of Canadian provincial premiers to acquire great repute by boldly and successfully challenging the government at Ottawa.

It was an old conviction of the Grits of Ontario that their province should extend to the Rockies. By the establishment of Manitoba Macdonald's government had commenced a process of division of the west by which, it was supposed, a large number of small provinces, puny in their powers, would eventually emerge. But the bigness of Ontario could not be denied. Between the two there was a great area in dispute: part of the land of Keewatin – the land of the bleak north wind, as it was known to the Indians. Rat Portage, later renamed Kenora, was the only place of consequence in the territory which contained considerable reserves of valuable timberland. In the time of Alexander Mackenzie an Ottawa tribunal had awarded it to Ontario, the argument hinging on the limits of Canada as ceded to Britain in 1763, but Macdonald, upon his coming to power in 1878, had refused to honour the decision. During the following years Ontario and Manitoba clashed in more than legal array. In the summer of 1883 Mowat sent magistrates and constables to contest Manitoba's jurisdiction at Rat Portage. Policemen of each province found themselves in the other's gaol. Ontario's constables were kidnapped and packed off on the long journey to Winnipeg, and the Manitoba gaol was set on fire. One incident of violence was reported as the work of both 'Mowat's carpet-baggers' and 'a Tory band of thirty-four ruffians'. Very unconstitutionally the Manitoba government ordered the Winnipeg Field Battery to the scene. But again Mowat won, this time his greatest triumph. When he returned to Toronto from London in September 1884, with the favourable opinion of the Privy Council in his portmanteau, he was received as a conquering hero who had humbled Ottawa in the dust.

The great era for the opening of the west seemed finally to have arrived with the eighties. The year 1881 saw the greatest immigration in Canadian history, and the traffic through the United States, from St. Paul down the Red River Valley, tripled in volume. Thousands of Ontario farmers, it was said, were preparing to join the colonization trains for Manitoba. There was no doubt concerning the future of Winnipeg. It stood at the front door of a vast new empire that would reveal new riches with the years. Its situation as a distribution centre for the entire North-west could not be excelled. Already there was talk of the short haul by rail from it to the open water of Hudson Bay. With its population of ten thousand, Winnipeg was ugly and unfinished, its main streets long, crooked, and flat as a billiard table. But land of questionable title on imaginary streets was selling at seven hundred and fifty dollars the running foot. High wages made the industrious independent, and the high cost of living eliminated the laggards who hoped to escape work. But all was not raw and materialistic. The city abounded with churches and schools, and to the north there would arise a university to which all religious denominations had pledged their support. From the time of the establishment of the province law enforcement had been secure. No gangs of vultures and land-sharks, whose activities made the American west so spectacular, were found here.

A railway ran from Winnipeg to Portage la Prairie. Westward the traveller was dependent on the jolting Red River carts and buckboards that smashed so readily on the prairie sandholes. The Saskatchewan was served by two remarkable steamers, the *Northcote* and the *Lily*, stern-wheelers about 130 feet long and drawing twenty-two inches of water. Occasionally they employed the huge spars and tackle that were carried on their decks for 'walking' and 'pushing' from shoals and sand-bars, looking like great grasshoppers or spiders floating on the river. The lovely valley of Qu'Appelle, which in the summer season bloomed with roses, was forlorn and neglected: only the occasional pocket of white men had taken possession for Canada of the country to the west of Manitoba. Battleford had recently been made the capital of the Northwest Territories, yet nobody was proud of the designation, for the Dominion government had not yet opened a land office. The white squatters were in the humour to encourage the more vocal malcontents among the Métis, who ever since 1870 had been migrating to the Saskatchewan, and at Ottawa Macdonald, fearful of the greed of land speculators, was in no hurry to legitimize the huge claims of those who hoped for easy riches.

The prairie between Battleford and Fort Calgary was still red man's country. Domestication, the consequence of the policies of the Dominion government, had made considerable progress among the Cree, though not to their great improvement. But the Blackfoot were still untamed, still capable of mobilizing two thousand braves, well-equipped and presenting a formidable, warlike array as they did for Lord Lorne at his crossing of the Bow River in September 1881. Calgary itself was an outpost of the cattle industry from over the border. Cattle-breeders were emphatic in their point of view that the land was worthless for agriculture.

Macleod could produce Canada's best version of a wild west. The famous Camoose House, kept by an ex-trader, ex-preacher, and squawman, was the resort of all the whisky vendors, bull-whackers, and mule-skinners of the region who called themselves ranchers.

Guarded by the few hundred constables of the North West Mounted Police, the west was fairly in Canada's grip, despite the possibility of new Fenian raids and of the overflowing of American immigrants who might establish American claims by actual possession. Until Sitting Bull led his tattered lodges back over the border in July 1881, there was always a danger that American forces would cross the line in order to apprehend him. But the Police had managed the expatriate Sioux as well as they had kept their own Canadian Indians in order and had persuaded them peacefully to return to American territory.

Convinced that the west needed only publicity to fill its unpeopled plains, Lord Lorne proceeded on a tour in 1881 as far as the foothills of the Rockies, taking with him a large number of British and Canadian newspapermen. His efforts were singularly successful. Even *The Times* of London, always convinced that there was little above the commonplace in Canadian life, came around. A country, it said, that had been declared to be hopelessly sterile by the only authorities supposed to know had been shown to be exactly the opposite of what had previously been believed. The best lands in Canada had been left for the last immigrants.

III

The grip on the west could be made permanent and sure only by the modern method of economic exploitation – the construction of a railway. Through the years of the early eighties Macdonald anxiously contemplated the fitful construction of the American Northern Pacific on its slow progress from St. Paul to Seattle. Railway-builders had by this time learned that a railway could grow and make money for its shareholders only by establishing a monopoly of control

THE GREAT COMBINATION.

Let Monopoly tremble in its boots!

From a print in the Public Archives of Canada.

over the traffic of a territory. New and unexploited areas of virgin soil such as the Canadian west, obviously the resort of tens of thousands of immigrants in the approaching years, challenged the ambitions of monopolizers, and the men of the Northern Pacific had their eyes on the territory to the north of the forty-ninth parallel. If they could drain off its traffic the west would come within the American commercial orbit and Canadian sovereignty would become increasingly dubious.

Commercially, British Columbia had always been a part of the American hinterland. San Francisco was its metropolis and a whole generation of merchants and traders of Victoria were oriented to it. Canada had failed to hold to the union bargain of 1871. The government of Alexander Mackenzie had honoured it only by piecemeal and unsubstantial tokens, having no conviction that a railway line to the Pacific through British territory could be justified either by engineering or by commercial realities. At Victoria the government of George Anthony Walkem, calling for 'the terms, the whole terms, and nothing but the terms' of union, was resorting to expediencies that Macdonald called blackmail. The Vancouver Island party in provincial politics wanted more than anything else a railway from Nanaimo to Esquimalt which they declared Canada should build as a penalty for its failure. Secession was a powerful cry and behind secession there was a disposition, not overt but nevertheless real, to seek annexation to the United States. In the spring of 1881 a provincial delegation, headed by the blustering Amor de Cosmos, left Victoria for London to seek repeal of the union. Until a railway could be constructed to the Pacific, British Columbia would gravitate to the United States. The 'very British' upper crust of society would find it difficult to keep things in hand until the steel link with Canada should pierce the Rockies.

But Macdonald had swung into action. The Canadian Pacific Syndicate, organized in 1880, headed by George Stephen, was moving swiftly. In Parliament the Grits were vehement, certain that the C.P.R. contract represented the surrender of the natural resources of the west to a corporation whose influence would be much greater than that of the Hudson's Bay Company had ever been. Yet Edward Blake, so verbose and self-righteous, had declined an open debate on the great contract with the Minister of Railways and Canals, Sir Charles Tupper, and there was little doubt that the temper of the country favoured Macdonald's sanguine point of view. Stephen made a number of epoch-making decisions completely at variance with the gloomy economic and engineering calculations in which the Grits had been so prone to indulge. He would run his line along the swamp and muskeg of the Lake Superior shore, always considered the most hazardous and expensive route. Instead of building north through the Rockies by the Yellowhead Pass he would go farther south in order to intercept the anticipated invasion of Canadian territory by the Northern Pacific. In August of 1882 this gamble was justified by the exciting telegram from Major Rogers which announced a convenient pass through the Selkirks where no tunnel would be required. These short cuts would reduce both the costs and the time taken to fulfil the contract.

When William Van Horne joined the Canadian Pacific Company in the spring of 1882 the work of exploration, survey, and construction moved at what seemed like lightning speed. New techniques for track-laying quickened the completion of the easy prairie section from Portage to the Rockies. From Port Arthur hundreds of men worked to the eastward, and the frightening complications of the lake shore, so feared by the experts, did not materialize. Over the rough obstacle of the Canadian Shield, through the difficult country by which La Vérendrye and the first French voyageurs had made their way to the prairies, the railway moved, by-passing the myriad lakes and swamps, spanning the many portages. Communities of workshops and shanties dotted the route, and almost everywhere the bagpipes skirled to give inspiration. Up the valley of the Fraser, from Emery's Bar to Savona Ferry, Andrew Onderdonk and his imported army of Chinese labourers blasted their way. Stephen had announced 1886 to be the year of completion of the entire line and when the last spike was driven in a remote pass of the Rockies, named Craigellachie in respect to the Scottish antecedents of Stephen and his cousin, Donald Smith, the mood was one of self-congratulation but not of surprise. In the view of those who thought of Canada as a real entity – there were few scoffers now – the work of Confederation had been consummated.

Yet the triumph was achieved painfully. The construction

proceeded so rapidly that the facilities for financing it were outpaced. The tens of thousands of immigrants expected did not move into the west to provide the C.P.R. with revenue by purchase of the twenty-five millions of acres of land the company had been awarded by its contract. Stephen, self-confessedly, was like a man walking along the edge of a precipice. In March 1884, the government came to the aid of the company to save it from its creditors. But Macdonald had to combat in Parliament not only the Grits to whom the whole story of the C.P.R. was one of reckless misappropriation of the national heritage. His own majority was dubious as the credit of the Canadian government became plighted to that of the C.P.R., as the whole destiny of Canada became more and more synonymous with the company's success or failure. Quebec Conservatives blackmailed the government for local concessions in return for their support for the required financial measures in Parliament.

Much of the trouble was caused by the malignant rivalry of the Grand Trunk. It had first been indifferent to the idea of opening up the west by a railway, but when Stephen secured lines through eastern Ontario to Montreal, when he moved on to Quebec City by acquiring the line along the north bank of the St. Lawrence, when he entered Toronto and tapped the Grand Trunk monopoly in parts of southern Ontario, the Grand Trunk opened its talons. Because the government was committed to the success of the C.P.R., Ottawa was Stephen's citadel. London was the battleground on which Sir Henry Tyler and the board of Grand Trunk directors could fight the C.P.R. with assuredly greater prospects of success. It was intolerable to the Grand Trunk that this new upstart, the spoilt darling of the Canadian government, should compete with it for funds for Canadian development, and its hostile propaganda helped to destroy Stephen's prospects for getting money on the London market. The great news media of the world – Reuters, the Associated Press, *The Times* of London – all played the game of the scribblers who seemed determined to destroy the credit of the C.P.R. and with it the credit of Canada.

Early in 1885 the government again had to come to the aid of the company. The pay car was ready to leave for the west but there was no money. This crisis was averted by the news that rebellion on the Saskatchewan had been ended by the rapid transportation of Canadian soldiers to the scene of conflict over the railway which Parliament and the nation had seemed on the point of repudiating.

IV

The results of the election of 1882 reflected the prosperous and contented state of Canada. But the C.P.R. crisis of 1884 reflected a turning for the worse. In the summer of 1883 the land market in Manitoba had suddenly broken, and panic replaced the buoyant optimism that had reigned at Winnipeg for five years. Embattled farmers of Manitoba, where the population had risen to over seventy-five thousand, organized themselves for protest, blaming Ottawa for all their troubles–the high tariff on American agricultural implements, the high freight rates they paid to the C.P.R., which enjoyed a monopoly over the grain traffic, the alleged exactions by the Ogilvie monopoly of grain elevators, the laborious intricacies of Ottawa's policy for the sale of land. The real remedy for the trouble lay not in anything Canada could do. The rich, black soil required no cultivators so long as the price of wheat on the great exchanges of the world remained miserably depressed. The great days of the west had not yet come. Almost simultaneously an industrial slow-down struck the east. Bear markets ruled at New York and London. By the summer of 1884 bad times had come to the Treasury, and Tilley, the Finance Minister, reported to Macdonald that revenues were diminishing.

The months of late 1883 and early 1884 marked a minor turning-point in Canadian history. For five years prevailing tendencies had moved in the direction of greater unification and towards consolidating the work of Confederation. Now the winds had shifted. New forces were arising that could lead to disintegration. Ruling Canada became a business of holding hard to what had been accomplished rather than creating new industries and forming new provinces. Population failed to grow at a satisfactory rate. Immigration dwindled and, in London, Galt failed to interest the British government in the proposal to move the surplus and unwanted population of Ireland to Canada for the purpose of forming new Manitobas in the west. Again natural increase seemed to be totally absorbed in the movement to the United States.

As success faded, politics lost the veneer of good humour and joviality that had been so notable in Macdonald's halcyon days. The aging Prime Minister, fondly contemplating retirement amid more plenteous times, could not find a willing successor who could carry the party's confidence. He was rapidly becoming a lone survivor of the old guard who had made Confederation. Sir Charles Tupper, preferring to be on the fringes of politics and succumbing to the importunities of his wife, who enjoyed the refinements of titled English society, took the office of High Commissioner in London in 1883. His violent, sometimes coarse, counter-attacks upon the Opposition during the great moments of debate in the House of Commons were sorely missed by the Conservatives. Tilley, in poor health, was becoming a spent force. Sir Alexander Campbell, Macdonald's old law partner, wanted to retire. Nobody of Cartier's stature had appeared to manage the large bloc of Quebec Conservatives in the House. Macdonald had accomplished all he could for Confederation. He now had no choice but to hold on to office, in poor times, until a strong and acceptable candidate for the leadership should appear. D'Alton McCarthy, the highly qualified young barrister of Orillia, had to remain in his large practice to pay his debts. John S. D. Thompson of Halifax was induced to enter the Cabinet as Minister of Justice in 1885. He had all but one of the necessary qualifications for leadership. It was not so bad that he was a Roman Catholic. But a Protestant turned Roman Catholic, however able and moderate, could not instantly overpower the prejudices of the great Orange contingent of the party. For the leadership and the Prime Ministership he would have to wait.

Macdonald was on the look-out for talent of all kinds and did not care where he found it. There is an account of how, one summer day in the 1880s, he drove into Kingston and tied his horse to a hitching-post half a block away from Municipal Hall, the stage for the old parliament of the Province of Canada, from which he could hear a clear, mellifluous voice, pitched in good, strong cadences. He enquired about the speaker and was told that it was George Foster from New Brunswick lecturing on temperance. 'Get him into politics,' said the Prime Minister. A few months later the young university teacher was in politics and but a few months more had passed before he was Macdonald's Minister of Marine and Fisheries.*

The first great testing time for Confederation was at hand, and Macdonald was fortunate in the quality of the opposition that faced him. The Liberal party had no real discipline and no grand conviction. Ousted from the leadership in 1880, Alexander Mackenzie, not really aged, though broken, held to his rigid principles and could not compromise as the march of events impelled elasticity of belief and action. Through the entire decade he faithfully cherished the great principle that Toryism was the personification of evil, but became increasingly helpless as the muscles in his throat refused to voice his contempt for his infuriatingly successful rivals. Edward Blake, the leader, was eloquent, high-minded, and negative. He professed to believe during the Canadian Pacific debate that the west was merely 'a sea of mountains'. By his determination to be in the forefront of opinion on the development of Canadian nationhood, particularly on Canada's right to make trade treaties of her own, he failed to help the cause of his party and sometimes created in the public mind the impression that he was disloyal to the Empire. The Liberals offered wisdom without hope and failed

* Told to the writer by the Rev. Dr. G. M. Young of Fredericton. Dr. Young was a brother-in-law of Sir George Foster and died in 1963 at the age of 96.

to find the flair that was necessary to win the electorate's confidence. Sir Richard Cartwright's fatalism of economic thought was a dead weight to the party in its disjointed and uninspired struggles. There may have been many reasons for the Conservatives to lose elections, but the Liberals presented no alternative that seemed attractive.

The dictum that Canada is a difficult country to govern was already proverbial in the eighteen-eighties. Regional cross-currents often threatened to upset the constitutional and party structure that held Confederation together. The farmers of Manitoba showed no gratitude to the government and to the C.P.R. that had linked their country with the outside world. They wanted other links as well, principally to the south. Their resentment was concentrated against the monopoly clause in the C.P.R. contract that guaranteed the company freedom from competition for a period of ten years. Macdonald was compelled to accede to their demands in 1888. Then, in return for their support of financial measures of assistance to the C.P.R., Maritime members of Parliament successfully demanded their 'short line' from Montreal to Saint John through Maine, while Quebec, largely by reckless and improvident subventions to railways, had gotten into such financial difficulties that the Dominion government was constantly called to her relief. Her politicians, according to an unfavourable comment of the time, could be bought and sold like steers by the railway contractors who lurked about the committee rooms of government. And as for the most powerful region of all, it was already customary in Toronto blandly to identify Ontario's interests with those of 'the nation'.

Intrusions from the outside sometimes made the management of Parliament more difficult. Racial as well as religious causes contributed to the diversity of the scene. The Irish Home Rule movement of the early eighties converted the Canadian Irish into a homogeneous element in politics. Right across the country they were acutely aware of the tensions in their native land, and they organized themselves to demand of the Canadian government some kind of action that might persuade Britain to moderate her Irish policy. In countless constituencies their votes could be mobilized to win or lose seats for the government.

To keep power Macdonald was compelled to yield to their demands, consenting to the passage in Parliament of resolutions favouring Home Rule for Ireland. Canadians, it was argued, had suffered from Fenian outrages and, out of their federal experience, had the right to advise the British government on how to solve the Irish constitutional problem. But masterfully he took the sting from the resolutions that were prepared in their original form by one of the most violent sympathizers of the Irish extremists, Timothy Warren Anglin of New Brunswick. Taking advantage of the rules of procedure, he steered them through in drastically amended and much more moderate form. Even so, they reached Britain at the time of the horrible Phoenix Park murders and drew angry replies from all British circles, official and non-official. The British government virtually told Canada to mind her own business. The Canadian Parliament, suggested *The Times*, was guilty of levity of thought and had passed the resolutions merely for electioneering purposes. Goldwin Smith, rejoicing in what he thought was a clear illustration of the sham of British loyalties in Canada, told *The Times* that the whole affair had been an electioneering dodge to win the Irish vote. 'You see the real value of the loyalty of colonial politicians.'

The affair created embarrassments and demanded explanations, but Macdonald, having taken a gentle tilt at the British, had the Irish vote delivered to him in the elections of 1882. A few extremists continued to cause mild alarms. The new Governor General, Lord Lansdowne, who arrived in 1883, was threatened with assassination for the prominent part he had played in arousing the resistance of the Irish landlords to the Home Rule movement. Many Canadians became partisans of either 'the tyrannical landlords' or 'the cowardly Fenian assassins who hocked horses and maimed cattle', but as the Irish agitation at home became more subdued, the Irish in Canada became more quiescent.

V

All these problems were minor, compared to the first great crisis of Confederation, which originated on the prairies in the eighties. Ottawa was slow in coming to grips with fundamental problems of the organization of the west, particularly the disposal of land. While the Canadian Pacific was being constructed over the southern prairie, discontents to northward attained the dimensions of a rebellion. Around Battleford, the Métis of the Saskatchewan, who had migrated there following the Red River episode of 1870, again became exposed to the exercise of governmental authority. Again Canadian surveyors divided the country into square sections, ignoring the historical predilection of the Métis to strip farms fronting on the river. Still the government persisted in refusing land-scrip to the Métis, preferring to believe that their claims were fraudulent, as, indeed, in many cases they were. At Battleford white settlers themselves encouraged the Métis to adopt their truculent attitude. Macdonald considered the whole fraternity of the north Saskatchewan a band of blackmailers, and would take no action. His agents in the west warned of impending troubles, but the Prime Minister held to his great conviction that time was the healer of difficulties of this kind.

Early in 1884 a delegation of the people of the Saskatchewan, headed by Gabriel Dumont, rode off to Montana for the purpose of inviting Louis Riel to take the leadership of this mixed community that contained Scots and other racial ingredients as well as French Métis. The leader of the provisional government of the Red River had lost no prestige among his people with the passing years. He was articulate, even eloquent, gifted with a capacity for putting bold and resolute plans into action. What was to become more novel was his capacity to see visions and to dream dreams. The great question as to whether he was patriot or scoundrel, sane or insane, can be dismissed with the observation that there is a little of each of these in all men.

Riel believed in the possibility of establishing a half-breed nation in the west. But following his return to Canada his demeanour was at first orderly, for his activity consisted chiefly of urging upon the government civil measures that would assure his people of their rights. Having established his ascendancy, he employed it for private purposes. At the very moment the government was about to honour the demands of the half-breeds for land-scrip, which, Macdonald believed, they would spend on whisky, Riel intimated that he was willing to leave Canada if his own personal claims to land in Manitoba, valued at one hundred thousand dollars, were bought out for thirty-five thousand. Ignoring this blackmail, the government reinforced the North West Mounted Police and took measures to appease lesser lights among the Métis.

Coupled with this cupidity, never revealed to his followers, Riel exhibited a fanaticism suggestive of a Moslem Mahdi in the desert. He described himself as a prophet destined to lead 'the New Nation' to freedom. He would divide the west among the Catholic nationalities of Europe. As excitement mounted on the Saskatchewan his faith became more unorthodox and schismatic, reflecting to some extent the competing tendencies in the Catholic world. The records of his errant imaginings may be dubious, but according to one authority he would destroy not only England and Canada but Rome and the Pope. Apparently rejecting the new orientations of Leo XIII, he would make Bishop Bourget, leader of Quebec's ultramontanes, Pope of 'the New World'. Alarmed by these eccentricities, his clerical mentors of the Saskatchewan, especially Father André, deserted him.

On March 17, 1885, Riel established a provisional government with himself as president and Gabriel Dumont as adjutant-general. A few days later a detachment of Mounted Police under Superintendent Crozier, attempting to establish control over the country about Duck Lake, proved to be unequal in marksmanship to the Métis. Twelve police were killed. This battle, so trifling in dimensions, began the Saskatchewan rebellion and reopened the whole question of the future of the Canadian North-west. Though the white settlers turned against him, behind Riel were the Cree and the Blackfoot, who could sense the last opportunity to contest the complete domination of the plains by the white man. With considerable reason Riel could boast of American assistance, for the frontier was lined with Fenians and irresponsible expansionists who would make what they could of trouble in Canada.

Sensing real crisis, the kind of crisis that could undo so much of what had been done for Confederation, Macdonald acted swiftly. By March 27 Major-General Frederick Middleton, the British commander of the Canadian militia, reached Winnipeg. On the night of the same day he left for Qu'Appelle with the Winnipeg Rifles. Within the next few weeks he had under command a force of over 3,200 men, drawn chiefly from the militia battalions of Quebec and Ontario. Colonel Thomas Strange, a retired British officer who was cattle-ranching near Calgary, led a force of westerners down the Saskatchewan from Edmonton to Fort Pitt, where he joined the eastern formations. These rapid movements were made possible only by the near-completion of the C.P.R. The Métis were unready and unable to deal with the overwhelming forces that so suddenly converged upon them.

After four days of fighting, Batoche, the rebel stronghold, was stormed and taken by Middleton on May 12. The rebels fought well but they were overpowered by numbers. On May 15 Riel sullenly emerged from hiding and surrendered to a small scouting formation. This was the first purely Canadian military enterprise in history and the triumph heartened the nation at a time when little else, not even the certain completion of the C.P.R., could give it heart. In Quebec, where the hierarchy of the Church gave its blessing to the expedition, the jubilation was as great as elsewhere. British and American newspapers had written forebodingly and disparagingly of a long-extended war in the west, but the rebellion had been quickly crushed by what appeared to be the remarkable effort of a united Canada. Yet, when the year 1885 was out, it was disunion that emblazoned the Canadian scene. Riel was tried for treason at Regina and convicted. The defence rested its case on insanity, but Riel himself, in his highly emotional address to the jury, repudiated this contention. The Crown invoked the famous McNaghten judgment to show that the accused, at the time of the crime, had been able to distinguish right from wrong.

The great question was not that of Riel's guilt but one of whether or not the government should act on the jury's recommendation for mercy and commute the sentence of execution. During the trial excitement had risen in Quebec. For all his failings, Riel was a Frenchman. In a strange, mystic kind of way his career was symbolic of the rapidly receding hopes for a French Canada in the west, of the idea, dominant at Confederation, that the west could be bilingual. The fact of Riel's insanity was accepted as an excuse for his violent eccentricities. It was noted with bitterness that his English-speaking secretary, Jackson, had been found insane and allowed to escape across the border. Mercy had been extended generally to other rebels, even to Gabriel Dumont. Within the Cabinet, in Parliament, and throughout Quebec, French-Canadian opinion welled up in the conviction that the government should act mercifully and commute the death sentence.

Yet opinion favouring the execution was the stronger. In Ontario the feeling was that Riel should hang, not so much for his recent treason as for the alleged judicial murder of Thomas Scott, the brash young Orangeman who had been shot at Fort Garry in 1870. Revenge for Scott was the great impulse that moved opinion not only in Ontario but all through English-speaking Canada. Was it reasonable, men argued, to spare the life of a blackmailing scoundrel who was responsible for the deaths of thirty-eight Canadians in a rebellion that cost the country five million dollars? The recommendation for mercy became primarily a matter of politics, though the judicial apparatus was kept in motion until the end. Twice Macdonald suspended the execution. From July until November the great decision hung in the balance while convulsive fits of feeling became more notable on each side of the Ottawa River. On November 11 opposition among Quebec members of the Cabinet was overcome. Interpreting the decision brutally, it was a question of political analysis. Quebec's opinion was less certain than Ontario's. By commutation of the sentence Macdonald would lose more seats in Ontario than he would gain in Quebec should he decide on mercy.

All this time Riel had waited in prison, daily visited by medical practitioners and spiritual advisers, retracting his heresies but announcing new fantasies of nocturnal interviews with an angel. His priest, declaring he was not responsible, readmitted him to the communion of the Church. On November 16 the sentence was executed and the trap sprung. Macdonald could not bring himself to believe that the gibbet at Regina could become the symbol for the great tragedy he had always sought to avert – the division of opinion in Canada on the basis of racial antipathy. His career had been a succession of triumphs for the idea of the confederation of races. Yet the execution of Riel was to unloose new forces which he, in his remaining lifetime, would be unable to master.

VI

At Ottawa the affair of Riel apparently blew over easily and much as Macdonald had anticipated. Blake, making a seven-hour speech in the Commons, was tactically outmanoeuvred. Seventeen Quebec *Bleus* deserted the government, but twenty-three English-speaking Liberals refused to vote for the motion deploring the passing of the death sentence. Many Quebec Conservatives, Sir Hector Langevin told Macdonald, felt it necessary to deliver one vote against the government. The bishops and archbishops of the province sorrowfully held to the point of view that Riel's execution was justifiable.

But Ottawa and its allies in the hierarchy lost the leadership of French-Canadian opinion. On November 22 the greatest mass meeting in the history of Canada was held at the Champ de Mars in Montreal. There the eloquent Wilfrid Laurier burst the bonds of Liberal refinement and constitutionalism by declaring that he, too, had he lived on the banks of the broad Saskatchewan, would have shouldered a musket and fought with Riel. Ultramontane *Bleus* and radical *Rouges* united to proclaim the monumental injustice that had been inflicted on the French race and to mourn the death of Riel, who, on this great occasion, became a deathless symbol of the martyred French groups of the west now passing under English domination. The hero of the afternoon was not Laurier but Honoré Mercier, a Liberal newspaperman and politician, who professed to see great urgencies in the hour and could present greater necessities. 'Riel, our brother' had died because of the fanaticism of Sir John A. Macdonald and the treason of the Quebec cabinet ministers, who, privately opposing the execution, had nevertheless collaborated in the act in order to keep their portfolios. The French race, said Mercier, could redeem itself only by uniting in the formation of a national party. The cheering on the Champ de Mars was so loud that the artist Robert Harris, who had just completed his picture of the Fathers of Confederation, could hear it as he leaned from his window a mile and a half away. He was not the only English-speaking Canadian who would condemn 'this murder for policy'.*

The formation of a purely French-Canadian party was a solution of vengeance, a program of practical action that ran counter to the whole Canadian tradition. It affronted the memories of Lafontaine, Cartier, and all other French-Canadian leaders who had believed that the two races could work together within a single constitutional system. It offended the sensibilities and faith of Laurier who said that Riel at his worst was a subject fit for an asylum, at his best a religious and political monomaniac. But Le Parti National came into existence. Its philosophical basis was a mystic faith in the virtues of the French race, of memories of how Charlemagne had championed the papacy in the Middle Ages, of

* From a letter in possession of the writer.

the great tradition of St. Louis and Joan of Arc and of Champlain and Brébeuf. Mercier had been something of a *Rouge*, tinged with anti-clericalism, but it was easy for him to identify his violent racism with a militant Catholicism. In the provincial elections of October 1886 the Conservatives lost their majority, and out of the confusion that ensued in the legislature Mercier emerged as the leader of a new Quebec government early in 1887.

Le Parti National spared no pains to convince its following that it was anti-British and anti-Protestant, determined to avenge the insults and injuries of the past. The English-speaking reaction was no less violent. The Toronto press led the van of the counter-attack, professing to believe that Mercier's ascendancy in Quebec was the prelude to the break-up of Canada, reminding its readers that they were the successors to the conquerors of 1763, warning that they might be compelled to fight in order to retain the fruits of the conquest. These strenuous threats and retorts inspired Mercier to still greater excesses in his own utterances. To an alert and prejudiced Protestant public his legislation suggested the coming of a life-and-death struggle between the two races. Anticipating a great cry of the future, he warned French Canadians that the propaganda of the Imperial Federation League might result in the sending of their sons to die for the British Empire 'from the icefields of the North Pole to the burning sands of the Sudan'. For friendship he looked to Rome, Paris, New York, and Brussels, never to London and Ottawa. He behaved like a head of state and, as his policies gained popularity in Quebec, the hierarchy regarded him more warmly. Far in the depths of the minds of Mercier and some of his supporters was the dream of a French state, not merely French-Canadian but Franco-American as well, that would include the 350,000 French Canadians of New England as well as those of the St. Lawrence. It was candidly believed by many Franco-Americans at the time that Confederation was like a house of cards and would soon collapse. Out of the debris an independent French state might arise.

The Jesuit Estates Act, passed in the Quebec legislature in 1888, sustained the racial strife that the execution of Riel had engendered. Within its own context it was a reasonable measure. Ever since the eighteenth century, when the Jesuit Order had been suppressed by papal decree, its vast properties in Canada had been administered by the government, largely in the interests of education. Returning to Canada in 1831, the Order had steadily regained influence in French Canada, powerfully contributing to the ultramontanism of Bishop Bourget and becoming embroiled in Quebec's tangle of Church-State politics. An agitation arose for the return to the Order of its property. This, Mercier was prepared to stop by buying out its claims for a monetary compensation. Other religious orders pressed for shares in the financial returns which were to be devoted to education. So scrupulous was Mercier in apportioning the funds that he reserved sixty thousand dollars for the Protestant Committee of Public Instruction.

Fierce Protestant reaction throughout Canada was aroused by the stipulation in the Act that the Pope should decide upon the distribution of four hundred thousand dollars to Catholic foundations. Papal authority was invoked in the Act's preamble and it became evident that the Bishop of Rome was about to dispose of property rights in a British country. Through the nineteenth century, Protestant Canada had developed with the doctrine of separation of Church and State as one of the cardinal articles of its belief. The Church establishment and system of tithes in Quebec were regarded as alien and outmoded. In extreme Protestant circles the Jesuit Estates Act was described as insulting to the character of Canada and to the intelligence of its people, and threatening to Protestant populations in other parts of the country. Eastern Ontario, said an editorial in the Toronto *Mail,* would become the victim of French and priestly aggression and be detached from Protestant civilization.

The immediate outcry in Ontario was for disallowance of the Jesuit Estates Act by the federal government. Weighing carefully the political odds as well as the legal considerations, Macdonald decided against it. Disallowance would merely strengthen Mercier in Quebec and deepen the increasing gulf between the two races. At this stage the initiative in maintaining the cultural and racial conflict passed to Ontario. There came into existence the Equal Rights Association, an organization whose objectives, if realized, would force French Canada to the will of the English-speaking majority, would deny to Catholics the 'privilege' of separate schools financed by public money, would refuse to French-Canadian clergy any influence in civil affairs – would make of Canada a melting-pot in which English-speaking, Protestant, secular culture would be supreme. The Jesuit Estates Act passed to the theatre of the House of Commons, where the motion of the Orange Colonel W. E. O'Brien, demanding disallowance, gained but thirteen supporters. But throughout rural Ontario, the west, and the Maritime Provinces they were widely acclaimed as 'the noble thirteen'. English-speaking Canada, too, acquired a well organized bloc of embittered extremists.

Racial conflict spread to other quarters. In 1889 D'Alton McCarthy proceeded west and toured Manitoba, advocating anti-French measures in a province where the French language stood on a legal footing equal to that of English. In 1890 Thomas Greenway, the leader of Manitoba's government, an aggressive politician who was seeking a new basis of popularity amongst the overwhelming English majority, brought to the legislature a bill that denied the official character of French as a language and abolished the system of separate schools, contrary to the guarantees of the Manitoba Act of 1870. In the same year McCarthy successfully introduced to the House of Commons a bill which could have effectively destroyed the equal status of the French language in the Northwest Territories and precipitated a division in which party lines were broken down and race voted against race for the first time in Canada's history. Simultaneously attacks were made in the House of Commons on the use of the French language in the schools of eastern Ontario.

VII

The cultural conflict between the two great races of the country was not the only reason why men were saying, in the last five years of the decade, that Confederation could not last. The concept of Canada as a unified state received a whole succession of damaging blows from a cluster of provincial premiers of whom Mercier was merely an outstanding example. The Judicial Committee of the Privy Council at Westminster had placed such heavy emphasis on the Property and Civil Rights clause of the British North America Act that it was becoming possible to think of Canada as a loose league of provinces. Mowat's legal victories were considered by his supporters to be the commencement of the process by which the authority of Ottawa could be subordinated to provincial pride. The authority of Ottawa, in the minds of the Grits of Ontario, could be identified with the sinister methods, the unscrupulous tactics, the loose moral character of Sir John A. Macdonald.

From the east there emerged another threat. In 1884 William Stevens Fielding, the editor of the *Nova Scotian*, a product of the old anti-Confederate school of Howe and Annand, became head of the government at Halifax. Disappointed hopes and bad times rejuvenated the old conviction that Nova Scotia was entitled to a destiny of her own, that her prosperity could be found in an oceanic and international economy, freed from the tariffs and railways of a continental state. Temperamentally Fielding was cautious. But in 1886, after an unsuccessful attempt to extract larger subsidies from Ottawa, he introduced to the legislature resolutions favouring Nova Scotia's secession from the union, coupling them with the other old plan of a union of the Maritime Provinces and the secession of all three. Not only did he succeed in this, but he went to the people on this drastic program and routed the Conservative opposition. The first open challenge to the union of British North America, sanctioned by the people of a province in an electoral contest, had been made.

Honoré Mercier enjoyed the support of a goodly number of provincial premiers when he called a constitutional conference at Quebec in October 1887. His objective was to bring about a general surrender of powers from the Dominion to the provincial governments. The provinces, it was reasoned, should appoint half of the members of the Senate for life. The federal power of disallowance of provincial legislation should be abandoned. Larger financial subsidies should be paid by the Dominion to the provincial governments that would enlarge their spheres of influence. Mowat, the pre-eminent champion of provincial rights, was present. Fielding, though refusing to compromise on his grand objective of secession, agreed to take part. John Norquay, though he had always been Macdonald's man, had his back to the wall in Manitoba and felt compelled to participate for the purpose of securing the removal of the C.P.R.'s monopoly over the traffic of the west. From New Brunswick there came Andrew G. Blair, the leader of a hard school of legislative trimmers who declined party labels. He had risen to eminence as a non-party man, but by 1884 he had deemed it politic to wear a Liberal tag. Six members of his cabinet called themselves Liberal-Conservatives.

Macdonald's answer to the passage of the resolutions at Quebec, which would, if carried out, change the whole character of the Dominion, was a highly conscious profession of masterful inactivity. The Parliament of Great Britain would amend the British North America Act only following the joint address of the Senate and the House of Commons of Canada. The two provinces of British Columbia and Prince Edward Island had been unrepresented at Quebec. The Dominion government had abstained from taking part. The conference, therefore, could be said to have absolutely no legal basis or any basis of consent on the part of the people of Canada. As the provincial premiers returned to their strongholds to proclaim the new dispensation and to introduce to their legislatures the Quebec resolutions, some appreciably modified and weakened, Ottawa's attitude was one of aloofness and gentle disdain. Acting on their own, the provincial premiers could accomplish nothing.

Initiative in the affairs of Canada had fallen into the hands of a new school of provincial politicians whose stages, originally intended to be miniature, had become marvellously expanded. Yet Macdonald could not be dislodged from his central and commanding position. In February 1887, realizing that time was working against him, he went to the country and emerged the undoubted victor in a short, sharp campaign. The Liberals seemed constitutionally incapable of taking advantage of the enormous underlying factors working in their favour. Canada was in a humour for new departures. But Blake stultified the Liberal effort by violently breaking with a free-trade wing of the party, led by Cartwright, on the issue of commercial union with the United States. In spite of the logical appeal of free trade he could not bring himself to betray the interests of the manufacturing belt, extending from Montreal to Sarnia, that the National Policy had so notably developed. In this he was supported by the aging titan Alexander Mackenzie. The idea of Canada not merely as a nation but as a national economy, bound together against its great neighbours by a tariff fence, survived a great peril in this election of 1887. In moments of despair, or something akin to it, when all commercial activity seemed incapable of rousing itself from a cloying depression, closer relations with the United States could exercise a general appeal. In 1887 the idea of nationality appeared to come at a high price. The only good explanation for the Conservative victory was the ineptness and indiscipline of the rival party, a factor on which Macdonald could count heavily. Out of the Liberal discomfiture there came a new leader, Wilfrid Laurier.

The electoral victory brought no new enthusiasm and freshness of ideas to the Conservatives. As the decade drew to a close the strength of the government seemed more and more to rest upon the aging Macdonald. Confident Tories had acquired the habit of saying that he would never die, but in 1887 he was seventy-two and new strains had come to the problem of holding Canada together. Corruption in the Department of Public Works struck down Sir Hector Langevin and intensified the prejudice of many Canadians that the vocation of politician was sinister and dishonest. While heads hung in shame at Ottawa no Canadian could take an ebullient pride in the character of his country. The Imperial Federation League, by stimulating within a thin band of the population a violent desire for the closer integration of the British Empire, antagonized the French Canadians and gave to Mercier and his separatists new reason for the cry that Canada as a nation could not function. To this highly emotional appeal Macdonald never acceded. Galt, McCarthy, and George Foster succumbed to the blandishments of Imperial Federation, but the Prime Minister could see in these real obstacles to the integration of Canada as a state.

Old tensions from across the border acquired new form as the Americans, less outwardly hostile than in former years but apparently no less cunning and underhanded, seemed to snatch at every opportunity to weaken the slender foundations on which Canada was constructed. The government at Washington began to seize Canadian sealing vessels in the Bering Sea, putting forward the pious pretext of conservation but at the same time permitting its own sealers to operate from the Pribilof Islands. James G. Blaine, the American Secretary of State, who had risen to political affluence as a baiter of Britain and as a hero to the Irish vote, deepened the insult by professing to regard Canada as a colony, by attempting to deny Canadian participation in the negotiations that followed with Britain. For years almost all Canadians had nourished hopes for freer trade with the United States. Macdonald and the Conservatives, though committed to the policy of high tariff on manufactured goods, had watched for openings that would enable them to bargain with Washington for lower rates on Canadian farm produce. These aspirations were dealt a cruel blow by the McKinley tariff of 1890, which especially penalized the importation of Canadian cereals. The old cry that Yankee politicians were attempting to starve Canada out, the deep suspicion that they were using commercial policy to force Canada to sue for annexation, acquired fresh poignancy.

Canada was a North American country with but two abiding marks of distinction – its British institutions and its bilingual culture. In 1890 there was no certainty that the constitution of 1867 could restrain the tensions that divided the two great races. Confederation, it could soberly be argued, had reached its limits. Perhaps the solitary mark of grandeur on the bleak and unpromising scene was the withering but unflagging figure of the Prime Minister. For twenty years he had been a favourite target for moralistic propagandists as well as professional politicians. But behind the veneer of cynicism and worldly wisdom, beneath the deep knowledge of men's frailties gained from a long career of public administration, there were faith and constancy. To his life's mission, the building of a nation from sea to sea, he was holding hard.

4. The 1890s

JOHN T. SAYWELL

We have come to a period in the history of this young country when premature dissolution seems to be at hand. . . . How long can the present fabric last? Can it last at all? All these are questions which surge in the mind, and to which dismal answers only suggest themselves.' As the decade opened, there were many Canadians who agreed with Wilfrid Laurier, leader of the Liberal Opposition. The high hopes of the founding Fathers had not been fulfilled. The statecraft of veteran Sir John A. Macdonald, the charcoal sketch of the Canadian Pacific across a still-unsettled west, and a slim volume containing the ever-increasing tariff schedules seemed to be the only tangible instruments of Canadian unity. Yet the old Conservative's fingers were weakening and losing their grasp, and the instruments of the National Policy were blunted and suspect.

Provincialism, unequivocally supported by the Judicial Committee of the Privy Council in the nineties, threatened the delicate fabric of unity, with a cancerous decentralization, dissolution, or annexation as the price of its triumph. However gradual its pace, the economic growth of the country was creating a sharply divided society; the overture promised a fully orchestrated symphony of class consciousness and conflict. Between English and French Canada lay a gulf of incomprehension bridged only by the necessities of politics. Bigotry was widespread, finding outlets in the traditional French-English and Catholic-Protestant conflicts, in hostility to any strangers in the land, and in sharp rivalries among Protestant sects. The tone of the nineties was rough and discordant.

While bigots fanned the embers of racial and religious controversy in readiness for a new conflagration and even a cynical population was increasingly disturbed by mounting evidence of gross political corruption, the central issue as the decade opened was the question of Canada's commercial policy. A growing disenchantment with the National Policy of tariff protection had been reinforced by the slump of the late eighties. Low yields and low prices led to meagre returns for the farmers. Manufacturers attempted to relieve the pressure on profits by increasing that on the workers. While bank presidents informed shareholders that debt and mortgage payments were being met, post-office savings banks reported a marked decline in the number of depositors and the size of the balances. The Liberals looked to Sir Richard Cartwright's utopia of Unrestricted Reciprocity, which was to open up American markets by removing tariff barriers between Canada and the United States. D'Alton McCarthy tempted Tories with the virtues of Imperial Preference, to enlarge trade within the Empire through a structure of preferential duties. Macdonald and the National Policy Conservatives prepared once again to defend their beleaguered fortress.

By late 1890 Sir John had concluded that his maxim 'time

and I against any two men' would have to be set aside. Only a modern economist could have seen in increased government revenues, increased imports, and an upswing in export prices the early signs of a turn in the business cycle. Far more obvious was the threat of another bad harvest and, worse still, the fear of the McKinley tariff that was to close the United States to Canadian exports. Ahead too were the well-documented revelations of party scandals and the threat posed by the Manitoba Schools Question to the unbelievable Basilica-Lodge alliance on which the party rested. For the moment, however, the Liberals were more divided than the Conservatives. Mercier's nationalistic, extravagant, and corrupt policies in Quebec had alienated many English Canadians, and important elements in the party, led by Blake and Mowat, were dragging their heels over Unrestricted Reciprocity, dubious themselves of its consequences for Canada.

As early as 1889 Macdonald had realized that economic statistics would be impotent weapons with which to defend the National Policy, and that his opponents could only be felled by psychological warfare. Patriotism and loyalty to a Canada within the Empire – a war cry, not a weapon – would have to be the issue. Canadians would be forced to choose between collective survival as a Britannic community or possible individual betterment as Americans. Macdonald's polarization of the trade issue in terms of loyalty ('A British subject I was born') and treason ('a deliberate conspiracy, by force, by fraud, or by both, to force Canada into the American union') had already been attempted by Colonel George Denison and the Imperial Federation League and had been used to good effect in a by-election in South Victoria.

In the short campaign that followed the snap dissolution on February 2, 1891, the Conservatives were ordered to hammer home loyalty versus treason. So boldly stated it seemed believable, even to dyed-in-the-wool Grits. Moreover, Catholic ecclesiastical declarations against annexation seemed only to have one meaning. The silence of Blake and Mowat added to the uncertainty and suspicion. Far more was at issue than political allegiance. There was, said J. C. Patterson of the Toronto *Mail*, in asking Canadians to place patriotism above partisanship, nothing less at stake than the survival of a superior culture. What Canadian could be so diabolical, he asked, as 'to throw Canada, with her lofty ideals of religious, political and civil liberty, her noble educational institutions, her unstained judiciary, her pure social and domestic life, her high standards of commercial integrity, into the arms of the United States which to put it mildly, in all these particulars, stands on a much lower level?'

Of course loyalty could not be expected to carry the entire election. Traditional methods of patronage and promises–even promises of a tunnel to Prince Edward Island–were called into service. The financial and industrial community was alerted to the dangers of reciprocity, although, feasting as it did on duties and bounties, it was unlikely to need the reminder. The C.P.R.'s Van Horne wrote publicly to Drummond of the sugar trust–as if he needed to be told–that the interests of manufacturers, financiers, transportation officials, and the working men lay with the National Policy, and later could boast that not one C.P.R. employee in a hundred was doubtful.

The combination of conventional weapons and psychological warfare was irresistible. Loyalty–not boodle or Sir Charles Tupper, confessed the Liberals–swept the Maritimes. The Conservative popular vote rose in Quebec, although the Liberals capitalized on Tory dissension to gain seven seats. Reciprocity had too firm a hold among the farmers of south-western Ontario to be broken, but elsewhere the Conservatives triumphed easily. Significantly enough, many of the victorious Conservatives were members of the Imperial Federation League, and in eastern Ontario the central issue of the election was often overshadowed by the Protestant Equal Rights campaign and anti-Jesuit agitation. Conservatives swept the cities, despite the disaffection of the working class, and were eminently successful along the main line of the C.P.R. For the last time Macdonald had given his party a comfortable victory. In June even time deserted him. The Old Man and his era passed away, although his party remained in office five more years, under the last election he had won for them.

II

Whatever else it accomplished, the election did not solve the problems of the Canadian economy. Publication of the census of 1891 confirmed the most gloomy suspicions and dismayed its readers for, despite the boom years of the early 1880s and immigration levels not exceeded until after the turn of the century, population growth had not even kept up with the natural increase. Prospects for the 1890s seemed bleaker. The birth-rate was falling. Immigration declined and remained well below emigration as Canadians flocked to the farms and factories of the United States. Increasing urbanization–about 6 per cent a decade between 1880 and 1900–was accepted as a beneficial effect of the National Policy in central Canada. Until late in the decade, however, there were few optimistic signs in the Maritimes and the prairies. In Manitoba and the North-west low prices, unusually dry years, and the difficulty of finding methods of cultivation suitable to semi-arid lands served as a process of natural selection. But while some deserted farmhouses and almost empty settlements were the marks of failure, the increasing use of machinery and experiments with windbreaks, seeding, and summer fallowing were gradually bringing the land under man's control. Beyond the mountains British Columbia, not yet integrated into the Canadian economy, enjoyed its first boom since the Cariboo gold rush. American enterprise and capital, encouraged by the generous policies of a government of entrepreneurs, opened up the rich mineral lands of the southern interior and began the war of devastation on virgin timberlands. And American railways threatened to confirm the dictate of geography and turn much of the province into the hinterland of a commercial empire based on Spokane or, if J. J. Hill had his way, Tacoma.

There was generally a modest improvement in Canada's economic conditions between 1891 and 1893. Reasonably good harvests, an increase in the value of agricultural products, and diversification which enabled many farmers to take advantage of urbanization and an expanding British market aided agriculture. While the United States was the chief beneficiary of this expanding British market, following the end of the slump of the 1880s and the inability of the Russians to maintain food exports, increased Canadian sales to Britain helped to offset the American barriers of the McKinley tariff. The volume of business grew and, while some business suffered from over-expansion and severe competition, good profits were reported in banking, manufacturing, and transportation. Improved economic conditions were undoubtedly one reason why the Conservatives won back eighteen Ontario seats (and lost only three) in the carefully staggered and well-managed by-elections between 1891 and 1893.

But a downturn began late in 1893, and the middle years of the decade were bleak. The crash of 1893 had an unsettling effect on the financial world. Agricultural production and prices fell. A British embargo on live cattle and the competition to horses posed by increasing use of electricity dealt the farmer further blows. Contraction was marked in banking, manufacturing, transportation, and construction. Banks reported that farmers were borrowing, not buying, and falling behind in mortgage payments. Business failures increased; there was a general pressure on profits. Wages fell and unemployment increased. In June 1896 the general manager of the Bank of Commerce gloomily reported that for the first time in years 'we have not been able to take a forward step' and that the year had 'been one of constant anxiety and almost unexampled difficulty in making profits and avoiding losses'. For another sector of society there was perhaps some consolation when beer fell to an all-time low of 32 cents a gallon in 1896 – indicative of the level of commodity prices. The trough was reached in 1896 and early 1897. It was little wonder that Laurier was convinced that the Liberals could win the 1896 election, if only the distorting race and religion issue could be removed from national politics.

The pace of industrial growth fell sharply in the nineties, but the role of the large firm became more important as the depression stimulated efficiency and consolidation. Mountting popular criticism of monopolies, combinations, and price-fixing was based on more than suspicion. Avoiding such areas as textiles (where it was well known that a cotton combination flourished behind a constantly higher tariff and paid dividends of 32 per cent) a select committee in 1888 found: a grocers guild in league with an association of sugar refiners; an association of coal dealers that fixed prices, made identical bids on public tenders, and awarded the contract to the company that paid the highest premium to the association, and drove out competition; an association of oatmeal millers to fix prices, establish quotas, and buy out competitors; and organizations to control the production and price of binder-twine and barbed wire. An anti-combines bill introduced by a Conservative back-bencher was taken over by the government, watered down, and sent to a committee whose members readily yielded to the lobby that descended on Ottawa before it was passed; it was then sent to the Senate, where it was further emasculated. The act was not only half-hearted, it was fraudulent; so frequently did the words unlawfully, unduly, and unreasonably appear that the measure actually weakened the old common-law restrictions on combinations, and was an inducement rather than a deterrent to them – unless one accepted the official government view that the common-law restrictions were so severe that no judge would convict. (At some point a clause was inserted that removed the protection given to trade unions in 1872.) Such an act did nothing to alter the trends in business organization established in the eighties and intensified in the nineties.

III

As the plutocracy grew, so too did the class consciousness of its employees. Until late in the decade the times were not auspicious for rapid trade-union growth, and, given high unemployment, the Yellow Dog, the Ironclad, or the Agreement must have been powerful instruments in the hands of management. Wage rates were depressed and working conditions for men, women, and children were often inhumane; withheld wages or payment in kind or in truck were commonplace. As a royal commissioner commented in 1889 'there seems to be no idea of any obligation existing between the employer and his operatives, any more than the mere payment of wages. To obtain a very large percentage of work with the smallest possible outlay of wages appears to be the one fixed and dominant idea.'

The large mass of the working class, crowded into city slums, was unorganized, and the trade unions – Knights of Labor, local unions, or the Trades and Labour Congress – were largely ineffectual as a political pressure group. Repeated demands for a wide range of protective or remedial economic, social, and political legislation went unheeded in Ottawa. Mowat proved more responsive in Ontario, and there by the mid nineties legislation concerning hours and conditions of work, workmen's compensation, and some of the social consequences of urbanization had been placed on the statute books. Increasingly, however, working men looked to some form of political action. Gradually a left-wing program began to emerge. Except in British Columbia, however, the movement for independent political action was fitful and ineffectual.

The new urban proletariat found few sympathizers or champions. While in literary realms Archibald Lampman and D. C. Scott lashed out at the squalor and injustice of the new industrial society, there was nothing comparable in Canada to the American muck-rakers. Some religious leaders realized that they were losing contact with what one of them called 'the unconverted masses', but churches and chapels seemed too established to make the structural and ideological adaptations necessary to meet the challenge. Classes, wrote the editor of the *Christian Guardian* in 1884, 'must exist as long as there are different degrees of thrift, intellect and religious education in a community', and the antagonism to the church among the lower classes, he felt, was 'to some extent the outcome of the feeling of the unsuccessful and the needy against those who are successful and comfortable'. Their energies absorbed by denominational conflict and their funds by the construction of magnificent buildings housing high-rent pews, the organized churches left the work in the streets and slums to the revivalist movement of the 1890s and the Salvation Army, which mushroomed in the industrial cities. By the middle nineties more thought was being given to social questions. Some Methodists, for example, grudgingly accepted the legitimacy of trade unions, although not the right to strike, and even allowed that a reduction in hours worked might not be matched by an increase in sin. And in 1894 the Methodist Conference even declared its sympathy with 'the struggling masses everywhere' and affirmed hopefully that 'when society had become impregnated with the teaching of Jesus of Nazareth, trusts, monopolies, heartless combinations and oppressive economic conditions shall have been superseded by universal brotherhood'.

The 1890s also witnessed the first stage of the agrarian revolt in Canada. Rural Canada was slowly losing its paramountcy. In 1880 over 75% of the population was rural; by 1900 37.5% was urban. In some rural counties in Ontario there was an absolute decline in population. Parents watched the family unit being broken up as sons and daughters headed for the godless fleshpots of the cities. Economic hardship made more acute the bitterness felt towards the producers of farm goods and implements, sheltered by a high tariff and combining to fix prices. Since the 1870s the Grange had stimulated the development of a rural class-consciousness and had undertaken a wide range of social and economic activities to demonstrate the advantages of collective action.

The movement had declined in the eighties, largely because of its unwillingness to accept political action.

When an American organizer for the Patrons of Industry, an American farmers' association with social, economic, and political objectives, appeared in Ontario in 1889 he found the field ripe for expansion. By 1892 there were 1,400 lodges with 30,000 members and by 1894-5 over 50,000 members, including 5,000 in Manitoba and the North-west. By 1891 the Patrons had severed their American connection and had started to work on a national political program. Their major concern was the tariff, and in 1893 they presented a petition with over 40,000 signatures calling for tariff reform. By this time the Patrons had successfully entered the political field in Ontario and Manitoba. In the Ontario election of 1894 the success of seventeen Patrons indicated the extent of agrarian discontent. But like the Progressives a generation later, the Patrons found their reluctance or inability to be a party and their preference for the Liberals over the Conservatives a barrier to effective action. Moreover, although united on major economic issues, the Patrons were divided over the racial and religious issues that emerged in the mid nineties, as well as over prohibition. The high hopes for the federal election of 1896 were not realized, as only three Patrons were elected. By 1900 the Patrons were a spent force and were unable to field a single candidate. Their revolt against the economic and social biases of the National Policy, however, was to remain a permanent force in Canadian politics.

Competing with the Patrons for farm support was the Continental Union movement, which got under way late in 1891. Inspired by Goldwin Smith and supported financially by wealthy American annexationists, the advocates of continental union found a ready audience among the farmers of south-western Ontario. Support given the movement by Liberals enraged Oliver Mowat, who even charged that the Toronto *Globe* had become an annexationist organ, and he warned Laurier that if continental union was 'to be the policy of the Dominion Liberal party, I cease to be a member of it'. The reaction against continentalism, the effect of Blake's West Durham letter with its doubts that unrestricted reciprocity could be combined with independence, and repeated defeats in the by-elections convinced the Liberals that a change in policy was essential before the next federal election.

IV

The occasion was the national Liberal convention in Ottawa in June 1893. Elected chairman, Mowat used his address to emphasize the British connection and warn that any notion that the convention disagreed with him on such a matter 'would cause a sufficient stampede from the reform ranks to make our success at the next general election out of the question'. Laurier too emphasized his loyalty, but added that 'the commercial interests of England are not the interests of Canada'. After a battle over the critical tariff resolution moderate Liberals were victorious. The Liberal tariff was to be based not upon the protective principle, but upon the requirements of the public service, and would be 'adjusted as to make free, or bear as lightly as possible upon the necessaries of life, and should be so arranged as to promote freer trade with the whole world, more particularly with Great Britain and the United States'. A second resolution underlined the importance of broad and liberal trade relations between Canada and the United States.

The new platform was the first stage in the ultimate Liberal acceptance of the main principles of the National Policy. Almost at once it had its effects. As William Mulock wrote from Toronto, 'it is conceded that our platform is proof against the disloyalty cry while the moderate character of our trade policy fails, apparently, to create alarm in monetary circles'. Old friends lost in '91, he added, 'are all coming back'. And by late 1894, while Cartwright was wooing the Patrons, Laurier was cultivating what financier George Cox called 'the leading financial men in this Province'.

Criticized from all sides, the Conservatives were aware that every effort would have to be made to increase Canadian prosperity within the framework of the National Policy. In 1892 the five-year-old act creating the Department of Trade and Commerce was proclaimed, and the elderly Mackenzie Bowell was appointed Minister. The Department gathered statistics, appointed trade commissioners, and encouraged Canadian exporters, and Bowell followed a trip to Australia by hosting the 1894 Colonial Economic Conference. While Bowell could describe attacks on the trusts 'as a species of socialism' he and the Minister of Finance, George Foster, undertook a survey of the tariff in the summer of 1894 in response to universal criticism. As Foster reported to the Prime Minister: 'Bowell and I have done Montreal, Toronto and Hamilton in Tariff and shall polish off St. John and Halifax and Quebec week after next. . . . It is hard work, but it is doing good. The interests like to talk out the various subjects and we get many good pointers and some information. . . . What fools the Opposition have been. If they had struck tariff reform and gone into . . . details they would have made it hot for us.' To cool down criticism the government introduced a new schedule in 1894 which lowered the duties on such items as farm implements, binder-twine, nails, wire, and fencing. The reductions had little effect on the public, but gravely disturbed the manufacturing community. The editor of the *Canadian Manufacturer* asked in disbelief why Foster should have felt it necessary 'to deal such a fearful blow to his political friends and supporters', but trusted that the rates would soon be revised 'to conform to the requirements of the country and the expectations of the manufacturers', which clearly were synonymous. That trust kept most of the business community loyal to the Conservatives in the election of 1896.

V

Far more menacing than the clash of socio-economic interests was the failure to respond to the challenges of a pluralistic society. Within a decade of Confederation Pierre Chauveau had written, 'English and French, we climb by a double flight of stairs towards the destinies reserved for us on this continent, without knowing each other, without meeting each other, and without even seeing each other, except on the landing of politics.' In the 1880s the landing of politics had become increasingly turbulent and in the 1890s was a battleground of bigotry where race battled race, and creed fought creed.

Although it stopped short of the rack and the stake, the Protestant hatred of Catholicism was intense. 'Jesuit! Jesuit! Jesuit! Dislike of the Jesuit is part of the blood and bone of these people,' wrote the editor of the *Globe* in 1889. Orange Lodges, the Equal Rights Association, and the Protestant Protective Association (later called the Canadian Protective Association), an offshoot of the American Protective Association, were openly determined to rid the country of the menace of Catholicism. The churches were officially less outspoken, but religious bigotry was a major obstacle faced by every non-denominational institution. Bitter rivalries and hostilities even divided the Protestant sects.

The religious conflict was overwhelmed and to a large extent absorbed by the more serious ethnic conflict. While many English Canadians doubtless shared Goldwin Smith's view of the habitant as 'a French peasant of the Bourbon day . . . simple, ignorant, submissive, credulous, unprogressive', what was fundamentally at issue was not individual incomprehension, but two widely different conceptions of the nature of the Canadian nation. Many English Canadians in their search for a meaningful nationality adopted the pan-Anglo-Saxonism that afflicted late-Victorian England. In a nation so defined and among a majority firm in the belief in racial superiority there was little room for French Canadians. The great question facing Canada, trumpeted D'Alton

McCarthy, is 'whether this country is to be English or French – and it is this problem and the apparently insoluble character of the difficulties that it presents that are driving people openly to look on annexation as the only means of escape.' Imperial Federationists, many of them members of the Equal Rights Association, were of the same mind. John Charlton confided to his diary that 4,000 Montrealers gave him the greatest applause when he 'asserted that a successful French nationality on the North American continent was a hopeless dream, for that question had been settled on the plains of Abraham'. 'I would suggest that if the other provinces are maintained out and out English,' wrote another Ontario Liberal to Premier Greenway of Manitoba, 'French must disappear from Quebec. There would be no overflow places for the French to go and knowing this, the French would learn English'. 'I am satisfied that sooner or later this crisis had to come,' wrote John Willison. 'It may be that Confederation will be the main sufferer.'

Impotent when national politics centred on race, facing the politics of the 'reserve' doctrine, and with its survival openly threatened, French Canada resorted to every defensive mechanism at its disposal. And many French Canadians, like the young Jules-Paul Tardivel, must have dreamed 'd'un Canada français autonome, d'une vraie Nouvelle-France. . . . A l'heure marquée par le Dieu des nations . . . formeront un vrai peuple . . . et dans cinquante ans peut-être, il [Quebec] prendra place parmi les nations de la terre.'

The celebrated Manitoba Schools Question sprang from and helped to crystallize sentiments about the duality of Canada. The issue arose in 1890 when an English-Protestant majority in Manitoba deliberately removed the legal linguistic and religious privileges or rights of a French-Catholic minority there. As confirmed in the Northwest Territories two years later, the action made it clear that wherever possible the majority was determined to make the public schools the vehicle for creating a Canadian nationality which, without definition, would be English. In French

Canada the issue became 'une question nationale, une question de notre avenir comme race, de la position que nous devons occuper dans la Confédération'. In English Canada it was much the same. Tragically, the objectives were diametrically opposed. Here lay the dilemma facing the federal government, empowered by the constitution to protect minority rights.

The Conservative party was ill-equipped to face such a crisis. Macdonald had been losing his touch in his last few years, and had not only failed to contain the McCarthyites, but had also refused a necessary reconstruction in Quebec. After his death, his successor as Prime Minister, Sir John Abbott, persuaded Langevin, Macdonald's chief French-Canadian lieutenant, to offer his resignation in return for a lenient report from the committee investigating the McGreevy political scandal in which Langevin was implicated, but refused to promote the strongest Quebec Conservative, J. A. Chapleau, to the position of Quebec federal leader. Abbott, however, soon tired of the game–'if it were not for the deputations wanting money and lands, and the people wanting situations and plunder, I should get on pretty well'–and gave way to Sir John Thompson in November 1892. Under pressure from the Ontario wing, where he was already suspect because of his conversion to Catholicism, Thompson refused to yield to Chapleau's demands and unwisely sent him to Spencer Wood, the luxurious residence of the lieutenant-governors of Quebec, from which pinnacle Chapleau continued to exert an enormous influence on Quebec politics. His replacement was the ultramontane A. R. Angers, whose brilliance and integrity were matched only by his impotence in the constituencies. Thompson's appointment of Clarke Wallace, Grand Master of the Orange Order, might have balanced the government, but it was unlikely to facilitate a settlement of the schools question.

Thompson was dead and the lacklustre Mackenzie Bowell was Prime Minister when, in January 1895, the Judicial Committee of the Privy Council ruled that the federal government had the right to take remedial action on behalf of the

Manitoba minority. For the next year the Cabinet was rocked by resignations and revolts as Bowell and his colleagues proved unable to take a firm and united stand. In March Sir Charles Hibbert Tupper resigned when Bowell reversed a decision to go to the country and secure a mandate for remedial action, but was persuaded to return by Sir Donald Smith and Senator Drummond. In July the three French-Canadian ministers threatened to resign when the Cabinet refused to answer Manitoba's refusal to restore separate schools by introducing remedial legislation. Angers fulfilled his threat, but Caron and Ouimet came to heel after a visit from Drummond 'in his role as peace-maker and purse-bearer'. In December Clarke Wallace left office, after months of publicly advocating national schools while the government was committed to remedial action. In January seven English-Canadian ministers resigned in a calculated attempt to force the Prime Minister to resign in favour of old Sir Charles Tupper, who had journeyed from England to be on hand at such a time. But the Governor General, falsely assuming that the resignations were designed to prevent remedial legislation, refused to accept Bowell's resignation. The Prime Minister's belated success in securing a replacement for Angers, the fear that Lord Aberdeen would call on Laurier, and Bowell's agreement to resign after the session brought an end to the Cabinet crisis. But a prolonged filibuster prevented the Conservatives' remedial bill from passing before Parliament was dissolved.

The Liberals were as divided as the Conservatives but enjoyed the immense advantage of being in opposition. For six years Laurier remained silent, confessing that 'it was impossible to take a bold and well-defined attitude without breaking the unity of the party. Indeed such a rupture may be unavoidable in the end. But to exhibit the spectacle of a divided opposition would have been simply playing the game of the government.' By the fall of 1895 he had gone no further than to recall the fable of the man who shed his coat for the sun, not the wind: 'if it were in my power, I would try the sunny way.' And in moving rejection of the coercive remedial bill on March 3, 1896, he assured the House that his policy would be based 'not upon grounds of Roman Catholicism, not upon grounds of Protestantism, but upon grounds which can appeal to the consciences of all men, irrespective of their particular faith . . . .' Meanwhile in Quebec Israel Tarte could promise that Laurier's sunny ways would provide the best deal for the Manitoba minority and that his victory would 'relever le prestige de notre race'. And in Ontario Liberals could pledge that provincial rights would be inviolate under a Liberal Prime Minister.

The Quebec Liberals were afraid that old Sir Charles Tupper, who took over from Bowell in April, could entice Chapleau back into the Cabinet with the offer of the Quebec leadership. But Chapleau rejected the offers and Angers, selected in his stead, recruited the entire French-Canadian wing from the ultramontanes, thus insuring that many moderate Conservatives would swing to Laurier. However, it was not the ultramontanes the party relied on to win the election in Quebec, but their ecclesiastical allies; lacking political leadership the Conservatives turned to spiritual. The Quebec bishops had long demanded the restoration of separate schools, and the influential Father Lacombe had publicly stated early in 1896 that 'the episcopacy, like one man, united with clergy, will rise up to support those who may have fallen in defending us'. After endless correspondence, the reconciliation of serious internal divisions, and anxious soul-searching the bishops issued a *mandement* to be read without comment in the churches commanding the faithful to support only those candidates solemnly pledged to support remedial legislation. 'Ce grave devoir s'impose à tout bon catholique,' intoned every parish priest on May 17, 'et vous ne seriez justifiables, ni devant vos guides spirituels, ni devant Dieu lui-même, de forfaire à cette obligation.'

Conservatives were disappointed and Liberals relieved, for the *mandement* was weak. Although its intent was clear, and some priests made sure their parishioners understood 'la pensée intime' of the bishops, it did not prohibit Liberal support, and all but eight Liberal candidates signed a declaration supporting remedial action. Far more to the taste of the Quebec Conservatives was the action of Bishop Laflèche, who denounced Laurier's March 3 speech as 'l'affirmation du Libéralisme condamné par l'Eglise la plus catégorique qui ait jamais encore été faite à ma connaissance dans une assemblée législative de notre pays. . . . L'homme qui parle ainsi est un Libéral rationaliste,' support of whom would be a mortal sin. But Laflèche stood alone and the power of the *mandement* was not sufficient to overcome the absence of political leadership. Laurier and the Liberals swept to a decisive victory in Quebec.

The bishops were not alone in taking a stand. Protestant conferences had declared unequivocally against Catholic schools, and the pulpit was a vehicle for political education. A Methodist minister in Western Ontario informed his flock that a Liberal vote 'would stare the voter in the face at Judgement Day, and condemn him to eternal perdition', while a Presbyterian divine assured Clarke Wallace that 'the country is with you in its truer conscience and God is, and the Pope and the Devil are not.' In Ontario suspicion of Laurier was probably stronger than doubts about the Conservatives, and many Conservative candidates openly and with Tupper's permission refused to support remedial action. The total Ontario Liberal vote and the percentage of the Conservative popular vote fell, as 30,000 voters followed McCarthy or the Independents and another 30,000 voted for the Patrons of Industry. The net result was a draw as both Liberals and Conservatives won forty-three seats in the big English-speaking province. Elsewhere the Liberals made substantial gains, an indication perhaps that the racial and religious controversy was less intense. Over-all the Liberals emerged with a comfortable 118-88 margin over the Conservatives.

The Manitoba Schools Question was not the only, and in some areas it was not even the main, issue in the election of 1896. Bad times, trade and tariff policies, agrarian and working-class discontent, Liberal indications of sympathy for prohibition, Conservative disintegration, and, with falling revenues and strict orders from the Minister of Finance in 1895 to cut out all unnecessary expenditures, a decline in the extent of patronage and boodle, all played their role. The schools question cut across these issues and, probably for all time, made a firm analysis of the election impossible. However enigmatic, the election did bring one period of Canadian political history to an end. The next four years were to see whether the Liberal revolution could be consolidated.

VI

The Laurier Cabinet reflected the basis on which the party had been re-organized and the victory won. The appointment of W. S. Fielding rather than Cartwright as Minister of Finance and the selection of William Mulock, William Patterson, and R. R. Dobell (all sympathetic to the major principles of the National Policy) confirmed the pledges concerning commercial and fiscal policy. The entry of Mowat guaranteed loyalty and religious moderation. The presence of Tarte and the virtual exclusion of the old *Rouges* strengthened the still-tentative alliance with moderate conservatism in Quebec. The presence of strong provincial figures–Mowat of Ontario, Fielding of Nova Scotia, Blair of New Brunswick, and Sifton of Manitoba–suggested that an era of centralization had passed. The only serious criticism of the Cabinet came from Quebec, where *Le Temps* described it as 'la plus profonde humiliation nationale qui eût pu être infligée à la race française', and *Le Monde*, recalling Laurier's promise to base his policy neither on race nor on creed, commented bitterly, 'M. Laurier a tenu sa promesse; il a oublié qu'il est Canadien français et catholique.'

Laurier's first challenge came from Quebec, where the shocked bishops were determined to mount a counter-attack. Conciliation depended upon a favourable settlement of the schools question and Laurier sent an ex-Conservative and respected Catholic, Judge Routhier, to Manitoba to soften up the Catholic community. Clifford Sifton's deferred Cabinet appointment and Greenway's desire for better terms, in addition to the greater willingness of Manitoba Liberals to negotiate with their federal counterparts, facilitated a compromise. And by mid November a settlement had been reached whereby instruction in faith and French were allowed under certain conditions. But the hierarchy was in no mood to accept a compromise which Archbishop Bégin described as an 'abandon unjustifiable des droits les mieux établis et les plus sacrés de la minorité catholique'. At the same time L. O. David saw his tract on the clergy placed on the index because he described Laflèche's action during the election as a subversion of political liberty and constitutional government, while Ernest Pacaud's *L'Electeur* was forbidden to Catholic readers because he reprinted extracts from David's pamphlet.

Laurier had already realized that no solution to the problem would be found in Canada. As in 1877, an appeal would have to be made to Rome. Armed with a lengthy statement from Liberal members of Parliament, which outlined the issues involved and emphasized the Catholic dilemma in a democratic pluralistic society, Abbé Proulx left for Rome. The bishops entrusted their case to four of their members. As Proulx wrote from the Vatican, 'presque tout le Canada va se transporter à Rome; ce serait bien plus simple qu'un seul, au nom de Rome, se transportât au Canada.' Charles Fitzpatrick, Laurier's Solicitor-General (a leading Quebec Liberal, and once counsel for Louis Riel), also hastened to Rome. So earnest were his devotions and so successful his diplomacy that Mgr. Merry del Val was sent to Canada. Like Mgr. Conroy two decades earlier, del Val soon saw the realities facing the Catholic minority in Canada. Thus, while the encyclical *Affari Vos* refused to criticize the hierarchy and described the settlement as inadequate, it urged Catholics to accept it as partially satisfactory and to work to secure additional improvements. The bishops could hardly continue their relentless struggle with the Liberals, and in time Laurier's friendship with Archbishop Bruchési and other prelates not only lessened the hostility but made Liberalism almost respectable.

Meanwhile, the government had turned to the equally pressing problem of economic policy. The Liberal victory had had a further unsettling effect and the winter of 1896-7 was a low point in the recession of the mid nineties. Soon after taking office the government reduced the interest rate in its own savings banks to three per cent and lowered it again the following year. After discussions with the Americans, Fielding, Cartwright, and Patterson held tariff hearings in the major industrial centres. When the new tariff was presented in 1897 the Cabinet had obviously not only agreed with Sifton that 'the free trade theory, which has already been shattered' should 'not be permitted to stand in the way when it is clearly not in our business interests', but had found the manufacturers' case almost as impressive as had the Conservatives. While many duties were lowered in the interests of the farmer and the consumer, the general level remained high and the protection of such basic industries as textiles and iron and steel remained undisturbed. To offset free-trade criticism the Liberals included a broad preferential system with reduced rates for countries offering reciprocal privileges. The double schedule had little effect, however, for despite British preference the United States continued to improve its position in the Canadian market.

The 1897 tariff both placed export duties on nickel, copper, and lead and held out the offer of reciprocity with the United States. This ambivalence ended after the failure of talks at the Joint High Commission and the enactment of the highly protective Dingley tariff. The offer was deleted in 1898 and the Canadian government threatened to place a duty on the export of logs and pulpwood if the Americans placed a tariff on newsprint. At the same time the Ontario government prohibited the export of logs cut on Crown lands in a further attempt to strengthen Canadian manufacturing and force Michigan lumbermen to mill in Canada. A federal subsidy to the Canadian Pacific to build the Crow's Nest Pass line into the Kootenays was not only a lever to secure reduced freight rates to the prairies, but was also designed to contest American commercial control of the southern interior of British Columbia.

These measures coincided with the rapid growth of American capital investment in Canadian natural resources and the establishment of branch plants in significant numbers. By 1897 American direct investments totalled about $160 million: $55 million in each of mining and manufacturing, $18 million in agricultural enterprises, $13 million in railways, $10 million in marketing, and $6 million in oil. The pace of investment quickened during the prosperous years at the end of the decade when the *Economist* estimated that another $100 million was poured into mines, forests, and manufacturing.

Increased American investment was only one manifestation of the new prosperity of the late 1890s. Recovery was slow through the later months of 1897, but by 1898 virtually all indices–prices, government revenue, exports and imports, immigration, construction–moved forward. The boom has usually been attributed to the 'conjuncture of favourable circumstances'–technological changes, freight rates, gold supply, end of the American frontier, increased urbanization, rising prices, and increased rainfall–which made possible the full development of the wheat economy of the prairies. The western boom was by far the most significant aspect of a general economic advance, and in attracting millions of immigrants and billions of dollars in capital investment in the next decades it provided an immense stimulus to manufacturing, lumbering, transportation, banking and insurance, and service industries, including even the coal, iron, and steel industries on the eastern seaboard.

Such rapid expansion intensified the socio-economic consequences of industrialization and urbanization. Concentration of economic power increased, as men such as George Cox could consolidate an interlocking empire of banks, trust and insurance companies, brokerages, and railways. Combinations and monopolies flourished, undeterred by the 1889 legislation or the provision in the 1897 tariff that protection could be removed if it encouraged monopolies. Although warned in advance of the consequences, the Liberal government made minor changes in the regulations concerning the transportation and sale of crude oil and kerosene which, with preferential treatment from the Grand Trunk and the Canadian Pacific, enabled Standard Oil to present its subsidiary, Imperial, with a virtual monopoly of the central Canadian market. (Ironically, seventeen manufacturers, including Massey-Harris and Dominion Bridge, cried to Laurier that 'since the Standard Oil Company secured the control of the product there has been a tendency to curtail the supply and reduce the quality as well as to advance the price materially.') Trade unions grew in number, size, and power. Labour-management relations became increasingly tense and bitter. Evidence published by the young Mackenzie King revealed that nothing had changed for the better since the 1889 Royal Commission report. In the west farmers mounted an offensive against inadequate grain inspection, elevator monopolies, lack of branch lines, and price syndicates.

The government had more pressing problems than industrial or agrarian unrest. In July 1897 ships docked at Seattle and San Francisco with the news – and the gold to back it up – that in the previous summer Lying George Carmack, Skookum Jim, and Tagish Charley had found a mother lode on the Klondike. In the spring of '98 thousands of prospectors and camp followers tempted fate on the Skagway Trail, the Chilkoot Pass, and the treacherous waterways leading to the Klondike. By the summer Dawson, with 18,000 inhabitants, was the largest Canadian city west of Winnipeg. With surprising ease the Mounted Police established their authority, but the civil administration was less successful in minimizing inefficiency and corruption.

Conflicts over territorial jurisdiction, customs fees, and bonding privileges in the north strained Canadian-American relations to the breaking-point, and there were frequent rumours of an American military expedition to the Alaskan panhandle. Attempts to find or manufacture an all-Canadian route, such as the ill-fated Yukon railway, failed. But the

Canadian government hoped that because of the ill-defined panhandle boundary they could manufacture a case for control of the heads of inlets and access to the overland passes. Diplomatic negotiations failed and discussions at the Joint High Commission in 1898-9, which merged with talks concerning sealing, the fisheries, and reciprocity, were fruitless. By 1903, when a quasi-judicial tribunal rejected the Canadian case, the rush was over. But the anti-American feeling caused by the boundary controversy stimulated Canadian nationalism and imperialism in the last years of the century.

VII

Even prosperity could not blunt the edge of racial tension and conflict that re-emerged in the late nineties, largely as a by-product of Canada's relations with Britain. Until the late 1880s discussion of Anglo-Canadian relations had turned largely on constitutional and economic questions. A few Canadians were quickly caught up in the early phases of the imperial federation movement in England, and in 1885 formed the first branch of the I.F.L. in Canada. The League languished for several years until it became the instrument through which loyalists cultivated imperial sentiment as an antidote to continentalism or annexation. As the British League declined the Canadian flourished. Most of the members were Tories, but by 1896 many of the leaders, such as Colonel George Denison, Principal Grant, and D'Alton McCarthy, had become supporters of the Liberal party. As Denison wrote to Lord Salisbury, the imperialists were delighted with the 1897 tariff. 'They [the Liberals] have come out straight in favour of the Imperial idea, have wrapped themselves in the old flag to the intense satisfaction of all parties except the extreme partisans in the Conservative ranks. . . .'

Laurier's conduct at the 1897 imperial pageant of Queen Victoria's Diamond Jubileee delighted the Canadian imperialists. His vision of a French Canadian at Westminster and his heady references to imperial representation were far more eye-catching than his careful motion at the conference that relations were for the moment satisfactory and would remain so as long as Canada remained a colony.

Yet this newly awakened imperial enthusiasm was a serious threat to Laurier's object 'to consolidate Confederation, and to bring our people long estranged from each other gradually to become a nation'. Imperialism seemed to be strongest in circles inhabited by the Noble Thirteen, the Equal Rights Association, the Protestant Protective Association, and the advocates of national schools. Imperialism was in many ways the reverse side of English-Canadian nationalism, and another instrument in the forging of a Canadian nationality – 'We are Canadians, and in order to be Canadians we must be British' declared the annual meeting of the British Empire League in 1898. Racism and social Darwinism were explicit or implied in the literature of these nationalist-imperialists. George Parkin, for example, could subtitle his book *Imperial Federation* 'The Problem of National Unity'. Like countless other English Canadians, Parkin echoed Chamberlain's boast of 'that proud, persistent, self-asserting and resolute stock that no chance of climate or condition can alter and which is infallibly destined to be the predominating force in the future history and civilization of the world'. It was unlikely that many French Canadians could share this view of Anglo-Saxon superiority and supremacy.

Just as many Canadians shared the doctrines of racial supremacy and conflict – even business reports reflected it – that underpinned much of the late-Victorian western imperialism, so too did they exhibit many other symptoms of the disease. Military writers were prominent and military ardour increased. There was a greater interest in athleticism and combative sports, the ultimate sport of course being war. The press of Canada showed many of the signs of the so-called yellow press in Britain and the United States, leaving some bewildered greybeards to marvel at the new vicarious interest in gossip, sports, crime, and war. Nor was it surprising that in Canada, as in Britain, the new evangelism was carried forth under the militant banners of the Salvation Army, with its journal *The War Cry*, and to the rousing strains of Sir Arthur Sullivan's 'Onward Christian Soldiers'.

VIII

Many of these tendencies in western civilization could be shared by English and French Canadians alike. In Rhode Island the young Canadian Olivar Asselin could encourage recruiting and he raced to join the colours when the Spanish-American war broke out, just as thousands of English Canadians living in Canada flocked to the American consulates to participate in the adventure against Spain. While some Canadians were uneasy about the Anglo-Saxon bond that drew England and the United States together, most were pro-American and endorsed racial solidarity. The *Mail and Empire*, however, warned that further absorption of Latin territory would, because of intermarriage, ultimately weaken the race and 'the dominating influence of Anglo-Saxondom will become less powerful'. The same paper also commented on a banquet in Montreal under the headline 'They Cheered for Spain – French Canadians show their sympathies in the crisis'. If this was true, French Canadians were reacting as did continental Europeans to Anglo-Saxondom's determination to conquer and cleanse the world.

Back in Quebec a year later, however, Asselin wielded his pen to denounce Canadian participation in Britain's war to conquer and cleanse the Boer Republics in South Africa. For the Boer War moved the question of Anglo-Canadian relations from the levels of visions or logic to those of reality and emotion. Once again it revealed the conflicting ideas about the nature and future of Canada, demonstrated the divergence of French and English views, and confirmed the weakness, if not the impotence, in times of crisis of a cultural minority in a democratic majoritarian state.

In Britain, the Colonial Secretary, Chamberlain, and the imperialists saw the war as an admirable opportunity to demonstrate imperial unity and establish a precedent for the collective imperial defence that had been rejected at the 1897 conference. In Canada, English Canadians were overwhelmed by imperial fervour and regarded resolutions of sympathy and frenzied flag-waving as inadequate expressions of loyalty or solidarity. They wished to identify and participate, however vicariously for most of them, in a triumphant war. French Canadians could not identify. As the Governor General, Lord Minto, wrote of Laurier, who felt the war was just, 'the Frenchman in him precluded the possibility of any British enthusiasm – there was not a spark of it.' And as *La Presse* observed, 'Canada is for us the whole world; but the English-Canadians have two countries, one here and one across the sea.' Moreover, many French Canadians either did not believe in the justice of the war or tended to identify with the Boers, whose collective survival, like theirs, was threatened. To English-Canadian demands for a contingent, Israel Tarte replied 'not a man, not a cent for South Africa'.

Laurier's policy of 'parliament will decide' was much less successful in his hands than in those of his Liberal successor, William Lyon Mackenzie King. 'It is not constitutional authority that the Government lacks to send Canadian troops to the Transvaal,' thundered Hugh Graham's Tory-imperialist Montreal *Star*, 'it is moral courage to do its duty at the risk of offending a disloyal element, which objects to any action that tends to strengthen the bonds which unite England and Canada.' 'The French rulers of Canada are holding back the loyal Canadians,' trumpeted its Toronto counterpart, the *News*. 'This Dominion is in the grip of foreigners who have no taste for British advancement. Their ideas are not those of the Anglo-Saxon. They would cast off their allegiance to Britain's Queen tomorrow if they dared. Only a wholesome fear of what would happen to them at the hands of the more virile people of Ontario and the West restrains them.' As usual Laurier sought a compromise that would divide Canadians least. After a stormy two-day session of the Cabinet, with Tarte's resignation in the balance and

Mulock once stalking angrily from the room, the government authorized a contingent, later followed by another, to be organized and equipped by Canada but paid for by Britain. The action was not to be regarded as a precedent, but the nationalistic-minded Henri Bourassa knew a precedent when he saw one, and resigned his seat in protest. The seed of future tragedy was sown.

Laurier had planned an election for December 1899, but the furor over the war forced him to postpone it. Since 1896 the Liberals had won virtually every by-election, yet the party was not in a good position for an election. The sessions of 1899 and 1900 had been unsatisfactory. Irish Roman Catholics were disaffected. Prohibitionists felt betrayed, and were not convinced by Laurier's arguments that the slight majority for prohibition–slight because Quebec had voted overwhelmingly against it– was insufficient, or that the government could not afford to lose seven million in revenue from taxes on liquor. The neutrality of the C.P.R., a power in seventy-five constituencies, it was said, had been lost. Some businessmen felt that the government was too sympathetic to labour. The party organization in Ontario was hopeless. The Conservatives, on the other hand, had benefited from the fierce energy of Tupper and, thanks to generous donations from the Grahams, the Drummonds, the Danbys, and the Gooderhams, had an efficient paid organization and ample funds. Liberal pundits believed their party would win in the Maritimes, Quebec (where the Conservative cry 'Laurier is more imperialistic than Tupper' sounded absurd), and in the west, but would be lucky to hold their own in Ontario.

The pre-election speculations were close to the mark. Liberal strength increased substantially everywhere but in Ontario. With excessive simplicity Liberals and Conservatives alike attributed the results in Ontario to the race and creed cry. Conservative campaigners, while seldom attacking Laurier openly, had fastened on the allegedly disloyal Tarte, describing him as the real master of the administration. 'The writing of the leading opposition papers in Ontario has been positively wicked,' wrote Lord Minto, 'simply aiming at stirring up hatred of French Canada.' The Sons of England, Orange Lodges, and the P.P.A., converted into the 'purity association' and assisted by the A.P.A., became branches of the Tory party. Emotion-charged demonstrations for returning veterans a week before the election set a tone that lasted through election day.

After the election the Toronto *World* gloated that 'it was the voice of the lion saying "thus far and no further".' And Charles Eaton of Bloor Street Baptist Church wrote to Laurier that 'I am sadly convinced that the chief menace to the future of Canada is the unreasoning blind bigotry of English-speaking Toryism, and pardon me if I venture to say that you cannot overestimate this danger – I cannot suggest a remedy because the evil is not amenable to reason, but I hope the good sense of the rest of Canada will avert a calamity.'

Laurier was despondent, and again wondered if a French-Canadian Catholic could successfully lead a national party. But he tried to look hopefully on it all, as he asked Bourassa in the House, 'Can we not hope – I ask my honourable friend himself – that in the grave shall be buried the last vestiges of our former antagonism?' Unfortunately, neither good sense nor countless graves were to overcome antagonisms or avert future calamities.

5. The New Century

H. BLAIR NEATBY

In 1891 Goldwin Smith had seen no future for the Dominion of Canada, composed as it was of four separate regions cut off from each other, and doomed to remain the backward and impoverished northern fringes of the continent. But now, at the turn of the century, pessimism was outmoded and Canadians had become braggarts. When the Chambers of Commerce of the British Empire held their congress in Montreal in 1902, the delegates must have been surprised to learn that they now found themselves 'in the largest and chief commercial city of the Dominion of Canada – a city which is at once the London, the Liverpool, the Manchester, the Birmingham, the Leeds, the Bradford, the Sheffield, the Northampton, the Oxford, the Cambridge of North America'. So exaggerated were

UP AGAINST THE SOLID FACTS !

From *Laurier Does Things*, 1904.

many of the claims made by citizens of the Dominion that another British visitor at this time commented that it was difficult to talk to Canadians about their country; 'They have been told so often what a fine country they have, they tell themselves so often what a fine people they are, that any touch of criticism, even amid general admiration, is resented as though it were a studied slight.' Canadians had become vociferous optimists and the Canadian question was no longer whether Canada would survive but rather how populous and how prosperous it would become.

There was much to justify the optimism. Prosperity was the central fact of the first decade of the century. The *Canadian Annual Review* was founded at the beginning of the decade to provide each year 'a summary of current progress in a country now steadily growing in importance', and each succeeding volume did present an impressive record of economic progress. The economic foundations of the Dominion seemed so secure that Sir Wilfrid Laurier's boast of the twentieth century belonging to Canada seemed more an appraisal than a prophecy. At the end of the decade the spiral of material progress was still ascending.

But if prosperity was the central fact, it does not fully explain the changes in Canada during the decade. Some Canadians did not share in the sense of national achievement because they had no share in the benefits of prosperity or because they were dissatisfied with their share. Farmers and labourers resented the profits of businessmen and manufacturers; the Maritimes and the prairies were jealous of the greater prosperity of central Canada; French Canadians were disturbed by the increasing influence of English Canada. Authors who described Canada at the end of the decade still saw prosperity as the major theme but they now wondered whether material progress alone could nurture a nation-state. The multi-volume history *Canada and its Provinces* was in preparation by this time. The decision to write such a history was proof of national pride, and the editor, in his preface, was still enthusiastic about the visible signs of economic growth. But pride was now tempered by the warning that 'the national character is not moulded exclusively by economic causes' and that 'the danger of sectionalism, in spite of material success, is greatly to be feared, unless this destructive tendency is met by the positive and constructive idea of the Nation'.

The harsh truth was that the nation was not yet built. The leaders of the scattered British colonies in North America had created a political union in 1867 and by the first decade of the new century an integrated transcontinental economy – an economic union – had been shaped. But some of the fundamental divisions within the union still remained and prosperity had brought new divisions into focus. National pride was there, and a new-found assurance that Canada would survive and prosper, but there was as yet no way of knowing what Canadian society would be like or what kind of nation-state Canada would become. Canadians were still searching for a sense of national identity.

I

And high above the sea and lands,
On peaks just tipped with morning light,
My dauntless spirit mutely stands,
With eagle wings outstretched for flight.

Frederick George Scott

The Canadian spirit took flight with the flocking of immigrants to the Canadian prairies. For years, even before Confederation, this 'great lone land' had created hopes and fostered national ambitions. Canadian politicians had forestalled the northward expansion of the United States by taking over the Hudson's Bay territories and by luring British Columbia into the union, and had then linked these regions to the St. Lawrence with the steel ribbons of the Canadian Pacific Railway, but the National Policy, the grand design of a transcontinental economy, depended on making the western lands productive. The tariffs had been imposed, the railway built; all that remained was prairie settlement. For a generation the high hopes had been frustrated; now in the first decade of the new century the settlers came and the grand design became a reality.

There were fewer than half a million people living on the Canadian prairies at the beginning of the decade, most of them in what was then the tiny province of Manitoba. Ten years later the prairie population had trebled and homesteaders could be found in all the arable regions of the prairie. The density of settlement would increase in the following decades and settlers would push northward into the Peace River country, but 'the last best west' of North America was no longer a frontier by 1910. The railway lines that criss-crossed the prairies were knotted every few miles by villages, with grain elevators in each village to receive the harvest. Some communities, favoured by nature or by railways, became distributing centres. Saskatoon, for example, was little more than a general store on the South Saskatchewan at the beginning of the century, linked with the outside

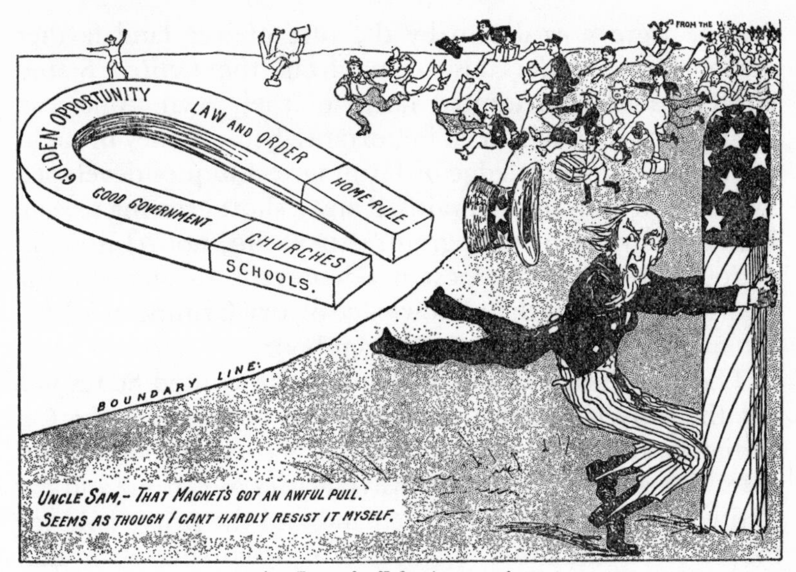

An Irresistible Attraction

From *Laurier Does Things,* 1904.

world by a branch line running south to the main line of the C.P.R. at Regina. In 1902 Saskatoon was organized as a village, although the storekeeper later recalled that 'it was a hard struggle to effect this, the ordinance calling for twenty houses within a mile square. By counting all the shacks we managed it.' Then the settlers established themselves on the prairie lands to the south, and soon two new railways, the Grand Trunk Pacific and the Canadian Northern, crossed the river at Saskatoon and opened up new territory to the west. Saskatoon was incorporated as a town in 1903 – although they had difficulty in finding the necessary nine councillors who had the qualification of a year in residence. By 1905 it had received a city charter and by the end of the decade it had a population of almost twelve thousand, a university was being built, and Saskatoon was no longer a frontier community.

It was not difficult to attract settlers in these years. Nearly all of the free homestead lands in the United States had been occupied by 1890, and land-seeking immigrants from

Europe were now drawn by the lure of free land farther north. Many settlers also came from the United States, farmers' sons who wanted farms of their own. American immigrants were of special importance because they brought with them the knowledge of farming techniques developed for a region with limited rainfall and a short growing season. Unlike European immigrants, they did not cluster in national colonies but located homesteads throughout the prairie region, and their knowledge of 'dry-farming' methods was quickly acquired by their neighbours.

The disappearance of free land in the United States was not the only factor that stimulated settlements on the Canadian prairies. Wheat-farming was becoming more profitable. The growth of large industrial cities in Europe and the United States increased the demand and the prices paid for food. At the same time, large-scale manufacturing meant that the cost of the lumber and farm machinery required by the homesteaders did not rise as quickly. Technological advances also provided other advantages. Ocean freight-rates fell, and so wheat could be shipped to Europe more cheaply. A farm in the Canadian west was now a far more attractive venture than it had been before.

The Canadian government had long been ready to welcome immigrants to the prairies. As early as 1870, when the province of Manitoba was created, the federal government had retained control over its natural resources; it would retain the same control over the lands in the provinces of Saskatchewan and Alberta when they were formed in 1905. In this way the federal government could grant any bona fide settler a free homestead of 160 acres without any interference from the governments of the three prairie provinces. Other prerequisites for orderly settlement had also been provided before the turn of the century. The Indians had been located on reserves, the North West Mounted Police were enforcing the law, the Canadian Pacific Railway had been built, the land had been surveyed, and municipal and territorial government had been established. Immigrants would not be coming to a turbulent and lawless frontier.

This did not mean that the Canadian government calmly waited for immigrants to come. Sir Clifford Sifton, Minister of the Interior from 1896 to 1905, was a dynamic salesman. Sifton gave priority to advertising Canadian homesteads in the United States, and exhibitions of Canadian farm products at American state and county fairs, combined with free railway excursions to the Canadian west for American newspaper editors, helped to destroy the myth of a 'frozen north'. In Europe, the British Isles had provided most of the emigrants that had peopled the New World in the nineteenth century, but by this time British emigrants came from industrial cities rather than rural areas and these newcomers needed a long period of apprenticeship before they could become successful farmers. Sifton shifted Canadian publicity to rural areas in central Europe. There were growing criticisms during the decade of a policy which established colonies of central Europeans in western Canada, colonies which brought prairie land into production but which preserved languages, customs, and a way of life that were different and alien. Sifton ignored the criticism. 'I think', he said, 'that a stalwart peasant in a sheep-skin coat, born on the soil, whose forefathers have been farmers for generations, with a stout wife and a half-dozen children, is good quality.' It was enough for Sifton that these immigrants would grow wheat on what had been unproductive prairie sod.

Under Sifton, the Department of the Interior did more than advertise the opportunities in the west to attract immigrants. Departmental regulations were simplified and even ignored in order to make it easier for the immigrant to become a settler. Clifford Sifton, himself the son of an early immigrant to Manitoba from Ontario, had no sympathy for red tape. 'One of the principal ideas western men have is that it is right to take anything in sight provided nobody else is ahead of them,' he once wrote. 'As a rule it is sound policy for the government to fall in with this idea and encourage the people to go ahead.' Newcomers to the prairies had enough problems to face, building barns and houses, 'sod-busting', surviving cold winters and arduous summers before they had a crop to sell. Under Sifton's administration they were at least spared many of the frustrations of red tape and officious bureaucrats when filing homestead claims and earning title to their land.

The life of these new settlers in western Canada differed greatly from the pioneer life of an earlier era. The settlers were not pioneers in homespun, growing their own food, cobbling their own shoes, making their own furniture, and living a self-sufficient life. From the beginning they expected to share in the advantages of an industrial age. The first homes might be log cabins or sod huts on the treeless plains, but such accommodation was always considered temporary. Most farmers either began with or soon moved into frame houses built of lumber sawed in Ontario or British Columbian mills and roofed with cedar shingles. Clothes, kitchen utensils, and farm machinery were usually imported from eastern Canada. Settlers usually had vegetable gardens and pigs and chickens for their own use, but they were far from self-sufficient. They were businessmen who produced a product that might be sold to consumers on another continent, and who lived on the profits of their enterprise.

II

This kind of farming meant that settlers were completely dependent on efficient transportation services. Railways made prairie settlement possible. When a fierce blizzard cut off the train service to many prairie communities in the spring of 1907, the pioneering families faced the possibility of starvation or of freezing to death until the tracks were cleared of snow. Only railways could bring in the food, fuel, and equipment on which the settlers depended; only railways could move out the millions of bushels of wheat that they grew. Canoes and Red River carts had served in an earlier era, but the iron horse created this wheat kingdom.

Railways extended beyond the settled areas at the beginning of the decade, but in the next few years railway construction failed to keep pace with settlement. In 1900 railway lines fanned out west of Winnipeg in the province of Manitoba; in the Northwest Territories there was the Canadian Pacific with the 'Soo Line' south to the United States and branch lines running north from Regina and Calgary. The flood of immigrants in the next few years, however, meant that the only available homesteads were soon thirty or forty miles from the nearest railway. And as early as 1901 the combination of an increased acreage under cultivation and a good crop showed that the Canadian Pacific's single-track line from Winnipeg to Fort William and its limited supply of box-cars could not handle the harvest. Some of the grain had to be stored on farms over the winter in what became known as the 'wheat blockade'. The need for more railways was glaringly apparent.

The farmers' demands for better railway facilities fell on receptive ears. Many Canadian businessmen were now convinced that long lines of box-cars would soon be needed to carry the wheat from the prairies and wanted to share in the profits; a visit to the west in 1902 convinced Edmund Walker of the Canadian Bank of Commerce that 'the extent of land for agriculture exceeds even my fondest hopes . . . within four or five years every railroad in the country will have to double-track its lines to handle the traffic.' But private investors would still be inclined to wait until the existing traffic ensured an adequate return on their investment. Canadian politicians were not prepared to wait for private enterprise to take the initiative because any delay would retard settlement. As Sir Clifford Sifton wrote to a friend, 'I think for the government to shut down on railway policies would be a suicidal policy. . . . Twenty years ought to see at least twelve million people in Canada. But if this result is to be accomplished, small ideas of cutting off expenditures on railways and public works will have to be dropped. For myself I am altogether in favour of going ahead.' With politicians ready to subsidize railway construction and with entrepreneurs willing to build, it is not surprising that railway mileage increased dramatically during the decade.

This eagerness for railways did not answer the question of

how many lines should be built, who would build them, and where they would be located. Each western farmer wanted a branch line as close to his own homestead as possible, but the farmers had developed a deep-rooted suspicion of the Canadian Pacific, which they blamed for the wheat blockade and which they believed had taken advantage of its monopoly to provide inadequate service at extortionate rates. Political pressure from the west ensured that governments would favour rivals of the Canadian Pacific. These rivals, however, had ambitions that went beyond providing railway services for new prairie communities. They wanted to create transcontinental railways, carrying the lucrative long-haul traffic to and from the west.* Added to this was the fact that Canadians in other parts of the country also wanted railways. The federal government could largely determine what railways would be built because railway construction depended on federal subsidies, but the many pressures and the optimism of the period meant that more than prairie railways would be built.

Donald Mann and William Mackenzie were the first to take advantage of the situation. Mann was a tough, barrel-chested construction boss, while Mackenzie was a small and neat business promoter; the two combined to form one of the most amazing partnerships in Canadian affairs. At the turn of the century they already owned a few short lines in Manitoba which went by the name of the Canadian Northern Railway. The Canadian Northern was a frontier railroad, cheaply constructed, using old steam-engines and box-cars bought second-hand from other railway companies, and depending for revenue on such local traffic as the hauling of firewood into Winnipeg. But these two men were ambitious and daring. They applied to the Manitoba government for a subsidy to build a line from Winnipeg to the Great Lakes and so create an alternative outlet to the Canadian Pacific

* Few people realized at the time that wheat would continue to be shipped through the Great Lakes, because even after paying storage costs over the winter it was cheaper than shipping grain all the way by rail.

from the prairies. The Manitoba government was more than willing and even subsidized the construction of the section located in the neighbouring province of Ontario. By 1902 the Canadian Northern extended to Port Arthur on Lake Superior. An English traveller gave a description of Fort William and Port Arthur soon after–'the shanties, the miry roads, the railway tracks in chaos, the humped elevators, the snorting and evil-odoured engines'–but he also commented that here was the wheat funnel of the world.

But for Mackenzie and Mann this was only the beginning. They had visions of a transcontinental railway. Money was no obstacle because federal and provincial governments were generous and private investors had confidence in Canada and in these two men. By 1910 Mackenzie and Mann had borrowed more than two hundred million dollars and their railway consisted of some three thousand miles of track, mainly in western Canada, with construction under way across the Rockies to Vancouver and across the Canadian Shield to eastern Canada. Even in this era of optimism, this was a fantastic achievement. The partnership of Mackenzie and Mann had shown that there was scope for the talents of daring entrepreneurs in the Canada of the twentieth century.

The Canadian Northern was not the only railway to expand in this decade. The Grand Trunk Railway had benefited from the prosperity in central Canada after years of near-bankruptcy–but Charles Hays, the aggressive general manager, was not satisfied; he wanted the Grand Trunk to get a share of the traffic of western Canada. As early as 1902 he proposed that the Grand Trunk build a line north of the Great Lakes to Winnipeg and beyond Winnipeg across the northern prairies and the Rockies to the Pacific. It would have been more logical for the Grand Trunk with its eastern network to combine with the Canadian Northern and its western lines, but Hays was not interested in 'that little bunch of lines up around Winnipeg', and in any case Mackenzie and Mann were too ambitious to merge with the Grand Trunk. The directors, shareholders, and bond-holders of both railways were so optimistic about the future of western Canada that they were ready to take the financial risk of building two new transcontinental systems.

Charles Hays's plans for the Grand Trunk depended on government aid; without federal subsidies there could be no western extension. Hays did not need to worry about a receptive hearing at Ottawa. Sir Wilfrid Laurier was even more eager than the Grand Trunk to have railways built. He justified his sense of urgency in a speech in the House of Commons:

> We cannot wait because the prairies of the North-west, which for countless ages have been roamed over by the wild herds of the bison or by the scarcely less wild herds of red men, are now invaded from all sides by the white race. They came last year one hundred thousand strong and still they come in still greater numbers. Already they are at work opening the long-dormant soil; already they are at work sowing, harvesting and reaping. . . . We consider that it is the duty of all who sit within these walls by the will of the people to provide immediate means whereby the products of these new settlers may find an exit to the ocean at the least possible cost and whereby likewise a market may be found in this new region for those who toil in the forests, in the fields, in the mines, in the shops of the older provinces. Such is our duty; it is immediate and imperative.

With such a vision of the future, it is not surprising that Laurier welcomed discussions with Charles Hays. But Laurier's vision created a serious complication. He wanted a railway that would be a national railway carrying Canadian goods through Canadian territory, and so strengthening the National Policy. In the speech already quoted he gave vivid expression to the nationalist view that the United States must be excluded from the western traffic:

> Heaven grant that it is not already too late; Heaven grant that while we tarry and dispute, the trade of Canada is not deviated to other channels and that an ever vigilant competitor does not take to himself the trade that properly belongs to those who acknowledge Canada as their native or adopted land.

Unfortunately for the Grand Trunk, its Atlantic terminus was Portland in the state of Maine. There would be no federal aid until there was some assurance that the Grand Trunk would not deflect Canadian traffic to an American seaport.

Laurier therefore made a counter-proposal to the Grand Trunk. The federal government would give subsidies if the Grand Trunk would build a railway sweeping north in an arc from Winnipeg to Quebec city, bridging the St. Lawrence and extending to Moncton. This would ensure an all-Canadian route and also have the advantages of opening up new areas for French-Canadian settlement in northern Ontario and Quebec and of winning popular support in the Maritimes. If this proposal was accepted, the government would then be ready to subsidize Grand Trunk construction west from Winnipeg to the Pacific.

Charles Hays did not like this proposal because western goods would not travel on the old Grand Trunk lines in southern Ontario. But Hays could not be stubborn; he was intent on westward extension and he needed federal aid. It was finally agreed that the federal government would build the line from Winnipeg to Moncton, which was named the National Transcontinental, and would lease it to the Grand Trunk when it was completed. The government then agreed to guarantee the interest on a large part of the money borrowed by the Grand Trunk for the construction of the line west from Winnipeg to Prince Rupert.

These arrangements involved the construction of some 3,500 miles of railway. Still to come were the branch lines that would funnel the prairie wheat to the main Grand Trunk line. Construction was well advanced on most sections of the main line by the end of the decade, although the railway would not be completed until 1914, and the bridge across the St. Lawrence at Quebec, after collapsing twice during construction, would not be opened until 1917. The total cost of construction would be more than $250 million, with the federal government spending $60 million of this total on the National Transcontinental and guaranteeing bonds to a total of $75 million on the western line. Canadian nationalism could be expensive. At the time, however, few politicians or observers worried about the cost; the economic boom, partly induced by the huge expenditures on railways, seemed to justify any extravagance.

John A. Macdonald's National Policy had encompassed more than prairie settlement and railways. It also involved a protective tariff to exclude foreign manufactures and so ensure a monopoly of the growing prairie market for goods manufactured in Canada. The Liberal party had argued for lower tariffs in the days of Macdonald, but accepting the National Policy meant accepting the principle of protective tariffs as well. The imperial preference had lowered the tariff on imports from other parts of the British Empire, but even this lower tariff still provided adequate protection to Canadian manufacturers. In 1907 an intermediate tariff was introduced, falling between the general tariff and the imperial preference, which was useful for negotiating trade agreements with other countries, but again the protective principle was preserved. Growing demands for freer trade from western Canada worried the government later in the decade and led to reciprocity negotiations with the United States, but even these talks involved free trade in natural products rather than in manufactured goods. Economic nationalism effectively smothered the free-trade sentiments that Liberals had espoused in a less prosperous era.

The three-fold National Policy was truly national in this decade because it linked all of the hitherto isolated economic regions of Canada by creating an interdependent economy. While the production of wheat spiralled, the value of manufactured goods produced in Canada more than doubled; iron and steel, lumber and coal, and minerals were produced in greater quantities than ever before. In spite of the flood of immigrants to the prairies, the urban population increased more rapidly than the rural population, and Ontario and Quebec grew in numbers almost as quickly as the three prairie provinces. It was true that the benefits of the National Policy were not evenly distributed–manufacturing in the Maritimes actually declined, with the exception of the iron and steel industry there, which was stimulated by railway construction – but although regional differences attracted some attention, regional jealousies were tempered by the increased prosperity in all areas.

Industrial expansion meant more than increased production. The structure of Canadian industry was also being modified. The typical manufacturing enterprise in Canada had been owned by a family or a small group of business associates. By 1910 many of these companies had become or had been absorbed into large and impersonal corporations. The Canada Cement Company, for example, was formed by a horizontal merger of the major cement firms in the country; the Steel Company of Canada was a vertical merger which combined blast furnaces, rolling mills, and finished iron and steel products. All such mergers were made possible by the expanding Canadian market; large-scale production and greater specialization now seemed both possible and profitable.

This consolidation of industry required talents much different from the technical ability or salesmanship of successful businessmen of an earlier era. The new 'captains of industry' were financiers and promoters, often with little knowledge of the manufacturing process but with the daring and skill to negotiate large mergers and with the confidence of the bankers and investors who supplied the capital. The outstanding example of such a promoter is Max Aitken, later Lord Beaverbrook. Aitken was twenty-six years old when he moved from Halifax to Montreal in 1907. He was already director of Royal Securities Corporation and the trusted adviser on investments of many wealthy businessmen. Within the next three years Aitken had promoted the merger of three huge corporations – the Canada Cement Company, the Steel Company of Canada, and Canadian Car and Foundry, with an authorized capital of almost one hundred million dollars – and had found investors to provide the necessary funds. Aitken himself showed little interest in these corporations after they were formed. 'I am a builder,' he explained. 'When the building is finished I do not stay in it but move on to build another.' The financial success of the firms he built testifies to his talents as a promoter as well as to the opportunities for large-scale enterprises in this decade of expansion.

III

The 'wheat boom' was not an unmixed blessing. J. S. Woodsworth, a young Methodist minister in Winnipeg, was outraged by the abject poverty and degradation of immigrant labourers in the city, and the slum conditions he saw at the All People's Mission in North Winnipeg were duplicated in most Canadian cities. Woodsworth, however, was an exception; most Canadians turned a blind eye to the tenements or blamed the plight of this urban proletariat on their lack of initiative or their taste for alcohol. Even the slum-dwellers themselves were virtually untainted by the heresy that poverty might not be their fault.

There were, however, more privileged groups who became increasingly dissatisfied during the decade, and who were able to organize and take collective action to improve their lot. Wheat farmers, who were producing the staple commodity on which the prosperity was founded, were convinced that others were growing wealthy at their expense. The more skilled industrial labourers begrudged the difference between their wages and the owners' profits. The collective action of each of these two groups reflects the growing complexity of an interdependent society and the emerging tensions of class conflicts.

Prairie farmers in this decade showed a remarkable talent for collective action. In spite of their varied racial backgrounds, their linguistic and religious differences, and the immediate problems of transforming a homestead into a farm, these settlers quickly found that they shared common interests. They all faced the challenge of a rigorous climate and the dangers of drought, frost, and grasshoppers. They grew the same crops for the same remote market, which meant they shared the same suspicion that they were being exploited by railways and elevator companies, or by manufacturers, bankers, and politicians, who seemed to control market conditions. By the end of the decade the sense of being an economic group had largely transcended the divisions of race and creed.

Farmers first organized to protect themselves against the most obvious form of exploitation. Grain elevators were an essential link in shipping wheat to the distant market. Farmers could sell their grain to the elevator company, or, if they had a thousand bushels or more, they could pay the elevator company to load their grain in a box-car for shipment to Winnipeg, where it would be sold through the Grain Exchange. Farmers were soon convinced that elevator companies were taking advantage of the situation by giving dishonest weights, offering low grades for the grain, and levying excessive charges for storage. Farmers who might have travelled ten miles with a wagon-load of wheat and who needed the money were in no position to refuse the offered price and take their wheat home again.

The most obvious grievances were eliminated by the federal Grain Act of 1900 which prohibited excessive handling and storage charges and appointed an inspector to prevent improper weighing and grading of the grain. Farmers, however, still believed that they were being exploited by the elevator companies. These companies were theoretically competitors for the farmers' wheat, and in most villages there were two or more elevators beside the railroad track. In practice there was no competition, for the companies had formed an association and offered identical prices and terms for the grain. Farmers were convinced that this association was a conspiracy against them but soon discovered that the law offered no redress because the courts ruled that it was not an 'undue' restraint of trade. Disillusioned by this decision, the farmers decided to take direct action.

E. A. Partridge provided the initiative. Partridge had come to the prairies from Great Britain in the 1880s, and had built a sod hut as his first home. He was a socialist who believed that the farmers were involved in an inevitable class struggle against the vested interests of capitalists and politicians, and although few farmers shared his philosophy their immediate sense of injustice was so intense that many responded to Partridge's agitation for collective action. It was agreed that a co-operative association should be formed to buy a seat on the Grain Exchange. Farmers could then sell their own wheat on the Exchange and end their dependence on the elevator companies.

This simple solution encountered a series of obstacles. The federal government first refused to incorporate the Grain Growers' Grain Company on a technicality, and the farmers' organization had to be satisfied with a more limited provincial charter. Then, after a seat on the Grain Exchange had been purchased, the officials of the Exchange disbarred the company on another technicality. The company was reinstated but only after a public outcry had persuaded the Manitoba government to exert some pressure on the Exchange. Farmers were more convinced than ever that the protection of their interests depended on their own collective action.

Collective action naturally meant political action in the prairie provinces, where most of the voters were farmers and where provincial governments reflected this fact. The seat on the Grain Exchange did nothing for farmers who did not grow enough wheat to ship a carload to Winnipeg; they still had to sell to the elevator companies. By the end of the decade some farmers were agitating for provincially owned elevators. The Manitoba government agreed to purchase and operate some elevators, and the Saskatchewan government appointed a royal commission to investigate the idea. On the prairies at least, collective action meant that provincial governments, whether Conservative or Liberal, quickly became farmers' governments.

The farmers' organizations were less effective in federal politics. Farmers had long argued that the protective tariff benefited Canadian manufacturers at their expense. Wheat producers had to sell their product abroad but they had to buy such things as farm machinery from Canadian manufacturers because the tariff excluded foreign competition. They saw little justification for a policy that prevented them from buying similar machinery in the United States at lower prices; it was easy to believe that manufacturers in eastern Canada were taking advantage of the monopoly that the tariff created. Local Grain Growers' associations and their organ, *The Grain Growers' Guide*, led a sustained attack against the policy of protection. The federal tariff policy, it was argued, was a form of economic imperialism designed by the vested interests of central Canada to hold the west in tutelage.

This version of the National Policy was not readily accepted at Ottawa. The national Conservative party had long been committed to the protective tariff and its position was not significantly modified during the decade. Westerners had more confidence in the federal Liberal party, which had free-trade traditions and was in office, but as years passed without major tariff reductions there was growing disillusionment with both national parties. The reins of political power, it seemed, were securely held by 'big business', and western protests were being ignored. 'The only hope of the farmers in Canada,' *The Grain Growers' Guide* asserted in 1910, 'is to realize that they have no more to expect from one political party than another. They must step aside and secure men to represent them who will stand out boldly in the interests of farmers at all times.' If the federal Conservatives and Liberals continued to represent eastern interests it might be necessary to organize another political party to represent the west.

By 1910, however, the Liberal government at Ottawa was at least aware of the danger of independent political action by the farmers. Sir Wilfrid Laurier made a western tour that year and was impressed by the petitions for tariff reduction that were presented at every stop. Later in the year a mass delegation of some eight hundred farmers came east with the same request; such a formidable demonstration by an organized pressure group was so unprecedented that the event became known as the 'Siege of Ottawa'. The readiness of the government to discuss a reciprocity agreement with the United States was clearly a response to this agitation.

IV

The farmers were not the only economic group to turn to collective action. The decade saw trade-union membership grow from some twenty thousand to more than one hundred and twenty thousand. Union activity was piecemeal and the benefits gained in one craft or one industry had little effect on the majority of unorganized workers, but some workers at least were responding to the tensions of an industrial society. More significant than the improvements in working conditions was the pattern of union affiliations that emerged, and the shaping of a government policy in industrial disputes.

The Canadian labour movement at the turn of the century was largely the northern expansion of the American labour movement. Although there were Canadian trade unions, most locals in Canada belonged to international unions with their headquarters in the United States. These 'international unions' can be explained by the earlier development of trade unions south of the border and by the fact that whether they lived north or south of the border, workers in the same crafts had the same problems and wanted the same working conditions. The political boundary, however, created serious complications. The Trades and Labour Congress of Canada had been formed to act as a spokesman for all trade unions in the country and to bring pressure on Canadian legislators for the benefit of all workers. Union rivalries in the United States, however, disrupted union activity in Canada. In 1902, in a test of strength within the Canadian Congress, the unions affiliated with the American Federation of Labor expelled Canadian unions if international unions of the same craft existed, and also expelled any international unions not affiliated with the Federation. The result was that from 1902 the Trades and Labour Congress was little more than a regional division of the American Federation of Labor.

American influence was not accepted without opposition. The national pride and the national ambitions of Canadians in the decade were shared by some Canadian workers. The Canadian Federation of Labour was founded by the Canadian trade unions as a reaction against the subservience of international unions to American leadership. Yet another development was the organization of Catholic trade unions among French-Canadian workers in Quebec. These locals were usually organized and directed by a parish priest, and the religious rather than secular concept of the rights of workers was an illustration of the cultural difference between English and French Canada. Like the Canadian Federation of Labour, however, the Catholic unions had only a small membership by the end of the decade. To the extent that labour was organized in Canada, it was still an extension of an American movement.

The federal government took an active interest in labour problems in these years in spite of the weakness of trade unions. This concern was not with organized labour directly. An employer was not required by law to negotiate with a union; he could dismiss union organizers and replace them by more submissive workers at any time. But the government did want to prevent strikes that might interfere with the National Policy. A labour dispute involving railway workers, for example, could disrupt the national economy; it is no coincidence that the labour policy of the federal government was first formulated to avert railway strikes.

W. L. Mackenzie King was the architect of this policy. Mackenzie King was young, energetic, and ambitious, with an active interest in industrial relations. As Deputy-Minister of Labour in 1900, at the age of twenty-six, and later as the first Minister of Labour, he had his ideas put on the statute-books. King believed that strikes could be avoided if employers and workers behaved like reasonable men, for it seemed obvious to him that both parties to a dispute would suffer if work stopped. At the same time, King did not believe in coercion; he saw that there could be no industrial stability if either employers or workers were forced to make concessions against their will.

King's solution to this dilemma was government intervention to delay strikes until employers and workers had tried to negotiate a settlement. The Railway Labour Disputes Act of 1903 allowed the Minister of Labour to forbid a strike until the dispute had been investigated by a board that he appointed. The railway company and the workers then presented their arguments before the board. Neither party had to accept the recommendations of the board – there would be no direct coercion – but King believed that the public hearings would force each side to present a reasonable case and that reasonable arguments on both sides would make a peaceful settlement possible. The publicity given to the investigation and to the recommendations of the board would also help to persuade each party to reach an agreement.

A few years later this policy was extended. A coal-miners' strike in Alberta in 1906 threatened to bank the fires in railway steam-engines and prairie homes. The Industrial Disputes Investigation Act of 1907 broadened the policy of compulsory investigation to include mines and public utilities.

This form of government intervention in labour disputes continued to be the policy of the federal government for many years to come. It did not prevent strikes, because the company or the workers could refuse to accept the recommendations of the board. But by permitting the workers to present their case effectively it did give some recognition to the rights of labour and helped to eliminate the worst forms of exploitation by employers. In later years, organized labour would object to a policy that might prevent strikes from being called at the most effective moment, but in this decade government mediation in any form was a radical innovation.

V

Derrière deux grands boeufs ou deux lourds percherons,
L'homme marche courbé, dans le pré solitaire,
Ses poignets musculeux rivés aux mancherons
De la charrue ouvrant le ventre de la terre.

Il s'imagine voir le blé gonfler sa grange;
Il songe que ses pas sont comptés par un ange,
Et que la labourer collabore avec Dieu.

William Chapman

This scene of rural bliss has little in common with the English-Canadian poet's metaphor of a dauntless spirit outstretched for flight, and during this decade the contrast in the attitudes of French and English Canadians was to become even more marked. French Canadians did not share the nation-building enthusiasm of their compatriots because to them prairie settlement and industrialization seemed remote and almost irrelevant. Instead of sharing the optimistic vision of spiralling national prosperity, many of them believed that nothing in the French-Canadian way of life had changed, and, what was more, they believed that nothing would or should change. The few who sensed that their society was being affected deplored the changes. Life on the remote prairies or in industrial cities seemed morally inferior to the idealized family life in the rural Quebec parish. French Canadians, always conscious of their distinctive identity, were becoming more defensive and more than ever determined to preserve their traditional way of life.

The great migration to the prairies in this decade did not include many French Canadians. There had been a time when some of their leaders had hoped to create a second Quebec in the Canadian west. French-speaking Roman Catholics had been an important group in Manitoba when it became a province in 1870, and the provincial constitution had included guarantees for their language and for Roman Catholic schools. In the years that followed, however, few French Canadians had migrated west and the English-speaking majority in the province had revoked these guarantees. Manitoba had become a second Ontario rather than a second Quebec, and the bitter controversy over the Manitoba Schools Question had shown that Manitobans were determined to live in an English-speaking province with non-sectarian schools. It was clear to French Canadians that their form of Canadian society was not welcome in the western province.

Nor was there any warmer welcome in the newly created provinces of Saskatchewan and Alberta in 1905. Provincial status involved little change for the people of the Northwest

Territories. The Territorial Assembly already controlled local administration, having won a form of responsible government, and had already established English as the language of the Assembly and the courts. French Canada had little interest in the discussions as to whether there should be one province or two, whether the federal government would retain control of Crown lands, and how large the provincial subsidies would be, and the final decisions on these issues roused no serious opposition. The federal government created two provinces and retained Crown lands–federal control of land policy would ensure that free homesteads would still be given to new settlers–but in exchange the new provinces received generous subsidies. Only the schools question provoked heated debate.

From the point of view of the people in the Territories there was no problem. A series of Territorial Ordinances had transformed the original dual system of Protestant and Catholic schools into one in which a single department of education administered both 'public' and 'separate' schools, with little difference between the two except in the teaching of religion. Roman Catholic students could be taught by Roman Catholic teachers in the separate schools but these teachers were expected to qualify for a teaching certificate by attending the same normal school as the public school teachers, and for the teaching of most subjects they used the same textbooks as the public schools. The people in the Territories had accepted this modified system of separate schools without any serious criticism and it was taken for granted that the same system would continue after provincial status was conceded.

Sir Wilfrid Laurier, however, was not satisfied with this arrangement. He feared that the Protestant majority in the new provinces might introduce administrative changes in the future that would further reduce the Roman Catholic character of the separate schools; the events in Manitoba ten years before convinced him that the minority needed a constitutional guarantee of their rights. Laurier did not raise the question of the language of instruction–he seems to have taken it for granted that the west would be an English-speaking region—but he did insist on a constitutional guarantee that there would be no interference with the religious character of the separate schools. Roman Catholics in this part of Canada were to be assured of schools of their own faith. Thus the first draft of the legislation creating the new provinces was designed to protect the separate schools from secular pressures by the provincial departments of education.

This guarantee almost defeated Laurier's government. Sir Clifford Sifton argued that this legislation would really restore the completely separate and dual system of schools that the people in the Territories had already rejected. Sifton himself resigned from the government in protest. W. S. Fielding, the Minister of Finance, threatened to resign. Robert Borden and the English-speaking Conservatives denounced this interference with the right of the provinces to choose the educational system they preferred, and strong protests came from the Territories. On the other hand, many French Canadians insisted on this guarantee for the Roman Catholic minority in the west; English-Canadian opposition to the legislation only confirmed their fears that without such a guarantee separate schools would be suppressed.

The government survived because Sir Wilfrid Laurier yielded to English-Canadian pressure. He did not believe that any constitutional guarantee would be effective if the majority in a province was not prepared to accept separate schools. In the long run he was sure that minority rights depended on the tolerance of the majority and he was sure that there would be even less tolerance if he tried to coerce the majority. He therefore introduced an amendment to the legislation which declared that the existing separate school system would be preserved but which left the administration of the schools under the control of the new provincial governments. Most of the Liberals, whether English- or French-Canadian, accepted this compromise and the amended legislation was approved.

The compromise was accepted but it was not applauded in French Canada. French Canadians could not share in the national enthusiasm for prairie settlement if English was to be the dominant language of the region and if separate schools were to be almost indistinguishable from non-confessional public schools. Henri Bourassa, the grandson of Louis Joseph Papineau and a brilliant young French-Canadian orator, had little confidence in the tolerance of the majority. He had tried to persuade Laurier to force the original legislation through the House of Commons even if it meant the resignation of many English-Canadian Liberals from the party, and the amendment which Laurier called a compromise Bourassa called a surrender to Protestant fanatics. Bourassa was joined by French-Canadian Conservatives in the House, who denounced Laurier's policy and who also denounced the official policy of their own party for the same reason.

The bitterness at being treated like aliens and foreigners in the western provinces of their own country survived long after the political crisis had ended. The French-Canadian Conservatives under F. D. Monk seriously considered separating from the English Conservatives in protest, and the break came a few years later with the next crisis. And Bourassa reported that many French Canadians had come to believe that only in Quebec could they be themselves:

> I regret every time I go back to my province to find developing that feeling that Canada is not Canada for all Canadians. We are bound to come to the conclusion that Quebec is our only country because we have no liberty elsewhere.

VI

Even in Quebec, however, prosperity had brought many changes. Montreal was both an industrial and a transportation centre, and the growing importance of transatlantic commerce, which was one aspect of the 'wheat boom', meant that Montreal, as Canada's major Atlantic port, was directly affected by prairie settlement. One visitor has left this impression of his first sight of Montreal after a voyage from Europe:

> Montreal! There is the city, swathed in smoke, like Sheffield itself. Through the dust-pall pierce factory chimneys and church spires and mammoth grain elevators. The docks are full of shipping, the winches are busy, and the cranes swing. Bales and machinery are being hauled from that ship. Grain is rushing in a yellow stream into that. Cattle are hoisted into another. Lumber rafts surround a fourth. There is the uproar of a busy town. Before you land you hear the shrill buzz of the racing electric cars, and on the great bridge spanning the river, nearly two miles wide, rumbles an express of the Grand Trunk Railroad.

But Montreal was not French Canada. Some fifty years earlier half the population of this city had been English-Canadian; it was now predominantly French-Canadian in numbers, but the French Canadians, mainly labourers who had migrated from rural areas, had little influence in the city. The railways, the banks, the commercial houses, the industrial firms – all were English-speaking institutions, owned and directed by English Canadians or by Englishmen or Americans. The workers might be French Canadians but they had no voice in the management or the policies of these firms. A prominent Frenchman noted that

> Visitors may pass whole weeks there, frequenting hotels, banks, shops, railway stations, without ever imagining for a moment that the town is French by a great majority of its inhabitants. English Society affects unconsciousness of the fact, and bears itself exactly as though it had no French neighbours. They seem to regard Montreal as their property.

Montreal was still an English enclave in French Canada.

French Canadians showed little resentment at this alien domination of Montreal. French-Canadian leaders, then as always, were intent on *la survivance*, the preservation of French-Canadian society. They feared that the distinctive qualities of this society could not survive in an urban and industrial world. Montreal meant more than the dangerous association with English Protestants; it also meant a materialistic way of life which was a threat to the ties of family and faith. As an influential churchman said in 1902:

> Our mission is not so much to manipulate money as to wrestle with ideas; it consists less in lighting factory fires than in keeping alight the luminous hearth of religion and making it shine from afar. . . . While our rivals claim . . . supremacy over industry and finance, we are eager above all for the honor of the faith and the victory of apostleship.

With this view of the destiny of French Canada, Montreal was alien territory and the French Canadians there seemed already lost to French-Canadian society. The Quebec in which they could be themselves lay outside of Montreal.

The champions of *la survivance*–churchmen, politicians, and journalists, many of whom lived in Montreal–reacted to the dangers to French-Canadian traditions by extolling the virtues of rural life. They appealed to their compatriots to remain untainted by contact with the English language, the Protestant religion, and the materialistic way of life, and they painted an idyllic picture of French Canadians tilling the soil and going to mass, with all the moral values of a close-knit family life. To the leaders of French Canada, *la survivance* meant the preservation of this rural society.

This ideal had one serious flaw. The children of large families grew up and had families of their own and the family farm could not support them all. For generations there had been a steady exodus from rural Quebec to the textile towns of New England. As Franco-Americans, these emigrants lived in an English-speaking and urban world; it seemed only a matter of time before they lost their language and their faith. In this decade Montreal probably absorbed a higher proportion of the rural emigrants, but Montreal was little better than New England to the defenders of *la survivance*.

To most French Canadians the answer seemed obvious. The sons who left their fathers' farms must clear more land and establish new rural communities in which the traditions of French-Canadian society would be preserved. This had been the solution advocated by French-Canadian leaders for generations. It had been the policy of George Cartier, of Bishop Bourget, of Curé Labelle, and of Honoré Mercier, and it became the policy of Sir Wilfrid Laurier and Henri Bourassa. The National Transcontinental railway was seen by Laurier as a colonization railway opening up new areas south of the St. Lawrence between Moncton and Quebec City, as well as in northern Quebec and in northern Ontario. European immigrants, he argued, would go to the prairies. Only the French Canadians were prepared to carve farms out of forests, and hence 'all the forest lands in Quebec and even in Ontario are the patrimony of French Canadians'.

It would be many years before the limitations of this colonization policy were understood. The soil that produced the northern forests did not yield bountiful cereal crops, and August droughts and September frosts made every springtime seeding a gamble. The settlers who moved north had to supplement their income in the early years with pick and shovel on railroad construction gangs or with axe and saw in logging camps, and even after their farms were cleared they still depended on winter work to survive. Louis Hémon, writing just after the end of the decade, described the life of the Chapdelaines in the Lake St. John area, the three sons spending the winters in logging camps to earn the only cash the family received, and returning in the spring to 'make land':

> The forest still pressed hard upon the buildings they had put up a few years earlier: the little square house, the barn of planks that gaped apart, the stable built of blackened logs and chinked with rags and earth. Between the scanty fields of their clearing and the darkly encircling woods lay a broad stretch which the axe had but half-heartedly attacked. A few living trees had been cut for timber, and the dead ones, sawn and split, fed the great stove for a whole winter; but the place was a rough tangle of stumps and interlacing roots, of fallen trees too far rotted to burn, of others dead but still erect amid the older scrub.

And yet after a few more years of toil, when the farm was cleared, the Chapdelaines would still be off to the *chantiers* in the winter in order to survive. Small wonder that the

Maria Chapdelaines of the province were sometimes tempted by the distant glamour of a crowded city.

Nonetheless, the colonization of northern Quebec and adjacent territories remained the accepted solution to the problems of French Canada. Henri Bourassa was one of the advocates of northern settlement. Bourassa was not a narrow French-Canadian nationalist, for he believed that Canada should be a bicultural country–a country in which French and English communities should have equal rights from the Atlantic to the Pacific. But he was sadly disillusioned by the debate over separate schools in Saskatchewan and Alberta. In 1907 he withdrew from federal politics to concentrate on the problems of colonization in the province of Quebec. Here at least was a part of Canada where French Canadians could be themselves.

Bourassa knew that these northern pioneers had grievances, but instead of blaming poor soil he blamed the provincial government at Quebec. He believed that this government was impeding colonization by leasing large areas to lumber or pulp-and-paper companies and thus excluding settlers. Bourassa won popular support by championing the rights of the colonists. His campaign drew support from those who wanted to strengthen a rural French-Canadian society, as well as from the French-Canadian nationalists who resented the activities of English-Canadian and American corporations in northern Quebec. If the other provinces were to be English-Canadian, rural Quebec at least should remain French.

Bourassa did not overthrow the provincial Liberal government by his attacks but he did alter the political balance within French Canada. He and a few young Liberal followers found ready allies within the provincial Conservative party. The collaboration of Bourassa and Monk on the schools question was soon duplicated by the collaboration of Bourassa and the French-Canadian Conservatives in Quebec on the colonization issue. This alliance was a protest against both of the national parties, which always seemed to heed English-Canadian demands and to ignore the interests of French

Canada. It was, in fact, the beginning of a sectional French-Canadian party and its emergence was a response to the growing isolation and estrangement of French Canadians from their English-speaking compatriots.

This isolation might have reduced friction between the two societies except that the isolation could never be complete. French Canadians, like the farmers in western Canada, found that they were affected by the policies at the federal as well as the provincial level. In the past the divisions between English Canadians and French Canadians at Ottawa had been blurred by the structure of the national political parties, in which cultural differences were tempered by party loyalties. The alliance between Bourassa and Monk and the Quebec Conservatives, however, meant that the party loyalties for this group coincided with French-Canadian loyalties, and within the federal Conservative party the withdrawal of the French-Canadian wing meant that this party was more and more an English-Canadian party. A clash between the two societies on a federal issue would be less easy to cushion because of this changing political alignment.

VII

It was not long before the clash occurred. Early in 1909 the British government announced that the tremendous expansion of the German navy constituted a critical threat to British security. The development of the torpedo had transformed naval tactics, and the emphasis was now on large capital ships with big guns that could engage the enemy at long range. The development of the Dreadnought, with its strength, speed, and twelve-inch guns, made older battleships obsolete. By 1909 German construction of this new type of capital ship threatened to outdistance British construction. Public opinion forced the British government to undertake a major naval construction program, with eight new Dreadnoughts to be laid down in 1909 and a total of eighteen within three years. The 'naval scare' of 1909 quickly became an issue in the British Dominions. The Royal Navy had always been the first line of imperial defence and the tremendous cost of this construction program convinced many people, both in Great Britain and in the Dominions, that the cost should be shared. In Canada, the question was whether the federal government would respond to this pressure.

Sir Wilfrid Laurier had successfully avoided any naval expenditures until 1909. The British Admiralty had pressed for contributions to the Royal Navy at the Colonial Conference of 1902, arguing that 'the sea is all one and the British Navy therefore must be all one'. Laurier however had argued that such contributions would be incompatible with Dominion self-government. How could the Canadian government control its defence expenditures and its defence policy if it had to pay levies to the Royal Navy? He admitted that Canada should take more responsibility for naval defence but announced that his government was contemplating a local naval force. Nothing was done in the years that followed because there had been no popular support in Canada for any form of defence expenditures. Since the choice between a contribution to the Royal Navy or building a separate Canadian navy was certain to be controversial, Laurier preferred to procrastinate. The 'naval scare' of 1909 forced the government to act.

The Naval Service Act of 1910 was Laurier's response; there would be a Canadian navy which at the same time might become part of the Royal Navy. This compromise was designed to satisfy most Canadians but at the same time it accurately reflected Laurier's view of the proper relations between Canada and Great Britain. Laurier was a staunch defender of Canadian autonomy but to him autonomy did not mean separation from the Empire. He believed that the Royal Navy contributed to Canadian security, and if British naval supremacy was in danger that it would be in the interests of Canada 'to support England with all our might'. To him, Canadian autonomy meant that Canadians would decide whether to participate in a British war – there would be no automatic commitment–but it also meant, in case of a major war, that Canadians would decide to be at Britain's side.

The Naval Service Act therefore declared that the Canadian government had the authority to place the Canadian naval force at the disposal of the British Admiralty in time of war, and the naval force itself was designed so that it could be easily integrated with the British army. The Act thus asserted a Canadian autonomy that was neither colonial subordination nor national independence.

This compromise was unacceptable to the Conservative Opposition. English Canadians were becoming more conscious of their ties with Great Britain; this was the era of Kipling and jingoism, and it was also a time when the major role played by the British market and British capital in the 'wheat boom' strengthened the emotional ties. Many expressed horror at the implication that Canada might refuse to participate in some British war. R. L. Borden argued that 'such inaction or declaration will amount virtually to a declaration of independence'. Other Conservatives argued that the new naval force would be inadequate–they called it 'Laurier's tin-pot navy'–and demanded a direct donation of the cost of two Dreadnoughts to Great Britain. In effect, the Conservative Opposition was advocating a closer commitment to participation in British wars than Laurier was willing to accept.

Laurier's compromise, however, was equally unacceptable to many in French Canada. French Canadians had few ties with Europe; as Bourassa said, they were French in the same way that the Americans were English. To them, the attachment of English Canadians to Great Britain was a form of colonial subservience and a proof of their failure to develop a true loyalty to Canada. In 1899 Bourassa had denounced Canadian participation in the South African war because he felt Canada's interests were not involved, although at the time most of his compatriots had been able to tolerate the idea of a Canadian contingent of volunteers. French Canadians were less tolerant a decade later. Not only was their isolation more complete but they had become more suspicious of English-Canadian motives. F. D. Monk argued in the House of Commons that Canada was in no danger of attack and so the only possible reason for spending money on a Canadian Navy was to strengthen the Royal Navy. The Canadian navy might be Canadian in time of peace but English Canadians would make sure that it was British in time of war. In Quebec Bourassa joined Monk in denouncing the Act as a betrayal of Canadian autonomy. In contrast to Borden's position, these French-Canadian leaders were advocating a greater separation from Great Britain than Laurier was willing to accept.

The Drummond-Arthabaska by-election in the fall of 1910 showed that many French Canadians shared the suspicions of Bourassa and Monk. Laurier opened the constituency to challenge the opposition in Quebec to the Naval Service Act, but the opposition proved to be unexpectedly strong. The constituency, long a Liberal stronghold, elected an independent candidate who had campaigned against Laurier's naval policy. The federal election of 1911 would prove that this was not an isolated incident. French Canadians, like the western farmers, were ready to support a third party because neither of the two national parties seemed sensitive to their special outlook.

VIII

In retrospect it must have seemed to most Canadians that the decade had justified the boast that the twentieth century would belong to them. The 'Dominion from sea to sea' was no longer a mere geographical or political expression; physical regions with distinctive natural features and provinces with separate histories were now bound together by interdependent economic activity. New railways were crossing the continent and nurturing new towns and cities, and the 'wheat boom' dispelled the fears of earlier decades that Canada was an artificial creation that could never become a nation.

But although Canadians in 1910 no longer doubted that the federal union would survive, they were still uncertain about the future. Prosperity had linked regions but it had not erased the divisions. The context of regional rivalries had changed but the divergence of regional aims and aspirations had not been resolved. Material progress had not created a sense of common purpose or common identity. National unity continued to be the slogan of every Canadian politician because unity of purpose was still no more than an elusive goal.

6. Through the First World War

ROGER GRAHAM

At the outset of the second decade of the twentieth century, in the late autumn of an age, violent winds of trouble were beginning to blow in distant quarters of the globe. But, accustomed to relative order and tranquillity, conditioned by good fortune and their prevailing outlook on life to anticipate continued progress, the Canadians had no more reason to guess than most people, and perhaps much less than many, that mankind was about to pass over one of the great watersheds of history into a time of war and revolution, of profound moral and intellectual unsettlement, and of almost unremitting anxiety.

Of course they were not oblivious to all that was happening in the world. There was much newspaper talk, for example, of the ambitions of Kaiser Wilhelm II, self-styled

'Admiral of the Atlantic', whose imperial German navy challenged British mastery of the seas. Disquieting reports came from places far away and only vaguely apprehended: St. Petersburg and Belgrade; Bosnia and Bulgaria; Salonika, Constantinople, and Fez. But in the view of most Canadians, these clouds appeared small, on a remote horizon. The naval challenge struck closest to home, and they argued about it heatedly, but it seemed inconceivable that Germany, for all her military might, her industrial capacity, and her imperial swagger, could successfully dispute the sea supremacy of the vast maritime empire of Great Britain. As for the mad ambitions and absurd rivalries of the Balkan kingdoms and principalities, the chronic violence and obscure intrigues of North Africa, the dim, mysterious rumblings in the Russian Empire, these could hardly be of real danger to a country as securely situated as Canada. Minor wars might be fought but major crises would be averted or, if not averted, solved by diplomatic accommodations. With power balanced between two rival alliances of great European states a large, all-consuming conflict was hardly imaginable. So it doubtless seemed to most Canadians in that year of grace 1911; so it seemed in the years thereafter until the news from Sarajevo destroyed the illusion in 1914 and brought an epoch to an end.

For Canada, these were years of hope abounding, of spacious visions and happy expectations. The population was growing at an unparalleled rate, thanks chiefly to the swelling wave of immigration that had begun to roll about the turn of the century and was now approaching the crest it would reach in 1913, when over 400,000 people, the biggest number ever, settled in Canada. A large proportion of these newcomers found their way into the great, sparsely settled stretches of the prairie provinces, that 'last, best west' of which Sir Wilfrid Laurier had spoken, thus adding flesh and sinew to the thin frame of the country. Harvests, production, and construction were all increasing prodigiously. The most striking accomplishment was the building–with generous public financial assistance–of two new transcontinental railways to serve what, with more enthusiasm than good judgement (they fell on evil days a little later and had to be nationalized), were thought to be the needs of a rapidly developing, increasingly prosperous nation. One could not guess that the boom would shortly end, to be revived only by the grim demands of war; one could not anticipate the fact that easy optimism and confident faith would soon give way to doubts and sullen disillusionment, and the near-fracture of a country that in 1911 looked so fit and so secure.

Nor was it to be imagined when that year began that a startling political upset was in the offing. The decade, in fact, was bounded at either end by a political milestone, the defeat of Laurier at its start and the retirement of his successor, Sir Robert Borden, as it drew to a finish. The Laurier government looked as strong when 1911 opened as any government had a right to be after fourteen consecutive years in power. The Liberal party had won four general elections in a row, won them handily, and Laurier himself had come to be almost as much a national institution as a mere leader of men. With the country progressing splendidly there appeared to be no compelling reason for a change of government, and yet, before 1911 was over, Laurier was defeated. He lost because of fears created by two of his major decisions. Both decisions had a bearing on Canada's relations with Great Britain and one bore on the equally explosive subject of her relations with the United States; both therefore touched the emotions and aroused passionate debate.

The first was Laurier's naval policy. As an alternative to direct contributions of men and money to strengthen the imperial fleet, of the sort advocated for some years past by the British Admiralty, he proposed that Canada assume responsibility for her naval security with a navy of her own, which, however, might be placed at the disposal of Great Britain in time of emergency. It was a compromise and it caused widespread dissatisfaction. Criticisms came from two opposite directions. There were many in English-speaking

Canada who, while not necessarily against a separate Canadian navy in principle, believed that only by outright cash contributions to build up British naval power could Canada effectively aid in meeting the immediate and actual danger, the menacing growth of German strength on the seas. To them Laurier's policy was ineffectual and unrealistic, a weak-kneed surrender to anti-British elements in the nation. The policy was attacked with equal bitterness but for quite contrary reasons by the French-Canadian Nationalists, led by Henri Bourassa. In their view the establishment of a navy under the terms of Laurier's Naval Service Act of 1910 was hardly less obnoxious than the gifts of money so much desired by the Admiralty and so zealously advocated by many Canadians. In the absence of any conceivable threat to the naval security of the country, they argued, the expense of acquiring and maintaining a naval force would be unjustified. Worse than that, possession of such a force would needlessly involve Canada in imperial adventures that were no concern of hers, especially since it was stipulated that Canadian ships and their crews might be handed over to Britain in the event of war. This last feature of the policy convinced them that Laurier was, as they had long suspected, *un vendu,* that he had sold out to the imperialists and betrayed his own people. These, by and large, were also the opinions on the matter expressed by F. D. Monk, the leading French-speaking Conservative in federal politics.

The second of Laurier's fateful decisions at that juncture was to discuss with the Americans the possibility of reciprocity in trade between Canada and the United States. Thus was revived a project that for nearly half a century, ever since the abrogation of the Reciprocity Treaty of 1854, Canadians had talked about a great deal and from time to time attempted unsuccessfully to promote. Discussions were succeeded by actual negotiations and the result was a formal agreement which was to be implemented by concurrent legislation in the two countries. It provided for free trade between them in natural products, as well as in a selected list of semi-finished and fully manufactured articles, and for reciprocal tariff reductions on a number of other goods as well. These arrangements were approved by the American Congress, which more than once in the past had balked at reciprocity with Canada, but in the Parliament at Ottawa and in various parts of the Dominion a formidable antagonism to the scheme began to take shape. The parliamentary Conservative party seemed at first to be somewhat disconcerted by the agreement–as much so as the government was pleased with it, for its terms looked very favourable to Canada. However, as evidence of opposition mounted and as signs appeared of a serious split in the Liberal party over the issue, with a group of prominent Toronto Liberal businessmen issuing a manifesto denouncing the agreement, the Opposition in Parliament began a filibuster against the scheme that was carried on in the midst of an increasingly acrimonious and emotional debate across English-speaking Canada.

Faced with resourceful obstruction of his measure in the House of Commons and without a closure rule enabling him to bring it to a vote, Laurier at length decided to appeal to the country, and Parliament was dissolved. In the ensuing election campaign critics of the agreement attacked it not so much on purely economic grounds as because it would bring Canada too much into the orbit of the United States, would in fact place her political independence in jeopardy. It was a disloyal policy, they contended, likely to lead to the severance of Canada's ties with the mother country and her annexation to the United States, a charge given some truth by the numerous annexationist statements made by men of some prominence in American public life and by certain American newspapers. Meanwhile Quebec was ringing with denunciations of Laurier's naval policy. There the Nationalists made common cause with the Conservatives against the Liberal party, with the result that Laurier's hold on his own province, the foundation of his long power, was seriously weakened. Thanks to this, to their gains in some other provinces, and to their near sweep of Ontario, the Conservatives came into office with a commanding majority.

The new Prime Minister, Robert Laird Borden, was a Nova Scotian who had become leader of the Conservative party in 1901. Less elegant and less brilliant than Laurier, he had little of the urbane charm and eloquence of his great adversary. However, Borden brought distinguished gifts of his own to the office: patience and persistence, courage and common sense, strong convictions about duty and honour, and solid integrity. He was to need all these personal resources in the years of storm and stress during which he led his country.

Borden's troubles began to appear even before the outbreak of war in the summer of 1914. Most important in the immediate political sense was the loss of much of the support in Quebec that he had enjoyed in the election. The Conservative-Nationalist alliance in that province was an unnatural union that began to dissolve shortly after the purpose for which it had been formed – the defeat of the Laurier administration – was achieved. Its dissolution was hastened, though not entirely caused, by the decision of the new government to replace the Laurier naval plan with an outright cash contribution to the enlargement of the British navy. Parliament was to be asked to appropriate $35,000,000 for the construction of three large battleships which would be units in a single imperial fleet. This was strenuously objected to by Monk, who held the Public Works portfolio. Failing to persuade the Prime Minister to submit the question to the voters in a referendum, Monk resigned from the Cabinet. The alienation of Quebec from the Borden government had begun. As it turned out, though, the contribution of the three ships was not made. Borden's Naval Air Bill ran into stormy weather in the House of Commons, the Liberals obstructing its passage just as the Conservatives had that of reciprocity in 1911. With the aid of a new closure rule, the handiwork of a young, ambitious, and able back-bencher from the west by the name of Arthur Meighen, the Bill was finally approved by the Commons, only to be rejected in the Senate, where the Liberals were in control.

II

Although the naval issue revealed a deep cleavage in Canada over the general subject of imperial relations, when war finally broke out in Europe in 1914, Canadians were united in believing that they must join forces with Britain and her allies. With the British declaration of war on Germany on August 4, Canada was then automatically at war as well, and most Canadians heartily approved of this arrangement. It was thought that the war would be over and won in short order, would in fact be something of a glorious adventure. Few yet understood the extent to which the resources and the unity of the country would be tested. There was much display of patriotic fervour as young men, a large proportion of them recent immigrants from Great Britain, flocked to join up.

Everywhere in the Dominion people greeted the war with enthusiasm; crowds sang patriotic songs in the streets, and the Minister of Militia and Defence, Sir Sam Hughes, was deluged with offers of volunteers. Hughes, who always knew better than his professional advisers, discarded the carefully prepared mobilization plan for the Canadian Militia and substituted a scheme of his own whereby a Canadian contingent would be mobilized at Valcartier Camp near Quebec City. All during August and September volunteers poured into Valcartier, where, in spite of the bungling and bombast of the Minister, they were formed into the battalions of the Canadian Expeditionary Force. On the 3rd of October 32,665 men embarked for England.

At home the economy, which had lagged somewhat in a short pre-war recession, was mobilized to supply small arms and ammunition, boots and uniforms, food, metals and timber, medicines and bandages, horses and wagons. All across the land photographers' shutters clicked so that soldiers and their families might have something to remember each other by.

In England through that autumn and winter, the First Canadian Contingent trained in the wet misery of Salisbury

Plain, and, although the soldiers did not know it, the rain, mud, and cold of that desolate camp was to be a fitting introduction to the campaigns that lay ahead. Early in February the First Canadian Division, under Lieutenant-General E. A. H. Alderson, a British officer, arrived in France and was gradually introduced into the fighting line in the Armentières sector.

April 1915 brought the Canadians their first major battle. On the 22nd the Germans suddenly attacked in the Ypres Salient, advancing behind yellow clouds of chlorine gas which rolled over the French colonial divisions on the Canadian left. A gaping hole was torn in the Allied front, but the green troops from the Dominion stood firm. The Canadian line extended to provide a thin screen across the gap, and the German drive was halted. The fighting at this second battle of Ypres was a bitter foretaste of the heroism and sacrifice that was to come, for in four days Canadian casualties totalled 6,037.

Less than a month later the Canadian Division was back in the thick of the battle. In the middle of May at Festubert and in June at Givenchy, the Canadians were launched in suicidal frontal attacks against impregnable positions. Such attacks were to be the hallmark of Allied strategy for the next three years. In September 1915 a second division arrived in France, and in December a third division was formed.

The First Division had had its baptism of fire at Second Ypres. In April 1916 the Second Division was thrown into an equally confused and desperate battle for possession of the St. Eloi craters. The troops fought with their usual courage and tenacity, but bad staff work and inadequate commanders prevented them from gaining firm possession of the worthless holes in the ground that were their objective. The following month Lieutenant-General Sir Julian Byng replaced Alderson as Canadian Corps Commander.

The year 1916 was to be marked by a tremendous Allied effort on the Western Front. The Germans had been pressing the French hard at Verdun, and the British Commander-in-Chief, Sir Douglas Haig, intended to relieve this pressure by breaking through the German lines on the Somme. Before Haig was ready to mount his great offensive, the Germans launched a number of limited spoiling attacks, one of which overran some Canadian positions near Sanctuary Wood and Mount Sorrel. The Canadians were in no mood to accept such reverses, and on June 13 the First Division, attacking through a black night filled with driving rain, recaptured the lost ground.

For the British and Dominion troops, the history of the remainder of 1916 can be summed up in two ominous words – 'the Somme'. Fortunately, the Canadians had no part in the débâcle of the 1st of July, when Haig's soldiers advanced under a bright blue sky to meet the bloodiest repulse ever to befall British arms. The Newfoundland Regiment was there on the fatal first day of the Somme, being practically wiped out at Beaumont Hamel before the soldiers so much as reached the German wire, but the Canadian Corps was not committed to the holocaust until September. By then Haig was no longer aiming at a breakthrough and the offensive had degenerated into bitter, bloody, step-by-step slogging of a type never before witnessed on any battlefield. The Canadians attacked again and again – at Pozières Ridge, Flers-Courcelette, the Sugar Factory, Fabeck Graben, and Regina Trench. They gained their objectives, or most of them, but when the winter rains at last forced Haig to call a halt, the Canadians had lost 24,029 men.

By the end of 1916 it looked as though the war might go on forever and in all the belligerent nations the mood of the people had hardened into a sort of angry despair. The peace proposals that Pope Benedict XV made in December were rejected out of hand by both sides, for both the Allies and the Central Powers were determined to settle for nothing less than victory. In Canada too this feeling was apparent, although by no means all Canadians were deeply committed to winning the war. Profiteering scandals rocked the government; farmers and industrial workers were making unprecedented earnings; and angry voices in Quebec were beginning to repeat the Pope's condemnation of the conflict as 'this senseless carnage'. The men in France had little in common with the aspirations and emotions of the people at home. The daily tasks of the battle-zone demanded all the soldiers' energy, but by now the Canadian Corps had already been welded into a magnificent fighting machine with a corporate pride and confidence that later events were fully to justify.

Easter Monday, April 9, 1917, brought the first Allied-offensive success of the war on the Western Front. On that day the entire Canadian Corps of four divisions stormed forward in the early dawn against the imposing heights of Vimy Ridge. With driving sleet and snow at their backs, the Canadian soldiers crashed through three successive lines of German defences and reached the crest of the ridge by mid-morning. Before nightfall the name of Canada was ringing around the world, for the Allies, after so long being starved of success, were inclined to exaggerate the importance of this splendid, but minor, victory. Vimy Ridge became a symbol of Canadian achievement, and the pride engendered on the bloody slopes of that commanding hill did much to bring Canada to full nationhood.

That summer Sir Douglas Haig was resolved to strike again in the west. With irrational confidence he still hoped to achieve the final breakthrough that had so long eluded him. The British offensive was to be launched across the most difficult terrain on the Continent, the undulating low-lands beyond Ypres around Passchendaele. As a diversion, the Canadian Corps, now commanded by a Canadian, Sir Arthur Currie, was ordered to capture Hill 70 near Arras. On August 15 the Canadians took the hill in a dashing assault and held it firmly against all counter-attacks. Indeed, from the capture of Vimy Ridge on, the Canadian Corps invariably gained its objective every time it was committed to battle. Nevertheless, the fighting at Hill 70 had been costly. In ten days Canadian casualties totalled 9,198.

Worse was to come. Although Haig's Passchendaele offensive had met with no appreciable success, he persisted in his attacks long after all hope of victory had disappeared. The British had begun attacking on July 31 but there had been long pauses–coinciding, ironically, with the brightest, dustiest weather–in August and September. The autumn rains set in by the evening of October 7 and quickly turned the shell-drenched landscape into a muddy morass where movement was all but impossible. This did not prevent Haig from sending the Canadians to the Ypres Salient or from committing them to action on October 26. The nature of the fighting that autumn about Passchendaele defies adequate description. Men struggled forward to attack through waist-deep mud and icy water; the wounded often slipped off the greasy boardwalks to drown or smother in the mud; and all the while the Germans, who held the higher ground, saturated the entire area with shell-fire. Yet the Canadians struggled agonizingly forward to capture each successive objective. The last Canadian troops were not relieved in the Salient until November 20, by which time they had taken the ruins of Passchendaele village and were the possessors of an insignificant area of flooded swamp. The cost to the Corps had been 15,654 casualties.

By now, however, the war was drawing towards its climax. Russia, torn by revolution, made a separate peace with Germany in December, and large numbers of German troops were freed from the Eastern Front for deployment in the west. The United States had entered the conflict on the Allied side in April, but it would be midsummer of 1918 before significant numbers of American troops could take their place in the fighting line. Therefore, the spring of 1918 was a crucial time for the Central Powers. The German High Command decided to launch a last desperate offensive in the hope of winning the war before the weight of American manpower and industrial production could make itself felt. The German attacks began in March; great holes were immediately torn in the British front and the Allied line bent alarmingly back towards Paris. For the first time since the bright, adventurous summer of 1914 it appeared as though Germany might win the war within a matter of days.

During all this desperate fighting, the Canadian Corps was held in reserve, but when the German offensive was at last halted and the time for counter-attack came, the Canadians again formed the spearhead. The great counter-blow was launched on the morning of August 8 near Amiens. Canadian, British, Australian, and French divisions, utilizing surprise for the first time in an unimaginative four years, broke cleanly through the attenuated German lines and advanced joyously into open country. The battle of Amiens convinced the German High Command that the war was lost and that peace would have to be made. The end was now in sight, and all ranks of the Canadian Corps could sense that victory was almost in their grasp. Yet bloody, bitter battles still remained to be fought. The Canadian Corps was continuously used as the hard-hitting hammerhead of the relentless Allied assaults. The Canadians broke through the Drocourt-Quèant Line and the Hindenburg Line and then, in one of the most brilliant and daring conceptions of the war, advanced through the narrow funnel of the dry bed of the Canal du Nord to fan out on the far side in another victorious attack. By the end of October the harried German forces were everywhere falling back, with the pursuing Allies hard on their heels. When the Armistice brought an end to hostilities on the morning of November 11, the Canadians were on the outskirts of the Belgian city of Mons, almost exactly where, four years and three months previously, the British had first brushed against the enemy.

III

In every way the First World War had been the most tragic episode in Canadian history. Gone for ever was the old, pleasant, half-somnolent world, in which most Canadian communities had borne a striking likeness to Stephen Leacock's sunshiny little town of Mariposa. A terrible total of 61,326 Canadians had been killed, and 172,950 had been wounded. On top of that, national unity had been dealt a grievous blow by a prolonged and passionate controversy over how to maintain the supply of men for Canada's forces overseas.

The Canadian Corps was both a highly effective fighting force and the proudly regarded symbol of Canada's identity as a partner in the Allied cause, which made the question of maintaining its strength all the more vital. This problem, which became crucial in 1917, arose fundamentally from the unexpectedly long duration of the war, the shockingly high wastage of men at the front, and the fact that the Canadians were present in force and more or less continuously in action from early in 1915 to the very end of the struggle. Even under the best conditions at home these brute, inescapable realities might well have caused trouble in recruiting the needed reinforcements.

But conditions at home were not of the best, and the most serious feature of the worsening situation here was an ever-widening breach between Quebec and the rest of the nation. At the outset of the war the French Canadians were, by and large, at one with the mass of their fellow countrymen in the belief that Canada must participate to the fullest extent, a belief to which Laurier gave characteristically eloquent tongue. Other spokesmen of French Canada, in both Church and State, also expressed this conviction, as did the French-language newspapers, and urged the young men of Quebec to enlist, which many did. However, as time went by angry voices began to accuse the French Canadians of not contributing their fair share of men to the forces, and asserting that Quebec was lagging behind, with smaller numbers enlisting in proportion to her population than were coming from the other provinces. Not only that, it was pointed out, a substantial proportion of the volunteers from Quebec belonged to her English-speaking minority.

That there was such a discrepancy was true but there were reasons for it. If one left out of the reckoning the British-born recruits, most of whom lived outside Quebec and who supplied so large a part of the volunteers in the first two years of the war, and compared the response of native Canadians from the various provinces, the discrepancy was not

Crumbling

From *The Canadian Liberal Monthly*, October, 1916.

nearly so great. But in any case the people of French Canada could not be expected to answer the call to arms with quite the readiness and enthusiasm shown by their compatriots of British descent. Appeals to a sense of kinship and duty to Britain and the Empire did not touch their emotions in the same way. Nor had they their own comparable feeling of loyalty and affection for France, from which they had long been separated both politically and sentimentally; the argument that she deserved their aid in her hour of peril left them relatively unmoved. Indeed, to most of them Europe seemed quite remote, even irrelevant. The war as it dragged on came to look less and less like a noble crusade and more and more like another in the long series of struggles between the big European powers for wealth and territory. The French Canadian would willingly die for the defence of Canada, and especially of his homeland in the St. Lawrence valley, but he found it increasingly difficult to believe that Canada was in danger or that her defence might best be mounted in the muddy trenches of Flanders.

In addition to feeling isolated from Europe and uninvolved emotionally in its problems the people of French Canada felt antagonized and their tempers were frayed by certain errors of judgement made in recruiting and organizing the overseas force, errors for which the flamboyant, egocentric, and bull-headed Sam Hughes was largely responsible. As Borden's Minister of Militia until 1916, his failure in the beginning to establish distinctive French-speaking units and his policy of dispersing French-speaking recruits among predominantly English-speaking battalions annoyed the people of Quebec, as did his tendency to overlook qualified French-Canadian officers when promotions were decided. If his ingrained Orange prejudice and his suspicion of Quebec annoyed French Canadians, he had as remarkable a gift for annoying almost everyone with whom he came in contact. But, unfortunate as his influence was in many ways, the importance and seriousness of his errors were exaggerated by his critics. He was not the author of the manpower problem, only an exasperating aggravation of it.

A more serious grievance of the French Canadians, one entirely extraneous to the war but powerfully destructive of Canadian unity while it was being fought, was the Ontario government's policy of restricting the use of French as a language of instruction in the schools of the province. In the eastern and northern regions of Ontario, and to a lesser extent in the south-western corner, there was a marked concentration of French-speaking people. Acting on the finding of a commission of inquiry that children were graduating from some of the schools in these districts without an adequate knowledge of English, the provincial Department of Education in 1912 issued an administrative order – the notorious Regulation 17 – placing severe limits on the use of French in teaching. The strenuous protests of those directly affected by this policy found a noisy echo in Quebec, where the rights of the French-speaking minority of Ontario were widely regarded as more important and better worth fighting for than the cause of the Allies in Europe. Canadians were dying overseas, allegedly in defence of freedom, justice, and democracy, at the hands of the Prussian enemy. But should not justice, like charity, begin at home and the fight be waged against Anglo-Saxon 'Prussianism' in Ontario? Such was the cry raised by some leaders of opinion in Quebec, most insistently by Bourassa and his newspaper, *Le Devoir*. Here was a distraction for which the Dominion government was in no way responsible and which it was constitutionally powerless to remove. Borden's private representations to the authorities in Ontario urging a modification of the policy were rebuffed and the language issue remained alive to bedevil the country throughout the war.

Although the most alarming feature of the situation that developed during the war was the growing estrangement of Quebec and the evidence of hostility towards her elsewhere, a reluctance to enlist for overseas service was, needless to say, not confined to the young men of that province. War weariness and disillusionment became more prevalent everywhere. Furthermore, the war, by placing heavy demands on Canada's productive capacity, created a pressing need for labour on the farm, in the mines and mills, and in the factories and the forests. These all competed with the armed forces for men and it was not surprising that many men, despite the social pressures on them to enlist, preferred to remain employed at home rather than embark upon the hazardous and ill-paid life of soldiering.

The shortage of reinforcements for the army began to be serious in 1916, especially during the second half of the year, and in the early months of 1917 it became worse, with only about half as many men enlisting as were being lost in action.

Faced with this fact, knowing that its various efforts to stimulate recruitment had failed and finding itself under mounting bi-partisan pressure from English-speaking Canada to adopt conscription, the government was forced to reappraise its manpower policy. Borden himself had more than once stated that he had no intention of resorting to compulsory service and had tried to put the best possible face on the situation. By the spring of 1917, however, it was no longer possible to pretend that without conscription the additional soldiers could be found. In May of that year the Prime Minister came home from a visit to England and France convinced by discussions there and by first-hand observation that conscription would have to come.

Borden's announcement on his return of the fateful decision to abandon voluntary enlistment was followed shortly by efforts, at length successful, to construct a coalition cabinet of Liberals and Conservatives who favoured conscription. He first invited Laurier to join such a ministry, but Sir Wilfrid, unable to endorse the new manpower policy, declined. Discussions were then opened with a number of English-speaking Liberals and at last, in October, Borden completed the formation of the Union Government, a government in which the French-speaking people of Quebec were not effectively represented. In the meantime there had been stirring scenes and much eloquent oratory in Parliament. A bill embodying the principle of selective compulsory service was drafted and enacted after long debate between opposing forces which to a disturbing degree reflected the division between Quebec and the rest of the country. One of the most poignant features of those dramatic days was the desertion of the venerable Laurier by many of his leading lieutenants and followers outside of Quebec and the disruption of a party which under his leadership had become a great power in the land. But the unity and *esprit de corps* of the Conservative party were hardly less seriously injured by these developments. Its French-Canadian wing was almost totally alienated by conscription, and many dyed-in-the-wool Conservatives, both in Quebec and elsewhere, were bitterly opposed from the party standpoint to even a temporary coalition with their traditional enemies.

With party lines thus drastically altered, and with passions at a high pitch over the conscription issue and the increasing antagonism between Quebec and the rest of the country, the Union Government went to the polls in the autumn of 1917. It did so under a franchise that had been cleverly modified by another bitterly disputed enactment of the recent parliamentary session. This extraordinary measure, the Wartime Elections Act, was clearly designed to weight the electoral scales against the anti-conscriptionist opposition. By enfranchising the female near-relatives of men who had served or were serving overseas it added a significant number of voters who could be expected to support conscription. By disfranchising people who were of enemy alien birth or habitually spoke an enemy alien tongue, and who had not become British subjects until after March 1902, it removed from the rolls a class who on the whole had supported the Liberal party in the past and might be counted on to continue following Laurier now. This change in the suffrage presumably accounted in part for the great victory scored by the Union Government, whose candidates won a majority of seventy-one seats in the new House of Commons. But there was a most disquieting feature in the outcome of the voting. All but twenty of the eighty-two seats captured by the Laurier Liberals were in Quebec and that province therefore appeared to be pitted against the rest of Canada. Many of the utterances on both sides during the election campaign, indeed, not only indicated belief in the existence of such a confrontation but did much to separate the two peoples.

Enforcement of the conscription law, the Military Service Act, was most difficult in Quebec, where there was widespread evasion of the law. In Quebec City, there was rioting against it. However, the measure was also widely unpopular elsewhere, especially among those liable to service, as the very high number of claims for exemption in all provinces testified. The government's cancellation early in 1918 of certain exemptions hitherto granted, in particular those to farmers' sons, brought stormy protests. Seldom if ever had a policy given such apparently resounding electoral support encountered so much obstruction and aroused so much resentment among the populace. Partly because of this and partly because the Act was in force for only about ten months before the war ended, relatively few men–upwards of 80,000–were raised by conscription. Not much more than half of these actually went overseas and but a small number of those who did saw active service. It therefore made no significant military contribution, though it might have done so had the war continued longer, which seemed quite possible at the time conscription was adopted.

Although dislike of conscription was not confined to Quebec, in the main the issue did divide Canadians on 'racial' lines. At the height of the crisis of 1917-18 it appeared that the very survival of Confederation might be in doubt as the verbal violence of recrimination mounted on both sides. In the closing months of the war, however, a more moderate spirit made its influence felt. While the crisis left a lasting legacy of misunderstanding and distrust, with conscription remaining a potent political issue in Quebec for many years to come and affecting profoundly the course of Canadian politics, passions were in some measure subdued as with the end of the war new political developments and controversies took precedence.

IV

The post-war political situation was indeed new, and different from anything known before in Canada. Any expectations there may have been of a speedy return to 'normalcy' (equated by many people with pre-war conditions) were doomed to disappointment. For one thing those years witnessed an exuberant radicalism, especially in the western provinces, which in some of its manifestations was new in kind as well as in magnitude. For another, and this was partly an effect of the radical temper, the familiar party system, still suffering from the conscription issue, was being further weakened by a rebellion of the farmers against the two old parties, and even against the party system as such. New farmers' parties, or 'movements' as many of their supporters preferred to call them, were in the process of being formed, both in the provinces and on the national scene.

If there was an element of genuine radicalism in this resort to direct political action by the farmers, they were also in a sense driven by an impulse that was conservative, not to say reactionary. Though some of them exhibited a fondness for up-to-date reform ideas about direct democracy and group government, ideas largely borrowed from similar agrarian movements in the western United States, they were unconsciously reacting against the increasing domination of government and society by modern industrial capitalism. Making a desperate last-ditch stand in defence of the agricultural community, they were in a way political romantics attempting to preserve a fast-vanishing Arcadia. Of course they could also be hard-headed realists when it came to gauging their own immediate interests and determining how best to advance them. They had long since organized for collective action through various agencies to protect themselves from the ruthless exploitation practised by banks, railways, and grain companies. However, they had stopped short of creating their own political parties, relying instead on their united strength to put sufficient pressure on existing parties to secure the legislation they desired.

Before the war a lot of dissatisfaction with this method had appeared among the farmers, a growing conviction—strengthened by the defeat of the reciprocity agreement that most of them favoured—that both the Liberal and Conservative parties were dominated by groups hostile to the agricultural class and to the interests of western Canada in particular. Justice for the farmers, many of them came to believe, an influence in determining national policies commensurate with their numbers and importance, could only be achieved by electing their own candidates to Parliament, by presenting a united political front. Since agrarian influence in Liberal and Conservative councils was so slight, being invariably subordinated to the power of the great business aggregations of Ontario and Quebec, a new farmers' party there must be.

The process of its formation was interrupted by the war, the winning of which took precedence and which, in any event, by temporarily restoring agricultural prosperity, softened somewhat the anger and dissatisfaction of the farmers. At the same time, though, the creation of the Union Government facilitated the process by freeing many of its farm supporters from their allegiance to the Liberal party, which the majority in the west had followed before that time. This made it easier for them to find their way into the fold of the new agrarian political movement, instead of rejoining the Liberal ranks, when the day came to desert the Union Government. That regime they regarded as only a transitory war-time necessity. They not only disliked some of its measures, especially the conscription of farmers' sons and hired hands, but had little hope that in peace-time its policies with respect to the tariff and other domestic issues would be satisfactory from their point of view. In 1918 the Canadian Council of Agriculture, claiming to represent all the farmers in the country, adopted a platform known as the New National Policy. Two years later the National Progressive party came formally into being, made that platform its own, and, led by Thomas A. Crerar, an erstwhile Liberal from Manitoba who had resigned the previous year as Minister of Agriculture in the Union Government, prepared to appeal to the nation in the next general election. Meanwhile provincial farmers' parties were also being organized. In 1919 one of them, in Ontario, scored a sensational victory and, with the co-operation of a number of labour members also elected to the legislature, formed a government. The revolt of the agrarians was assuming large proportions, to some people alarmingly so. It was a new fact of political life which would have to be taken seriously.

The farmers were not the only ones who were more than usually restive at the end of the war. Their entrance into politics as a new force, though worrisome to the leaders of the old parties and to conservatively-minded people in general, was less frightening than the increasingly radical opinions popular in a section of the trade-union movement and the revolutionary talk indulged in by some of its leaders. In the past Canadian unions on the whole had been moderate in outlook and peaceful in methods. Of course there had been strikes and some violence in labour disputes but by and large little evidence of basic dissatisfaction with the capitalist system. When the war came to a close, however, such dissatisfaction was a good deal in evidence and, as with the discontent of the farmers, was most intense and most vehemently stated in the west.

There were varied and rather complex reasons for the disgruntlement of the western working men. For one thing they felt aggrieved by certain war-time policies, as well as by some economic consequences of the war and of the return of peace. Many of them, at least of those who did not enlist in the army, had opposed conscription, and many of the 'New Canadians' among them had been disfranchised for the time being by the Wartime Elections Act. A large proportion, whether unionized tradesmen or unorganized labourers, had been employed in the construction industry, which had been badly hit by the diversion of capital and materials to the war effort. In the absence of substantial, efficient, and well equipped industrial plants in the west to attract large war orders that would generate a demand for labour, many workmen sought refuge from adversity either in the army or on the land. Those who continued to be employed in the cities worked at wage rates rather lower than were paid in the east. Consequently they were especially hard hit by the war-time rise in prices, a rise made harder to bear by high freight rates, to which western Canadians had long since become accustomed but never reconciled. Thus much of the urban working class in the west did not benefit greatly, if at all, from the prosperity created by the war.

The situation was aggravated by the economic dislocations that occurred following the armistice in Europe. The abnormal war-time demand for many Canadian products ceased.

Large-scale unemployment was one of the results of this, and the rapid demobilization of the troops did nothing to improve matters, only adding to the surplus of labour. The federal government, in its plans for re-establishing the soldiers in civilian life – plans more generous and advanced than those of any other country, relied mainly on a scheme of assisted land settlement. But the results of this were disappointing. The vast majority of the returning veterans showed no interest in availing themselves of the help offered in acquiring land, preferring to take their chances in the cities and towns, where for the time being there were not enough jobs to go around. Hence at a time when the cost of living remained high a potentially explosive state of affairs was coming into being.

Its explosiveness was increased by disillusionment with the 'system' – with an economic mode, a structure of society, and a form of government which to many of the disenchanted hardly exemplified that democracy whose final victory in the world the war had been fought to ensure. Was it worth dying for a country, was such a country democratic, in which the personal sacrifices and material rewards of the war seemed to be so unequally distributed? One had only to contrast the lot of the privileged few, who made great fortunes, were granted titles of nobility, and controlled governments in their own interest, with that of the many who were expected to do the fighting and the dying for a soldier's pittance or to produce the materials of war for a subsistence wage. Nor did there seem, to those who saw things in this light, to be any prospect of a change for the better when peace returned. The propertied classes were firmly in command of the state. They had used and would continue to use their power to suppress the propagation of political, social, and economic doctrines with which they disagreed. They would continue to exploit those upon whose toil their wealth and security depended, resisting all efforts by the working class to improve its condition and to gain an influence in keeping with its size and value to the community.

From this unhappiness with the framework of government and society there flowed a more specific discontent: a rising impatience with the timid, cautious leadership of the national trade-union organizations in the east. These bodies, influenced by the views of Samuel Gompers in the United States and by the practice of American labour organizations, shunned direct political action through a distinctive labour party, depending instead on pressing leaders of existing parties for desired legislation and reform. But among the working men, as among the farmers, the conviction took root that because the old parties were controlled by the 'interests' this way of proceeding was bound to be ineffectual. The moral some of them drew was that a labour party ought to be formed, as in Great Britain. Others, though, more radical and less patient in spirit, turned away from that path in the belief that ballot-box democracy was an illusion that would trap the working class, instead of providing the sure means to power and reform.

They favoured, rather, the more dramatic and, as they believed, more effective weapon of the general strike. Sharing the outlook of the Industrial Workers of the World, a body strong in the western United States and much imbued with Marxist ideology, they looked forward to the creation of One Big Union which, speaking and acting for the whole of the labouring class, would use the paralysing power of the general strike to compel a surrender of power by the 'bosses' and bring about a socialist reconstruction. Some of them were given to heady revolutionary talk and to predictions that the Russian Revolution, which they greatly admired, would shortly be imitated in Canada. This did nothing to diminish the 'great Red scare' weighing heavily at that time on all those, mainly in the United States but also in Canada, who were haunted by the spectre of communism.

The strength of this radical movement seemed to make itself felt – to the consternation of many people – in a rash of strikes, some of them of large proportions, in various Canadian cities during 1918 and 1919. But the climax of it came in the Winnipeg General Strike in the spring of the latter year, a stormy episode precipitated by a dispute about collective bargaining in the metal and building trades. In a vote conducted by the Winnipeg Trades and Labour Council the workers in the whole city chose by an overwhelming majority to stage a general sympathy strike.

It lasted for several weeks, removed about 30,000 people from their jobs, and divided the residents of Winnipeg into two sharply opposed camps. It was finally ended, after some violence and loss of life had occurred, by the decisive intervention of the Dominion government, which became convinced that the municipal and provincial authorities could not control an essentially revolutionary situation. Several of the strike leaders were tried on a number of charges, including seditious conspiracy, and with one exception were convicted on all or part of the indictment. In retrospect it can be seen that all the bellicose talk about the strike being the start of a national Bolshevik revolution should not have been taken at its face value, that the strike was intended, not to touch off a revolutionary upheaval, but to gain acceptance of the principle of collective bargaining. Nevertheless, a case can be made for the view that a general strike, regardless of its leaders' intentions, must in order to succeed result in a usurpation of public authority–as happened to some extent in Winnipeg–and in that sense inevitably becomes a revolutionary act. In any case, considering the widespread fears excited by the Russian Revolution and the violent language used by some of the radical figures in western Canada, it was not surprising that many people in Winnipeg felt that they had been confronted by an overt revolutionary effort.

V

If most farmers and some industrial workers were restive and impatient with their lot, so too were members of still another large and underprivileged class – the women of Canada. Their organizations were as numerous and active as waves on the ocean, busy with all manner of worthy causes, mostly devoted in one way or another to moral uplift and reform. In fact women then appeared to have more of a self-conscious, collective will, more sense of power and mission, more verve and energy to accomplish their purposes than were to be seen half a century later when for the most part they had long enjoyed political and legal equality with men. Such equality, however, was denied them before the First World War and the prime objective of many of their organizations was to break the male monopoly of the franchise.

The cause did not receive anything like unanimous support from women – some were outspokenly opposed and many, perhaps most, were indifferent – but it was given devoted and effective leadership by a group of reformers, both male and female, whose efforts were crowned during the decade with remarkable, if as yet incomplete, success. These people regarded the vote as a fundamental right, of course, but not so much an end in itself as a means for the removal of the legal inferiority from which the sex suffered at the time, and for abolition of such other evils as liquor and the white-slave traffic. Not only that, the enfranchisement of women, it was argued, would have a salutary effect on Canadian public life, helping to cleanse it of corruption and baseness. The ruffianly behaviour natural to an exclusively male occupation would give way to something nobler if politicians had to justify their actions directly to the gentler sex and admit women to their hitherto closed society. Canadian advocates of electoral reform watched with interest the movements for female suffrage in the United States and Great Britain, and were much influenced by them. But the Canadian campaign was less marked by violence and disorder: there was no equivalent of Mrs. Pankhurst to incite rebellion, although that redoubtable feminist visited Canada to lend encouragement. However, the Canadians did not lack for zeal on the part of those women who took an interest in the subject.

Bodies specifically devoted to furthering the cause were established, such as the Canadian Suffrage Association, the Equal Suffrage Society, the Equal Franchise League, and the

Political Equality League, and were backed by other organizations such as the Women's Christian Temperance Union. Women prominent in the fight–Nellie McClung in Manitoba, Dorothy Davis in British Columbia, Flora Denison and Margaret Gordon in Ontario, to name a few–were indefatigable in addressing meetings and badgering public men. Resolutions were drawn up, approved by assemblies of women across the land, and presented to the politicians, demanding the removal of an unjust anomaly that was pithily described by one speaker as follows: 'The ballot to-day includes bad men and good men, men of all colours and even dead men, excluding only paupers, idiots, criminals, minors, and women.'

The response of most men to the pleas of the reformers was not very positive or encouraging at first. Perhaps many of them agreed with a British M.P., Lord George Hamilton, that to 'put women on an equality with men is contrary to Heaven's Act of Parliament, and to the everlasting law of Nature and of fact'. But Premier Sir Rodmond Roblin of Manitoba had a more flattering and guileful justification of his opposition. 'I think too much of woman,' he said, 'to have her entangled in the mesh of politics. She would be stooping from the pedestal on which she has sat for centuries.' Advocates of the suffrage, however, were willing to stoop in order to conquer. That famous pedestal was about to be vacated.

Considerations of reason and justice, it may be, are seldom wholly absent from politics in a well ordered democratic state –nor can politicians remain blind for too long to the party advantage that may accrue from extending the franchise to a large class thus far excluded. Whatever the causes, during the war the opposition to votes for women suddenly crumbled away in much of Canada. During 1916 and 1917 the five provinces west of Quebec all extended the suffrage and in the latter year came the partial enfranchisement afforded by the Wartime Elections Act. Before the 1917 election Sir Robert Borden promised that if he was returned to power he would introduce a measure granting the vote in national elections to all adult females, and in 1918 a bill to this effect was approved by Parliament. Women, for electoral purposes in the Dominion and in five provinces, were now officially distinguished from idiots, paupers, and criminals. It was a triumph of democracy.

One of the motivating impulses behind the women's suffrage movement, in fact one of the pronounced characteristics of Canadian sentiment in the century's second decade, was a fervour for moral reform. While it was much in evidence before 1914, it seemed to be intensified by the wartime atmosphere of sacrifice, self-denial, and righteous indignation against the foe. The 'Prussian tyrant' was the chief one, of course, but while the soldiers were waging that battle there was also a battle to be fought by those on the home front against other forms of evil, against crime and vice, drunkenness and indolence, and even, according to a few advanced reformers, against poverty and human hardship.

But of all the forms and causes of human degradation attacked by the moral reformers none was fought with greater enthusiasm, with more stirring eloquence and effectively concerted action, than the 'drink evil'. None was fought with as much apparent success.

Many social evils were considered to be produced or at least much aggravated by 'the curse of alcohol'. If it were conquered they would be much diminished. At the beginning of the decade the prohibitionist elements, among whom were numbered many so-called 'temperance' people, had made substantial progress. Prince Edward Island had a Prohibition Act in force, and elsewhere, under a variety of local option laws, the number of districts voting to become dry was increasing year by year. This partial success, though, did not satisfy such crusaders as Nellie McClung, the Reverend Ben Spence of Toronto, and J. H. Roberts of Montreal. They not only worked to increase the number of dry areas under the local option system but agitated for laws to 'ban the bar' in those that remained wet. Churches, with their clergy and their well organized women in the van, were joined by a number of prohibitionist groups such as the Dominion Alliance and the W.C.T.U. and by an assortment of moral and social reform leagues to marshal their forces for a mighty onslaught on demon rum. The war, far from diverting their attention, only intensified their efforts by affording them a number of additional arguments. The vast sums of money spent each year on beverage alcohol should be diverted to war purposes. The war demanded an end to self-indulgence. Canadians must be mentally alert and physically fit; was it not true that alcohol dulled the mind and wracked the frame? High productivity was required on farm and in factory; who could deny that strong drink caused absenteeism and inefficiency?

While the brewers and distillers fought a losing rear-guard action, backed by champions of individual liberty, disgruntled critics of the 'sin-hounds', and some trade-union leaders defending the right of the workman to his pint, the campaign for total prohibition was pressed through the war and through the victory. One after another the provinces, except for Quebec, enacted prohibitory laws, which were strengthened by federal Orders in Council forbidding the importation and interprovincial shipment of beer, wine, and spirits. The government of Quebec, where through local-option votes prohibition of sale had made substantial strides forward, was on the verge of following the lead of the other provinces, but held back when signs of a public reaction against the policy were seen. Indeed, after the war ended, evidence of dissatisfaction mounted in the rest of the country as well, and the anti-prohibitionists began to find new heart for the struggle. Certainly it proved to be one thing to enact 'temperance' legislation and quite another to enforce it. Spirits for medicinal, scientific, or mechanical purposes were permitted, along with sacramental wines, and soon stories multiplied about how the laws were being flouted by people with well disposed physicians. It was alleged, for example, that one doctor in British Columbia wrote more than four hundred liquor prescriptions a month. This kind of mal-practice, according to some reports, was much encouraged by the great, terrifying influenza epidemic in the fall of 1918, which took the lives of thousands of people. Many in the medical profession, it was claimed, displayed a quite unscientific faith during that emergency in the preventive and curative powers of alcohol. However, despite the difficulties of enforcement, and they were many, the spread of prohibition impressively demonstrated one fact: that a large, well organized, and vigorously led pressure group can wield enormous power, especially when it is able to take advantage of a prevailing mood like the determination and moral righteousness of war-time, and the desire to make some sacrifice, however small and unheroic, that would give one the sense of sharing in a noble cause and a grievous ordeal.

VI

When the ordeal of the war ended, Canadians, like the other victorious peoples, gave vent to their feelings of relief and thankfulness in exuberant celebration. Now, many thoughtlessly took for granted, life in its essentials would resume the old pre-war pattern. In some ways, no doubt, this expectation was fulfilled, but in other important respects the old order had vanished beyond recovery. The luxury of isolation from the controversies and conflicts of world politics, which Canada had enjoyed in the pre-1914 era, was gone for ever. Thanks partly to Borden's complaints during the war that he was not being properly consulted by the British on matters of policy affecting the whole Empire, Canada and the other dominions were given places in the small Imperial War Cabinet that was set up by Lloyd George shortly after he became Prime Minister of Great Britain late in 1916. Again owing in part to Borden's insistence the dominions were represented on their own account at the Paris Peace Conference of 1919 and were accorded seats of their own in the League of Nations established under the Treaty of Versailles. Such advances in status, such marks of recognition, were pleasing to Canadians, whose war effort did much to foster national pride. But as well as affording Canada recognition as something above a mere colony and conferring on her the right to be heard in the councils of the Empire and the world, these changes imposed upon her international obligations and responsibilities. For Canada the age of innocence was over.

In politics, the new awareness that the old order had disappeared was heightened by the departure of the two men who had dominated the scene in the war and pre-war years. Early in 1919 Sir Wilfrid Laurier died. He had sat in the House of Commons for nearly half a century, had led the Liberal party for over thirty years, and had been Prime Minister for fifteen. All Canadians, regardless of partisan feeling, sensed that his going marked the end of an age. His death was followed in the summer of 1920 by the retirement of Borden. The two, for all their disagreements, all the spirit with which they had done battle against each other, had a great mutual respect and liking. Under their direction Canadian politics had shown a certain civility, a quality of grace and gentlemanliness that was to be destroyed under their successors, whose intense personal animosities would loom large during the following decade.

The new Liberal leader was William Lyon Mackenzie King, who had been Minister of Labour in the last years of the Laurier administration. Aloof from politics for the most part during the war, he had been employed for much of that period by the Rockefeller Foundation to investigate labour-management relations. The work he did enhanced his considerable reputation as an expert in that field. Convinced that Laurier regarded him as his rightful political heir, and that he was ordained by Divine Providence to govern Canada, King managed to win the leadership at a national party convention in August 1919. Borden's successor was Arthur Meighen, who had come to Parliament in 1909 as a small-town lawyer from Manitoba. After first achieving prominence by his important role in the introduction of closure in 1913, he had gone on to become one of the three or four most active and powerful figures in the war-time government. Because of his acidulous manner in the House of Commons, where he was a highly skilled debater, and his close connection with so many controversial policies–including conscription and the related manipulation of the franchise in 1917, railway nationalization, and the suppression of the Winnipeg strike – Meighen had made many enemies during his rise to the top: too many, in the opinion of some Conservatives, for him to be a successful leader of the party. King and Meighen were as dissimilar as two men could be, in appearance, temperament, outlook, and style; and this lent a special fascination to the exceptionally bitter contest between them.

There was a marked contrast between the spirit and outlook of Canadians in 1920 and the confident optimism they had shown ten years before. At the opening of the decade they had looked forward with assurance to continued progress and prosperity, but when it closed the future seemed far less certain. It was not only that the changes in the structure, issues, and leading personalities of politics had unsettling effects. Nor did Canada's new status in the world, so gratifying to the national pride of her people, fully explain the air of misgiving and unease; for most Canadians failed to realize as yet that there was no longer any safe retreat from a world that remained more deeply troubled than they knew. In many ways, however, their collective experience during that time of stress and suffering had a sobering effect, bringing them face to face with harsh realities. They found satisfaction in Canada's contribution to victory in what the majority still regarded as a just cause, but some of them, at least, knew that victory had been purchased at a high price: at great cost of human life and disablement, and a strident renewal of the old antipathies of language and culture. They knew that during the war, perhaps in some obscure way as a result of it, there had begun to appear new, troublesome signs of social unrest, with accompanying class antagonisms that added a further dimension to the besetting problem of Canada – her fragmentation and lack of cohesion. They knew that their country faced difficulties in adjusting from a wartime to a peace-time economy, in finding markets for her goods and jobs for her people. All in all, in some undefined and perhaps indefinable way, life seemed to have become infinitely more complicated on the after side of the great divide of the world war. On New Year's Day, 1911, the Canadians had contemplated under sunny skies what looked to be a happy, satisfying future, with more people enjoying more of the good things of life than ever before. On New Year's Eve, 1920, they could only peer anxiously through mists of confusion and uncertainty into a doubtful future.

7. The 1920s

W. L. MORTON

Canada in 1920 entered the decade that stood between the Great War with its aftermath of revolution and the Great Depression with its sequel of disintegration. The Great War of 1914 had blown off the roof of nineteenth-century civilization. The walls and foundations still stood, cracked but erect, and the inhabitants of the western world lived on bravely in them until they too tumbled down in 1931, and men moved numbly into the spiritual tents and mental huts in which they have lived ever since, involuntary bedouins in a desert of the soul. The great myths of the nineteenth century, the century of modern Canada's creation, still glowed with life: order in freedom; stability in progress; truth despite contradiction; hope against despair. In the Canada of 1920, a colonial, imitative, and derivative society in which no idea had first been declared and only one or two discoveries had ever been made, these myths still flourished and the actual wreckage of war was far distant. The thunder of the guns was fading into a crackle of rifles in the forests of Russia and among the hills of Turkey. The growing hush was thought to be the return of day, a day that would restore the yesterday that had ended in 1914.

The decade, then, is defined in event by war and depression. The definition in character is a subtler matter. On a surface still troubled by war and revolution, waves of nostalgia ran back to the pre-war past. To resume the growth anticipated in 1914, to bring in immigrants, to break new fields, to turn out the new machines, to fill the long trains rumbling day and night to the seaports, to fill the wilderness with the prosperous and comfortable homes of a simple, democratic people, to realize at last the fantastic visions of the first decade of the century–these were the hopes renewed in 1920.

Yet the currents that were to flow from the decade of the twenties into that of the thirties were already running deep and strong. The dream of a Canadian nation like the American, the British, or the French had been dissolved. To the old happy acceptance of nationhood as the crown of civilized existence had been added the strange, disturbing doctrine of internationalism, the doctrine that nationalism was not enough, that nations must modify their newly asserted sovereignty and independence. And as emotional nationalism chafed against internationalism, economic nationalism abraded the imperial tie that for many Canadians was a sufficient internationalism. The former tension the Liberal party embodied, the latter the Conservative. The romanticism that had gilded Canadian art and letters was eaten into by a realism that made more astringent the bleakness of Canadian life and the harshness of the Canadian landscape. And Canadian churches, committed to a missionary and social role, found their foothold in the actual world narrowing rapidly between the erosion of a blind fundamentalism on the one hand and a popular scientism on the other.

In outcome this decade, therefore, was by definition an interim one. It stood between a century of uneventful intellectual and material progress, and one in which that progress had already begun to crumble, or to writhe perversely into forms and to flow in directions never intended. It was a decade of transition from a century in which chaos was steadily reduced to order to one in which order was to be increasingly disintegrated. The Canada that had been in 1914 did not return after 1920. After 1930 it was to be a very different country in aspiration, thought, and deed.

Very few Canadians sensed how deep the currents were running. Most were occupied in navigating the troubled surface waters. The first thing that stood out for all to see in 1920 was the post-war boom, a boom that had become an inflation. An abundance of money could not, after the expenditures of war and demobilization, purchase a sufficiency of goods. Agricultural and industrial prices were unprecedentedly high. Wages also were high, although salaries had not kept pace with rising prices. All seemed to prosper; few were really prosperous. The inevitable stresses of inflation therefore caused economic, social, and political discontent. The upward movement of the trade cycle set running by the demands of the war had reached its peak and was about to crest and break.

Deflation would then follow inflation. In the economic thought of the day this was regarded as being natural, therefore inevitable and right. The economy was thought to be self-regulating. Government controls on economic life had long been thought to be mistaken and even immoral, because controls would interrupt and distort the distribution of the resources of productive effort by the automatically adjusting free market in goods and services. The prevailing economic thought of the times therefore required that the government's control of parts of the economy devised since 1917 should be ended as quickly as possible, and that the process of deflation should be initiated. (That the latter was itself a matter of control escaped observation.) Thus it was possible for the editor of *The Canadian Annual Review* to write on the first page of the volume for 1920: '. . . the banks would have much to say in hastening a period of deflation and compelling the lowering of prices upon which the existing situation so largely turned'. Mr. Castell Hopkins, the editor of the *Review*, was neither an uninformed nor a reactionary man; he was rather a mirror of all that conventional men of affairs thought.

No one, of course, questioned then or would question now the need for deflation. The boom had become genuinely inflationary and the general interest required that it should be checked. But the particular mistakes of economic thought at the time were two. The first was the assumption that the existing economic system was a 'natural', that is, a non-political, one, and that no control should be exercised over it. Yet Hopkins's statement reveals that the banks did possess power to control the economy, that they deliberately exercised it, and that they were expected by men of business to do so. The second was that the means the banks used–the raising of interest rates on loans or the refusing of loans–did not have the effect of easing the throttle and slowly reducing the speed of the economy. Instead they had the effect of a sudden jamming on of brakes, and they brought the whole hurtling trade cycle to a grinding, shuddering halt.

The tightening of credit was, of course, the chief as well as the customary mode of producing deflation in 1920. But its depressing and indeed needlessly harsh effect was aggravated by the abolition of the last war-time government control: the Wheat Board, created to ensure a flow of grain to Britain in 1917 and used thereafter to stabilize the price paid to the wheat farmer and the wheat consumer. By 1920, when the price of the top grade of Board wheat was $3.15 a bushel at Fort William, it had come to be a guarantee that the western farmer would not only continue to enjoy the high prices of the immediate post-war period, but that he would be able to pay interest and principal on the debts incurred in increasing production and his standard of living. He desperately hoped that the Board might be continued to handle the crop of 1920, to moderate the inevitable decline in prices, and to win time to ease the load of indebtedness. But established opinion prevailed. The Board ended operations on August 31, 1920, and no amount of agitation by the grain growers' organization or the governments of the three prairie provinces was to get it restored. The price of wheat fell, and deflation swept over the western grain lands like a dust storm.

The special case of the Wheat Board, itself at once an expedient of the war and a prophecy of the future, illustrated the great weakness of the classical mode of deflating the economy. Not only did deflation bring the prosperity train to a shuddering stop; it fell with grievous and indefensible inequality on different segments of the economy. The working man, the farmer, and the small businessman were struck with the special force of a crushing blow. Major business was slowed but did not suffer severely, and the banks who had imposed the deflationary measures for the general good did not suffer perceptibly at all. No doubt that was why they administered so drastic a medicine with such philosophic calm and such unflinching courage.

II

Deflation, then, although an economic necessity, was applied in 1920 in a way that was socially intolerable and politically unacceptable. An old remedy was to produce both its expected consequences and a new resistance. Unemployment, a necessary aspect of deflation, was ceasing to be a price that people would willingly pay; farm foreclosures were a grim result not to be accepted without protest by a generation schooled in organization and enlightened with the gospel of economic co-operation. Labour would organize, farmers enter politics, as a result of the classical use of deflation like a surgeon's knife, without ether or antiseptic. This reciprocating stroke of old and new was a perfect example of the decade's essential character.

The year of deflation was therefore followed by a year of revolt. In the development of Canada, 1921 is indeed a watershed. It displayed, recorded in the decennial census, the results of the decade of the Laurier boom and the decade of depression, war, and inflation that had succeeded. The west had now been settled, the country's railway system completed, the east industrialized. Agricultural and rural Canada had reached its limits; industrial and urban Canada had become its equal, and was moving with a momentum that would carry it into first place. This momentous change, economic, social, and, as it was to prove, moral, was exhibited simply in the percentages for the totals of rural and urban population. These were: rural, 50.48%; urban, 49.52%. In this regard the decade was Janus-like, facing back to a predominantly rural past and forward to a predominantly urban future.

The balance of rural and urban populations of the agricultural and industrial economies was not, however, to be a peaceful equilibrium. The momentary equipoise indicated by the census meant that the fundamental struggle that had begun at least as early as the 1850s between the agricultural and the industrial interests of Canada, each seeking to ensure that national policy was in its favour, would only be intensified as the agricultural interest realized how formidable was the challenge to its place in the national life. For if Canada had always been mainly a rural and an agricultural country in population and in the nature of its economy, above all it was so still in sentiment and in morals. The twenties would witness a long battle between the two great interest groups of the country, the agricultural and the industrial.

Deflation had been urban and industrial in its inspiration, and, its incidence dramatized by the ending of the Wheat Board, it fell with particular weight on the countryside. Thus the great revolt of 1920 set the organized farmers against the old parties, parties led and largely manned in Parliament and the provincial legislatures by lawyers. The roots of the revolt ran far back into the farmers' organizations that had risen and fallen since Confederation. But the agrarian movement had gained strength and a body of doctrine with the rise of the Grain Growers' and United Farmers' organizations. Their original aims had been co-operation among their members and pressure on governments. But disappointments and necessities – the defeat of reciprocity in 1911, and the failure of the Union Government to take heed of the Farmers' platform of 1915 and lower the tariff – had strengthened the argument of those who urged that political action should be added to economic. Such political action, to avoid disruptions of the primary organizations, had to be on a non-partisan, non-political party basis. It had to be, as the word was, occupational. Already, the United Farmers of Ontario had captured the provincial government, and those of Alberta the government of that province. In Manitoba they had reduced the government party to a plurality. And already a separate 'Progressive' group had been formed in the House of Commons and a full and far-reaching political program framed, a program called defiantly 'the new National Policy'.

The fires were thus crackling in the bush and running on the prairies when the ending of the Wheat Board, and the refusal of the national government to restore it, prepared the dry and torrid weather that made possible a fire across the land. It was ignited when in June 1921, in a by-election in Medicine Hat, the government candidate was overwhelmingly defeated by a farmers' representative. Prime Minister Arthur Meighen, who had in 1920 succeeded Sir Robert Borden as Conservative leader, took note and called a general election in December 1921. The result was the return of sixty-five 'Progressive' members from British Columbia to Ontario, a sixty-five that might easily have been as much as seventy-five. The Liberal party had the larger number of members of the two parties, but with one hundred and seventeen were one short of half the House. Only fifty Conservatives were returned. The Progressives had not quite gained a balance of power, but they had upset the working of the old two-party system. They were in a position to bargain for the particular interest they represented, that of agricultural and rural Canada.

III

The farmers' revolt, however, was only part of the disruption of 1921. Even more important was the sectional character of the parties in the House of Commons. Thirty-seven of the Progressives themselves were from the prairies and they were always regarded, not wholly unfairly, as a sectional group. Of the Conservative party's fifty members, thirty-six were from Ontario, nine of those from Toronto. The Liberal party drew sixty-five of its members from Quebec, much of the remainder from the Maritimes, and only a sprinkling from across the rest of the country, some of them from constituencies in which the French vote was important. In short, the traditional parties had been disrupted as 'national' parties, and Parliament had become a congeries of sectional and occupational interests. Canada had reverted to its inherent parochialism.

Nowhere was this truer than in Quebec. There also, revolt was beginning. It was, however, a revolt masked by the provincial and federal Liberal parties. The revolt of Quebec spoke, if in muffled accents, through its unqualified support of the Liberal party, the party that had opposed conscription. Every French member, as every English member, from the province of Quebec was a supporter of the Liberal party. The revolt failed to speak through the provincial party because of the intellectual training and practical experience of the people who led it. By economic and political conviction they thought it necessary and even desirable to co-operate fully with the Anglo-Canadian economic ascendancy in Montreal. They could have no overt ties with a nationalism that was emotional and clerical, and that in its one clear purpose sought to end the unity of Canada, on which the fortunes of Montreal's business rested.

French-Canadian nationalism had grown steadily since the Red River resistance of 1870. It was, however, partly secular nationalism and partly ultramontane clericalism. Even when greatly inflamed by the Boer War, the revival of the schools question in Ontario and Manitoba after 1913, and the conscription crises of 1917, it remained clerical as well as secular in nature. Given the role of the Church in the maintenance of the French language and culture, there could be no other result. Yet the struggle to preserve French nationalism in Canada could not, ultimately, be only resistance to Protestant and English culture. It would have to become a revolt against the clerical, educational, and political regime in French Quebec itself. While, however, the leadership of the Quebec revolt still lay in the hands of clerics such as the Abbé Lionel Groulx, gifted and devoted scholar though he was, it would not fully realize its own nature or gain its goals.

One might argue that for French Canada to live fully and freely in Canada, it had to become a North American community in all respects – in the relation of Church and State, in the substance of education, in the character of its politics, in its attitude to the Vatican – and that until it did, its young people would remain handicapped in their choice of careers; its politics would remain corrupt and detached from popular life; the Church would carry a burden of responsibility for which it was not designed. During the 1920s, at any rate, the idea of a 'Laurentian' republic remained a romantic wish among a limited group of French nationalist idealists, the Liberal government of Prime Minister A. L. Taschereau remained the puppet of Anglo-American capital, and French aspirations were misunderstood and opposed in some parts of English Canada as aggression by the Roman Catholic Church. The practical political result was the return of a body of some fifty French members to Ottawa (including some men of notable talent such as Ernest Lapointe) who largely enabled the Liberal party to form the government of Canada and yet stood sufficiently apart from the views of their English-speaking colleagues that the government's conduct became essentially that of finding the least division between its French and English supporters. This brought a negative attitude in domestic affairs and a positive pursuit of broader 'national' rights in the external field.

IV

The sectional disruption of 1921 thus at bottom meant that English and French Canada cancelled one another out in politics, and the west was too inexperienced, too limited in its own aspirations, too deferential to the established leadership of the east, to resolve the deadlock. This situation was faced by the new Liberal leader, William Lyon Mackenzie King. King had to preserve the façade of national unity, to preserve it at all costs, and, if possible, to give it some substance. A highly trained sociologist, a creative civil servant, a politician who, in spite of misfortune, had reached the top – King was extraordinarily well equipped to lead a community moving from an agricultural to an industrial order. But because of the revolt in Quebec – not because of that of the Progressives – King had to set aside his special training and experience and devote himself to the negative politics of national preservation. In turning away from his training, he in fact reverted to himself, the grandson of the rebel of 1837, the son of an inadequate father and of a possessive mother who had spent her childhood in exile. He was a shy, lonely, highly respectable son of the Canadian middle class, trained to that class's devotion to hard work, self-discipline, and plain common sense.

Because of the political ancestry he cherished, King, moreover, was in one aspect a doctrinaire, wedded to the Grit ideas of popular democracy, responsible government, and the popular 'mandate'. These ideas he was sure he must realize in their final fullness in an independent Canadian nation and so justify the rebel grandfather whom his mother had adored. He had no idea that, logically developed, those ideas could lead to an irresponsible dictatorship of the Prime Minister. He did not comprehend that they could work to damage both Cabinet and Parliament, and even the Canadian federal structure – that they might bring government in Canada down to closed meetings of political chiefs. If emotions had not swayed his intellect, he might well have realized these things. As it was, by the fate of circumstance and his own personality, King was largely reduced to preserving national unity by the pursuit of expedience. Canada, with all its anomalies of nationality, class, and economic interest, was to be governed by the politics of opportunism.

V

The basic line of opportunistic politics was very simple. It consisted of keeping things as they were in Quebec and of attempting to win back the former Liberal voters in Ontario and on the prairies. No one then had any idea of how things might be really changing in Quebec–not even the nationalists. What Canadian politics required was, first, the negative condition that Quebec should continue to take a formal part in national politics. The second was a positive matter, the winning back of the prairie vote, for the things the western Progressives wanted were few and simple–the restoration of the Crow's Nest Pass Railway rates on grain, the re-establishment of the Wheat Board, the building of the Hudson Bay Railway, and the lowering of the tariff. These were not too remote from what the Liberal party could do without alienating any considerable Liberal or business support elsewhere. King had failed to bring the Progressive leaders into his Cabinet in an attempt in December 1921, but he was able to govern in the knowledge that, except on a few matters such as the above, the majority would support him in preference to Meighen and the Conservatives, or to a general election. Meighen and the Conservatives, for their part, were ostentatiously not opportunists – more so than their conduct warranted. Yet they made no overt advances to Quebec and few concessions in defending the National Policy of tariff protection as needed.

In these circumstances the King government met Parliament in four sessions. Its policy of expediency at home was made to seem positive by a nationalist policy abroad. In the Chanak affair of 1922 it refused to support the British government against insurgent Turkey. In 1923 it refused to allow the Commonwealth to become more than a meeting of governments at the Imperial Conference of that year. The signature of the Halibut Treaty with the United States earlier in the same year had shown a similar resolution, and ended the formal diplomatic unity of the Empire. For the same purposes of national assertion, lip service was given to the League of Nations.

The country in general approved this relatively insignificant nationalism. Quebec merely smouldered. The Progressive movement was beginning to disintegrate. The Crow's Nest Pass rates had been temporarily and partly restored. The Wheat Board had been refused, but the graingrowers had turned to the new idea of 'pooling' their wheat sales. Some slight gains had been made by political action, but the new form of economic action was drawing the farmer's attention, and his hope, away from politics. Politics would go back to the politicians. Above all, the distress of deflation was over. The crops of 1923 and 1924 were good, agricultural prices were once more rising, and business was reviving. The class and sectional distresses of the post-war deflation were subsiding, although some industrial unemployment remained, and Canadian life and Canadian politics might return to their usual pattern.

They indeed proceeded to do so, but the political beneficiary in the general election of 1925 was the Conservative party. It returned to Parliament with one hundred and seventeen members in a House of two hundred and forty-five. The Progressives elected only twenty-four representatives. And the Liberals were sent back with only one hundred and one members, one half of them from Quebec. The Prime Minister and a number of his English-speaking colleagues in the Cabinet were defeated at the polls.

The result might well have been a change of government, but King now revealed that octopus-like tenacity in keeping office that marks the true politician to whom the possession of power is everything because it alone makes anything possible. By means of loose agreement with the Progressives he continued in office, was then elected member for Prince

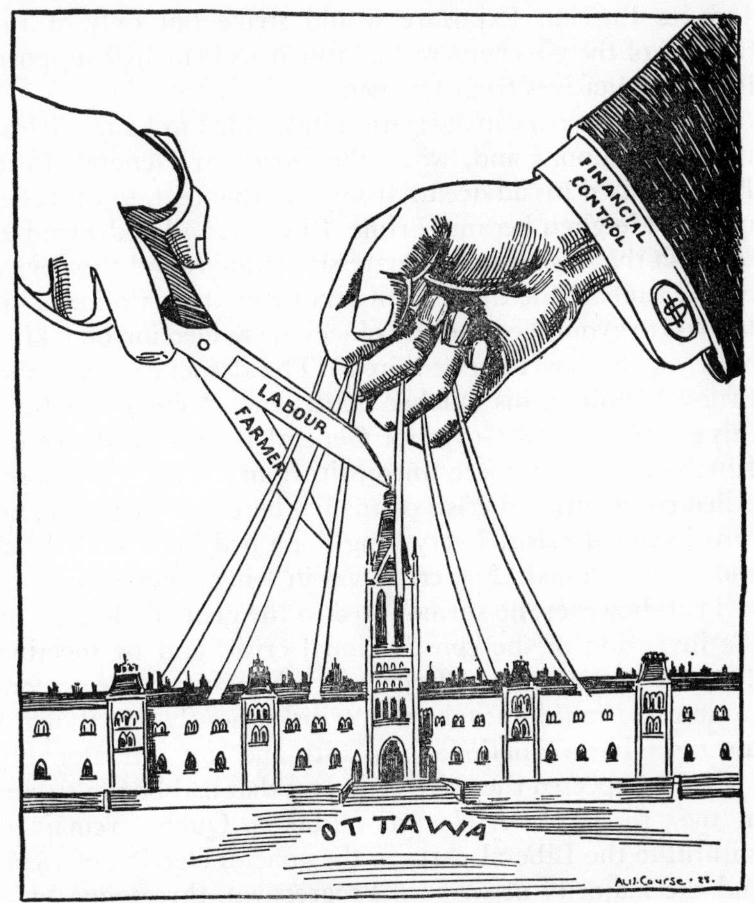

If we do not have public control over finances, we are going to have control of the public by financiers. We can take our choice.—Mr. Good, (Brant), Hansard, March 4, 1925.

From the *Weekly News*, Winnipeg, October 16, 1925.

Albert, and faced once more the triumphant and expectant Meighen. The master of expedients faced the master of words. King ought to have been destroyed by his experienced and brilliant opponent, because on the heels of electoral defeat came the revelation of government scandal. Investigation by a parliamentary committee revealed corruption in the Department of Customs, corruption that almost certainly involved the responsible minister, the Honourable

Jacques Bureau. Exposure would strike not only at the honesty of the government but also at its principal support, its representatives from Quebec.

The preliminary investigation indeed led to King's defeat in the Commons and, when the Governor General, Lord Byng, refused his advice to dissolve Parliament, to his resignation. Meighen became Prime Minister, and endeavoured to finish the session with Progressive support and the device of a Cabinet made up of ministers without portfolio. (This last was to avoid the necessity of seeking re-election on taking office, as the law then required.) The desperate King and Ernest Lapointe, his Quebec lieutenant, claimed that both this expedient and Governor General Byng's insistence on King's resignation were unconstitutional. This was the so-called constitutional crisis of 1926. There was, of course, no constitutional crisis. Everything done had been both legal and constitutional. The crisis was in King's own career.

That, however, he surmounted in the general election by the invention of the constitutional crisis, and by meeting demands of the western Progressives. Meighen made no concession. He could not take the 'crisis' seriously. He thought the tariff both a national necessity and not unreasonably high. He expected the wave of success that had begun to run in 1925 to continue. He was mistaken. Quebec remained faithful to the Liberal party in the general election of 1926, and the majority of western Progressives, threatened by a revival of the protectionist party, either supported the Liberal party openly or at least voted for its candidates.

One hundred and twenty-nine Liberals and liberal Progressives faced ninety-one Conservatives, nine Progressives, eleven U.F.A. members from Alberta, and three Labour members. King, with the ferocity of a cornered animal and a prodigious effort of imagination, had saved his career. And the class and the sectional antagonisms of 1920 were now to be both soothed by prosperity and blanketed by a national Liberal party, indeed by a return to the two-party system in Parliament. Only the U.F.A. and Labour members in the

Commons, the farmers administrations in Manitoba and Alberta, and the clerical and intellectual nationalists in Quebec, remained of all the tumult and revolt of 1920. Canada had survived the shock of the war and the strain caused by the transition from the old rural order to the new industrial one. The remainder of the decade would perhaps give Canada time to study and to find itself. One may venture to peer into the national mirror, note the lineaments of the face, and endeavour to see the mind and spirit behind the puzzled eyes.

VI

To look at the physical face of Canada as a whole in 1926, from the blue and sombre cliffs of Cape Breton and the sweeping shorelines and mountain horizons of the St. Lawrence cleaving Quebec, the woods and waters of Ontario, the rock and waters of the Shield, the long roll of the prairies, and the forest-clad slopes of the Rockies plunging to the Pacific, is to be struck by the way these vast horizons, these great reaches of land and rock and water were held together by a net of railways. Ships plied the great waterways, but distance made them seem few. Roads bound farm to farm, town to town, but were straight and narrow and mean. Few were yet sweeping, challenging highways. But the railways were everywhere, criss-crossing around the great cities, winding through the granite ridges and muskegs of the Shield, crossing the north with an imperious directness from Quebec to Prince Rupert. Four were even probing the farther north towards Hudson Bay, the Peace River, and the Mackenzie. Among the fields and villages of the Maritimes and central Canada the traveller crossed and re-crossed them. The camper in the northern woods came upon their steel spans silent over the rushing waters, their rails running with insistent purpose through the cleft forest. The farmer in the western wheat-fields worked within sight of the tracks that cut across the square survey from landmark to landmark of elevators. The great river valleys of British Columbia were scarred by their rights of way winding by cliffside and through timber stands.

The railway was the symbol of the Canada it had made possible and indeed created. The rolling plume of smoke by day, the echoing whistle by night, were the marks of the progress of civilization in Canada, whether by the riverside at Trois Pistoles, or in the sweeping grasslands of Battle River. And a potent symbol it was. Nothing had ever meant more to Canada. Nothing concerned more Canadians more. Nothing material in Canada more struck the eye with its might, majesty, and power than a great steam locomotive sliding with leashed strength into the station, or thundering with its long train through the countryside, the great strokes of its piston rods slashing the miles down like a scythe in the roadside weeds.

Nor was the symbolism merely picturesque. Canada had almost one mile of railway for every 200 persons. It had indeed built beyond its resources, and the collapse of the Canadian Northern and the Grand Trunk Pacific during the war had not been caused wholly by the conditions of war-time. One great task of the Union Government of 1917-20, and of its successor under Meighen, had been to prevent a collapse of national credit brought about by the collapse of the credit of the railways. Its efforts to preserve the credit and good name of the government left the government with the two railways on its hands, to which the Grand Trunk Railway was later added. The three were combined under one management as the Canadian National Railways in 1921. Whatever the financial cost, whatever the devotion to economic principle, the railway services of Canada had to be preserved, by private enterprise if possible, as in the case of the Canadian Pacific Railway, by government ownership if not. Now a great railway man, Henry Thornton, was endeavouring to make the Canadian National Railways a railroad system despite the diverse origins of its constituent railways, and to make it earn a profit despite the over-capitalization that was greatly excessive even after the sharp reductions effected by the reorganization of 1917-21. Canada, it was hoped, would yet grow up to the railways it had built.

In the old settled areas, however, the automobile lurching along dusty roads was a foretaste of a means of transport that would end the supremacy of the railway in Canadian life, and make impossible the slow reduction of deficits of the government railways by national growth. Growth in general had been going on in spite of deflation and the uncertainties of politics. In the long-settled areas some rural counties were losing population, but to the growing cities, or to the expanding wheatlands of the farmer, or to the new towns of the north. The pattern here of a small farm behind its fences of rail, stone, or stump, the farmsteads with their tree-shaded lanes down to the public roads–or in Quebec and the Maritimes with unpainted porches peering onto the roadways–was much the same; it was already old, sometimes gracious with trees and ivied houses, sometimes bare and dilapidated. The towns were lapping into the neighbouring fields. Sometimes a raw new factory took over an orchard or a barley-field, but most of them, in spite of their crude red-brick and smoking chimneys, fitted into the countryside. Only in the greater cities–Montreal, Toronto, Hamilton–did one hear the real clangour of industry, or in Vancouver encounter a pre-1914 rush of speculative building and suburban growth. Winnipeg, its tap-root of traffic cut by the Panama Canal, fretted in stagnation. Older Canada was fattening, rather than extending, the structure that the settlement of the west had built.

Growth as Canada knew it, in terms of prairie sod broken, or mine shaft opened, or mill site cleared, was taking place on the northern prairies and in the aspen-growth country of the Manitoba Interlake, in Saskatchewan north of its great river, or in the Peace River country of Alberta and British Columbia.

There the shifting farmer and the immigrant, following the grain belt as it was advanced north by new strains of wheat bred in the experimental stations, cleared the scrub and drove the breaking-plough. New fields were turned black, and the next year grew green and golden under the long sunshine of the north. And at the dam sites of the rivers coming down from the plateau of the Shield, new dams rose grey and rigid, to send waters down the whirling turbines summer and winter, to stroke from the dynamos the electric current for the mines and the pulp-mills. In Kirkland Lake and Abitibi the hard-rock miners were cutting ever deeper into the mineral rocks of the Precambrian Shield after gold, silver, and the base metals that American industry increasingly sought in Canada. And along the southern edges of the black-green spruce forests that lay across Canada like a hunting tartan, and on the tree-covered Pacific slopes, pulp-mills and paper-mills rose and gathered towns around them to print the daily records of the crimes, follies, and sports of men in a thousand American cities. To lumber and wheat, national growth was adding the metals, noble and base, and the paper that held together an urban and industrial civilization. The rocks the immigrant had passed by, the spruce woods the lumbermen had scorned, the water that had run untrammelled to the lakes, were adding new wealth to Canada, and a new population neither agrarian nor urban.

The northern wilderness immediate to settlement, hitherto the haunt of the miner and the summer camper, was yielding to exploitation. This much of untouched Canada had been opened by the new demands of industry and urban life and the great railways built to haul wheat. But the immense Canadian northland, flung out towards the Pole, remained beyond the reach of exploitation except in the old way of the trapper. The missionary, the fur-trader, and the Mounted Police lived or travelled in these vast wastes, in tent, igloo, or cabin, by canoe, snowshoe, or dog-sled, to serve Indian and Eskimo and to maintain the Canadian claim to areas yet unoccupied. The north was in effect a barren empire that Canada ruled and Canadians ignored. Their interests, like their railways, ran east and west, but rarely north.

Yet in the north also change was occurring, like the first summer thaw along the face of southward-facing Arctic cliffs. Oil had been found in 1920 at Fort Norman on the Mackenzie River, a first portent of the mineral riches of the Arctic. And now the Hudson Bay Railway, its roadbed abandoned since 1915, was reaching towards the Bay to begin a line of northern sea traffic and become a jumping-off place into the islands of the eastern Arctic. And most important of all, 'bush-flying' by means of planes equipped with pontoons for summer's open water and skis for the level ice of winter was opening the north to the surveyor, the prospector, and traffic as never before. Edmonton, Winnipeg, Quebec City–all suddenly saw the deep north as a new hinterland. The airplane was to bring the north into Canadian life with an immediacy and an intensity never known before.

VII

The face of Canada, so far as it had been altered by human action, reflected the material purposes of Canada. It did not, and fortunately, reflect the mind of Canada, except in so far as that was scientific. Science, particularly science applied to some material end, was solidly established and widely flourishing in Canada. The National Research Council, founded during the war, was now turning its efforts to building up the scientific establishment of Canada, and to distributing the government grants in aid of scientific research. The one dazzling scientific achievement in Canada during the decade was the discovery in 1922 by Doctors F. G. Banting and C. H. Best of the nature and function of insulin. It was perhaps in the national character that the discovery should have been in medicine, for in Canada the doctor enjoyed much of the reverence only the clergy had had, and many of the best men, mentally and morally, of earnest middle-class homes went into the practice of medicine as a vocation. But science went much beyond research. It had become the basis, with mathematics, of popular education in Canada, and as religion and the humanities declined in popular influence, science succeeded them, not only as a material utility but also as a world view.

Learning in the humanities did little to affect this change. In Canadian schools and universities, instruction in literature and philosophy was, in general, inhibited and dull, and well behind the movement of ideas and events in the world at large. In professional philosophy, the speculative idealism of the great John Watson of Queen's University still remained the chief philosophic influence in Canada, and particularly on theology and the life of the Church. But idealism, although it continued to be taught by R. C. Lodge in the University of Manitoba, was no longer to lead philosophy in Canada. Philosophy now took many forms, the chief being that of the historical understanding of philosophy of G. S. Brett of the University of Toronto. For the decade, however, philosophy became academic, its achievement that of laying foundations for later edifices. And the same was true of the study of literature and history. Historians were active in producing good and learned books, such as R. G. Trotter's *Canadian Federation* (1924) and Chester Martin's *Empire and Commonwealth* (1929). Others, such as O. D. Skelton, turned to political service in the Department of External Affairs. But the most publicly influential scholar, in part because of the nature of his science, was Adam Shortt, economist, editor, and adviser of government. Still lacking was a Canadian idiom for the discussion of ideas and affairs, the golden bridge between the detached world of learning and the committed world of action.

The public schools, on the other hand, were becoming steadily less concerned with academic training and more and more involved as agents of social policy. It was becoming their prime function, undeclared but imperative, to diminish the distinctions caused by home and class among their pupils, and to produce from diversity of background and national origin the social conformity a democratic society required. In the process academic excellence suffered before the demands of social mediocrity. The power to discriminate, to differ, to divine new relations, had to share the teachers' concern with the power to conform, to co-operate, to conciliate. The school of learning had become the school of manners, and, all unwittingly, the new generation was being prepared for the demagogue and the advertiser.

Literature in Canada was no prophylactic against change so fundamental and subtle. It was popular, optimistic, pragmatic, and romantic. Perhaps the most widely read novelist in English, Ralph Connor (Rev. Charles W. Gordon), was a clerical Jack London, combining violence with virtue in a recipe that sold thousands of volumes. His books contain not a single memorable character, or one noteworthy statement, but they had the great virtue that one could read them without ever being disturbed. Connor wrote for the less demanding members of the middle class; a similarly typical novelist, Sir Gilbert Parker, wrote for the more worldly of the middle class, for the established businessman and his family–novels of remote and aseptic action with the fruity accent and cigar-smoke atmosphere of the clubroom and the den. Such writers appealed to the romanticism, the desiccated nostalgia of a people raised on the romantic writings of Scott and Tennyson, of Longfellow, Lowell, and Whittier, and quite unused to an imaginative and searching discussion of their own society, and in their idiom. Literature was in Canadian experience unreal, and an amusement, never a criticism of life.

When an immigrant writer, Frederick Philip Grove, gravely and successfully attempted this task, his books were received in silence, or with self-conscious and damning praise. When a Canadian writer, Sara Jeanette Duncan, in *The Imperialist* (1904), for example, described Canadian life in realistic but by no means brutal terms, her book was not recognized for what it was, the beginning of a native criticism of life. In short, all sense of realism, and above all of tragedy, was lacking from Canadian writing, even from the excellent academic verse of genuine poets like Duncan Campbell Scott and Bliss Carman. In French and in English, Canadian writers and the Canadian literary idiom were derivative, sifted, and genteel. Only the poetry of E. J. Pratt in his *Newfoundland Verse* (1923) promised the emancipation of poetry from the polished and the soignée. Emancipation had yet to be won from rural conservatism and a Victorian prudery.

In art little was worthy of note except the painting of the Group of Seven. The art of these men was considerable in both execution and vision. It did open Canadian eyes to the northland and the character of the country. But it too was essentially derivative and romantic, and it caught the public eye, not because of its vigour and skill, but because, strong as it was, it too could be fitted into the prevailing local romanticism.

Art and letters, then, had done little, if anything, to resolve the fierce transition in Canada from a Victorian world of rural conservatism to the astringent, realistic, and abstract world of sophisticated, scientific, urban volatilism. Canada had not felt the psychological impact of the Great War, and it had escaped in consequence the smothering disillusionment that descended on Europe and the United States in the twenties. Thus the mind of Canada was floundering in a world it had not experienced; it could not prepare for the future because it had not caught up with the present. Hope there was in the work of Grove and the first novel of a new writer, Morley Callaghan–his *Strange Fugitive* (1928). It was a grim, overdone story, but a story, flatly reported, of bootlegging taken up as merely another line of business, and of urbanized people in Toronto who had neither tradition nor values, who were amoral creatures of appetite. Canada had indeed been strangely fugitive from reality all the decade.

VIII

If so backward in mind, what was Canada in spirit? The Christian churches in Canada had been and still were essentially missionary and 'pioneer' churches. They had not only to care for souls, but also to create a Christian milieu. They had created and were incorporated in the rural conservatism that still constituted the Canadian mind. The churches were therefore little prepared to deal with the new scientific, urban, and industrial culture that was changing the mentality and morals of Canadians in ways Canadians themselves could neither understand nor control.

The traditionalist as well as the fundamentalist churches were caught in this self-created prison. The Roman Catholic Church was concerned either with the cultural survival of French Canada or with the advancement of immigrant and depressed groups–Irish, Scots Highlanders, Ukrainians. It was a vast, arduous, and necessary task, called for by the basic ethics of Canadian life, never openly avowed, and continually pursued. The Anglican Church, the church of the northern missions and of the recent British immigrant to the west, was in the east, along with the Presbyterian, the garrison church of the Anglo-Scottish and Protestant Irish ascendancy.

The Protestant churches were also, sociologically speaking, bringing their congregations up to the middle-class status, again a necessary work of civilization and improvement. How true this was is shown by two things. One was the steady revolt of fundamentalist sects from the 'old line' churches; the other was the gnawing concern, best exemplified in the careers of Salem Bland and J. S. Woodsworth, of the Methodist Church with the 'Social Gospel', once proclaimed by Wesley himself and now re-awakened amid the great social changes of the century.

In all this social effort the churches became confused and lost control of events through their own self-induced contradictions. The traditionalist churches ignored the challenge of science and failed to adapt their world view to the new material culture that science and industry were forcing on society. The Protestant churches, with their fundamentalist roots, accepted the challenge of science and were shattered by it, and veered uncharacteristically to what was essentially a gospel of good works: social reform and prohibition. The Canadian churches, as fragmented as the country they served, were bankrupted intellectually and spiritually, not in the decade as such, but more definitely during the decade than before or after.

This was revealed by two events. One was Church Union. The succession of unions between the Methodist and Presbyterian churches was a Canadian phenomenon based on practical considerations, and it prepared the way for the union of the Methodist Church with the Congregational Church, and with the majority of Presbyterian churches. This great ecclesiastical event was nevertheless much more a matter of pooling resources and aiding the weaker rural churches than an exercise in Christian brotherhood or the ecumenical spirit. In many ways it was a Protestant rally against the steady growth of the Roman Catholic Church. Because it was these things it left the new church increased in numbers and in wealth, but uncertain in doctrine and weaker in spirit and influence than before.

The other event was prohibition, an enterprise of the churches, mainly the Protestant, and of the rural voters, and particularly the newly enfranchised women. In nothing did rural conservatism speak in more authentic accents. A contemporary journalist accurately observed: 'it is clear . . . that it has always been the countryside – its prejudices as well as its interests – that has been the prime factor in shaping Canadian legislation.' The abuses attacked by legislation were real and indefensible. The difficulties prohibition had to encounter were great because in Canada only the consumption of alcoholic drinks could be prohibited, not its manufacture and sale for export. Moreover, and this was the fundamental error, it was an attempt to enforce a moral code by legal means. The result was both the failure of the enterprise – not complete, because drinking habits were to be improved – and serious damage to the law itself, as in the shifting of the onus from the Crown to the accused, and to respect for the law and for law-officers. Bootlegging flourished in direct proportion to the degree of prohibition. The law was flouted and the police were corrupted. Fortunes were made, one at least still among the greatest in Canada. The unsophisticated morality which among many Canadians passed for religion had overreached itself and was discredited. The churches that had supported prohibition suffered too in loss of influence. And the way was widened for the advance of the secular spirit.

IX

What, then, was the central vortex of Canadian life in the decade of 1920-30? It was the opposing drives of what may be termed the nostalgic and the propulsive elements in Canadian society. Canadians, looking backward with sentiment, were being driven forward by desire.

The elements of the Canadian nostalgia were, first, a Christianity essentially missionary in impulse and rural in assumption. And then a rural conservatism that was materialistic, even primitive, and committed to simple living and moral endurance. What had been a necessity was defended as a thing good in itself. And beneath both of the religions of primitivism and rural conservatism was an unthinking individualism, essentially optimistic in spirit. A university president might question progress, but the popular mind in Canada accepted without thought the doctrine of continual, automatic progress, moral as well as material. One had only to persevere in the plain, hard way, and all would be well.

Such was the outlook, with varying degrees of sophistication and clarity, of the bulk of Canadian society, French as well as English, of the urban middle class as well as of the farmers, lumberers, and townsmen of the countryside and the frontier. Yet nothing could have been more illusory. Not only the great obvious changes wrought by the growth of cities and industry made that outlook unrealistic. The very acts of the farmer leaders, of the exponents of rural thought, of the behaviour of any prospering Canadian, denied the outlook. Every advance of science and industry was welcomed; none was questioned. The fundamental grievance of those who followed the rural life was that it lacked the amenities and advantages of urban life. The very changes sought would change rural life itself, would industrialize and urbanize it.

The spinning vortex, however, was working more than a change from rural to urban mores and values. The social structure was being altered to incorporate a permanent and organized labour force with its own values and its own outlook. The grim misery of the urban slums was forcing a new concept of social obligation and of the role of the state. The virtue of charity became a matter of scorn because of its inadequacy in the new conditions, and its social assumptions were intolerable in the new society. It was being replaced by the concept of social welfare, the beginning of the rise of the social worker, the advent of the service state. In the municipalities and the provinces human needs were to be met by public means and scientific training.

Such changes were happening, but were still anathema to the general conscience. Yet the slow extinction of social laissez-faire was being pressed also on economic laissez-faire. Free enterprise, still in the ascendant, was challenged by the spectacular rise of the Wheat Pools in the prairie provinces between 1923 and 1928, and by the persistence of labour representation in the Commons after 1921, the fruit of the Winnipeg General Strike of 1919. Few as they were yet in number, the shoots of a social democratic movement were struggling to the surface. If not socialistic in doctrine, they were socialistic in spirit. In 1927 the leader of the movement, J. S. Woodsworth, won his first victory in the passage of the Old Age Pensions Act, the act by which the government and people of Canada admitted that personal effort and private charity could not be left alone to provide for the care of every member of the community. It was the affirmation in personal affairs of the same principle the provinces had been asserting in industry, that human life could not, in all cases, be regulated by private contract and have all its needs met by personal effort alone.

Not less significant, perhaps more so, was a change of thought on monetary matters that had begun to trickle through the fissures of public discussion. The harsh deflation after 1920 had renewed interest in the monetary doctrines of American populism and in a new monetary theory propagated in England under the name of Social Credit. Both were forms of under-consumption thought. When the Canada Banking Act was reviewed in 1923 the Alberta Progressives had arranged to have the leader of the Social Credit movement, Major C. H. Douglas, called as a witness. Thus the principles of Social Credit were spread on a public document, to defy with its inflationary spirit the orthodox dogma of enforced deflation applied in 1920. This, and the writings of W. C. Good, Progressive member for Brant, on the cyclical theory of budgeting, ensured that as economic individualism was challenged by social welfare, financial orthodoxy was also queried, queried by principles which in more sophisticated terms Maynard Keynes was to make respectable and effective in the next decade.

X

The same wrestling of the nostalgic and the progressive occurred in literature and in thought, more faintly and less decisively. By the end of the decade romanticism had retreated to the pages of the ladies' magazines, or, heavily spiced with sin and realism, had entered into its euthanasia in Mazo de la Roche's *Jalna* (1927) and *Whiteoaks of Jalna* (1929). Grove and Callaghan among novelists, E. J. Pratt among poets, were recognized as the emerging artists because they spoke in tones of convincing realism and dealt with tragic as well as comic themes. And in thought there was some beginning of realization that the firm world of optimism was cracking, that progress was probably not automatic, perhaps not necessarily desirable. This failure of Canadian contemporary thought in general to grasp how the assumptions and values of the previous century had collapsed at least left the nation free to rejoice in the prosperity of the second half of the decade and in the victories of the political opportunism that had triumphed in the election of 1926. That was a victory of nationalism, but a superficial victory, for the troubles of Canada were more fundamental than nationalism could be. They were the difficulties of secular change–economic, social, and moral–and could be changed only by experience and suffering, not by the expedience of politicians. Nationalism was a mist that hung over the vortex of Canadian life; it was, in its drift and changes, lit by sunlight, eye-catching and seemingly solid, but it was in large part mist.

So far as it was not, what it was appeared through the rare insight of a writer, John Mitchell, to be known later under the pseudonym of 'Patrick Slater' for his tale *The Yellow Briar* (1933). Canada had become, so the title of Mitchell's book proclaimed, *The Kingdom of America*. It had, but did its people accept the fact, and would they give their allegiance to a king of Canada? This too was mist for two more decades at least.

Because, however, nationalism triumphed in 1926, that year and its successors saw the consequences of nationalism. These were the Imperial Conference of 1926 and the Dominion-Provincial Conference of 1927. The former declared, in the famous Balfour formula, the equality in status of the Dominions with the United Kingdom and set in train the achievement of equality of function enacted in the Statute of Westminster of 1931. In the acid of nationalism, Emppire had dissolved into Commonwealth. Because, however, equality of function would mean national control of the constitution, a matter of great importance to the provinces of Canada, a Dominion-Provincial conference met in Ottawa in 1927 to consider, among other things, the amendment of the constitution by a process wholly Canadian that would end the still necessary reference to the Parliament of the United Kingdom. The conference marked the beginning of the endeavour, not yet completed, to find such a process. It may also be taken as marking the establishment of the national-provincial conference as part of the working, if not of the formal, constitution of Canada. Both the failure to agree on a method of amendment and the continued use of the conference were to reveal how superficial was the nationalism of the decade, and how much Canada was a country *sui generis*. The basic truth was that the changing nature of the British Empire brought Canada face to face with the task of finding its own internal cohesion, whether in nationalism or in its own peculiar federalism. A percipient writer in *The Canadian Forum* saw as much, and wrote: 'If the [British] Empire were to fall apart, no cohesive force in the Canadian Confederation could hold it together.'

The logic of the nationalistic course was furthered in international affairs also. Not only was a British High Commissioner sent to Ottawa, to mark the new relations between Canada and the United Kingdom, but a Canadian minister, the Honourable Vincent Massey, was also sent to Washington in order that relations with the United States might be handled directly. And in the League of Nations, Canada, who had used the League in the assertion of its own nationality, itself declared by the 'Canadian resolution' that it would not have to go to the defence of other nations. This effectively ended Article X of the Covenant, by which all members of the League were committed to the defence of any member of the League. No Canadian supporter of the League, apparently, foresaw that the right of national self-determination might be used to destroy a state member of the League, such as Czechoslovakia, or indeed Canada itself. And few noted that as Canada became more independent of the United Kingdom it became more dependent on the United States.

No such thoughts disturbed the celebration in 1927 of the Diamond Jubilee, the sixtieth anniversary of Confederation. It was the avatar of a Confederation vindicated, of a nation restored to a unity, disturbed but not broken by the events of the preceding decade – the Great War and the conscription crisis.

Canada, therefore, rode the crest of opportunist politics, romantic nostalgia, and economic prosperity into the great and unintended deflation that closed the decade. The Liberal regime of Mackenzie King, having survived the hazards that might well have destroyed it, was content to survive.

The regime did nothing after 1927, and stayed busy doing it. Political expediency had paid off. The threatening forces of agrarian revolt and Quebec nationalism had been lulled. Abbé Groulx, although less aggressive than before or after, continued his essentially nationalistic studies, and the little group of U.F.A. and Labour members in the Commons were quieted if not silenced. Why do anything to arouse them, or to give the representatives of labour and agrarian discontent material for bitter speeches to the complacent benches in the Commons?

Not only the character of the political regime was responsible for this euphoria. Canada, with its practical instinct for material success, was sharing the great American boom. Even the farmers were relatively well off, and the record crop of 1928 seemed to put them beyond any need for complaint. More and more roads were built for more and more motor cars. The cities grew, particularly Vancouver, which surged ahead of Winnipeg in size. The country home became steadily more like the city home. What was needed but more and more effort in order to enjoy more and more of life in a country dotted with the well lit, well warmed homes of a simple and democratic people? Nationhood had been achieved, except for a few details. Germany was in the League, and the war forgotten. The United States was revealing with its usual exuberance what science and productive drive could do. War had been abolished by the Kellogg-Briand Pact of 1928, an amiable gesture inspired by Mr. Kellogg, whose name every Canadian knew, and by M. Briand whose pictures in the press were so friendly and reassuring. And in 1928 the Washington Senators had won the World Series, which proved that any good luck was possible in a peaceful and prosperous world. An unfortunate interruption – an accident, appalling, but an accident – the Great War and its aftermath, had been surmounted and left behind. Canada was once more on the high road it had been following in 1914.

Such was the mood of 1929. Then in October came the crash of the Wall Street stock market; shares tumbled in

Montreal and Toronto. Prosperity continued but only as a hope–the old car was not turned in, and the old suit was made to do. What had been forgotten since 1920 now reappeared in the news and grew steadily–the black disease of industrial and urban society, continuous mass unemployment. The financial and administrative structures of municipalities and provinces, not prepared for this dead weight of the new society, took the impact and shuddered. The spectres of the next decade, the unemployed, began to walk the city streets and ride the freight cars. And the great crop of 1928 had been sold to the Pools at levels too high to allow them to carry the loss on falling markets. The western grain crop, for a generation the great nourisher of the national economy, now became a national problem, and the carry-over a burden lightened only by the beginning of the driest decade the west was ever to know.

The decade thus ended as it had begun, with deflation. This deflation, however, was the result not merely of the ending of a post-war boom, it was the result of the ending of an epoch, that which had begun in 1815 when England had saved the world for industrial capitalism and the United States had opened the Mississippi Valley for the settler. The decade of 1920-30 was devoted to an attempt to continue that epoch. In it Canada had accomplished little that was positive and had learned little of the new realities. Some novelties had begun to stir: a political labour movement, strange ideas of Social Credit and cyclical budgeting, a saving realism in a few writers. Some social experience had been acquired, and prohibition had failed and been replaced by government control of the sale of liquor. City ways were not quite so alien and so menacing to rural conservatism. So much, it would seem, and perhaps no more.

But Canada had still to learn from the next decade that the world of 1914 was beyond all recall.

8. The 1930s

KENNETH MCNAUGHT

The grim world-wide financial collapse of 1929 dictated to Canada a basic condition of life in the 'hungry thirties' for which the country was unprepared. Both the politics and the economic growth of the twenties bequeathed basic political preconceptions which acted like a constitutional strait-jacket. The economic growth and collapse were constitutionally the concern of the provinces, and the provinces were still strong to defend their rights, or extend them, at the expense of the federal government. Lassitude seemed to hang over the weakened Government of Canada.

Prime Minister King, after weathering the political storms of the twenties, was reluctant to challenge the provinces by advocating any broad federal program to meet the depression. Moreover, he and his Liberal colleagues were by no means convinced that federal spending, subsidies to the provinces, and deficit financing were good policies *per se*. Quite apart from King's 'obsession with the sense of our constitutional difficulties', as J. S. Woodsworth put it, the Prime Minister was no further along the Keynesian path than was the ex-Progressive President of the United States, Herbert Hoover. Surrounded in his cabinet by men of basically conservative temperament, such as Charles Dunning (Finance), Ernest Lapointe (Justice), Peter Heenan (Labour), and Thomas Crerar (Railways), Mackenzie King doggedly defended the barren ground of rugged individualism. The government's response to demands for positive leadership was well illustrated by Heenan's remark that 'unemployment insurance will be adopted in Canada only after public opinion has been educated to the necessity for such legislation.'

Rattled by the mounting spirit of political discontent King compounded his sins of inactivity by dropping the injudicious remark that he would never give 'a five-cent piece' to any province with a Tory government. While he was irritated by the evidence of rising unemployment, falling wheat sales, and regional inequities, he vastly underestimated their political impact. Continuing to think in terms of tariff tinkering he called an election in the autumn of 1930. Long since laid to rest is the legend that he foxily anticipated defeat in order to saddle the Conservatives with responsibility for the worst of the depression. In fact he was confident of victory. His decision to go to the country was reinforced by contact with the occult and he recorded in his diary on the eve of the election: 'I believe we will win with a good majority.' He also noted his conviction that R. B. Bennett was 'not so good a leader as Meighen', and this personal misconception was to be a major cause of Liberal defeat. When the votes were counted the Conservatives took 49 per cent of the total, the Liberals (with Liberal-Progressives) 45.6 per cent. Minor parties and independents accounted for the remaining 5.4 per cent. This gave the

Conservatives 137 seats to the Liberals' 88. R. B. Bennett, the rich and bombastic bachelor lawyer from Calgary, was Prime Minister for the next five years.

The 1930 election spelled out the principal Canadian themes of the decade. Liberal defeat revealed that the country was not content to endure depression nourished only on memories of ephemeral prosperity. Bland promises of sound administration and retrenchment–'the record'–were met with loud cries for farmers' protection against New Zealand butter, retaliation against rising American tariffs, and, on the left, the demand for a more collectivist legislative philosophy. Although the Dunning election budget had increased imperial preference and provided for a response to American tariffs it had been mild in both directions. Bennett saw this and castigated the Liberals for 'timidity and vacillation'. Representing a party tradition that was not philosophically averse to positive government action he declared that he would use Canadian tariffs to 'blast a way into the markets that have been closed', put on foot large-scale public works, and assume the provinces' share of the cost of old-age pensions. Anticipating F. D. Roosevelt's 1932 assault on Hoover, Bennett thundered: 'Mackenzie King promises you conferences; I promise you action. He promises consideration of the problem of unemployment, I promise to end unemployment. Which plan do you like best?' Although the Conservative program was even less specific than Roosevelt's and in practice was to accomplish even less towards ending the depression, it did acknowledge the circumstances of the day. Together with the programs and activities of new federal and provincial political parties and of voluntary organizations, Bennett's blustering was an appropriate harbinger of a decade in which Canadians sought a new definition of national purpose. Despite, and partly because of, economic frustration, it was an energetic, speculative decade – one that created a new national sentiment and many of Canada's most important modern institutions.

The crucible of depression was certainly well heated. The ten million Canadians of 1930 were hit as hard as any comparable group in the world by economic chaos. In some respects, because of the boom of the late 1920s, the impact was much greater than in many other countries. The depression was also, because of the extent of the Dominion and the variety of occupations, very uneven in its incidence. Urban centres that had grown rapidly in the 1920s remained nearly static in the 1930s. Thus, many middle-class families suffered relatively little, while a swollen urban working class bore the brunt of lowered wages and unemployment created by business policies designed to protect prices rather than jobs. Yet, even so, the Atlantic provinces and the prairies undoubtedly reached the lowest depths in Canada.

For the country as a whole, both income and gross national product actually declined slightly over the ten years following 1929. But in the Maritimes and on the prairies the decline was catastrophic. The national net farm income plunged from $417 million in 1929 to $109 million in 1933 and by 1939 had only recovered to pre-depression levels. Hit by disastrous drought in the early thirties, as well as by shrinking external markets for wheat, the prairies suffered total economic collapse. Saskatchewan, the greatest of the wheat producers, had to apply for loans from the federal government, to meet even the provincial share of federal-provincial relief payments. The shock-waves from the western dust-bowls spread quickly through the national economy, affecting transportation, banking, commerce, and industry – and were not tempered by any substantial recovery of world markets.

For a country that was still overwhelmingly dependent upon exports of farm produce and raw materials the figures of foreign trade tell the story briefly. The total value of domestic exports was $1,152,416,000 in 1929, sank to $489,883,000 in 1932, and by 1939 had climbed back only to $924,926,000. For central Canada and British Columbia a fairly steady market for mine products (especially gold) and pulp and paper helped to ease the shock, but also aggravated the regional differences. The Maritimes, which had benefited little from the prosperity of the twenties, reached a near-subsistence level as fisheries, lumbering, and steel production withered. Fish exports, for example, fell from a 1929 value of $38 million to $19 million in 1932 and had reached less than $30 million by 1939. By 1933, in addition to the social devastation on the Atlantic seaboard and the prairies, approximately 23 per cent of the labour force was unemployed (compared to 3 per cent in 1929). This meant that, besides farmers, there were well over one and a half million Canadians without any source of earned income.

While the statistics are revealing, they fail to conjure up the reality of wasted lives, of long lines of forlorn men stretching away from the city soup-kitchens or shivering against the wind on the tops of freight cars as they rode hopelessly about the country in search of non-existent jobs. Nor do the abstract figures tell the real story of farms lost to mortgage companies, of the accumulated savings of a generation vanished with the sale of a fishing schooner, the closing of a corner store, the shutting down of a small plant. Least of all can the statistics portray the bitterness of newly pauperized classes forced to forgo amenities and even adequate food while the salaried and *rentier* groups suffered little. Highly protected industry and monopolistic control of prices served to emphasize the inequities of a chaotic capitalism. The social nadir was sketched briefly in the Commons by J. S. Woodsworth, who emerged in these years as the rallying-point for the country's conscience:

> In the old days we could send people from the cities to the country. If they went out today they would meet another army of unemployed coming back from the country to the city; that outlet is closed. What can these people do? They have been driven from our parks; they have been driven from our streets; they have been driven from our buildings and in this city [Ottawa] they actually took refuge on the garbage heaps.

The rumbling of political discontent that had reverberated through the election of 1930 grew louder as the depression deepened. In the west the old feeling of betrayal and exploitation brought forth new political groupings which grew naturally out of the background of Progressivism. In Ontario and British Columbia, provincial Liberalism threw up demagogic leaders and these provinces also sustained active branches of the new socialist party, the Co-operative Commonwealth Federation (C.C.F.). In Quebec, spreading unemployment led to a combination of social radicalism and French-Canadian nationalism. There, the urbanization and industrialization that had been stimulated in the twenties by English-Canadian, British, and American investment was exploited politically as evidence of growing foreign domination. In fact, urbanization was a factor in the decline of French-Canadian influence in the power élite of Quebec. Owing to lower rural educational levels, farmers' sons who went to the cities ended up in unskilled, lower-level occupations and thus emphasized the non-French control of Quebec's economic life. In the Maritimes, while new political movements failed to emerge, the sentiments that gave rise to the 'Maritimes rights movement' in the twenties continued to find vigorous expression in both the old parties.

Plainly, the breakdown of the Canadian system, both economic and political, required the definition and implementation of new policies at all levels of government. The municipalities and the provinces had discovered that their sources of finance were utterly inadequate to the roles imposed upon them by unemployment relief and general welfare as well as by the industrial and urban growth of the preceding decade. Many Canadians also felt that since the economic problems were nationwide in their impact the federal government should assume, or be given, power to establish more uniform levels of welfare and opportunity—in short, to establish a new 'national policy' with a strong tinge of collectivism. In this mood many French Canadians shared with English-speaking Canadians despite the extreme *nationaliste* politicking that emerged in Quebec under Maurice Duplessis.

II

The initial response of the new Bennett government to the national calamity was to convene a special session of Parliament early in September of 1930. Twenty million dollars was voted for emergency relief work to be administered by provincial and municipal governments, without any national plan being worked out, and the tariff was raised more sharply than at any time since the institution of the 'national policy'. While King was horrified by this 'fiscal irresponsibility', it did represent action, and there was no substantial opposition to it in the House. On the other hand it was action along archaic lines. While Bennett, as the offspring of an old New Brunswick Loyalist family, was prepared to use his power positively, he had had little preparation, as a corporation lawyer, for the socio-economic needs of a semi-industrialized country faced by the collapse of world markets. His argument rested on the assumption that he could provide 25,000 jobs by protecting Canadian industry and also use the tariff to bargain for the entry of agricultural and primary products to foreign markets. In practice this over-simple response had the same effect as did the autarchy adopted by other western nations at the same time. The Canadian trade balance was transformed from a deficit of $125,332,000 in 1930 to a surplus of $187,621,000 in 1935. Financiers on Bay Street and St. James Street found this gratifying, especially since the government also refused to devalue the dollar. Undoubtedly, too, the Tory fiscal policy saved some Canadian firms from bankruptcy (particularly by rigorous application of new anti-dumping features of the tariff) and thus protected some Canadian jobs. But while the policy lessened the depression in profits, dividends, and prices this very virtue militated against recovery in the vast areas of the economy that depended upon exports. And by keeping the price structure artificially rigid it added appreciably to the misery of millions of people living on relief or on drastically reduced incomes.

Allied to the initial tariff-monetary policies was Bennett's use of the Imperial Economic Conference, held in Ottawa in 1932, to wring concessions from the United Kingdom. 'From that Conference', declared the Governor General in his 1932 prorogation speech, 'may arise a power which will bring enduring harmony out of economic chaos.' Bennett had prepared his ground by almost acrimonious insistence during the 1930 Imperial Conference that while he firmly believed in an extension of the system of imperial preferences he also believed in 'Canada first, then the Empire'. Disavowing the Laurier-King principle that imperial preference in the Canadian tariff should be voluntary and unrelated to specific reciprocity in the British tariff, Bennett had irritated the Labour government by his suggestion that it was time for Britain to abandon free trade and construct a genuine imperial commercial system. But between 1930 and 1932 Bennett's position was markedly strengthened. Not only had negotiations with the United States, Germany, and France failed to produce any significant concessions, but in Britain Ramsay MacDonald had survived the collapse of his Labour government and emerged at the head of a National (or thinly-disguised Conservative) government that was very interested in regrouping the Empire-Commonwealth in the face of both economic and possibly military difficulties.

Thus, when the Conference assembled amidst much fanfare in Ottawa, the ebullient Canadian leader drove a hard bargain. With the Canadian tariff already raised by about 50 per cent Bennett agreed to raise the general level still further while exempting Britain from the second-round increases. He also agreed to lower the Canadian tariff on some significant items as a second way of increasing the imperial preference. But in return he got the British agreement to ban dumping of foreign goods in the British market, and to provide free entry for a considerable range of Canadian farm and primary products, as well as preferential treatment for others, ranging up to 33 per cent. In addition to the British agreement, bilateral trade pacts were worked out with other members of the Commonwealth.

In the years following the Ottawa agreements a considerable shift in Canada's trading pattern occurred. Britain and the Commonwealth took about 12 per cent more of Canada's total exports, but the continued failure to expand exports to the United States and Europe more than balanced this shift. One thing the agreements did prove: with determination the Commonwealth system could be fleshed out by trading benefits. In a world in which tariff warfare was painfully ubiquitous the Ottawa initiative showed some positive advantages. Had the tariff policies been accompanied by a mild inflation these advantages might have been enhanced by lowering the price of Canadian exports (as well as the cost of living) and thus improving Canada's competitive position in other foreign markets. The other Bennett depression policies, however, were framed within a hard-currency context.

In the most critical centre of economic collapse, the prairie west, a series of stopgap measures was applied. When the Wheat Pool, with its system of initial payments, was forced to wind up its operation in 1931, small subsidies were paid by the government for wheat brought to market in that year. This was followed by government purchasing on the open market – which failed to sustain prices to any appreciable degree – and in 1935, with over 200,000,000 bushels of government-owned wheat in storage, the Wheat Board was re-established to bring permanent order into the western grain economy. Aid to the provinces, to provide for relief of farmers and the unemployed, was continued, but its administration through provincial and municipal bodies was largely *ad hoc* and no system of co-ordinated public construction was worked out. In many of the relief camps for single unemployed men the conditions of life provoked rioting, while extreme distress in the cities created grave class tension. To these continuing problems Bennett's further responses were a curious mixture of government planning and outright reaction.

In 1934 Conservative legislation established the Bank of Canada in an attempt to give greater stability and order to the country's finances as well as to have a useful financial adviser to the government. However, the Bank legislation

If We Don't Sell Our Wheat Abroad

From the *Manitoba Free Press*, July 17, 1930.

was criticized by many because it provided for a much greater private than public equity in its stock ownership. It was not until 1938 that the Bank was fully 'nationalized', and in the meantime it served to bolster the restrictive credit policies of the private chartered banks. In the case of the railways, which were in sore straits because of reduced traffic, the government reorganized the C.N.R. and permitted a limited degree of pooling in passenger services with the C.P.R. But the full recommendations of the Duff Commission which had been appointed to examine the railway problem were not implemented, and it was not until 1937 that the C.N.R. was relieved of some of the huge debt burden with which it had been saddled for the relief of bondholders between 1917 and 1922.

The government also undertook one unsuccessful and two successful programs of national enterprise. Negotiation with the United States for the joint building of a St. Lawrence deep waterway was completed and signed in 1932, but failed to obtain ratification by the American Senate. A far more significant action was taken in 1932 when Parliament passed an act establishing the Canadian Radio Broadcasting Commission (renamed the Canadian Broadcasting Corporation in 1936). Although scarcely an anti-depression move, the development of public control over the airwaves was symptomatic of the new sense of national purpose that had grown with widespread discussion of the problems thrown up by the economic crisis. Across the country, groups of professional and business people either had been established or had rapidly increased in membership during the 1920s. Expressing a revived concern about the maintenance of political independence and the nourishment of cultural growth, such groups extended their activities in the thirties.

An outstanding example of such activities was the Canadian Radio League, which turned into one of the most successful pressure groups in Canadian history. With members in all the provinces and the support of key men in the political parties it was the work of this organization, more than any other single factor, that induced the government to frustrate the ambition of private interests, such as the C.P.R., which were preparing to commercialize radio on the basis of cheaply imported American programs. Enjoying support in both French- and English-speaking Canada the new publicly owned network provided services in areas considered of no value from a profit point of view. It also provided employment for musicians and actors, as well as developing an objective national news service and stimulating the exchange both of people and of ideas amongst the regions.

Implementation of public control and enterprise on the

airwaves rested upon a 1932 decision by the Judicial Committee of the Privy Council confirming federal jurisdiction in broadcasting. Another ruling of the Privy Council in the same year validated the 1927 Aeronautics Act, which asserted federal control of the airways. Both decisions seemed to express the general feeling that provincial powers had been overblown by previous legal decisions and economic trends. The mysterious ratiocination of the Judicial Committee had somehow reflected the new national feeling in Canada, and encouraged by the airways decision the government laid the basis of a national air-transport system, partly as a relief construction project. In 1937, under the Liberals, Trans-Canada Air Lines was chartered as a public corporation to operate intercity, transcontinental, and international flights. As with the C.B.C., where private radio stations were not eliminated but put under public control with the public corporation dominant in the field, so private air lines continued to operate, but with T.C.A. the dominant national line. In both cases the private sector was permitted to expand in later years and the debate about the virtues of mixing the two economic methods continues.

Despite a willingness to assert the directing authority of the federal government Bennett could do so only within a rigidly orthodox framework of 'sound money' and protection of investments – at least until the 1935 election. He could increase federal grants to technical education and raise the federal share of the cost of old-age pensions from 50 to 75 per cent (neither of which measures appealed to Mackenzie King), but when it came to proposals of inflation and 'unbalancing' the budget he was as the rock of Gibraltar. In 1932, when credit had all but disappeared in most sections of the economy, Bennett's Finance Minister, Edgar Rhodes, proclaimed increases in all forms of taxation, declaring: 'The preservation of our national credit is an indispensable prerequisite to the return of prosperity.' The proposal of the agonized western farmers, seconded by J. S. Woodsworth, that the dollar should be devalued and both currency and credit completely nationalized was rejected out of hand. The

King Liberals were equally horrified by this financial heresy, and as King told his nervous caucus, 'I pointed out how extreme it was, that I doubted if those who were for supporting it understood it, that it wd. make conditions worse if such a policy were adopted.'

Faced with radical proposals and deeply conscious of the inefficacy of his own policies Bennett was persuaded that Canada was on the verge of revolution. Moreover this fear was very personal. The Prime Minister was sensitive to the charges that filled the opposition air about his dictatorial methods of handling Parliament and caucus. He was furious at the widespread use of such terms as 'Bennett buggies' to describe horse-drawn farmers' automobiles for which owners could not afford gasoline, and 'Bennettboroughs' to designate the shanty-towns of tin and tar-paper where many relief families lived in the urban areas. When camps were established in 1932 for transient unemployed men their 20,000 inhabitants were placed under military discipline enforced by the Department of National Defence. When large delegations of farmers, or of unemployed, sought interviews with the Prime Minister they were either refused (on the ground that the government was already aware of their problems and proposals) or they were met with an exaggerated show of force. During the 1932 session when one such delegation declared its intention of meeting with the Prime Minister armoured cars were called out, the city police were reinforced, armed groups of R.C.M.P. were deployed on Parliament Hill, and a mounted detachment was posted in reserve behind the buildings. The delegation dispersed peaceably after a few hortatory words delivered by the Prime Minister from the Tower steps. Inside the House tempers flared as Woodsworth asked how much longer the people of Canada would stand the spectacle of a millionaire Prime Minister, surrounded by the military, lecturing 'poor people' because they did not speak to him in the most polite language.

Across the country many municipal and provincial governments and much of the press shared Bennett's view that protest groups and mass meetings of unemployed were, by definition, revolutionary in intent. The Minister of Justice, Hugh Guthrie, gave quick support to such local authorities in their war against the largely imaginary 'reds'. When financial incapacity forced the prairie and Maritimes governments to eliminate their police budgets, the R.C.M.P. was assigned the responsibility of police duty in those provinces, and in the bill that reorganized and expanded the R.C.M.P. provision was made for the swearing in of special unpaid constables whose recruitment was largely from the ranks of private industrial groups. In addition to stepping up its invigilation of the trade unions by 'labour spies' (despite the fact that union membership declined sharply between 1929 and 1936) the Justice Department ordered the Mounties to put a tight clamp on any large-scale movement of 'transients'. When a strike of British Columbia relief-camp workers led to a 'march on Ottawa' in 1935, the workers' delegates were stopped by the R.C.M.P. at Regina and turned back amidst scenes of bloody riot. Censorship of 'seditious' books was intensified through anonymous officers of the Department of National Revenue, and aliens (some of whom had lived in Canada for twenty years) were arrested without warrant for deportation without court trial or right of *habeas corpus*. Communists and radicals were jailed under the terms of Section 98 of the Criminal Code, which, like the authoritarian amendment to the Immigration Act, had been passed as a 1919 emergency measure and which gave an open-ended definition of sedition.

The development of such a semi-police state was opposed step by step by Henri Bourassa, the Quebec nationalist and social reformer, J. S. Woodsworth, and even Liberals like Ernest Lapointe, who seemed to forget Liberal acquiescence in the repression of Cape Breton coal-miners in the twenties. Woodsworth's motion to repeal Section 98 was met first by Bennett's attempt to refuse debate and then, simply by Guthrie's derogatory innuendo: 'If there was a reason to pass such a section in 1918 [sic], there is certainly a reason to keep such a section in force in the year 1933. . . . Section 98 is not in any sense a hindrance to any right-thinking person.' Those who spoke out against the drift toward totalitarianism were labelled red. In large measure this was because the proponents of liberty were also the chief castigators of the *status quo.* It was they who charged that the old national policies of high tariffs, balanced budgets, subsidies to transportation, coal production, and immigration, had ceased to work – or, rather, were working excessively well for the protected parts of the economy. Moreover, they pointed out, those policies had nourished the growth of monopoly and had led to a concentration of economic control in Montreal and Toronto that made virtually impossible an equitable distribution of the country's wealth – let alone the adequate realization of that wealth. As the Stevens Report on the spread of prices between the producer and the consumer put it in 1934:

> It [the Commission's evidence] has shown that a few great corporations are predominant in the industries that have been investigated; also that this power, all the more dangerous because it is impersonal, can be wielded in such a way that competition within the industry is blocked, the welfare of the producer disregarded, and the interests of the investor ignored.

Not only were there sharp contrasts between social classes within each of the regions and between the regions themselves, but there was an inability (stemming from constitutional as well as political inhibitions) to enact anything like adequate social reforms. Trade unions remained unprotected against limitations of their organizing and bargaining rights, unemployment insurance and other welfare legislation languished as abortive proposals while the government, like its predecessor, pleaded the limiting effect of the B.N.A. Act. Substantial transfer payments from Ottawa to the provinces remained unpredictable and thus an infirm basis on which to plan provincial welfare measures. The depression had made it plain that the federal division of legislative fields and financial resources – a division that had come under critical provincial review in the preceding decade – was totally unrealistic. Either the federal government would have to assume large new responsibilities or the provinces would have to be granted new jurisdictions and assured sources of revenue. To meet these complex problems of the constitution, the economy, and social welfare, new political parties sprang into being at both levels of government, and even the Bennett Conservatives (or, at least, Bennett himself) agreed by 1935 that reform would have to come. It was a part of the subtlety of this dynamic decade that a deepening reform sentiment led both to intensified nationalism and to strong expressions of provincialism in regions as different as Quebec and Alberta.

III

On the national stage the first and most significant of the new parties was the Co-operative Commonwealth Federation (C.C.F.). At its founding convention held at Regina in 1933 the C.C.F. adopted a platform announced as the Regina Manifesto, which condemned the capitalism system in its entirety and advocated a far-reaching program of social democracy. The Manifesto closed with the sentence: 'No C.C.F. government will rest content until it has eradicated capitalism and put into operation the full programme of socialized planning which will lead to the establishment in Canada of the co-operative commonwealth.' Horrified editorials in most of the country's press analysed the new party as a mixture of bolshevism and impractical idealism. In fact the C.C.F. was a natural outgrowth of previous Canadian experience and politics as well as a relatively moderate response to the savage impact of the crisis of capitalism.

In a political sense the new party was a grouping of farmers' protest organizations whose experience went back through the Progressive movement to the years preceding the First World War, of small urban socialist parties with an equally lengthy if less influential history, and of urban intellectuals. Trade unions as such were not founding partners in the C.C.F. although A. R. Mosher was a delegate to the Regina convention as president of the largest national railway union. With the spread of the C.I.O. in Canada after 1936, unionists became more active politically and in 1938 the first union affiliated directly with the C.C.F. This trend culminated in the establishment of the New Democratic Party in 1961, jointly sponsored by the Canadian Labour Congress and the C.C.F.

Ideologically the C.C.F. reflected many influences, all of which added up to a distinctive brand of Canadian socialism. Its first leader, J. S. Woodsworth, brought to the party a combination of British Christian socialism and Fabianism, the American Social Gospel, and political unionism of the British Independent Labour party brand. An ex-Methodist minister, he had sided with the Winnipeg strikers in 1919 and been charged with sedition for quoting from Isaiah. Elected to the federal Parliament in 1921 as the candidate of the Manitoba Independent Labour party, he had co-operated with U.F.A. and other Progressives in the 'Ginger Group' throughout the 1920s, seizing every opportunity to expound the rights of labour unions, the need for unemployment insurance and other welfare measures, as well as the virtues of socialism. From his experience in the House of Commons Woodsworth became convinced that the political left would have to accept the Parliamentary-party system as it existed. Other Progressives, such as Robert Gardiner of Alberta, came to agree with him. Thus the C.C.F. was from the beginning both a movement and a political party, although it was controlled by democratically elected conventions and ruled out election contributions from business sources. Elaborating Canada's history of railway, customs, and other kinds of party corruption, and with the contemporary Beauharnois scandal fresh in the public mind – a scandal in which both old parties were implicated in accepting money from the beneficiaries of the alienation of public power-rights in the St. Lawrence River – the C.C.F. appeal to party democracy and political purity cut deeply.

The party also benefited from the moral indignation and the nationalist sentiment of the thirties. With the General Conference of the United Church condemning the profit motive of capitalism, and many ministers of that and other denominations active in the new party, many of its club meetings and conventions took on the tone of evangelistic enthusiasm that had also characterized the early phases of Progressivism. Moreover it had the effective support of one of the period's many national-interest groups, the League for Social Reconstruction. Formed in 1932, the L.S.R. was a Canadian version of the Fabian Society with members drawn largely from the universities and the professions. Conceived in the midst of depression and doubts about the validity of the Canadian experiment, the L.S.R. emphasized the necessity of completing Canadian independence, retaining British legal and parliamentary institutions, and defining social purposes. The pamphlets, broadcasts, and meetings of the L.S.R., together with contributions to the small but influential *Canadian Forum,* did much to create interest in democratic socialism as an answer to planless capitalism, and it was a committee of the League that wrote the first draft of the C.C.F.'s Regina Manifesto.

Electorally the C.C.F. made rapid headway. By 1934 there were hundreds of C.C.F. clubs and locals across the country and a federated section of the party in each province. In British Columbia and Saskatchewan the C.C.F. had become the official opposition. In Manitoba, Alberta, and Ontario, C.C.F. candidates had won seats in the legislatures and in many municipal bodies. In the Maritimes the new party made some headway in the mining districts, but in Quebec the firm anti-socialism pronouncements of the Roman Catholic hierarchy blocked the party, and social protest in that province took a different form. In the federal election of 1935 the C.C.F. polled nearly 400,000 votes and elected seven M.P.s, including M. J. Coldwell and T. C. Douglas, both of whom were to become successors of J. S. Woodsworth as leader of Canada's social democratic party.

The influence of the C.C.F. was pronounced, not only upon the leftward trend of other party platforms in the 1935 election, but also upon the Liberal government after 1935. As with the earlier Progressive movement, Mackenzie King was conscious of the need to express a sufficient amount of nationalism and social-reform sentiment to prevent the socialists from achieving further gains. By 1940 the Liberals had secured an amendment to the B.N.A. Act that enabled them to provide a national system of unemployment insurance, the Criminal Code had been amended so as to guarantee the right to join a trade union, and the Bank of Canada had been nationalized. C.C.F. pressure in the provinces had also produced a considerable advance in welfare legislation and the movement for family allowances was well under way. In 1935 the C.C.F. vote would undoubtedly have been substantially larger had it not been for the splintering of the protest vote in that election. The ephemeral Reconstruction Party and the Social Credit Party between them took some 600,000 potential C.C.F. votes, and the division in the Conservative party over a sudden 'radical' turn taken by Bennett served further to distort the vote. All of this reflected the social-economic turmoil of the period.

One startling aspect of the 1935 election was the capture of seventeen seats by the new Social Credit party, with less than half the vote garnered by the C.C.F. This was possible because Social Credit took all fifteen of the Alberta seats (plus two in Saskatchewan). Behind this success in the foot-hills lay the political magic of a fundamentalist lay preacher, William (Bible Bill) Aberhart. Founder of the Prophetic Bible Institute of Calgary, Aberhart was an ex-Ontarian schoolteacher who had read the curious monetary theory of the English engineer, Major Douglas. To the simplistic idea that poverty in the midst of plenty could be ended by printing and distributing 'social dividends', which would keep purchasing power and productive capacity in balance, Aberhart added the evangelistic fervour of frontier revivalism. The new inflationary gospel of Social Credit was preached every Sunday over a province-wide radio network rented by the Prophetic Bible Institute in 1934. By election time in 1935 Social Credit organization was complete and huge audiences could be assembled to hear Aberhart announce: 'You remain in the depression because of a shortage of purchasing power imposed by the banking system. If you have not suffered enough, it is your God-given right to suffer more.' The gospel was close enough to that preached previously by the U.F.A. movement to strike a familiar note and new enough to give a sense of excitement to the brilliant hortatory powers of Aberhart. The older spokesmen for the farmers went down to defeat first in the August provincial election of 1935 and again in the October federal election. In provincial elections down to the present, Alberta has remained solidly Social Credit.

The astonishing political unity exhibited by Albertans can best be explained by the homogeneity of their social-economic structure. A society of more-or-less-independent primary producers, the majority of people in the province constituted a sort of rural *petite bourgeoisie* with an identical interest in loosening credit facilities and defending themselves against national protective policies that favoured the industrialized region of central Canada. Fundamentally the province's Social Credit governments have been conservative in their 'radicalism' – in the sense of claiming to protect private enterprise, whether on the farm, the ranch, or, more recently, the oil and natural-gas fields. But in the 1930s an attempt was made to give effect to some of the Social Credit election promises. Legislation was passed to license and tax federally-chartered banks, to issue 'social dividends', and (revealing the basically illiberal, one-party-state assumptions of Social Credit) to gag the press. All of these bills were eventually disallowed by the federal government or declared unconstitutional by the judiciary. Indeed, the fate of Alberta Social Credit legislation was one more sign of the growing emphasis in the 1930s on the need to assert federal powers. That it was also evidence of the influence of entrenched 'eastern' financial interests did no harm to Social Credit's political appeal in Alberta. At the federal level of government Social Credit's impact was not comparable to that of the C.C.F., and its Ottawa representatives remained narrowly interested in provincial rights and an impossible monetary policy. Like some other forms of North American agrarian radicalism, the movement exhibited a disturbing trend toward anti-Semitism and restrictions of civil liberty.

Worried political response to the depression was also evident in policy divergences made by the provincial wings of the Liberal party in British Columbia and Ontario. On the Pacific coast the Liberal T. D. Pattullo won office in 1933 with a Rooseveltian pledge of positive government. Having promised 'work and wages' in the campaign, Pattullo put on foot extensive public works, increased the scale of relief payments, subsidized mining and fishing, and secured legislation governing hours of work and minimum wages. It was the most energetic program of its kind in Canada during the depression, and, when the necessary deficit budgeting led to fiscal difficulties requiring either financial aid from Ottawa or a redistribution of revenue sources between the two governments, the resulting controversy caused a serious review of Dominion-provincial relations.

In Ontario the Liberals came to power in 1934 under Mitchell F. Hepburn, who thus broke the nearly thirty-year sentence of Liberal opposition. More 'populist' in some respects than the Social Crediters themselves, Hepburn was in a long Ontario tradition of liberal radicalism dating back at least as far as George Brown. It was the tradition of the businessman farmer of the south-western Ontario peninsula, able to attract the support of the province's rural interests, yet identified in actual policy terms with the merchant-manufacturing class of Toronto. At the outset of his administration Hepburn secured marketing legislation to protect the price of some farm products and even made a bid for labour votes with legislation to safeguard trade-union rights. But he moved steadily closer to the power élite of the Toronto Mining Exchange and the American branch plants. Much less willing than Pattullo to budget for a deficit in the interest of welfare and economic recovery, Hepburn with his rather uncouth and bumptious political hyperbole soon identified the growing trade-union movement, with its potential support in the semi-organized unemployed, as the major threat to Ontario's well-being. This threat he met by adding substantially to the ranks of the provincial police and thundering against the irresponsibility of radicals – amongst whom he drew no distinction between C.C.F.ers, the U.F.O. (which affiliated with the C.C.F. in 1934), Communists, trade-union leaders, and the unemployed.

The climax of Hepburn's anti-labour policy came with a strike against General Motors in Oshawa in 1937. Leaders of the United Automobile Workers, who were backed by the newly formed C.I.O. in the United States, were denounced by the Premier as 'foreign agitators', and the full force of the Ontario government was brought to bear in support of the American-owned company. Although the U.A.W. was eventually successful in its organizing drive, the managers of other American branch-plants, the northern mine-owners, and most of the mercantile community were not ungrateful to the little 'onion farmer'. While Hepburn lost from the Cabinet his two most liberal ministers (David Croll and Arthur Roebuck), he remained politically entrenched. In a bitter personal feud that broke in the late thirties between Hepburn and the re-established Mackenzie King, Hepburn retained the support of much Toronto business (including the ex-Liberal *Globe*, which was purchased by a mining millionaire in 1937 and amalgamated with the Tory *Mail*). It was only the overriding necessity of war-time federal leadership that finally enabled King to undercut his Ontario rival. In the process the provincial Liberal party was left in ruins and until at least 1948 the C.C.F. was the most serious opposition challenge to Ontario toryism – a challenge based in large measure on the growing strength of the unions, especially the C.I.O. unions.

The pattern of provincial political unrest was similar in Quebec, but there it was still further complicated by the growing industrialization which transformed many farmers into urban wage-earners. Moreover, racial nationalism was exploited by a clever political opportunist. In the 1935 provincial election the corrupt Liberal administration of L. A. Taschereau came within an ace of defeat and during the succeeding months a new party was formed. The *Union*

Nationale combined French-nationalist Conservatives and, incongruously, social-reform Liberals who were disillusioned by the utter indifference of the Taschereau government to the sordid social condition of the province. Under a master ex-Conservative politician, Maurice Duplessis, the *Union Nationale* won power in 1936.

Ignoring his electoral promises of reform and improved social welfare for the workers, Duplessis proceeded to consolidate his power. Making a system of corruption, he gave favours to the farmers and winked at the extension of control over economic resources by outside capital – the precise object of his most virulent pre-election attacks. Like Hepburn, Duplessis focused attention on 'radicals' and trade-unionists as the source of Quebec's troubles; and for good measure he rode forth against Ottawa in defence of the special Quebec rights. Like Aberhart, Duplessis aligned himself closely with his province's dominant religious orthodoxy and from it drew grateful support in his war against radical reformers. Symbolic of his method was the outrageous Padlock Law which permitted the seizure and closing of any premises suspected of being used to propagate communism. Communism was not defined in the law and it thus crippled attempts to establish the C.C.F. and to extend the limited range of the province's trade-union organization.

The Padlock Law was simply the most extreme expression of a quasi-police state. Duplessis found himself supported not only by the Church but also by a growing body of conservative opinion amongst the propertied classes. Clerical corporatism, stimulated by the success of General Franco in Spain, allied itself in Quebec to American capital and ran happily in harness under Duplessis. When Woodsworth in the House of Commons sought either federal disallowance of the Padlock Law or its reference to the Supreme Court, he declared that 'Twice every three days for six months the provincial police have carried out execution without judgement, dispossession without due process of law; twenty times a month they have trampled on liberties as old as Magna Carta.' The Canadian Bar Association petitioned against the Act, and a

Canadian Civil Liberties Union was founded with the first purpose of opposing such legislation; yet to Woodsworth's protests in the House, the Minister of Justice, Lapointe, would reply only 'In spite of the fact that the words are so unpleasant to the honourable member for Winnipeg North Centre, I do desire to say that the reign of law must continue in this country, that peace and order must prevail.' Lapointe prepared to order the R.C.M.P. to support Hepburn's anti-labour campaign in Ontario, and he was quick to act against the Alberta legislation affecting the federal powers in finance. Why, then, did he not protect the federal interest in criminal law and civil liberty?

The answer is complicated but important. While Canadian nationalism was at high tide and deeply anxious to define new national purposes and policies, Duplessis's power was based upon exploitation of the most powerful prejudices against such purposes and policies. Unwilling to change social policy in Quebec to meet new conditions he posed as the defender of French-Canadian rights against the threat of Ottawa's intervention and the tentacles of American ownership. Fear of Duplessis was a major part of the explanation for the failure to launch vigorous federal domestic policies in the late thirties as well as for the dangerous refusal of Mackenzie King to permit the debating or definition of Canadian foreign policy. The alliance of Duplessis and the Church, furthermore, effectively blocked the establishment of partnership between the C.C.F. and the social democrats in Quebec, thus further emphasizing the introverted separateness of the province and the political dangers which that involved.

IV

Ottawa's response to the political undulations in the provinces was governed by the outcome of the 1935 federal election. Major party programs in the election, in turn, were largely determined by analysis of the provincial trends. Mackenzie King decided that the Liberals would be most likely to regain power if they posed as the moderates in a sea of radicalism and racialism. With the slogan 'It's King or Chaos' the Liberals were to win a handy majority of seats with a minority vote almost the same as that with which they had lost in 1930. The events of the preceding twelve months made King's decision a clever, if not a very daring, one.

In the Conservative party Bennett found himself confronted by forces demanding an extension of positive federal action and the leader himself was gradually converted to this point of view. The Minister of Trade and Commerce, H. H. Stevens, argued that economic recovery was being blocked, and equitable distribution of purchasing power prevented, by monopolistic rigidities. When Bennett gave him a royal commission to investigate the methods by which retail prices were kept alarmingly higher than was justified by the wages of employees or the prices paid to producers and small manufacturers, Stevens made public comment upon the evidence as it was being assembled. Since some of the chief offenders were also supporters of the Conservative party an inner crisis resulted in the resignation of Stevens from the government. In 1935 the ex-minister led an *ad hoc* 'Reconstruction Party'. With a platform calling for regulation of business along early New Deal lines, Reconstruction candidates polled votes scattered across every province. Their total was about equal to that polled by the C.C.F., but only in Stevens's own constituency was it sufficiently concentrated to elect a member.

Despite the Stevens crisis the Prime Minister's brother-in-law, W. D. Herridge, continued the campaign to shift Conservative policy towards intervention in economic life. As ambassador to the United States Herridge was deeply impressed by the vigour and social purpose of Roosevelt's New Deal. Heeding Herridge's urgent call for government action to save the nation from the collapse of capitalism, and recognizing the political necessity of counterbalancing the favours that Conservative policy had granted to industry, Bennett acted with characteristic impetuosity. In a series of dramatic radio broadcasts early in 1935 he announced his intention of legislating a New Deal for the Canadian people. Conservative

Members of Parliament (who had not been previously consulted) and the country at large listened in astonishment as the Prime Minister declared that the capitalist system was responsible for the depression and for the continuing insecurity of millions of people, and that the system now lay in ruins. Only a total revamping of the system could enable it once again to serve the national interest. In the speech from the throne the reform program was again spelled out with the preface: 'In the anxious years through which you have passed, you have been the witnesses of grave defects and abuses in the capitalist system. Unemployment and want are the proof of these. Great changes are taking place about us. New conditions prevail. These require modifications in the capitalist system to enable that system more effectively to serve the people.'

Although Bennett declared that his inspiration came from reading the lives of Conservative reformers such as Lord Shaftesbury, in fact the program that he presented was derived from the whole reform tradition of the English-speaking people in the twentieth century and every part of it had been demanded by either Progressives or Liberals or C.C.F.ers in the Canadian Parliament. It stopped short of advocating the co-operative commonwealth of the socialists but was even more comprehensive than F.D.R.'s experiments – although, like the American New Deal, it was consciously designed to save capitalism. Its shock value lay in the fact that it sought to make use of the rising demand for a new national policy by deliberately asserting federal powers that by any objective reading of past judicial interpretation were bound to be contested and in most cases declared *ultra vires* of Ottawa's jurisdiction. As passed by the pre-election session the Bennett New Deal consisted of five principal acts – the Unemployment and Social Insurance Act, the Weekly Rest in Industrial Undertakings Act, the Natural Products Marketing Act, the Minimum Wages Act, and the Limitation of Hours of Work Act – together with several lesser bills concerned with farm and other credit, some of which were extensions of existing legislation.

The whole program horrified many supporters of the Conservative party in the business community, especially because it was accompanied by the threat of serious measures against price-fixing and the establishment of an economic council with potential regulatory influence. In the House the C.C.F. applauded and derided the new policy, claiming that it was inherently good in its reformism but that it stopped far short of adequacy and that it was worthless until there was assurance that the constitution would permit its implementation. Mackenzie King established Liberal election attitudes by castigating Bennett for the dictatorial manner in which he had 'insulted' Parliament by giving the speech from the throne in pre-session radio talks and imposing 'his' policy on a party whose caucus had not even discussed it.

The centre of the Liberal critique, however, was the charge that the whole program was a deliberate deception perpetrated in the knowledge that it would be disallowed by the courts. King declared that the government should have sought a judicial opinion and, if necessary, obtained an amendment to the B.N.A. Act before introducing such legislation. He challenged Bennett to 'tell this house whether as leader of the government, knowing that a question will come up immediately as to the jurisdiction of this parliament and of the provincial legislatures in matters of social legislation, he has secured an opinion from the law officers of the crown or from the Supreme Court of Canada which will be a sufficient guarantee to this house to proceed with these measures as being without question within its jurisdiction.' On the question of Liberal opinion about the inherent propriety of the Bennett social reform program King was cagey. On the one hand he argued that such legislation could come only after careful discussion with the provinces and determination of the division of powers. On the other he declared that the whole approach was wrong: 'I tell the Prime Minister that, if he wants to reform the capitalist system, the way to begin is by sharing between labour and the community as well as capital, the control of industrial policy. Let labour and the community, which are as essential to industry as capital, be represented around a common board to determine the policy that is to govern, and very soon these questions of maximum hours, minimum wages, sweat shops and other evils . . . will be remedied in the one effective way, namely, by the parties themselves who are directly concerned having an effective voice in the determination of the conditions under which they shall work.' While some historians have been quick to charge Bennett with insincerity in his sudden conversion, they have perhaps been less ready than the case warrants to charge King with insincerity manifested in his careful hedging of the Liberal position on reform.

The election was fought along the general lines of the throne-speech debate and the Conservatives lost sufficient votes as a divided party to carry the Liberals back to office. With the worst of the depression past, and bearing in mind the increasing business support for the Liberal party, King made it clear at once that he would act on social reform only after the constitutional position had been clarified. The Bennett legislation was referred to the Supreme Court in 1936. The Court's opinion that the main items affected fields of provincial jurisdiction and were thus unconstitutional was confirmed by the Judicial Committee of the Privy Council in the following year. The judicial decisions reversed the apparent trend of the aeronautics and radio cases of 1931 and ran directly counter to the sense of national emergency. Indeed, the Judicial Committee specifically refused the Dominion's argument that the residual powers of Section 91 of the B.N.A. Act – the federal responsibility for 'peace, order and good government' – and the enumerated powers to regulate trade and commerce were being used to meet a national emergency. Revealing an equally impenetrable logic the Privy Councillors struck a crippling blow at the authority of Ottawa in external relations by announcing that Section 132 of the B.N.A. Act was insufficient basis for the labour laws of the Bennett program. Enacted as fulfilment of obligations undertaken as a member of the International Labour Organization the hours and wages legislation was declared to infringe the powers of the provinces. The granting of power to Ottawa in Section 132 to carry out the duties of 'Canada or of any province thereof, as part of the British Empire, toward foreign countries, arising under treaties between the Empire and such foreign countries' was announced to have died with respect to any matter touched with a provincial interest – on the ground that Canada possessed the right to make her own treaties and that the I.L.O. agreement fell into this non-imperial category. Not only did this aspect of the decisions create mischief at the time, it was to be used, ironically, in the 1960s by anti-British Quebec nationalists as partial justification for claiming a large degree of provincial control over Quebec's external relations.

Rather than launch an immediate campaign for amendments to the B.N.A. Act to undo the erratic pronouncements from London, King welcomed the decisions as proof of his warnings about Bennett's high-handed and 'unconstitutional' policy. The return of the Liberals was also the occasion for intensification of the demands of provincial rightists. The provincialist case put forward at the 1927 Dominion-provincial conference seemed to be revived as strident claims to jurisdiction came from Quebec, Ontario, Alberta, and British Columbia. Even amendments that would have given power of indirect taxation to the provinces were dropped when they met opposition in the Senate. No agreement on a method of transferring to Canada the actual mechanics of amendment had been reached at a conference late in 1935, and when the Privy Council decisions of 1937 gave added strength to the provincialists' assertions, King appointed a royal commission to examine 'the economic and financial basis of confederation and the distribution of legislative powers in the light of the economic and social developments of the last seventy years'. While the problem of an agreed procedure on amendments was important the question of what amendments might be desirable was even more so, and King left this question in the lap of the commission, which was headed by N. W. Rowell and Joseph Sirois. Although the commission did not report until the spring of 1940 at a time when one might have expected an emphasis on war-inspired federal initiative, its research and the main lines of its recommendations had been well advanced prior to the outbreak of war.

The Rowell-Sirois Report was one of the principal expressions of the nationalism of the 1930s. Its brilliant analysis of Dominion history since 1867, with its special studies of economic, social, and constitutional trends, revealed a fresh understanding of the need for identifying and enabling new 'purposes of the Dominion'. Moreover the Report left no doubt that neither the French- nor the English-speaking founders of Confederation had anticipated the halting and ineffectual role assigned to Ottawa by the Privy Council jurists, some ambitious provincial premiers, and the investors of foreign capital. Reviewing the fiscal chaos, economic stagnation, and national frustration of the depression years, the Report made sweeping recommendations for redistribution of responsibilities and revenue sources – a redistribution which the commissioners believed would restore the balance of powers as originally conceived. Key controls over the economy were to be definitively in federal hands, as was the responsibility for essential services of national welfare such as unemployment insurance and relief. As further expression of national goals the existing system of provincial subsidies was to be replaced by national adjustment grants that would enable the provinces to maintain educational and social services at an average Canadian standard. In order to launch this ambitious and realistic plan without mortgages, provincial debts were to be assumed by the Dominion. To enable Ottawa to shoulder a revived federal planning role it was to enjoy exclusive rights to income and corporation taxes and succession duties.

Implementation of the Rowell-Sirois plan would have required a combination of amendments to the B.N.A. Act and policy agreements between Ottawa and at least a majority of the provinces. Such agreement was not reached. Throughout the Commission's period of research it was virtually boycotted by the governments of Ontario, Quebec, and Alberta, and when the Report was issued in 1940 these governments, supported by British Columbia, expressed marked hostility to the recommendations. At a Dominion-provincial conference called in 1941 to consider the recommendations in detail Premier Hepburn led a provincialist opposition that resulted in collapse of the conference. In 1940 the King government obtained an amendment to the B.N.A. Act empowering Ottawa to establish a nation-wide system of unemployment insurance, at least in part because it was worried by signs of growing C.C.F. support, but the war and post-war periods were to see only *ad hoc* adjustments to the federal balance of responsibilities and revenues. This outcome was of crucial importance to the future of Canada, for it meant that the nation was to emerge from the potentially unifying experience of war without a clear conception of the nature of its own constitution. It was an outcome that was the result of a too hesitant federal political leadership in the 1920s and 1930s – a leadership that feared the political risks of open confrontation of particularist provincial prejudices and feared equally the task of consolidating a public opinion that was ready for an extension of social democracy at the federal level of government. Bennett's conversion came too late to be credible, and King took only those steps that were essential to avoid immediate defeat. The technique of issue-dodging permitted the firm establishment of provincial governments allied in an essentially anti-national program of exploiting local sources of power – foreign investment that found provincial governments more pliable than Ottawa, narrow self-interest that denied the justice of equalization policies, and prejudices both of race and of religion. The same method of issue-dodging was highly developed in the field of external policy, and here the long-term results were to prove equally dangerous.

V

The problem of Canadian foreign policy in these years was intimately related to the problems of the constitution and the Liberal political tradition. In fact the speed with which the implications of the imperial conferences of 1923, 1926, 1929, and 1930 were worked out in the 1930s was very embarrassing to Canadian leaders, many of whom had not really thought out what they wanted to do with independence either in domestic or in external affairs. The Statute of Westminster, passed by the imperial Parliament in 1931, left Canada with only those restrictions on her sovereignty that she herself desired. Power to amend or repeal the B.N.A. Act was left in Westminster only because Canadians had not decided on an amending procedure acceptable in Canada, and appeals to the Privy Council were retained principally because some economic and some minority groups felt them to be a needed safeguard. To some extent the lack of confidence in purely Canadian control of the constitution stemmed from Mackenzie King's ambivalence towards Parliament – a policy that insisted on the one hand that in all matters Parliament must be the final arbiter, yet on the other hand endeavoured either to remove contentious issues from debate in the Commons or to present the House with virtual *faits accomplis*. The success that had attended King's 1926 appeal to the electorate in avoidance of a decision in the House seemed to encourage the Prime Minister's reliance on a kind of plebiscitary democracy through which the power of the Cabinet was enhanced while policy assumptions were left ill-defined.

The abdication crisis at the end of 1936 illustrated this trend in a precise constitutional context. One of the aspects of Dominion 'independence' asserted by the Statute of Westminster was the right of Dominion Parliaments to assent to 'any alteration in the law touching the Succession to the Throne or Royal Style and Titles'. Section 4 of the Statute declared that no British Act should apply to a Dominion 'unless it is expressly declared in that Act that the Dominion has requested, and consented to, the enactment thereof'. In accordance with these provisions, when Edward VIII decided to abdicate, the governments of the Dominions were all advised on December 9, 1936. The Instrument of Abdication was signed by the King on December 10, and the British

Parliament met to pass the legislation necessary to give effect to the abdication. In Canada, Parliament was not specially summoned to deal with this constitutional problem. Instead, the Cabinet requested the application to Canada of the British Act of Succession because there was not, in Mackenzie King's opinion, enough time to summon Parliament.

When the Canadian Parliament did assemble in January 1937, the government sought passage of an address of loyalty to George VI. C. H. Cahan for the Conservatives and J. S. Woodsworth for the C.C.F. protested the procedure as being government by Order in Council and a denigration of Parliament. Woodsworth argued that the address should not be passed until after the Succession Bill was debated and passed, and that the oath of allegiance to George VI should not have been administered to the members. Between the prorogation and reassembling of Parliament the King of Canada had been changed by order of the Liberal party. While there was no serious possibility of parliamentary rejection of the British Act the constitutional propriety of the Cabinet's action was dubious since the Order in Council, as Cahan pointed out, rested upon no statutory authority. Pursuing the logic of the situation, Woodsworth suggested that if the Prime Minister could decide such important matters unilaterally he could also declare war by the same method: 'Surely if the King of the United Kingdom can be distinguished for legal purposes from the King of Canada, then the recognition of the King of the United Kingdom as King of Canada can wait until there is time to call Parliament. If the selection of the King of Canada is of such minor importance, the question arises: why a King at all?'

Defending his course of action the Prime Minister reiterated his conviction that time had been of the essence and announced that 'If there ever was a time in British history when it was of importance that the unity of the British Empire should be demonstrated to all the world, it was when a question affecting the Crown itself was under consideration.' Like many of Mackenzie King's statements this one was heavily laden with ambiguity. A pronounced advocate of absolutely responsible government, he was particularly emphatic on Canada's freedom from imperial obligations. The course marked out during the Chanak crisis in 1922, and in the succeeding imperial conferences, as well as in the gradual growth of separate Canadian diplomatic representation abroad and disinterest in the League of Nations, continued after 1935. While the Bennett government had made it very clear that Canada would expend neither men nor money in support of any League endeavour to roll back Japan's invasion of Manchuria, and in other ways rejected the League in favour of a passive acceptance of British policy in international affairs, under King there was an even greater insistence on non-commitment.

In 1935 Canada's representative in Geneva, W. A. Riddell, proposed that the League add oil to the list of economic sanctions against Italy. Since the Mussolini war machine was absolutely dependent upon oil imports in its barbaric assault on Ethiopia, the 'Canadian' proposal would have brought that war to a halt and in so doing would have redeemed the League from the impotence to which Anglo-French policy was consigning it. Riddell, however, had misinterpreted the views of the new King government before making his proposal, and when news of his startling initiative arrived in Ottawa his action was quickly repudiated. When King explained his position in the House it was with the rhetorical question: 'Do honourable members think it is Canada's role at Geneva to attempt to regulate a European war?' Similarly, when in 1936 Germany violated the Versailles treaty by formally repossessing the Rhineland, King argued that Canada should keep out of the ensuing negotiations and defined Canadian 'policy' thus: 'the attitude of the government is to do nothing itself and if possible to prevent anything occuring which will precipitate one additional factor into the all-important discussions which are now taking place in Europe.'

King's evasions and his reluctance to have foreign policy even debated in the House sprang from his strong desire to keep Canada united. Fearful of arousing the deep resentment that swept French Canada during the conscription

THE SHAPE OF THINGS TO COME

From the paper *Cry Havoc,* in the Woodsworth Papers Scrapbook (1932-9), Public Archives of Canada.

crisis of the First World War and conscious of the readiness of Duplessis and other Quebec 'nationalist' politicians to use the lingering suspicion of English-Canadian 'imperialism' as a certain source of votes, King sought to avoid definition of his real policy. That policy was to commit a 'united' Canada to the support of British military action should the European peace be shattered in a war of aggression. Like other western leaders he continued to indulge in the wishful thought that Hitler could be contained by judicious appeasement without serious revitalization of the League and without a Russian alliance. In 1937 he talked with the German dictator, whom he completely misunderstood, and then went on to London, where he left Prime Minister Chamberlain in no doubt about Canada's support of Britain in the event of a European war. In 1938 he informed Chamberlain, upon the British leader's return from Munich, that 'the heart of Canada is rejoicing tonight at the success which has crowned your unremitting efforts for peace'.

In the country few people questioned King's policy. Lamenting the emasculation of the League, John Dafoe of the *Winnipeg Free Press* asked after Munich, 'What's the cheering for?', and in the Commons Woodsworth spoke for a Canadian initiative to reinvigorate the League. But even stronger than the voices that began to call for rearmament and recognition of the real threat posed by Hitler's Germany were those that spoke from the crest of North American isolationism. Taking their cue partly from the neutrality campaign in the United States and partly from the decade's surge of Canadian nationalism a probable majority of Canadians believed that their country could in fact remain neutral in the event of a European war. King did little to disabuse the public mind in this respect, while at the same time he himself never had any doubt about the decision that would quickly be taken in the event of war. While he parried the first British suggestion that Canada become the base of a Commonwealth air-training program he did not discourage further discussion of the subject and as early as 1937 began cautious increases in the military budget. The government also made no objection to the placing of large British munitions orders in Canada in 1938 while it declared in the House that 'we have no more information than is in the possession of the honourable members.'

With this policy of preparing to support a British war effort while continuing to deny such intention, King's chief Quebec lieutenant, Ernest Lapointe, was in complete agreement. Lapointe believed that although a British declaration of war was still legally binding upon Canada, according to the old Laurier formula the nature and extent of Canadian involvement remained a matter for Ottawa's decision. He also believed that Quebec would go along with a Canadian entry into war once the crisis arrived, but that it would be too risky to test Quebec opinion without the assistance of crisis pressures. Thus, like King, he was very short with parliamentary questions that sought to elicit the government's real policy. In 1938 when the Minister of National Defence, Ian Mackenzie, incautiously declared in public that Canada must stand by Britain, Lapointe was asked to say whether this was government policy. He refused to support Mackenzie and asked the questioner, 'Does my honourable friend want to split the country right away?' Conversely, when J. T. Thorson of Selkirk moved a resolution in 1939 declaring a Canadian right of neutrality, King refused to entertain it, with the now standard rhetorical question and brief comment: 'Why divide Canada to provide against a contingency that may not arise, or if it does, may not come until the situation has materially changed? The same consideration of the overwhelming importance of national unity which has led this government to decline to make premature and inappropriate statements of possible belligerency prevent it from recommending actions to declare possible neutrality.' Requests that the government should embargo shipments of strategic materials to the fascist nations and Japan met with the same response.

The King-Lapointe policy beyond doubt brought Canada into the Second World War without substantial overt division. Without a formal declaration of the right of neutrality Canada was, by the judgement of her own Minister of Justice, at war from the time of the British declaration on September 3, 1939. Yet the government acted as if this were not the case. In a special session of Parliament authorization for a separate Canadian war declaration was obtained with only J. S. Woodsworth rising to oppose the move in an unrecorded vote. Between September 3 and the Canadian declaration on September 10 the United States regarded Canada as neutral, but the legal right to that fictitious neutrality was established only with the declaration of war itself. While a number of French-Canadian members of Parliament voiced opposition to the war none rose to oppose the vote in the House. Clearly the majority accepted the leadership of Lapointe and the government's assurance that there would be no conscription. In English-speaking Canada in the years preceding the outbreak of the war many who had been supporters of neutrality began to shift their opinions as Hitler's implacable purpose became harder to deny, and by the summer of 1939 even the C.C.F., which was committed to neutrality by its preceding national convention, was deeply divided on the issue. The very successful visit of King George VI and Queen Elizabeth in the summer of 1939 also did much to undermine neutralist feeling amongst English-speaking Canadians and thus make possible a wider 'automatic' support of British policy.

Yet the extent of the 'unity' can be exaggerated. With a population slightly over eleven million there were still some 529,000 Canadians unemployed. Despite the signing of a trade agreement with the United States in 1937, which ended the sequence of tariff retaliation, and an extension of that agreement in 1938, which further reduced tariffs between the two countries, the Canadian economy was recovering but slowly from the long depression. As a result, many of the enlistments for the first Canadian Division were the products of relief camps and work projects for the unemployed who brought with them a feeling of resignation rather than patriotic enthusiasm. Again, the C.C.F. gave support to the war declaration on the assumption that Canada's contribution would be basically economic, and this was certainly true also of most of French Canada. For Quebec, 'unity' was represented by J. A. Blanchette who, for the government, seconded the Address in Reply to the Speech from the Throne: 'It cannot be reasonably contended, after due reflection, that it would not be wise to co-operate to a reasonable extent with France and England in the present conflict, taking into account, however, our resources, and our capacity, and without sacrificing our vital interests . . . .'

Unity had been bought by the methods of evasion. 'Our vital interests' was a phrase that meant different things to different classes and different regions and was given no precision by federal leadership. In Quebec there had been strong sympathy voiced for General Franco and for the cororatist form of government during the Spanish Civil War, while the war with Germany, when it came, was still widely regarded as another British imperial conflict. Failure to clarify a specifically Canadian relation to the events that led to the conflict, let alone to exercise any influence upon those events, meant that the nation drifted into the greatest crisis of the twentieth century by default. While the war appeared to 'solve' such problems as the right of neutrality, the slackness in the economy, and even the federal distribution of powers, and while it called forth extraordinary courage and organizing abilities from the Canadian people, in fact it merely swept under the table the unresolved questions of the thirties.

9. Through the Second World War

COLONEL C. P. STACEY

In the autumn of 1939 it was just ten years since the onset of the Great Depression; and Canada, not yet fully recovered from the long and debilitating struggle against economic misfortune, found herself plunged, for the second time in a generation, into a world war. It was the beginning of six years of conflict. Those years would bring the Dominion triumphs and frustrations, achievements and embarrassments, glory and sacrifice on foreign battlefields, and crisis and recrimination on Parliament Hill.

I

In September 1939 approximately 11,300,000 people lived in Canada, whereas the population when the First World

War broke out in 1914 had been less than 8,000,000. The worst of the depression was long over; yet in 1939 estimates of the number of the unemployed still ran as high as 600,000, the federal government was still spending great sums on relief, and many of the young men who would have to fill the ranks of the services in the new war had seldom or never had a steady job. Factory-owners, hungry for orders, were disappointed that the Canadian and British rearmament programs had produced so few. The national government's revenues, which in 1933 had fallen to the lowest point since 1918, had climbed by 1938 well above the then record-breaking total of 1929; but export trade was still depressed.

Canada's approach to war had paralleled Britain's. Economic disorganization had been accompanied by political uncertainty. Isolationism, nourished by the memory of the

Prophetic Harmony?

From the *Winnipeg Free Press*, April 1, 1939.

blood-bath of 1914-18, and with no politician daring to challenge it, had yielded very gradually to the realization that Hitler would be checked only by force. Political leadership was largely hamstrung by recollections of how the country had been split by the conscription controversy of 1917-18 and fear of a repetition of it. Only in the last week of March 1939, when Hitler, by tearing up the Munich agreement of the previous autumn, had made war virtually certain, was a temporary answer to this dilemma found. It was enunciated by Dr. R. J. Manion, the leader of the Conservative Opposition: 'full cooperation with Britain in wartime', but 'no conscription of Canadians to fight outside our borders in any war'. Three days later the Prime Minister, Mr. King, associated himself with this fateful formula.

In those days few Canadians drew much comfort from the new national status that had been won for their country by the soldiers of the old war. Under those lowering skies the fact that in 1931 the Statute of Westminster had established the formal independence of the Dominions within the Commonwealth did not seem a matter of dominating significance, any more than the fact that there were Canadian diplomatic missions now in Washington, Paris, and Tokyo. Canada's action–in contrast with 1914–in issuing her own declaration of war against Germany, and issuing it only on September 10, 1939, after one week of purely formal neutrality, was to appear perhaps rather more important in retrospect than it did at the time. What men asked themselves at the moment was what unknown horrors the war would let loose, and whether the always shaky unity of English and French Canada, so sadly buffeted two decades before, could stand the strain of this new conflict. No one sang 'Rule Britannia', as people had in 1914. Grimly, but of their own free will and in a spirit of reluctant resolution, the Canadians went into their second war against the formidable folk of Germany.

It fell to the third administration of Mr. Mackenzie King, formed in 1935, to lead the country through the whole six years of conflict. It was not a government of warriors, though it did include a number of men who had fought in the 1914 war, and one–J. L. Ralston–who had been a legendary battalion commander in the Canadian Corps and, it was said, would have got the Victoria Cross had exception not been taken to his having exposed himself in a manner unsuitable to his rank. King himself was the most civilian of men, and has been credited by one of his numerous official biographers with possessing a 'deep-seated and life-long' distrust of the army–not perhaps the best of qualifications for a minister conducting a great war. Until nearly the end of the struggle, the controlling factor in his military policy was the determination to avoid overseas conscription at almost any cost. But his was certainly an able government: possibly the ablest that has ever ruled in Canada. Such people as C. D. Howe, who as Minister of Munitions and Supply showed himself something of a genius in matters of war production, and J. L. Ilsley, the rugged Maritimer whose transparent honesty helped him as Minister of Finance to retain the liking and confidence of Canadians even while taxing them as they had never been taxed before, were not untypical of it. Angus L. Macdonald, the popular Premier of Nova Scotia, joined the Cabinet in 1940 as Naval Minister. Ernest Lapointe, the senior representative of French Canada, deserves a high place on the roll of Canadian patriots; and when he died in 1941 King, by what turned out to be one of his most fortunate strokes, was able to replace him with Louis S. St. Laurent, distinguished alike for ability and integrity.

Whatever else the government was, however, it was not glamorous; and glamour is a useful thing in time of war. King's own flabby person and personality carried little suggestion of forceful leadership. There was no one on the government front bench who could strike sparks from the House of Commons or the country. The ministers were, some of them at least, genuinely great public servants, but they lacked the capacity to inspire their countrymen. The most compelling Canadian personality of the war period was not a politician but a soldier–General A. G. L. McNaughton; and when, in an evil hour for himself, Mc-

Naughton went into politics, it was under conditions that made him ineffective. King was childishly incensed when Canadians spoke of 'our leaders, Churchill and Roosevelt'; but Canada possessed no personality to challenge those two, and it is possible that the strongly marked hostility of the Canadian forces to their own government (and to King particularly) was influenced by a certain embarrassment born of comparing the Canadian Prime Minister with the dynamic and dominating British and American chiefs.

II

The Canadian war effort had an unimpressive beginning. The military policy of limited liability, which London had finally thrown over in the spring of 1939, before the actual outbreak, ruled in Ottawa until the collapse of France over a year later. Peace-time ideas of economy and treasury control were still dominant; the program was tailored to the domestic political situation rather than to the menace posed by the enormously dangerous enemy whom Canada had chosen to challenge. Such policies can be safely indulged in only by countries with powerful friends and great geographical obstacles standing between them and their foes.

On September 1, 1939, orders were issued to mobilize the 'Mobile Force' of two divisions provided for in the Militia's existing Defence Scheme. Four days later, when great numbers of men had already been enlisted, the Chiefs of Staff were instructed that there was to be 'no stimulation to recruiting at the present time', and almost at once recruiting was suspended in a good many units. In spite of this official cold water, the men of the country came forward in their thousands. Patriots, idealists, adventurers, perhaps some who were merely hungry, they volunteered in numbers greater than the examining doctors could cope with. Over 58,000 were taken into the army in the first month. Many others were rejected, among them numerous old soldiers of 1914-18 who were anxious to serve once more but who could no longer meet the medical standards. Much smaller numbers were enlisted by the navy and the air force.

There were two provinces where recruiting was slow: Saskatchewan, basically agricultural and with a population containing large numbers of recent European immigrants, and predominantly French-speaking Quebec, still nursing the memory of the hated conscription measure of 1917. Yet French Canadians did enlist in very considerable numbers, and some French-speaking units were among the first to reach full strength.

Indeed, the dominant fact in these early days was the unity of the country. After the pre-war controversies and apprehensions it seemed hard to believe, and people who had had little sympathy with King's policy of avoiding commitments and postponing decisions were heard expressing surprised satisfaction with its results. Nevertheless it is evident in retrospect that the unity of 1939, vital as it was at that moment, was largely artificial. It owed its existence in great part to the government's policy of a 'moderate' war effort, and above all to its adoption of the Conservative leader's formula, the rejection of overseas conscription. But unfortunately moderate war is a contradiction in terms, and, as the struggle continued and the strain increased, the policy of limited liability was certain to break down, and the unity of Canada would break with it. Only a short war could have fully vindicated the King policies; and this war was to be a long one. For the moment, however, unity was remarkably complete, and in Quebec André Laurendeau, then a youthful extremist agitating actively against taking part in the struggle with Hitler, had the feeling of not being followed by the mass of his French-Canadian compatriots.

That the country in general was prepared for the moment to accept the King war policies was demonstrated by two political crises that arose within the first six months. Maurice Duplessis, the nationalist premier of Quebec, chose to call a provincial election on the issue of war measures infringing provincial autonomy; it came close to being a threat of a declaration of neutrality. The Quebec members of King's

Cabinet, led by Lapointe, met this really appalling menace squarely. Against the Prime Minister's advice, they proclaimed that if Duplessis were returned they would resign, leaving Quebec without representation in the Cabinet at Ottawa; at the same time they reaffirmed the government's pledge against overseas conscription. In the election of October 26, 1939, Duplessis was heavily defeated, and did not return to power until 1944.

The second crisis came on King's other flank, in Ontario. The premier of Ontario, Mitchell Hepburn (a Liberal, but bitterly hostile to King), put through the legislature in January 1940 a resolution condemning the federal government's war policies as weak and inadequate–precisely the reverse of the criticisms that had come from Quebec. King's response was to dissolve Parliament (which was nearing the end of its legal span of life) and appeal to the people. In the election of March 26 the government swept the country; it won every seat but one in Quebec and a majority of those in Ontario. King had made an acute calculation in going to the country before the war had entered a critical phase, before violent passions had been aroused, and at a time when his 'moderate' war effort still commanded general support. He was now firmly in power for the duration of the war. The Conservative parliamentary opposition was and remained extraordinarily inefficient and ineffective, and the most formidable threats to King's position, as time passed, came from within his own Cabinet, the results of the developing strain of the war.

The mainspring of Mackenzie King's conception of the national effort was his fear of conscription for overseas service and its adverse effects upon the country's unity and, doubtless, his party's chances of continuing in power. It followed that he was consistently hostile to a large army. He saw the Canadian contribution to the war as centring in the development of war industry (which in addition to enabling many Canadians to make money would keep them safely at home), with the military effort concentrated in the air force and to a lesser extent on the navy. Those services, he thought, were unlikely to make demands on manpower that might result in conscription. Nevertheless, these conceptions were in great part defeated: by the logic of the situation and the way the war developed; by the pressure of some of King's colleagues; and by the fact that the Canadian people, conditioned by memories of 1914-18, perversely persisted in thinking of a war effort primarily in terms of a fighting army.

By about the middle of September 1939 the government had decided upon the main lines of its military program, including the dispatch of one army division overseas; and on September 19 it announced it. The program also included a large air-training scheme, for which the British government had asked. But on September 26 that government broached a much bigger project–which became the British Commonwealth Air Training Plan. Had it been proposed earlier it is possible that no army expeditionary force would have gone to England that year; for the Canadian government, and King in particular, embraced the idea with enthusiasm and sought to make it the country's chief military contribution. An important contribution to victory it was, for in the end the Plan produced over 131,000 air-crew personnel (Britons, Australians, New Zealanders, and–the majority–Canadians). But it brought troubles in its train. Indeed, it broke the back of the Royal Canadian Air Force. The strength and energy of the R.C.A.F. were diverted into training in Canada, and when Canadian graduates of the Plan began to become available in numbers most of them were dispersed through the Royal Air Force remote from Canadian contact or control. Basically this was because in 1939 the Canadian government felt unable to spend the money to maintain them. The so-called R.C.A.F. squadrons formed overseas had, for a long period, partly Canadian air crew but British ground crew and British-financed equipment; and even the Canadian air crew were paid by the British taxpayer except for the difference between British and Canadian rates! As long as this situation lasted the 'Canadianization' program pursued from 1941 onwards by the energetic and compassionate Air Minister, C. G. Power, with a view to producing as far as possible a genuinely Canadian overseas air force, was largely illusory. After Canada, in 1943, assumed the whole cost of the R.C.A.F. overseas the program began to show more results.

The catastrophic Allied reverse in France in the early summer of 1940, the Dunkirk evacuation, and the French collapse marked a tremendous divide in the Canadian effort. Canada and the Commonwealth looked into the pit of defeat. The dollar suddenly ceased to seem important. Limited liability was abandoned – except in the important item of manpower, for the government continued to stand by the pledge against overseas conscription. The National Resources Mobilization Act of June 1940 authorized the use of compulsion for home defence. With the great army of France suddenly swept from the board, more divisions were desperately needed, and for a time, it seems, even Mackenzie King did not oppose the expansion of the Canadian Army or the dispatch of more troops overseas. Four Canadian destroyers – the whole available effective force – sailed across the Atlantic to join the fight in the waters around the British Isles. Similarly, an R.C.A.F. fighter squadron was hurriedly dispatched and fought in the Battle of Britain later in the summer. And with British orders for equipment pouring in, and the expanding Canadian forces themselves in great need of weapons, the Canadian economic front suddenly began to develop in a manner unknown in the early months of the war.

Starting late, and from a very narrow base – for the country had almost no peace-time munitions industry – the production effort did not reach its peak until 1943; but it achieved proportions far beyond anything hitherto seen in Canada. Whereas in 1914-18 no weapons had been made except Ross rifles, now a wide variety of small arms and guns, ships, and aircraft were manufactured. The outstanding achievement was in the automotive field; nearly 800,000 motor vehicles were produced for the Allied forces. At the summit of the effort in 1943, some 1,100,000 persons were employed in war industry, as compared with a total of

1,086,000 who ever served in the armed forces. The estimated gross national product at market prices rose from $5,598,000,000 in 1939 to $11,897,000,000 in 1944. The Dominion government's total expenditure was $553,063,098 in 1939, and was up to $5,322,253,505 in 1944. These statistics make the financial calculations of the government and its advisers in the first year of the war look timid indeed.

Canadians on the home front were lucky by comparison with the people of Britain, infinitely lucky by comparison with those in countries overrun by the enemy. Yet they did suffer privations, and some of them were more serious than the sad fate of being unable to buy a new car in the peacetime manner whenever they chose. Rationing did not appear on any considerable scale until after the further intensification of the war following the attack by Japan at the end of 1941, but during 1942 coupon rationing of gasoline and various foods began; for the rest of the war Canadians made do with half a pound of sugar each per week. Alcoholic drinks were in short supply. Clothing was not rationed, but production of civilian garments was controlled. The disappearance of silk and nylon stockings was a blow to women. The public, however, had reason to be grateful to the Wartime Prices and Trade Board, which operated the country's price controls. The Board, with proper pride, calculated that the cost of living in Canada rose only 19 per cent during the six years of the Second World War, as compared with 54 per cent in 1914-18.

Economic discomforts on the whole were cheerfully borne. They were minor compared to the sorrow and deprivation resulting from the prolonged absence overseas of hundreds of thousands of sons and husbands, the constant fear for their safety, the all-too-frequent telegrams bringing news of death or wounds suffered in action against the enemy by land or sea or air. And many a home was broken by the long separation, leaving tragic social consequences which are felt to this day.

III

'Senior Service' by virtue of British inheritance if not of Canadian history, the Royal Canadian Navy remained throughout the war the smallest and the least publicized of the three services, happy in that its operations seldom became matters of political controversy. Yet it grew enormously in the course of the conflict, and there were few seas where its guns were not heard before the war was over.

The navy of 1939–its fighting element comprised six destroyers–was far too small to fight an independent naval war. The Canadian government kept the ultimate control of the force, and Canadian naval units were not sent out of Canadian waters or transferred from one theatre to another without the consent of the Cabinet War Committee in Ottawa. In most situations throughout the war, however, Canadian ships served and fought under the operational control of the Royal Navy. There was one considerable exception. In the summer of 1941 the R.C.N. organized a Newfoundland Escort Force with headquarters at St. John's. Later in the year, as a result of arrangements made between Churchill and Roosevelt at their Argentia meeting, this force was transferred to U.S. naval command, even though the United States was still neutral. This arrangement lasted until 1943, by which time few United States ships were operating in the area. Then the Canadian North-West Atlantic command was set up and a Canadian naval officer took charge of operations in the ocean areas off Canada's east coast, subject only to the qualification that the United States retained strategic responsibility for the whole Western Atlantic.

The Royal Canadian Navy was mainly a small-ship navy; its main battleground was the North Atlantic and its chief antagonist the German submarines that sought to sever the vital line of communications joining the fighting forces and the factories of North America to the United Kingdom. The battle was fought with destroyers, corvettes, frigates, and minesweepers, supported by naval and still more by land-based aircraft. It was conducted under the grimmest conditions of peril and discomfort, on one of the nastiest seas in the world. The seamen who manned the ships sought relaxation in Halifax, a place they apparently did not find particularly agreeable. Perhaps their feelings found expression on VE day–the day of victory in Europe–when mobs in which sailors were prominent wrecked a good part of the city.

Before that day came the R.C.N. had destroyed, or shared in destroying, 27 German submarines. It had also been active in the naval war in European waters, taking part in the landings at Dieppe and in the Mediterranean, and making a very considerable contribution to the Normandy D Day and the operations that preceded and followed it. The tiny service of 1939 had expanded to a strength of about 100,000 men and women, and it was a commonplace that some of the best seamen were lads from the prairies who had never seen the sea until they went down to it in the ships of the R.C.N.

The Royal Canadian Air Force was much larger–roughly 250,000 men and women served in it–and its tasks were even more varied. Nearly 100,000 of its personnel were absorbed in conducting the great British Commonwealth Air Training Plan in Canada. A large Home War Establishment guarded Canadian coastal waters, fought submarines–at home and abroad the R.C.A.F. was credited with destroying, or sharing in the destruction of, 23 U-boats–and took part in the air operations against the Japanese in the Aleutian Islands in 1942-3. And overseas a total–ultimately–of 48 R.C.A.F. squadrons, becoming more and more truly Canadian as Mr. Power's 'Canadianization' policy made its slow and painful progress, fought the enemy around the globe. At the same time a great number of individual Canadians, graduates of the Air Training Plan, served in units of the Royal Air Force. The controversy goes on still as to whether a national squadron was more effective than one of these mixed R.A.F. squadrons in which air crew from half a dozen different Commonwealth countries served cheerfully together. Canadians did a great deal of air fighting but got only a limited share of air command. Only one operational air vice-marshal's appointment was available to them overseas – the command of No. 6 (R.C.A.F.) Group in the R.A.F. Bomber Command, which was formed at the beginning of 1943. The final strength of the Group was 14 squadrons.

Mackenzie King and his colleagues, when they authorized the heavy commitment of the R.C.A.F. to Bomber Command, certainly did not realize what this meant in terms of loss of life. No military task of the war took a more appalling toll than the strategic air offensive against Germany; none called for greater or more sustained fortitude than that demanded of the young airmen who made the long flights against Berlin or the Ruhr, carried out grimly night after night in the face of searchlights, radar, flak, night fighters, and all the concentrated resources of German defence science. This was a battle in which few of the casualties lived to be recorded as wounded or prisoners of war; the vast majority of those shot down died. No one knows how many Canadians served in Bomber Command; but just under 10,000 lost their lives in it. This (nearly double the Canadian Army's loss in the 20-month campaign in Italy) accounted for far more than half of the R.C.A.F.'s total of 17,000 fatal casualties – and for the fact that the air force had far more such casualties in proportion to its strength than either of the other services.

The air force and the navy were both fighting the enemy on many fronts and on an increasing scale before the army really got into action. Yet as we have already said the Canadian people certainly in some degree equated the war effort with the army. This may have been partly because the army was the largest service – all told, some 730,000 Canadians served in it – and therefore closest to the community as a whole. It was certainly due in part to national memories of 1914-18 and the Canadian Corps. But there was probably also a consciousness, if only a dim one, that the army, inheriting the old Corps' traditions, was the most national of the three forces. The Royal Canadian Navy was overshadowed by the Royal Navy and fought dispersed across the seas, often under British or American local command. The Royal Canadian Air Force overseas had a long struggle before it achieved something like national status. But the overseas Army – until the great aberration of 1943 – served as a national body, under a leader of vivid personality whose Canadianism was very evident. In action it fought under British higher headquarters – the Eighth Army in Italy, the 21st Army Group in North-West Europe; but it fought in united national formations.

National spirit had moved strongly in the old Corps, especially in 1917-18 under Sir Arthur Currie; but this new Army was in one sense more genuinely Canadian. Of the men of the Canadian Expeditionary Force of 1914-18 only 51.3 per cent were Canadian-born. In 1939-45, no less than 84.6 per cent of the Army's personnel reported Canada as their native country.

Its experience was also quite different. The C.E.F. was involved in heavy fighting from the spring of 1915 onwards. The overseas force in the second war, which had expected to join the British Expeditionary Force in France in 1940, found itself condemned by events to years of garrison duty and training in England. During those years it was built up, under General McNaughton's direction, from a single half-trained division of infantry to an efficient small Army of two corps, comprising five divisions (two of them armoured) and two independent armoured brigades.

Not the least interesting phenomenon of these garrison years was the development of the Canadians' relationship with the British people. It began badly in the cold winter of 1939-40, the days of the 'phony war', when 'boredom, homesickness and a feeling of not being really needed' led the soldiers to write letters about England that shocked the censors who read them. Then came the Battle of Britain and the 'blitz', and the British people and their country suddenly began to look much more admirable to the troops. As the months passed, individual Canadians found their way into British homes and in many cases became almost members of the family. By the spring of 1944 the censors were reporting that in a batch of nearly 12,000 Canadian letters 'not one adverse comment' on British civilians had been seen. And when the war was over Canadian servicemen brought some 43,000 wives home from the British Isles. It was an extraordinary episode in social history and Commonwealth relations.

Only in December 1941 did the Canadian Army fight its first battle, when two battalions took part in the hopeless defence of Hong Kong against the Japanese. These troops were sent from Canada and had nothing to do with the force in England. That force had its baptism of fire in the bloody and unsuccessful raid on Dieppe (August 19, 1942). Both these tragic operations, followed as they were by further periods of inaction for Canadian troops, produced bitter, violent, and ill-informed discussion in Parliament and outside it. As time went on and the Army was still not fighting, demands that it should fight were heard in the press, on the platform, and at the council table. Ralston, the Defence Minister, and Lieut.-General Kenneth Stuart, the Chief of the General Staff, took this line. General McNaughton, commanding the First Canadian Army in Britain, was opposed to fighting for the sake of fighting, and had no doubt that the morale of his men would withstand even more prolonged inaction. He acquiesced when the Canadian government prevailed upon Mr. Churchill to insert the 1st Canadian Division into the order of battle for the Sicilian invasion in the summer of 1943. That autumn, when Ralston and Stuart, with the rather reluctant assent of Mackenzie King, got the British government to force upon the Allied Mediterranean command a Canadian corps headquarters and an armoured division that they did not need and did not want, there was almost an open break. At that moment the British War Office raised the question of McNaughton's fitness to command an army in the field. They were no doubt sincere in feeling that the heavy military and quasi-political responsibilities of the past four years had told upon him. At any rate, this, coming simultaneously with his difficulties with his own government, made McNaughton's position impossible, and he was forced out. The command passed after an interval to Lieut.-General H. D. G. Crerar, a competent and experienced Canadian professional soldier who had been commanding the Corps in Italy and who was now to command the First Canadian Army through the 1944-5 campaign in North-West Europe.

After its long period of inaction, the Canadian Army had its fill of bloody fighting in the final phases of the war. There is no need to relate in detail the story of its part in the great campaigns that began in Sicily in the south and in Normandy in the north. The battle honours on its regiments' colours will tell the tale for ever: Sicily, the Hitler Line, the Gothic Line; Normandy Landing, Caen, Falaise, The Scheldt, The Rhineland. Although the Canadian government at a remarkably early date began to ask for the return of the Corps that it had insisted on sending to Italy, the war with Germany was nearly over when the two segments of the Army were reunited under General Crerar's command in North-West Europe. British and other troops filled the gap in the First Canadian Army while the 1st Canadian Corps was fighting in the British Eighth Army far to the south. If one counts English, Scots, Irish, and Welsh, nearly a dozen nationalities fought under Crerar; and though the Canadian divisions were always the Army's solid core, the smooth and loyal cooperation of these varied national elements against the common enemy was a particularly inspiring element in its campaign.

Though the Germans were on the defensive by the time the Canadian Army got into major action, and the two campaigns in which it played its part were in general an unbroken series of victories, victory seldom came easily. The fierce house-to-house struggle at Ortona in December 1943, the desperate little fight beside the frostbound Maas at Kapelsche Veer in January 1945, may stand as types of bloody local operations; the figures published by Field-Marshal Montgomery, showing that the two Canadian infantry divisions had heavier casualties than any other divisions under his command in Normandy, testify to the burden Canadians bore in the major battles. Yet the total loss was far below that exacted by the carnage of the Western Front in 1915-18; the Army's fatal casualties in the Second World War, including deaths from natural causes, amounted to about 23,000.

IV

Canada was in 1939 a formally independent country, as she had not been in 1914. It remained to be seen how much this independence meant in practical international terms in the midst of a great war, when a nation's status is measured less in constitutional formulas than in the numbers of divisions it places in the field.

The war in its first stage (1939-40) was conducted on behalf of the Allies by an Anglo-French Supreme War Council. It appears that Canada never either sought or was offered a seat on this body or any direct relationship to it. For a country bent on a 'moderate' war effort and having no desire to be pressed to do more, this modest policy may have had a practical appeal. At any rate, except that the established diplomatic relations with France continued, Canada's relation to the direction of the war was through the Commonwealth channel; and that channel itself was not very active. A minister (T. A. Crerar) visited London in the autumn of 1939; there was day-to-day liaison through the High Commissioner in Ottawa and London; but when in the spring of 1940 the Chamberlain government in England proposed a conference of Commonwealth prime ministers, Mackenzie King successfully discouraged the idea. He argued that it would be politically difficult for him to leave Canada and that he should be available there 'in the event of a situation arising in which he might be called upon to assist in maintaining the most friendly relations between Great Britain and the United States'.

After the French collapse which shortly followed, Canada continued to take a similar line. The war was conducted by the British War Cabinet (but increasingly, in practice, by the new Prime Minister, Churchill, and the three Chiefs of Staff), with limited consultation with the Dominions. Australia wanted an Imperial War Cabinet as in 1917-18; Churchill and King unitedly – though clearly from different motives – opposed it. The importance of the United States to British victory was obvious; and King continued to see himself as playing a vital part in relations with that country. He was a whole-hearted adherent of the theory that saw Canada as the 'linchpin' of Anglo-American relations. For a time in 1940 it seemed that that theory held the field, and King scored an independent point with his meeting with Roosevelt in August and the issuance of the 'Ogdensburg Declaration'. This certainly initiated a new era in Canadian-American relations, and few dogs on either side of the border barked against it. But the linchpin theory suffered a serious setback, and King himself a severe shock, in August 1941, when Churchill and Roosevelt held their meeting in the waters of Newfoundland without previous consultation with or notice to him. For a short period of the war Canada had been Britain's strongest ally; that period drew to a close when Hitler attacked Russia in June 1941, and its western twilight ended abruptly on December 7, 1941, when the bombs that fell on Pearl Harbor blew the United States into the war. Thereafter Canada was a very junior partner and sometimes treated with scant ceremony.

The Combined Chiefs of Staff, set up early in 1942 to co-ordinate the military effort of the alliance, was a purely Anglo-American committee. Canada, as a considerable munitions producer, sought membership on the Munitions Assignment Board, which allotted completed stores among the Allies; her application was rejected, though she might have achieved limited membership. She did become a member of two of the four Combined Boards that supposedly co-ordinated other aspects of Anglo-American war affairs (the Combined Food Board and the Combined Production and Resources Board), but these were not really very powerful or important bodies. Canada, in common with other 'middle powers' of the alliance, was excluded from the great strategic conferences where war policy was decided. This applied even to the two conferences held at Quebec in 1943 and 1944, but the point did not greatly trouble Mackenzie King. 'I said to Ralston,' he wrote in his diary, 'the important thing was to have the meeting held at Quebec. That, of itself, would cause all else to work out satisfactorily.' Having the conference held on Canadian soil seemed to him a great political advantage to himself and to his party. That Canada had no voice in the higher direction of the war he regretted, but he never made a very serious protest.

V

We have referred to the adoption by both major political parties in 1939 of the formula 'no conscription for overseas service'. Neither departed from this formula in the general election of the early spring of 1940. But from the time when the war was intensified following the collapse of France demands were increasingly heard from English-speaking Canada for not merely the home-defence conscription authorized by the new National Resources Mobilization Act (above, page 283), but unlimited conscription. At the Cabinet table Colonel Ralston was mentioning such conscription as a possible if remote future requirement as early as April 1941. The attack by Japan eight months later produced an immediate agitation for repeal of the section of the N.R.M.A. forbidding the use of compulsion in connection with military service abroad. And after much soul-searching Mackenzie King decided that the best course was to appeal to the people in a plebiscite to release the government from its pledges against overseas conscription. This was announced when Parliament met in January 1942.

The result was a serious rift between English and French Canada, shattering the precarious unity of 1939. French-speaking Quebec considered (with good reason) that the 1939 pledges had been mainly addressed to itself, and took the view that the government was now trying to wriggle out of them by the device of a plebiscite in which the vast majority of voters would be English-speaking. For the first time the element in Quebec actively opposing the war found itself possessed of a popular and powerful issue. The *Ligue pour la défense du Canada* was formed to encourage French Canadians to vote 'No'. André Laurendeau, once discouraged by the public reaction in 1939, now found the movement growing 'like an avalanche'. And in the vote taken on April 27, Quebec isolated itself. In the country as a whole 2,945,514 people voted 'Yes' (for release) against 1,643,006 voting 'No'. In Quebec the proportion was reversed: 376,188 voted 'Yes'; 993,663 voted 'No'.

King had no intention whatever of actually introducing compulsory overseas service unless and until he was forced to; but the government proceeded to amend the National Resources Mobilization Act by removing the prohibition on such service. The result was the resignation of one French-Canadian minister, P. J. A. Cardin. At the other extremity of the Cabinet, J. L. Ralston resigned in a dispute over the procedure to be followed if circumstances demanded the actual application of compulsion. He was prevailed upon to stay; but his resignation remained in King's hands. Under the amended act, conscripts were sent to serve in various areas of the North American zone, but none were dispatched to Europe until late in 1944.

It was the heavy infantry casualties in Normandy in 1944 that precipitated the final conscription crisis. 'General service' enlistments (as distinct from compulsory call-ups for service in Canada) had fallen off seriously since early in 1943; and when the Normandy battles took a heavier toll in infantry, and a lighter one in other arms, than the Allies' calculations had anticipated, the supply of trained infantry reinforcements overseas was not equal to the demand. In Canada, however, there were thousands of trained conscript infantrymen who refused to 'go active'. The immediate overseas expedient was to 'remuster' men of other corps as infantry and give them emergency training. The result was that inadequately trained men were sent into battle. Colonel Ralston made a quick visit to the fighting fronts and returned to Ottawa on October 18 to recommend that the trained 'zombies' – the opprobrious term some too-clever person had coined for the conscripts – be sent overseas. King was not yet ready to consent. After prolonged wrangling, the Prime Minister, remarking that he still held Ralston's 1942 resignation, dismissed the Defence Minister on November 1. Ralston was succeeded by General McNaughton, who had been his bitter enemy since his own dismissal a year before, and was now prepared to make a final attempt to make the voluntary system work.

The attempt failed. After three weeks during which the great majority of the 'zombies' continued to resist appeals to them to accept general service voluntarily, the Chief of the General Staff (Lieut.-General J. C. Murchie) and the other military members of the Army Council reported on November 22 expressing the considered opinion that the voluntary system could not meet the immediate reinforcement problem. Mackenzie King seems to have told some of his confidants later that this action by the generals represented a grave threat to constitutional government and that, faced with something like a military revolt, he was 'struck dumb'. This is poppycock, though King almost immediately convinced himself that it was true. Actually, he had come by November 22 to feel that overseas conscription, which he had opposed so long and so bitterly, had become a necessity if his government was to survive. Public opinion in English Canada had taken a long time to harden on the conscription issue – the defeat of the conscriptionist Conservative leader Arthur Meighen by a C.C.F. candidate in a Toronto constituency in February 1942 was evidence of this – but now it was virtually unanimous. The Army was at last in full action, and it must be supported. This feeling was powerfully reflected in the Cabinet. When King heard from McNaughton the news of the generals' advice, the superstitious Prime Minister wrote in his diary,

> This really lifts an enormous burden from my mind as after yesterday's Council it was apparent to me that it was only a matter of days before there would be no Government in

> Canada. . . . As I look at the clock from where I am standing as I dictate this sentence, the hands are both together at 5 to 11.

The following day the government tabled in Parliament an Order in Council providing for the dispatch overseas of 16,000 conscripts – approximately the number required to fill the reinforcement pools overseas.

King and his government and party were saved. One minister – C. G. Power – resigned. Ralston, who probably could have brought the Prime Minister down and, in the light of the treatment he had received, could scarcely have been criticized for doing so, supported the new policy. The House of Commons gave King a vote of confidence – though 34 French-Canadian members of his party voted against him. There was a wave of desertion among the conscripts – 7,800 were missing at one point – and there were what amounted to mutinies (a word avoided at the time) in some of the camps in British Columbia, where great numbers of home-defence troops had been concentrated in 1942 to provide against a Japanese menace that existed only in the excited imagination of the people of the province. But nearly 13,000 conscripts were actually sent overseas, where those who got into action performed much like any other reinforcements. Thanks to their arrival, and to the fact that casualties in the final phase were fewer than had been feared, the Canadian divisions were fully up to strength in their last battles.

King had overcome the most serious challenge he had ever faced. For the rest of his time in office his power in his party and in Parliament was more absolute than ever. He suffered only one humiliation – not a serious one, though it had about it a flavour of poetic justice: his defeat, by the service vote, in his own constituency of Prince Albert in the general election of 1945. It was McNaughton, whom King had used to save himself, who paid the price. The general failed of election to the House of Commons in a by-election and subsequently in the general election, being defeated by nonentities. He had deserved better of the Canadian people. He resigned the

National Defence portfolio in August 1945, after the defeat of Japan. It was the measure of that extraordinary man that this reverse was not the end of him. He was to go on to a further distinguished career of many years in the public service.

Although the servicemen apparently could not bring themselves to vote for Mackenzie King personally, they – and other Canadians – did vote pretty heavily for his government in that general election of June 1945, held after the defeat of Germany. (The armed services have voted Liberal ever since.) The country was evidently satisfied, on the whole, with King's conduct of affairs. At any rate, it was not prepared to turn him out in favour of the 'Progressive Conservatives' led by John Bracken, a former Manitoba premier who, though chosen leader in 1942, had followed the curious tactic of not seeking a seat in the House of Commons until the general election. The Liberal majority was materially reduced, but not to the point of danger. The Co-operative Commonwealth Federation, which King had once thought more dangerous to him than the Conservatives, got only 28 seats, almost all in the West.

VI

There was no post-war 'slump' in any extreme sense after 1945, though in 1945-6 there was a material decline in employment from the 1944 peak. By 1947 there was again 'full' employment. The gross national product at market prices rose from $11,759 million in 1945 to $15,450 million in 1948. The post-war years were essentially an extension of the period of economic growth initiated by the war, and as usual prosperity brought contentment and political stability.

On the whole, it was remarkable how smoothly and easily the country's one million service men and women were absorbed back into the civilian economy. The generous veterans' benefits accorded them contributed to this while at the same time giving the economy a fillip. Educational benefits brought many thousands of ex-service students into the universities, whose resources were strained as they were not to be again until the sixties. Although Canada remained a country whose prosperity depended on staple exports, the economy in which the new graduates found places was more industrialized than before the war; and industrial expansion continued. With it, inevitably, came increased urbanization. The census of 1951, which indicated an increase of population from 11,507,000 to 14,009,000 in the past decade, also showed that 62.9 per cent of Canadians were now town-dwellers as compared with only 54.4 per cent in 1941. A change in the definition of the terms 'urban' and 'rural' between the two censuses had the effect of somewhat exaggerating the change, but it is clear that the pace of urbanization had greatly quickened.

A new element on the Canadian peace-time industrial scene was the continuance of some of the defence industries created during the war. The fact that Canada was now maintaining much larger defence forces than before 1939 contributed to this. Some of these production facilities were directly owned by the national government, others (the aircraft and shipbuilding industries in particular) owed their continued existence mainly to government orders and encouragement.

Among the industries rapidly 'reconverted' from war production to peaceful purposes, none was more notable or more representative than the automotive industry, whose war-time achievements had been so striking. At the end of hostilities the demand for civilian cars was enormous, and the industry's resources were strained to cope with it. And the statistics of production rose year by year: from 104,819 cars and trucks 'made for sale in Canada' in 1946, to 262,775 three years later. The number of motor vehicles registered in Canada rose similarly – from 1,497,081 in 1945 to 2,290,628 in 1949; and the increase continued rapidly thereafter. The motor car was no new thing in 1945; but it was the generation after the Second World War that was to feel the full impact of the revolution wrought upon society by the internal-combustion engine. In 1939-45 it had added a new dimension to warfare, enabling campaigns to move across the map at a speed hitherto unknown; but at the same time it produced a new set of tactical problems, threatening to destroy the mobility it created simply by strangling the armies in their own traffic jams. It was now to do the same for civilian communities. Millions of dollars' worth of super-highways were required for cross-country movement; great cities found themselves throttled by increasing motor traffic, and were forced to spend more millions to provide new high-speed routes to carry it in and out; the death-toll in accidents rose steadily with the number of cars on the roads; and Canada's expensive railways, so grossly overbuilt early in the century, found themselves faced with ruinous competition from highway transport just when increasing population seemed to hold out the hope of genuinely economic operation.

In another respect too the motor industry was representative of the trends of the time. A British official history of the Second World War remarks, truly enough, 'The industry of the Dominion was dominated to an undue extent by automobile production. . . . Moreover, the whole of this industry and a large part of the others had been created by American firms. . . . The dependent character of Canada's industrial development was betrayed at many points.' These tendencies were reinforced after the war; indeed, the Canadian economy as a whole acquired an increasing dependence on the United States. Between the two world wars the United States had displaced Britain as the chief non-resident investor in Canada; and between 1945 and 1949 the total U.S. investment in Canada rose from $4,990 million to $5,906 million. By 1948, 39 per cent of Canadian manufacturing industry was controlled by residents of the United States. The figure increased sharply in subsequent years, and it was in the fifties that Canadians became painfully aware of the situation and began to be vocal about it; but the trend was well established long before 1950.

Another trend was a modest movement in the direction of the welfare state. Mackenzie King liked to think of himself as a social reformer and the friend of the working man; and within rather narrow limits he can be so regarded. His third administration passed at least two fairly notable pieces of social-security legislation. An amendment to the British North America Act passed in 1940 to establish the right of the Dominion Parliament to establish unemployment insurance – which had been successfully challenged in the courts – was followed immediately by the enactment of the Unemployment Insurance Act. In 1944 came the Family Allowances Act, providing what was popularly called the 'baby bonus' – a monthly payment to parents of up to eight dollars for each child under the age of sixteen. There was long discussion of a non-contributory system of old-age pensions; but the Old Age Security Act did not become law until 1951 (following yet another amendment to the B.N.A. Act) – twenty-four years after the Dominion's first ineffective old-age pension act, and forty-three years after Lloyd George's act in Britain.

VII

The conscription question, which did so much harm in 1917-18, had a less damaging effect in 1942-5 on relations between French and English Canada. The conscription policy of the First World War was introduced and administered with little regard for the feelings of the French-Canadian minority. In the Second World War the country was ruled by a prime minister whose power was largely rooted in Quebec, and who made it the cornerstone of his war policy to avoid overseas conscription, or at the very least to postpone it to the last moment. Although the French-Canadian extremists hated King as much as the English-speaking conscriptionist extremists did (it is interesting that the former were largely quite young men, while the latter frequently belonged to the 1914-18 generation), it is evident that the French-Canadian community as a whole recognized King's government as far more satisfactory from their point of view than any that could conceivably replace it were it defeated. When King was finally forced to accept overseas conscription to keep his Cabinet together, many Quebec members, we have seen, voted against him. Nevertheless his party continued to control the federal representation from Quebec; and it was largely thanks to him that the country came out of the war somewhat less divided than it had been in 1918.

Within the armed forces themselves 'French' and 'English' got on rather better than their civilian compatriots did. It was in the services that many a Canadian actually met for the first time members of the other section of the community. It would be idle to claim that the result was always to the advantage of national unity; but most people who were there would probably say that it was oftener good than bad, and sometimes it was very good indeed. The comradeship of the battlefield was an admirable solvent of traditional prejudices. Even among servicemen in Canada who never saw a battlefield, there were good effects. The men from Quebec who served in British Columbia came home with a heightened sense of Canadian realities (and it may not be out of place to remark, on the evidence of those in the best positions to know, that it was not French-Canadian soldiers who organized the disorders in the west-coast camps in 1944).

The Province of Quebec in the post-war era remained under the *Union Nationale* government of Maurice Duplessis. In the election of 1944, which brought him back to power, the electors rejected not only the Liberal ministry of Adélard Godbout, but also the ultra-nationalist, anti-war *Bloc Populaire*. Duplessis's strength lay mainly in the rural areas. His policy within Quebec may be described as authoritarian and anti-intellectual. Towards Ottawa he took an intransigent attitude, refusing, for instance, to co-operate in the construction of the Trans-Canada Highway (authorized by a federal act of 1949). Nevertheless it seemed evident that the events of 1939-45 had done little if any permanent damage to the relations of French and English Canadians. So far as English Canada was concerned, there had probably never been a time when there was so much disposition to understand Quebec and co-operate with her. And in 1949 a French-Canadian, Roman Catholic prime minister won the greatest electoral victory in the Dominion's history.

VIII

In the sphere of Commonwealth relations the independence of Canada was already almost complete; but in certain matters of detail it was widened. In 1947 the Canadian Parliament passed a statute of this tendency: the Canadian Citizenship Act established for the first time a status as Canadian citizen additional to that of British subject. The year 1949 (after King's actual retirement) saw two other measures. The Judicial Committee of the Privy Council in London ceased to be the highest court of appeal for Canadian cases; these would now stop at the Supreme Court of Canada. Had this been done earlier it would have been well for the powers of the central government. The other measure was the amendment of the British North America Act to permit further amendments to be made without reference to the British Parliament in matters not affecting the powers of the provinces.

Relations with the other point of the North Atlantic Triangle contained many more uncertainties than those with Britain and the Commonwealth. Intimate contact with the United States dated only from 1940 and the Ogdensburg Declaration, which announced the establishment of the Permanent Joint Board on Defence, Canada–United States. King undoubtedly was proud of the part he had played in bringing about this *rapprochement*, and considerable evidence is now available to document his tendency to overvalue the American connection and undervalue the British one. This tendency was probably natural to him, but it was encouraged by O. D. Skelton, the isolationist and anti-British Under-Secretary of State for External Affairs, who, until his death in 1941, was King's closest adviser. Nevertheless King's experience as the war proceeded seems to have somewhat moderated his enthusiasm in this direction; he became aware, for instance, of the assurance with which American officers operated in the Canadian North, acting as if they were on their own soil and sometimes omitting even lip-service to Canadian sovereignty. And the President with whom King had been on terms of a degree of personal friendship vanished from the scene in the spring of 1945. In these circumstances the war-time co-operation between the two countries continued into peace-time, but it was hedged about with safeguards. The statement issued jointly by the two countries in February 1947 announcing that military co-operation through the Permanent Joint Board would go on emphasized that the collaboration would be 'limited' and that pains would be taken to protect each country's sovereignty. The only new joint activity undertaken in the North in King's time was a modest program of weather stations.

Perhaps more important for the future was the government's changing attitude towards international organization and collective security. Canada played an active if modest part in the organization of the United Nations in 1945. Her representatives were not pleased with the attempts of the great powers to ensure a dominant voice for themselves in the new body – only great powers were invited to the Dumbarton Oaks conference where the plan was drafted, and the constitution of the Security Council gave each great power not only a permanent seat there but a right of veto – but they did not lead a crusade on the subject. In marked contrast to her attitude towards the League of Nations between the wars, she did not object to the U.N.'s being allowed to have 'teeth' to help it keep the peace. And Canada was glad to be elected a temporary member of the Security Council for the years 1948 and 1949.

More striking events were coming. As the Cold War between East and West took shape, the Canadian government made no attempt to isolate itself from it. As early as the autumn of 1945, the revelations of Soviet espionage activity in Ottawa as well as other Allied capitals had shocked the Canadian government and people. The year 1948 produced alarming developments: the *coup* that brought the Communists to power in Czechoslovakia, the Soviet blockade of Berlin. Canada had no share in the improvised Anglo-American airlift that maintained the life of West Berlin; but as discussion developed in and between western capitals on the desirability of forming some sort of western alliance to check the further advance of communism, the Canadian government took an active lead in the movement. It was apparent now that new men and new ideas were stirring in that government; whether they met any resistance from the Prime Minister it is impossible to say. Until 1946 the portfolio of External Affairs was held by the Prime Minister himself; but in September of that year Mackenzie King resigned it and Louis St. Laurent succeeded him. Just two years later an able and popular professional diplomatist, Lester B. Pearson, was prevailed upon to join the King Cabinet; he took the External Affairs portfolio, St. Laurent returning temporarily to the Department of Justice, of which he had formerly been Minister. As early as April 1948 (shortly after the *coup* in Czechoslovakia) St. Laurent declared that the best guarantee for peace was 'the organization of collective defence' under British, American, and French leadership; and no party in the House of Commons seriously challenged the proposition. In June the Vandenberg Resolution, incorporating the same principles, passed the U.S. Senate. In August St. Laurent became leader of the Liberal party; in November he succeeded King as Prime Minister. In April 1949 the North Atlantic Treaty was signed by twelve nations, including Britain, the United States, France, and Canada. The Dominion thus committed itself to an alliance whose members agreed to 'maintain and develop their individual and collective capacity to resist armed attack'. In pursuance of this obligation, Canada in 1951 and later years was to contribute an infantry brigade and an air division to the European forces of the North Atlantic Treaty Organization. Co-operation with the United States outside of NATO was also advancing. By 1949 'an early warning system to cover certain vital approaches and areas' was being developed in the North.

It is evident that the five years after the war – and especially, whether by coincidence or not, the period immediately preceding and following the retirement of Mackenzie King – witnessed a revolution in Canadian external policy. The policy of 'no commitments', which had ruled until the outbreak of war in 1939, had been entirely abandoned in favour of defensive alliances. The commitments that pre-war governments had refused to make to Britain had now been made to an alliance in which Britain was a partner; and it was fairly evident that there were other commitments, unpublished and perhaps undefined, to the United States under arrangements stemming from those of 1940. At the same time, as we have seen, Canada was maintaining armed forces very much larger than it had kept up before 1939. Neither aspect of the new policy was meeting any real criticism from Parliament or the public. The Second World War and the advent of the atomic age had clearly had a powerful effect upon the outlook of the Canadian people and their government.

External relations were a constant source of anxiety; internal relations – in the sense of relations between the Dominion government and the governments of the nine provinces – also presented unsolved problems, chiefly financial. The Royal Commission on Dominion-Provincial Relations (the 'Rowell-Sirois Commission') had reported in 1940, recommending a new basis for the division of revenues and responsibilities, but several provinces, notably Ontario, would have nothing to do with it. After the war the Dominion succeeded in negotiating individual financial agreements with seven provinces (all but Ontario and Quebec), but these were stopgap arrangements and no final and general solution was achieved.

In 1949 the nine provinces became ten. Newfoundland had stood aside at the time of the original Confederation in 1867, and thereafter when opportunities for union arose they were rejected by one party or the other. Union between Canada and Newfoundland was one of the good results of the Second World War.

It was perfectly obvious that the island of Newfoundland was an area of first-class importance to the security of Canada, and indeed of North America at large. Its significance for transatlantic aviation was clear long before the Second World War. Yet before 1939 Newfoundland had no defences whatever; and the island had lost its dominion status in 1934, when economic disaster forced it to call upon the United Kingdom for help, and government by an appointed commission was instituted. From the outbreak of war there was close co-operation between the Newfoundland and Canadian governments; and at the time of the French collapse in 1940 Canadian troops and aircraft were sent to the island, and an agreement was made placing Newfoundland's forces under Canadian command. Almost simultaneously the 'destroyers-for-bases deal' between Churchill and Roosevelt gave the United States military bases in the island, and U.S. forces began to arrive there early in 1941. For the rest of the war there were essentially two separate defence organizations – Canadian and American – in Newfoundland. The Canadian Army garrison rose to a total of nearly 6,000 men. Mackenzie King was very conscious of the importance of protecting Canada's permanent interests in the island.

War-time contacts no doubt somewhat diminished the Newfoundlanders' old anti-Canadian prejudices. After long debate the island's people went to the polls in 1948 to decide their future. Three choices were before them: continuance of commission government, revival of responsible government, and confederation with Canada on terms that had been discussed with Ottawa. Commission government was eliminated, but a second referendum was required to decide between the other two possibilities. It resulted in a small majority for union with Canada. Essentially it was a victory of the 'outports' over the commercial community of St. John's. Final terms of agreement were signed on December 11, and the union became effective at midnight of March 31–April 1, 1949. There were seven Newfoundland members in the new Canadian House of Commons that assembled later in the year; and the first premier of Newfoundland under the new regime was the formidable and irrepressible 'Joey' Smallwood, who had led and won the battle for union with the Dominion. The union brought Canada the completion of her 'natural boundaries', a piece of territory of great strategic importance, and some 325,000 excellent citizens. It brought Newfoundland more security than she could create for herself, and the benefit of the Canadian social services, the payments under which were a useful stimulus to the island economy.

Confederation with Newfoundland provided a final triumph for Mackenzie King, for, though he had retired before it was completed, the vital arrangements had been made under his administration and he had actively encouraged the project. At the same time it was a very auspicious beginning for the government of the new prime minister, Louis S. St. Laurent.

> He to the Commons' feet presents
> A Kingdom for his first year's rents.

The advent in 1948 of the Dominion's second French-Canadian prime minister seemed to encourage the hope that an era of good feeling might lie ahead. He was a very different person from King: a married man with a large family, of whom several had been in the services during the war. Unlike King, he enjoyed not only the respect but also the warm affection of many of his colleagues and subordinates. But he seemed to have many of his predecessor's political gifts, and in the general election of June 1949, as we have already said, he and his party won a victory unparalleled in Canadian history. The new Progressive Conservative leader, George Drew, a former premier of Ontario, was no more fortunate than John Bracken had been; his party got only 41 seats to the Liberals' 193, and 25 of the 41 were in Ontario. The Liberals remained what King had made them – the only party with a solid base in every region of Canada.

Mackenzie King died on July 22, 1950. Very few people, it would seem, had loved him; not many had even liked him; some had entertained an almost psychopathic hatred of him; but vast numbers had voted for him. He had some unpleasant characteristics; we know more about them now than we did when he was living. As a political strategist and tactician, however, he has perhaps no equal in Canadian annals. His greatest political achievement was doubtless the creation and maintenance of a genuinely national party. There were

Canadians – probably a good many of them – who were not partial to King but who nevertheless voted for him and his party simply because it *was* a national party and the only one in the field.

As a statesman, King left his mark on his country and his times, and for better or for worse the mark was deep. His zeal for national unity – a thing good in itself, but in the circumstances of the day particularly good for the Liberals and for King – may not have rendered the country more genuinely united than it had been before, but at least it helped to prevent an explosion that would have made things much worse. Above all, he had left Canada a more independent community than he had found her. How genuine national independence can be in a world cowering under the threat of the Bomb, or how far independence even deserves to be considered a good thing in a world that has suffered so much from the destructive power of nationalism, are questions for the philosopher rather than the historian. Perhaps the measure of King's achievement will be found in the use his country makes of the status which – with the powerful assistance of thousands of more ordinary Canadians wearing various colours of battledress – he did much to win for her.

10. The 1950s

WILLIAM KILBOURN

It was a time of prosperity and civil peace. On the surface at least, the structure of society and politics appeared to change little. The values and influence of a small self-perpetuating upper middle class held sway over French and English Canada. Labour dug in to consolidate its gains or cut its losses, after the militancy and violence of the forties in the auto and steel and asbestos industries. The power and leadership of big business was not seriously challenged. The universities were hotbeds of quietism. The Protestant churches, if one looks no deeper than the newspaper, appeared to spend a good deal of energy fighting their old enemy, drink, and some of their money at least on full-page ads against proposed new violations of the Protestant Sabbath. Perhaps most people were simply content to live in decent and comfortable obscurity, aspiring to an affluence almost within reach, and to think as little as possible about the searing experience of depression and global war they had lived through for twenty years and might momentarily be plunged into again.

In the realm of applied ideas, a thoroughgoing pragmatism held sway. One economist complained that the Gordon Report, for which most of Canada's best economic brains had been mobilized, contained no new philosophy of growth, not even a basic new approach to economic policy. In most spheres of government the predominance of the federal power and the secondary role of the provinces was widely taken for granted. The expanding federal civil service, now administering the welfare state introduced in the 1940s, continued to exhibit its customary professional skill and competence. Its life style remained that of the archetypal Ottawa man who 'did nothing by halves which could be done by quarters'. Politics was dominated by the spirit of Mackenzie King, who was indeed still alive in 1950. His two chosen successors followed him into the Liberal party leadership, and his self-appointed disciple from Prince Albert succeeded to the leadership of the Conservatives. The dominant political style of the age was either that of iron-bound dedication to adopted positions and principles, in the manner of C. D. Howe or George Drew (it was, after all, the age of Churchill and Dulles, Stalin and Pius XII), or else, more successfully, the style of firm avuncular blandness practised by St. Laurent, Eisenhower, and Macmillan. The most successful Canadian politician of the decade managed to combine something of both styles. If hyperbole may be permitted, it can be said that John Diefenbaker stood in general for morality and strong principles, like George Drew, and in particular for nothing, like Louis St. Laurent. Even his astonishing victory in 1958 may be partly attributed to a nostalgic popular yearning for a past that was already gone, or regarded as another manifestation of the Canadian custom of having only one national, governmental party at a time.

Yet if one looks closely there were already signs in the fifties of the political activism and new directions of the years that followed. The pace and scope of economic growth were so great that they were bound to create far-reaching changes in the structure of society and business. The economic élite of the 1960s were perceptibly different in background and outlook from their counterparts in the 1940s. The heads of the major industrial companies and of the banks and the railways were no longer so predominantly recruited from the topmost echelon of Canadian society. The new men of influence in the churches and the professions, the universities, and the senior civil service also appeared to come from a broader spectrum of society.

If such changes in the structure of social power and prestige came slowly, there were other kinds of change during the 1950s – in culture and technology and the man-made environment – that amounted to nothing less than a revolution. In 1950 Canadians lived in a world without tranquillizers and polio vaccine, jet travel and computers, super highways and shopping plazas, metro government and pedestrian malls. Several of Canada's vast new suburban municipalities still consisted in 1950 mostly of farms and bush, gravel roads and village stores. Cities like Kitimat and Schefferville in the northern wilderness had not even been conceived, let alone built. Television, stereo, transistors, beatniks, Sunday sports, Stratford, the Canada Council, and abstract art were not yet part of Canadian culture.

Names that were to become household words in Canada during the next decade or so – René Lévesque, 'Wacky' Bennett, K. C. Irving and Robert Stanfield, Pierre Berton, Harold Town, Nathan Cohen, and Marshall McLuhan – were in 1950 scarcely heard of or unknown. Jean Lesage was a young back-bencher in the House of Commons. Paul-Émile Léger was teaching theology in Rome. Such nineteenth-century giants as John Dewey and William Randolph Hearst, men who had profoundly influenced the lives of all English-speaking North Americans, were still alive. George Bernard Shaw was still being heard from; so was B. K. Sandwell. A dozen of the Privy Councillors appointed by Laurier and

Borden were living. T. T. Shields still thundered against French Canadian popery from his Jarvis Street pulpit, as if the fires of the Inquisition had but recently been lit; and for Jehovah's Witnesses and Roman Catholic liberals in Duplessis's Quebec, Dr. Shields was not entirely wide of the mark.

During 1950 the voices of Rawhide and his troupe of friends were becoming familiar to Canadians, much to the alarm of a prominent ecclesiastic and historian, who called their radio program 'a public avowal of irreligion that Godless Soviet Russia could hardly improve upon', and an M.P. who denounced the CBC for cluttering its airwaves with these 'ravings'. Other leading Canadians were more concerned that the CBC had begun to squander its money at the horrifying rate of $3,000 a week (about two per cent of what an opera on television cost in the sixties) on a new forced diet of culture for Canadians called CBC Wednesday Night.

At the turn of the half-century, in January 1950, a *Maclean's* Magazine article predicted that in the coming year the British Labour government would be re-elected with Sir Stafford Cripps telling people to eat less, that the French cabinet would reshuffle itself seven times, that the St. Lawrence Seaway project would be re-opened for discussion for a short time, only to be deferred once more, and that the Toronto subway would be two feet closer to completion. Canada's population, it went on, 'now about thirteen millions, would, owing to immigration, emigation, births, deaths and sheer exhaustion, increase to about thirteen millions'. The same article looked ahead over the next half-century to Monday, January 1, A.D. 2000, when, 'with the Toronto subway completed and the housing shortage finally solved, some politician, speaking by ultra-radio to the entire population of Canada (thanks to immigration, emigration, etc., now about thirteen millions) would affirm that "the twenty-first century belongs to Canada".'

The head of the Canadian state in 1950 was King George VI, represented in Ottawa by a British Governor General. Canada was a member of a United Nations with only about half the members it had admitted a decade and a half later, and of a Commonwealth dominated by Britain and the four white Dominions. Canada was taking the unprecedented step of sending troops to Europe in peace-time as part of its obligations under the new NATO alliance. But the idea of a Canadian presence in Korea or Viet Nam or the Gaza strip would have seemed at the very least improbable – as improbable as a Russian victory over the American space program, over Canadian hockey teams, or over the spirit of Joseph Stalin.

Obviously from the vantage-point of the 1960s, the physical and spiritual world that Canadians lived in a decade earlier could seem very remote indeed. Perhaps one final example will suffice to sum up the difference and suggest the pace and scope of change. Imagine a typical Canadian university as it was just after the Second World War veterans graduated and the temporary disruption and excitement they brought had passed. In the early fifties it was still a quiet liberal-arts college, perhaps run by the church, but in any case essentially the same place its founders had built at the turn of the century. The students all knew each other, and the subjects and courses they took were pretty much the same ones their parents had taken there before them.

By the mid sixties, however, the original Gothic halls were almost lost in a vast university city of glass and concrete. Several professional schools, a new art gallery, and the elegant polygon of a nuclear reactor now graced the campus. Honours courses were offered in subjects unheard of in 1950 or only mentioned in science fiction. The church had relinquished its control and handed over its university as a gift to the people of Canada, yet there were more courses in religion than ever before, now taught as an arts subject by professors of several faiths and of none. There were more Ph.D. candidates than there had once been freshmen, and it was quite possible for the average staff member not to know everybody in his own department. A young lecturer's starting salary had moved up from about $2,000 to $7,000, more than the president earned back in 1950.

The federal government began giving support to Canadian universities for the first time during the fifties, and the rising cost of universities (many of them newly founded), along with the even larger cost of expanding school systems, made education much the largest item in provincial budgets. By 1960 the universities were the very centre of an opulent urban society whose attitudes were being studied and programmed by social scientists and computers, and whose way of life was being altered beyond recognition by automation and electronics and a new industrial alchemy which seemed capable of turning any substance into anything else.

II

The raw statistics of that new society's growth in Canada are formidable. The gross national product doubled between 1950 and 1960 from eighteen to thirty-six billion dollars, and appeared certain to double again well before the 1960s were over. The difference is all the more impressive when one remembers that 1950 was regarded as a year of unparalleled prosperity, while Canadians were glad to see the last of 1960, the worst year of unemployment since the days of the great depression. The value of manufactures produced nearly doubled during the decade, and the value of services rose two and a half times over.

Among the primary industries, Canada maintained her position as producer of half of the world's newsprint, which was still her largest export, and by 1960 she was producing a billion and a half dollars' worth of pulp-and-paper products annually. The most important growing edge of the economy, however, was unquestionably in mining and oil. With the opening of new fields in Alberta, crude-petroleum production increased five times in volume during the decade. So did iron-ore production thanks to the development of vast deposits in Labrador and northern Quebec, with the remarkable result that Canada moved from the position of being a net importer in 1950 to that of one of the world's great iron exporters in 1960. Planning for Canada's first atomic-power station began in 1955, and a year later Canada had become a leading uranium producer, though in the total picture this development was perhaps relatively less important than the continued growth of such giant operations as those of the Aluminum Company of Canada and the International Nickel Company.

The sixty billion dollars' worth of new housing and other buildings constructed during the decade was more than double the total value of buildings put up during the quarter-century before 1950 and probably greater than the value of all the buildings put up since Confederation. The demand for building materials, as well as for such consumer goods as new kitchens and cars and television sets, led to vast new investment in the Canadian steel industry. Far from cutting back capacity and production, as it had been forced to do in the twenty years that followed the First World War, the steel industry achieved an amazing fivefold increase in the same period after the Second World War.

The one great exception to the unprecedented growth during the 1950s was in agriculture, which could still at the beginning of the decade be described as Canada's most important industry. The dollar value of agricultural production remained the same in 1960 as it had been in 1950 – 1.7 billion – and the number of Canadians employed on the farm actually declined. An increasing number of people during the decade were, relatively speaking, reduced to rural poverty, and there were Canadians outside the cities, many of them Indians, who survived on the edge of bare subsistence. Their problems were left to a later period to identify and solve. The fifties ended forever in Canada the predominance of the small mixed farm and the hired man who lived in, the plough horse, and the hand-stooked wheat in the fields, which were a familiar sight during the Second World War. Even so, the aggregate of farm production increased during the fifties. The bumper wheat crops of the earlier part of the decade ran over four times larger than those of the first great western wheat boom before the First War. Agriculture, like other industries, moved rapidly along the path of mechanization and automation. It was the great demand for farm implements, in fact, that provided one of the initial sparks of the post-war boom.

Such prosperity was not expected. The Great Depression of the thirties had never really ended but had rather been absorbed into the war effort. Few Canadians could escape the nagging fear that in peace-time it would inevitably return. There were many reasons why it did not. Keynesian fiscal and monetary policies, ignored or disdained during the early thirties, were now understood and accepted, however difficult they might be to put into effective practice. Such new sources of consumer purchasing-power as the old-age pension and the baby bonus were now available. The Central Mortgage and Housing Corporation made it possible for thousands of Canadians to become home owners for the first time. Consumer demand was sustained throughout the decade by a dramatic rise in the birth rate, which by 1955 was up to 27 per thousand, one of the highest rates in the world; and nearly a million and a half immigrants arrived in Canada during the 1950s. There was a better distribution of wealth: wages in manufacturing, for example, rose by about 75 per cent during the decade. Because the Second World War had been financed by taxation and people's war savings and because inflation had been kept rigidly in check by price control, there was far less dislocation in the post-war period than there had been after the First War. In spite of the great pressure caused by the rapid expansion of the fifties, the consumer price index was only 28 per cent higher in 1960 than it had been in 1949.

In spite of all this, there were times during the decade when it seemed that the prophets of doom might be right after all. The two brief recessions of 1948-9 and 1953-4 were each followed by periods of rapid expansion, but the economy experienced three sharper and longer setbacks between 1957 and early 1961. The growth of real per-capita income slowed down to less than two per cent. The numbers of unemployed during 1960 approached the level of 1939. The daily average number of shares traded on the Toronto Stock Exchange in

1960 was down to two million, compared to six million in the boom year of 1956. The flow of immigrants slackened off, but not the exodus of emigrants to the United States. By 1960 the total population of this second-largest country in the world was still only eighteen millions.

The improvised and unplanned character of much of the expansion that took place between 1949 and 1957, besides the very speed of it all, goes far towards explaining the period of painful readjustment that followed. Canadian investors tended to concentrate on the two extremes of investment in blue-chip stocks and bonds on the one hand, and gambling on volatile penny mining stocks on the other. Partly because of an unsuitable tax structure, they paid all too little attention to the intelligent use of risk capital in investment opportuni-ies between the two extremes. So, too, many Canadian manufacturers and labour leaders moved easily from a depression psychology to its opposite. Some assumed that almost anything they could make could be sold no matter what its price. They were encouraged further in this by shortages caused by the Korean war. By 1957 such easy proliferation of high-cost operation and inefficiency met its nemesis. European and Japanese industries were now fully recovered after the dislocation and destruction of the Second World War. They had the extra advantage, in competing with Canadians, of the high value of the Canadian dollar, now riding about 5 per cent above the American. This was all the more serious because the greatest Canadian expansion of the early fifties had taken place in the primary and export industries, which were the most vulnerable to change in the economic climate. However, once some of the inefficiencies had been shaken out of the economy by 1961, once demand had caught up with the vast investment in industrial capacity made during the middle fifties, and above all once the American economy recovered from its own less serious recession, Canadian economic growth resumed. From the perspective of 1966, looking back over what was already the longest single period of sustained and balanced growth in the whole of Canadian history, the economic troubles of the later fifties can be seen as those of readjustment rather than depression.

More than ever before, however, Canada's economic destiny since 1950 has become tied to that of the United States. In the decade before the Second World War, Britain had been Canada's best customer, but by 1956 the United States bought more than three times the amount of goods purchased by Britain in Canada and accounted for 60 per cent of all Canadian exports. From the United States came some 70 per cent of Canada's imports, reaching a high point of 4.1 billion dollars in 1956, which made Canada a better customer of the United States than the whole of Europe or Latin America. While there was a rise in the percentage of Canadian trade with Britain during the later part of the decade, the economic ties with Britain were by 1960 far more tenuous than they had been a decade before. The percentage of direct British investment in Canadian branch plants and subsidiaries declined from 20 per cent to 15 per cent of the total of all external direct investment. The five-per-cent difference was accounted for almost entirely by new European investors. The American percentage of direct investment remained steady at about 75 per cent throughout the decade, but its absolute increase in crucial areas was striking. Direct American investment in Canadian manufacturing plants, for example, went up from less than two to more than four and a half billion dollars, and half of Canada's manufacturing industry was American-controlled by 1960. In fact the sheer number of American subsidiary firms had reached such a point by 1965 that the giant privately owned Canadian company, Eaton's of Canada, was advised to drop the last part of its name, because the words 'of Canada' had now become interchangeable in the public mind with 'American branch plant'.

Many people regarded the growing integration of the Canadian and American economies in the post-war period as a big step towards the inevitable disappearance of Canadian independence. After all, it had been the east-west pattern of communication and transport which, ever since the fur trade shaped the political boundaries of the country, had fostered and maintained a separate national identity. The two most dramatic changes in transportation were the building of the St. Lawrence Seaway and the Trans-Canada gas and oil pipelines. The Seaway helped fulfil that age-old dream at the heart of Canadian history, the Empire of the St. Lawrence, by bringing major ocean shipping two thousand miles into the interior of the continent. The pipelines were heralded as a new version of the Canadian Pacific Railway, bridging the difficult passage between east and west across northern Ontario with government help, and so tying western resources to the markets of central Canada. Certainly the flow of oil and gas across the country pointed ahead to a day when pipelines would become perhaps the most important of all bulk carriers, moving not only gas and liquids but solids as well across the country. But both developments also linked Canada more closely than ever to the United States. The Seaway's most important single new cargo was Canadian iron ore brought from Labrador and northern Quebec to the heartland of the American steel industry south of Lakes Erie and Michigan. The Trans-Canada pipelines also opened up the possibility of the export of oil and natural gas to the United States and pointed ahead to another energy export, hydroelectric power, from two of the largest sources in the world, Labrador's Churchill Falls and the giant Columbia River.

Nevertheless the fifties did see certain developments which unequivocably strengthened Canada's traditional east-west pattern. The most important of these was the construction of a 4,000-mile microwave network by the Canadian Broadcasting Corporation, the longest in the world, and the establishment of national television service from coast to coast. The fifties saw a revolution in the technology of passenger travel. By 1960 the airlines were carrying five and a half million passengers annually, a number equal to almost a third of the country's population. And on April 1 of that year, the first jet aircraft went into service on the Toronto-Vancouver run, cutting to five hours what was still a three days' journey by train, and preparing the way for still larger volumes of passenger air travel during the sixties. If a community is made more viable by the face-to-face meeting of its leaders from hundreds of different scattered political, commercial, professional, and religious groups, then this giant, sprawling, divided nation received at last, in the second half of the twentieth century, the form of passenger travel suited to its size and nature.

Since airplanes cannot tow steel beams, however, and since giant trucks are inefficient long-distance carriers, the railway age, which had given birth to Canadian confederation, was far from over as the nation's second century began. Before the end of the decade the railways showed the first signs of emerging from the ailing and archaic condition in which they had languished for nearly two generations. They moved into a successful battle against an aging union's blind protest against automation – the firemen's strike of 1958. They purchased Canada's first industrial computer and put plans on the drawing-board for automatic freight yards to sort trains by electronic control panels. And they bought up transport companies in order to integrate trucks and piggyback into a unified system of transportation. By the end of the decade, the age of the steam locomotive was over and the last of the great 6000-class engines had gone to the scrap-yard or the museum. The Canadian National had redesigned its public image and was painting its new symbol on everything from box cars to dinnerware. There were even signs that it might soon begin to lure back passengers that had been lost to the automobile.

The automobile, of course, was one of the prime symbols and facts in the vast economic and social change of the mid century. It stood for the aspiration of everyone to a life of affluence and leisure, for private rights over public, for the dissolution of old communities and traditional values. It had also killed more Canadians by 1960 than had the Second World War, and its demand for space and pavement was a voracious consumer of provincial budgets and urban land.

Of all the decade's social change, however, the urban revolution and the new values and styles that came with it was probably the most significant. Canadians had slowly been turning into an urban people ever since 1867. But even as late as 1939 one Canadian worker in three was employed in agriculture, and the figure was still as high as one in four at the end of the Second World War. By 1960 it had dropped to one in eight. Over half the labour force was employed in the urban-oriented service industries, and the chief place of work for those who lived in the countryside was in the towns and cities. According to the 1961 census, two out of every three Canadians lived in urban areas. Most of the decade's new immigrants went not to the farms but to the cities. Canada's dozen largest metropolitan areas grew by half their former size in the short space of ten years. As dormitory suburbs grew round old cities many times larger than the original core, the down-town areas suffered from abuse and neglect, and local governments designed for a horse-and-buggy age were totally inadequate to the needs of the vast new conurbations. Canadians were made aware for the first time that their precious resources of land and air and water did not exist in unlimited abundance, that they were using their skies as vast garbage dumps, drinking sterilized sewage from their streams, and facing the day when their peach orchards and vineyards would go the way of the passenger pigeon to extinction. By the decade's end, thanks to the very gravity of the problems, a few promising signs of solution had already appeared: conservation authorities and the first forms of regional planning, down-town redevelopment, and better public transit, some of it underground, and the separation of pedestrian and cars. Some solutions, of course, such as the tearing down of old houses in favour of prisonlike new apartment blocks, were worse than the disease. Not only did much new building cost far more than rehabilitation of the old, but its bleak sameness produced a kind of soul-destroying mass accidie. Other solutions such as metropolitan government and large-scale amalgamation came just in time to prevent the total breakdown of municipal services.

Nowhere did the decade effect greater changes than in the

character of metropolitan Toronto. For the first time it became a cosmopolitan centre for the whole of English-speaking Canada. Toronto acquired the somewhat dubious distinction of being the fastest-growing big city in North America, in population, tax assessment, construction, and retail trade – almost anything you could name. Plans were laid for the construction of the world's widest multi-lane expressway, through what was recently the farming country of North York and what would be by the end of the sixties the geographical centre line of the metropolitan area. Specialists in business and professions that had scarcely existed before in Canada set up offices in Toronto. The city became one of the world's largest centres of television and radio production. Canadian trade publishing became a big business for the first time as publishers added dozens of new Canadian titles, including paperbacks, to their lists, where previously they had survived almost entirely on a diet of school texts and books imported from abroad. Canadian advertising agencies increased the dollar volume of their business three times over during the decade, and the quality and quantity of their design staffs many times more than that.

Toronto had once been a stronghold of the religion of Empire and the Orange Lodge and the W.C.T.U., but by 1961 less than half of the people of the central city were British in racial origin, and Roman Catholics outnumbered Protestants. Toronto became one of the world's large Italian communities. The post-war immigrants played an important part in transforming the parks and shops and supermarkets, the restaurants and coffee houses, and the downtown bohemian villages. One successful place displayed a sign that read, 'If you like home cooking, stay home.' Toronto became known as one of the best places on the continent for jazz groups and folk singers to make a living. That time in the 1940s when Torontonians who wanted a weekend of excitement and night life took off for Buffalo was a distant memory. 'Returning to Toronto', wrote a British visitor in 1959, 'was like finding a Jaguar parked in front of the Vicarage and the padre inside with a pitcher of vodka martinis reading *Lolita*.'

III

Canada experienced a revolution in the arts during the 1950s. The old indifference and neglect of the depression and the war years gave way to an atmosphere of excitement amid the wealth and leisure of the new decade. Metropolitan newspapers from coast to coast for the first time devoted extensive news coverage to the arts, and a few of them even began to employ a roster of serious critics. Richer patrons and more powerful pressure groups appeared to promote the cause of the arts and the condition of artists.

Perhaps the most important new generator of interest and creative friction was CBC television, which began in 1952. Not only the newest of the lively arts itself, and to some degree a creator of artistic sophistication in the mind of a large public, it provided employment for a great variety of people whose chief vocation still lay in one of the traditional arts. The apotheosis of cultural promotion came in the 1961 rally of the Canadian Conference of the Arts at which large numbers of artists, critics, patrons, academics, officials, and arts councillors, representing every type of art, craft, and locality in Canada, were stirred up together for three days at the O'Keefe Centre in Toronto.

Taking up a recommendation of the Massey Report of 1951, the Canada Council was created in 1957, and many municipal and provincial governments have followed this federal move with new and increased support for the arts. Although the Department of Transport's enlightened policy in the design and furnishing of its new airports was the exception rather than the rule, it did point ahead to various forms of discriminating governmental and business patronage during the 1960s. Even the universities began to take the role of patron more seriously during the fifties, as the separation between the academic world and creative artists began to disappear.

The new awareness of a crisis in North American education was graphically demonstrated when Sputnik and the Edsel, the rival symbols of East and West, were launched in the same month of 1957. But the need to train the senses and the imagination as well as the mind was one to which most educators were still blind. Even the Canada Council's funds were directed primarily to universities and scholars rather than to artists. Although it spent its budget of one million dollars a year for the arts with superb discrimination and noticeable effect, this amount was only a third of what one single European company, the Vienna State Opera, was receiving annually from its government, and one-fifth the amount that Canada's Department of National Defence was spending annually on military bands. (The latter, curiously enough, did help to subsidize art in a roundabout Canadian way, by supplying several local orchestras with good brass players they could not otherwise have afforded.) Few serious Canadian performers acquired an income-tax problem during the 1950s. No good creative writer made even a bare living out of his writing alone, and the best composers were lucky if royalties paid for the paper they used for their scores.

In 1950, Samuel Marchbanks (alias Robertson Davies) pointed up the plight of the Canadian theatre in a letter to an aspiring playwright, Apollo Fishhorn, Esq.,

> What is the Canadian playhouse? Nine times out of ten, Fishhorn, it is a school hall, smelling of chalk and kids, and decorated in the Early Concrete style. The stage is a small raised room at one end. And I mean room. If you step into the wings suddenly you will fracture your nose against the wall. . . . The lighting is designed to warm the stage but not to illuminate it. . . . Write your plays for such stages. Do not demand any procession of elephants, or dances by the maidens of the Caliph's harem. Keep away from sunsets and storms at sea. Place as many scenes as you can in cellars and kindred spots. And don't have more than three characters on the stage at one time, or the weakest of them is sure to be nudged into the audience.

Yet in 1960, just ten years later, one critic could complain that halls of exaggerated vastness were being built, while intimate productions – reviews, readings, repertory theatre, and chamber music – were what directors wanted to put on.

The new friends of the arts were accused of having an edifice complex, and certainly many enterprises seemed to benefit civic pride and the construction industry more than the artists themselves. Nevertheless, artists did reach new audiences during the fifties, in new theatres like those in Vancouver, Edmonton, Calgary, and Stratford, and some of the more complex art centres of the sixties such as those in Montreal and Charlottetown were already in the early planning stage. The climate for the performing arts had changed drastically during the decade, as had the quality of what was being produced.

Native professional theatre appeared in strength for the first time, replacing the American road companies and the amateurs who competed in the Dominion Drama Festival, which was no longer now the most significant training-ground for actors and audiences. The companies of Stratford, the Théâtre du Nouveau Monde, and the Manitoba Theatre Centre, to be followed later by repertory companies in Halifax and Vancouver, along with the tours of the Canadian Players and the National and Royal Winnipeg Ballets, and the various summer festivals, all generated new interest and high standards.

The opera school of the Royal Conservatory was training literally dozens of fine singers who were to find employment later in the opera houses of Europe, or in the short but excellent seasons put on by the Canadian Opera Company, although the appearance during the fifties of such superb musicians as Glenn Gould, Maureen Forrester, Lois Marshall, and Jon Vickers did underline the fact that Canadians were as yet better as interpreters than as creators of great work in the performing arts. In some fields, particularly film and television drama, Canadians usually had to go to London and New York if they were to reach the top of their profession. In film production, apart from the stimulus of television, there were no major new departures such as the forties saw in the flowering of the National Film Board and the genius of Norman McLaren, and the sixties in the long-overdue beginning of feature-film production in Canada.

The late 1940s may have marked an all-time low for the visual arts in Canada, particularly in design, from typography right through to the architecture of whole new environments. Painting, with the exception of the work of a few isolated veterans and newcomers, was in the doldrums. Canadians were still largely living off the spiritual capital of the Group of Seven, whose best work had been done by 1920. There was little encouragement for new directions from either private or public patrons. As the Massey Report pointed out, there was a staff of exactly four full-time professionals at the National Gallery, while by contrast the art museums of Toledo, Ohio, had twenty-six, and Worcester, Massachusetts, forty-three. Yet before the fifties were over, several dozen good new painters had appeared and were selling their work at new commercial galleries like the Isaacs in Toronto; the best of them were being exhibited at the world's major exhibitions and had indeed twice won the national group award at the Guggenheim International. The National Gallery had experienced a transformation at the hands of Alan Jarvis.

By the end of the fifties the design profession too had achieved new standards of excellence. The worst of the post-war insurance companies and housing subdivisions had been built, and the impact of a number of new architects of the calibre of Arthur Erickson, Robert Fairfield, and John C. Parkin was being felt upon the environment.

IV

Though she still lacked certain attributes of sovereign nationhood, both legally and psychologically, and though she possessed less than half of one per cent of the world's population, Canada nevertheless emerged from the war years and their immediate aftermath as the fourth most powerful nation on the earth. The nations of continental Europe, which had now suffered defeat and enemy occupation on both sides, still lay ravaged and exhausted from their ordeal. Japan and China had been fighting for a decade, and the long Chinese civil war only reached its real conclusion in the first week of 1950. Indonesia had just emerged from its war of independence against the Dutch, and India and Pakistan from the terrible blood-letting of their partition. The independence of the new nations of Africa lay in the future.

Beside the might of the two superpowers, the U.S. and the U.S.S.R., and that of Britain, whose war-time courage and sacrifice had given her status for the time being nearly equal to theirs, Canada's power seemed almost insignificant. But because she was not one of the great powers, and because she possessed the unique if unearned advantage of being a wealthy western nation without an imperial past, Canada had an important role to play as a presence in international disputes.

By 1950 Canada was in spirit, word, and deed thoroughly committed for the first time to an internationalist position in peace-time and to new and unfamiliar responsibilities in the world community. Mackenzie King himself had never quite been able to grow out of that slightly smug, slightly fearful attitude of North American isolationism with which he so well mirrored Canadian opinion for two decades between the great wars. King had delivered the *coup de grâce* both to the older, imperial form of Canadian internationalism, and to effective action by the potential new form, the League of Nations. But in the post-war era, King's French-Canadian external affairs minister and successor, Louis St. Laurent, allayed his fears, and spoke for a new Canada. Perhaps his first and most important act as Prime Minister was to answer the threat of the Cold War by committing Canada to the NATO alliance and to a new role in a strong Atlantic community. St. Laurent, in turn, gave complete support and great scope to his foreign minister, L. B. Pearson, who personally represented the new spirit of Canada's small but highly respected diplomatic corps. Pearson during the 1950s became the first Canadian politician well known abroad and the first to play a major role in world affairs. As the decade opened, Canada had just finished her first term on the United

Nations Security Council, to which she would be re-elected again in 1958, and in 1953 Pearson was elected president of the General Assembly.

It is fair to say that at the end of the forties the climate of Canadian opinion in respect to the great questions of war and peace was one of anxiety in a world of immobile positions and rigid attitudes. The Cold War had come early to Canada when Igor Gouzenko walked out of the Russian Embassy in Ottawa with enough documents to prove the existence of an elaborate Soviet spy ring against her allies.

The Stalinist *coup d'état* in Czechoslovakia in 1948 finally hardened North American opinion in the belief that a new military alliance with Europe was needed. In that year, 51 per cent of all Canadians, according to a Gallup Poll, believed that a third world war was coming and that it was coming soon. Mackenzie King in his last year in office acted as if he were one of them. Specifically, he was afraid that it was coming in Korea (a thing that seemed at that time most unlikely), and he threatened to resign if Canada's involvement in the U.N. commission on Korean elections was not withdrawn. It took a counter-threat of resignation by St. Laurent himself and a highly unorthodox appeal by Pearson through the Canadian ambassador in Washington to President Truman to persuade King to allow Canada to fulfil this U.N. responsibility.

King's fearful prophecy – the result, it turned out, of a conversation he had had with his late friend Franklin Roosevelt through a spiritualist medium in London – was not entirely wide of the mark. The Korean war broke out on June 25, 1950. Of the sixteen United Nations members whose forces went to South Korea to resist aggression, Canada's contribution was exceeded only by those of Britain and the United States. Canadian soldiers were not finally withdrawn from Korea until 1955. Canadian diplomats in Geneva and New Delhi contributed to the negotiations that led to Communist China's release of U.N. war prisoners. The outbreak of the Korean war in 1950 thus marks the beginning of a fundamental shift of interest and focus in

Canadian extra-continental foreign policy from an almost exclusive concern with Europe to one that included other parts of the world, particularly Asia. Canada's membership, with Poland and India, in the Indo-China Control Commission which emerged from the Geneva conference of 1954 was indicative of this new role in Asia. In spite of her refusal to recognize the new Peking regime because of the feelings of her principal ally, Canada maintained tenuous but significant contact with China. A Canadian cabinet minister, James Sinclair, had meetings in 1955 with Chinese leaders in Peking, and Canadian business and university leaders have been there regularly since. The *Globe and Mail* correspondent in the Chinese capital was the only North American newspaperman in Peking during the whole decade; he was followed by CBC reporters and film-makers in the sixties. The most important single Western hero and saint of the Chinese revolution, other than Karl Marx himself, was the Canadian doctor Norman Bethune. Trade negotiations led to the huge wheat contracts of the 1960s. It was clear enough that Canadian relations with China were one area of sharp if subdued difference between Ottawa and Washington, particularly from the time of Canada's plea for restraint during the dangerous confrontation between the two great powers over the offshore islands of Quemoy and Matsu in 1955.

Canada's new role in world affairs is particularly illustrated by her function in what was increasingly 'an Afro-Asian commonwealth of nations'. Canada went far towards making such a Commonwealth possible when at the end of the forties she persuaded Britain and Australia to accept the idea of a new kind of association that could include republics that owed no allegiance to the Queen, and this of course was to be the pattern for new members in the future. In 1950 Commonwealth members met at Colombo and a new foreign-aid scheme was born, by which Canada was to provide India with an atomic reactor among other things, Pakistan with the Warsak dam, and other Asian members with supplies and technical personnel. Although the per-capita Canadian contribution to all foreign aid lagged disturbingly behind that of Britain and the U.S., it did gradually increase during the fifties and sixties to one half of one per cent of the gross national product.

Canadian participation in Afro-Asian affairs was more that of a disinterested observer than it was in Europe. She did not, for example join the South-East Asia Treaty Organization, preferring to maintain a position like that of Nehru's India. This position proved to be valuable during the Suez crisis of 1956. It enabled Canada to initiate and mount support for the idea of a United Nations Emergency Force, and to supply both the commander and the largest military contribution once the force was formed.

Although Pearson was denounced by some Conservative anglophiles at home for siding with Nehru's India rather than with Britain in her hour of need, it was obvious that Canada emerged from the crisis, as did the United Nations, with the grudging or approving acceptance of all parties concerned.

Five years later when another crisis in Commonwealth relations arose, the Conservative Prime Minister was to go further than the Liberals earlier thought feasible or proper. John Diefenbaker sided with Indian and Afro-Asian members against Britain and Australia, and so determined South Africa's departure from the Commonwealth, and the potential rebirth of the Commonwealth as a true multiracial partnership. Even the declared intention of the new Conservative government to achieve closer relations with Britain by means of a shift of Canada's foreign trade away from the United States and back towards Britain failed to materialize during the later part of the decade. The Conservative foreign minister, Howard Green, however, did his best to pursue an increasingly independent foreign policy for Canada, and one that was more disliked in Washington than anything the Liberals had done. Although his and Canada's efforts may not have contributed directly to the atomic-test-ban treaty that was finally achieved in 1963, they did represent, in concert with the policies of many other nations, the real if intangible pressure of world opinion encouraging the two great powers to arrive at their agreement.

The years of Conservative power after 1957 saw a certain decline in Canada's relative influence in world affairs, for which the Conservative government cannot be held responsible. The change in her world position was, in fact, inevitable once the recovery of Europe was accomplished and the rise of the Asian nations had begun. Even Canada's ranking in 1962 (estimated by R. A. Sutherland of the Defence Research Board) as eighth or ninth among the world's military powers could lead Canadians to an exaggerated sense of their own importance. Canada's position as a middle power, however, pursuing an independent foreign policy within the limits of the Western alliance, remained significant and valuable. Without it her role in the Congo and Cyprus and her military and educational contribution in East Africa, particularly Tanzania, would have been impossible. It was not so much a matter of her physical strength *vis-à-vis* the great powers – a relatively small quantity can hardly be compared to something like the absolute – but rather a matter of function. There was a series of jobs to be done that no great power, especially one with an imperial past or present, could possibly perform.

The central problem and concern of Canada's foreign policy during the 1950s, however, remained that of her relationship with the United States. More than ever before Canada seemed in danger of losing her identity in the American cultural sphere of influence and becoming completely dependent on the United States for her economic well-being and military defence. Ever since the Japanese attack on Pearl Harbor in 1941 brought the United States into the war against the Axis powers, the defence of North America, from the Alaska Highway to the American base in Newfoundland, had been treated as a single problem. After the war, Canada became the chief frontier and buffer state, another potential Belgium, on the bomber and missile path between the United States and the Soviet Union. Early co-operation in schemes of northern air defence culminated in the signing of the agreement to build a series of radar stations across the Canadian Arctic, the Distant Early Warning Line, which was to be entirely paid for by the United States. With the DEW Line's completion in 1959, there were more American military personnel in the Canadian north than there were Canadian. The NORAD agreement for North American air defence was signed in 1958, after a joint command with an American in charge and a Canadian deputy had been set up in Colorado Springs the year before. The magnificent Avro Arrow, whose production was cancelled in 1958 before it could cost the nation half a billion dollars it could not afford, was the last Canadian attempt to develop a major weapon for the western alliance. After that the Canadian armed forces were almost completely dependent for the development of complex new weapons systems upon American industry and upon military research done by such bodies as the RAND Corporation. In return, Canadian factories were given a share as sub-contractors in joint Canadian-American defence production projects and, in effect, became an integral part of the American military establishment. None of this precluded an independent Canadian initiative at the United Nations or in any other situation of crucial concern to Canada, but did require the exercise of a mature blend of forbearance and firmness in relations with the United States of a kind rarely demanded or forthcoming from the Canadian public in the past.

There were, moreover, a number of areas in which the direct conflict of economic interest was inevitable. Canada was replaced as the world's leading wheat exporter by the United States, thanks to the American department of agriculture's support prices, while Canadian farmers saw their unsold surpluses growing larger and larger. American lobbies saw to it that imports of Canadian oil or any other commodity that seriously threatened American producers were severely restricted by means of tariffs and quotas. The problem of flood control on the Columbia River and the use of its vast hydro-electric potential was also an occasional source of friction, until some questionable Canadian compromises began to move negotiations towards final settlement in the treaty of 1964.

Potentially, American ownership of Canadian branch plants could lead to their use as an instrument of American foreign policy, although such actual cases as that in which the Ford Motor Company of Canada was prevented from participating in Canadian-Chinese trade may have been the exception rather than the rule. Growing Canadian trade with China and Cuba, at a time when American trade embargoes existed and American diplomatic recognition was withheld, were inevitably causes of friction. They were undertaken for the economic advantage of Canada and of two powers unfriendly to the United States, and they were the reflection of a pragmatic Canadian approach to politics and world affairs that differed sharply from that of the United States.

American attitudes and policies towards communism during the decade contributed further to difficulties already inherent in the situation. Canada's foreign minister (in company of course with several American leaders) was consistently described by the Chicago *Tribune* as a pinko and by North America's largest newspaper, the New York *Daily News*, as being soft on communism. At the height of Joseph McCarthy's reign of terror, in January 1954, two of his colleagues, Senators Jenner and McCarran, arrived in Canada for the purpose of questioning the former Russian Embassy clerk, Igor Gouzenko. Although the incident resulted from Gouzenko's own initiative, and the senators were required to operate not in their usual free-wheeling public manner but in closed session under Canadian rules, there was criticism in Canada that they should have been admitted at all. McCarthy soon passed from the scene, but American attitudes and practices which had made him possible did not. The staff of the Senate's permanent subcommittee on investigations indulged in repeated acts of public vilification which led in 1957 to the suicide of one of Canada's most respected public servants, Herbert Norman.

The appearance of the radical right in all its virulence

served to underline the fact that Canada, in spite of being a thoroughly North American society, was also a society with qualities quite different from that of the United States. These qualities, produced by a fundamentally different history, were rightly cherished by Canadians. But in addition to feeling a justifiable pride, Canadians also covered their own envy and sense of inadequacy, in the face of the real achievements of American democracy and economic progress and culture, by identifying things American with the worst of American television, with the infiltration of Mafia mobsters into Canada, and with the tactics of Teamster Union officials.

Towards the end of the decade and on into the sixties there was a growing public debate in Canada about ways and means of preventing Canada from being totally absorbed into the American sphere of influence. Pressure groups mounted campaigns to prevent Canada from acquiring nuclear arms, particularly the American Bomarc missile with nuclear warheads, or to have her opt out of the Western alliance in favour of a neutralist position. One influential journalist, Charles Lynch, proposed the donation of the Canadian armed forces to the United Nations. Another, James Minifie, wrote a best-seller which invited Canada to decide whether she wanted to be 'Peacemaker or Powder-monkey'. The Conservative government expressed an intention to reduce Canadian dependence on American imports, and the Liberals on their return to power in 1963 managed to outreach the Conservatives in experimenting to reduce American economic influence in Canada. Ways of taxing Canadian editions of American magazines were tried, withdrawn, explored by royal commission, and tried again. The overlords of Canadian radio and television, the Board of Broadcast Governors, required television stations to put on a schedule that was at least fifty-five per cent Canadian in content.

V

Canadian–American relations were inextricably bound up, as they so often had been in the past, with the central political issues of the 1950s and after. The period's greatest turnover in political power, the Diefenbaker victory of 1957, could hardly have taken place without strong feeling among some sections of the public that the Liberal government had been too willing to let American business shape the Canadian economy, to tolerate the excesses of McCarthyism where they affected Canada, to accept the foreign policy of John Foster Dulles, and to join the United States against Britain during the Suez crisis.

Except for a few months following the Diefenbaker victory of 1957, Parliament in the 1950s was dominated by a powerful government with a huge majority at its back. The landslide victories of the Liberals in 1949 and 1953, after which they outnumbered the official Opposition by 190 to 41 and 170 to 51 seats respectively, and the even more astonishing Conservative triumph of 1958 in which the tables were turned on the Liberals, by 208 seats to 49, led to further erosion of a parliamentary system that was already ill suited both to the structure of Canadian federalism and to the needs of the Canadian situation in the middle of the twentieth century. The role of the back-bench M.P. receded in importance, and there was little compensating committee work for him to do of the sort that helped the American congressman play such a powerful and effective part in the process of government.

The official Opposition, not only because of its numbers but because of the experience and calibre of its members, was hard put to look like an alternate government. The Opposition was further handicapped by the fact that it rarely represented more than one major section of the nation. In the Parliaments elected in 1949 and 1953, the Conservatives were largely an Ontario party, led by the old-fashioned Tory, George Drew of Toronto. In turn the Liberals in 1958 suffered the staggering loss of all their members from the four western provinces, and the majority of their former cabinet ministers and parliamentary assistants. They were in numbers predominantly a French-Canadian party, with no members from English-speaking constituencies outside Ontario and Newfoundland.

Elections had turned into something very close to plebiscites on the performance of the Cabinet and on the personality of the party leader. Canada, it seemed, only wanted one national party at a time, expressed in a powerful cabinet that represented a consensus of the different parts of the country. For purposes of government the Cabinet seemed more like the extension and superstructure of the federal civil service than of its party in Parliament. In fact, Mackenzie King and the Liberals had established a tradition whereby the public service was one of the main routes to position in the Cabinet. Another route was a distinguished career outside politics entirely, which was the way taken by the two dominant figures in the Liberal Cabinet of the fifties, Louis St. Laurent and C. D. Howe.

Louis St. Laurent seemed by 1957 almost more of a national president or reigning monarch than the head of a political party. His courtly presence and firm but subtle grip on power lent the office of prime minister a dignity and respect and nationwide acceptance of a sort it had never had before. His corporation lawyer's penetrating mind and pragmatic approach to the problems of government enabled English Canadians, particularly businessmen, to regard him as their country's leader and as one of themselves. For his own people his presence in office helped him heal wounds as old as the hanging of Louis Riel and the English rejection of Laurier in 1917, and to move French Canada out of its spiritual isolation. Though he was never a French-Canadian political leader, let alone a *chef*, in the manner of either Lapointe or Duplessis, his prime-ministership formed a useful period of transition between the old servility of the past and the mature, proud, but self-preoccupied nationalism of the future. St. Laurent helped English Canada too to grow out of the attitude of colonial dependence in which it had prolonged its adolescence. The decision to appoint the first Canadian Governor General was St. Laurent's, and it was fitting that the first amendment to the British North America Act made without reference to Westminster should have been introduced in Parliament by his government.

As the Liberal regime entered its third decade of continuous power in 1956, its failure to read the mood and temper of the times, its poverty in new ideas and men, and its assumption of a kind of administrative divine right grew too great even for a prosperous and complacent Canadian public. Ironically, the downfall of the St. Laurent government was prepared by the most powerful and effective minister who has ever served in a Canadian cabinet. After a successful career as university professor, engineer, and head of his own construction business, C. D. Howe had played the central role in managing Canada's economy during wartime and the difficult period of readjustment that followed. In the fifties he was general manager of the post-war boom. He still held some of the war-time powers he had been granted under the Defence Production Act, though their extension was limited as a result of Opposition protest in 1955. In 1956 he had set his heart on the construction of the world's longest natural-gas pipeline–his version of the C.P.R.–to unite the industry of the east with this vital new source of energy in Alberta. In order to build it to a tight schedule, he persuaded the Liberal Cabinet to put the necessary legislation through Parliament by means of a misuse of the rule of closure. The wild and bitter debate that followed brought Parliament to life again and firmly registered an impression of Liberal arrogance in the public mind that was to last for many years to come. (It was also, less happily, the precursor of obstructive abuse of their privileges by some members of the parliamentary opposition in the following decade.) The overthrow of such a competent and experienced government during boom times, however, seemed so little likely that Canada's national magazine could put its post-election issue to bed over a week before the election with a lead editorial on the tasks facing the new Liberal administration. Yet on June 10, 1957, the Conservative party gained a narrow plurality at the polls over the Liberals and in 1958 went on to the greatest triumph in Canadian parliamentary history. More than anything else this astonishing turn of events was due to the impact of one man whose style and temperament were suited to the occasion, and who knew how to make the most of them.

In replacing George Drew, who was forced to retire because of ill health in 1956 after years of devoted service in the wilderness, John Diefenbaker remade the Conservative party in his own image. It became a party of protest–against big business, big government, the intellectual establishment, and the status quo. Of neither British nor French stock, he was the first unhyphenated Canadian to be prime minister. He brought into politics the sort of people who had not been there before–a Chinese M.P., an Indian senator, a Ukrainian minister of labour, and from the biggest group of second-class citizens, the first woman to hold cabinet rank. The city of Hamilton was plastered with 'Martini for Diefenbaker' signs in 1958 for the election of the first Italian parliamentary secretary in Canadian history. Diefenbaker was also the first English-speaking leader to whom French Canada was to give its trust since Macdonald–an astounding 61 per cent of Quebec's vote in the 1958 election.

Diefenbaker was a genuine folk hero, a battler like Harry Truman, David assaulting Goliath, a vindicator of Parliament and people, the poor newsboy who talked to Sir Wilfrid Laurier early one morning in 1909 and knew then he would be prime minister some day. He was for the little man; he was the outsider, who had to survive nine defeats before he gained the success he always knew would be his. He failed to get elected mayor of Prince Albert; he was defeated four times in federal and provincial elections before he finally entered the House of Commons in 1940; and he was twice rejected by his party for the House leadership before they turned to him in 1956. 'The weird manic grandeur' of his

"Howdy Sheriff"

From *Toronto Daily Star Cartoons,* by Duncan Macpherson.

public manner, larger than life, was balanced by the warmth and humour, by the feeling for local tradition and the fundamental verities, by the earnest intimacy streaked with a talent for mockery, of his private conversation. As he said himself, his greatest sins were those of the heart; they were not cold or mortal ones and most people for a time were as willing for him to indulge them as he was.

The difficulty was that heartfelt feelings if they were to last had to be translated into thought and action. Strong slogans and nostalgia for the simpler days of Canada's rural childhood were no substitute for hard decisions, particularly during the difficulties of recession and unemployment which arrived at the beginning of Diefenbaker's term of office. He kept putting off decisions himself, yet he would not trust his colleagues, especially the stronger ones, to make decisions of their own. He kept testing the winds of public opinion for every breeze blowing in his favour. That egocentricity and mystic relation with the common man that had made him a leader blossomed into a consuming jealousy of rivals. 'Dear John' became 'Ivan the Terrible'. With an overwhelming majority behind him, he still acted as though he were Leader of the Opposition.

Though Diefenbaker ended the decade still in an apparently unbeatable position, his own shortcomings as a prime minister, underlined as they were by Canada's economic troubles, were taking their toll. In 1960, for the first time, public-opinion polls showed the Liberals ahead of the Conservatives in the projected percentage of the popular vote. The new Liberal leader, L. B. Pearson, who had never been completely identified with the old ways of King and Howe, succeeded after a shattering start in rebuilding his party and attracting a wide variety of uncommitted opinion to him. As a means of finding policies, his Kingston Conference in 1960 may possibly have been the idle, ivory-tower occupation for which it was mocked by the *Globe and Mail*. But as a political symbol to attract a variety of thoughtful Canadians and as the unintended instrument for finding workers and candidates for the next two elections, it was an unqualified success. The Nobel-Prize-winning diplomat began to look like the head of an alternative government; and the very thing for which he was most criticized, the failure to act like a professional politician, worked partially in his favour.

Canada's Fabian socialists, the C.C.F. party, had also been shattered by Diefenbaker's victory in 1958. The party lost its western agrarian base, and was reduced to a corporal's guard of members from the heavily unionized sections of British Columbia and Northern Ontario. This suggested the obvious move towards a closer link with the labour movement which was itself entering a new period in its history.

In 1956, following a similar move in the United States, the old conservative Trades and Labour Congress and the industrial-based Canadian Congress of Labour were merged in the Canadian Labour Congress under the presidency of Claude Jodoin. After the C.C.F.'s most effective parliamentarian, Stanley Knowles, was defeated in 1958, he was made C.L.C. vice-president and from this position he played a prominent role in preparing the way for the founding convention of what was to become the New Democratic Party. Although that party was only able to attract between ten and twenty per cent of the popular vote in the early sixties, at least it ensured the survival of the old C.C.F. in a new and more urban form. It also served as a reminder that the 1957-8 Parliament of minorities, which was the exception in the fifties, would prove to be the rule of the following decade, and it provided a new and vital role for what was often the most effective and valuable group of M.P.s in the House.

However, the most important of all secular trends in the political history of the 1950s was the increasing strength of the provinces and their governments, after the war-time and post-war period of centralization and increased federal power. New economic and social conditions required greater government activity in areas that had been defined by the courts and the B.N.A. Act as matters of provincial concern, in everything from education to highways to the social services. By the end of the decade the provincial civil services began to change from small second-rate organizations, often ridden with patronage, to the large and sophisticated operations that were needed. The increased provincial power of the sixties was forecast in Quebec's nationalism under Duplessis, even though it was disguised in an outmoded and semi-Fascist form, and in the new prosperity of Alberta and British Columbia, as they developed their mineral and forest resources.

The provinces also continued to play one of their traditional roles in Canadian history, that of providing an effective political opposition to the federal government. The first sign of revolt against the national Liberal monarchy came

"Dig You Later, Pops"

From *Toronto Daily Star Cartoons*, by Duncan Macpherson.

with the Conservative victory under Hugh John Flemming in the New Brunswick provincial elections of 1952, and this was followed by the victory of Robert Stanfield in Nova Scotia in 1956. The new pattern in British Columbia was established in 1952. Both the traditional parties there practically disappeared from the scene, and the contest from then on was between a right-wing, free-enterprise Social Credit party under Premier W. A. C. Bennett and a socialist party, the C.C.F., which had come within one seat in 1952 of being the new government. Again in 1960 it was within striking distance of victory in the first trial run for the forces that formed the New Democratic Party in 1961. By 1960 no fewer than five provincial Liberal governments had been thrown out and the only one left was that of Premier Joseph Smallwood of Newfoundland. In 1960 this same trend began to move against the federal Conservative party, with the Liberal victory of the young Acadian Louis Robichaud in New Brunswick. Thanks in part to the enterprise of the man whom Robichaud eventually had to oppose, K. C. Irving, New Brunswick had already begun to recover from the economic stagnation in which it had lain almost since the time of Confederation. Nova Scotia, too, under Premier Stanfield, developed a policy of attracting new industry. Foreign firms such as Volvo and Canadian companies such as Clairtone moved in to take advantage of planned industrial estates, tax concessions, and relatively low labour costs. In Newfoundland, Premier Smallwood had also used the instrument of the state to undertake various experiments in the development of provincial resources. But outstripping all these in its national significance, both for economic and for political change, came the triumph of the provincial Liberals over the old Duplessis machine in Quebec in 1960. The decade thus ended with the appearance of the most dynamic and revolutionary government ever to take power in Canada, and the beginning of a new chapter in the history of relations between the country's two founding peoples and cultures.

11. The 1960s

LAURIER L. LAPIERRE

Canada – to borrow Arthur Lower's words – is the 'substance of things hoped for'. And the things most hoped for in Canada often involve the reconciliation of irreconcilables: the ideals of the nation and *la nation*, of east and west, of federal and provincial claims; all within a framework complicated by size and lack of unity of purpose, economic disparity and social inequality. The 1960s were no exception to this general rule.

Indeed the attempt to make one whole out of the varied pieces of the Canadian mosaic seems to have been particularly taxing during this decade. This was no doubt due in part to the absence of dynamic national leadership and to the dislocation of power that necessarily followed. But above all, it was due to the re-emergence of a militant French-Canadian nationalism which has managed to turn the entire edifice of Confederation inside out. In fact, the shape of the sixties has been dictated by Quebec's *révolution tranquille,* the reactions it has generated, and the adjustments it has imposed on the rest of the country. For the first time in their history, perhaps, Canadians are being seriously asked to define themselves as a people and to evaluate Canada as their *patrie*. The sixties have proved their *crise de conscience*.

From January 1, 1960, to November 8, 1965, three federal elections and fifteen provincial elections took place.* Of these eighteen elections, nine were held before the expiration of the usual four-year term. In each of the elections held before the end of the traditional term of office, the need for a 'workable majority' was given as the primary reason. The provincial governments were more successful in this search than their federal counterpart. In fact, one of the dominant characteristics of Canadian political life in the sixties was the apparent bankruptcy of federal leadership. More and more, Canadians tended to view the federal government with suspicion and appeared to be unable to make up their minds about its role within Canadian society.

In many ways this feeling was understandable. By 1957, the gigantic task of transforming a war economy into one for peace-time had been accomplished. Canadians began to concentrate on the immediate necessities of their daily lives: education, social services, and security. Because the constitution and the courts have given the provinces prior responsibility in education and social security, and because provincial governments are closer to individual citizens than Ottawa, they were considered better instruments to fulfil these immediate needs than a distant federal government. This development coincided with the appearance on the provincial scene of a new breed of politician, more alert, dynamic, and

* This article has taken January 1966 as a terminal date. Since the end of 1965, Quebec (where Mr. Lesage was defeated by the Union Nationale), Prince Edward Island (where the government also changed hands), Manitoba, Newfoundland, and British Columbia also held elections.

in touch with popular feeling than those on the federal scene. In contrast, Ottawa was increasingly dominated by old men, a trend that has continued in spite of the promises of 1958 and the Diefenbaker era, and the discovery of the American New Frontier at the beginning of Mr. Pearson's regime.

In 1958, John G. Diefenbaker was re-elected with the largest majority ever recorded in the annals of Canadian political history (208 seats out of a House of 265). After the many decades of Liberal rule, which had ended in the pipeline debate and Black Friday, the Canadian people wholeheartedly placed their trust in Diefenbaker. They looked forward to the realization of a policy which he had enunciated on February 12, 1958: 'Sir John A. Macdonald ... opened the west. He saw Canada from East to West. I see a new Canada – *A Canada of the North*!'

Four years later, on June 18, 1962, a federal election left Diefenbaker with 118 seats, and a year later, April 8, 1963, another election further reduced his following in the House of Commons to 95 seats. Although the man himself was still to be a powerful presence on the political scene (to the surprise of almost everyone, except himself), the Diefenbaker era had ended.

Many reasons have been offered for Diefenbaker's demise. Many Canadians believe that his chronic indecision and his determination to make the Conservative party a personal instrument of power alienated the bulk of his followers. His handling of Canada's acquisition of nuclear war-heads serves as a good example.

By the commitments made by the Diefenbaker administration in 1957 (the establishment of the North American Defence Command and the new NATO role of 'strike and reconnaissance') Canada, it was generally admitted, had accepted a defence policy based on nuclear arms. By the beginning of 1963, $685 million had been spent on new planes, rocket installations such as the BOMARC sites in North Bay, Ontario, and La Macaza, Quebec, and other equipment designed to receive nuclear war-heads. However, the Diefenbaker government appeared incapable of making up its mind to purchase the war-heads. Cabinet ministers such as George Hees, Douglas Harkness, and Pierre Sévigny insisted on fulfilling Canada's nuclear commitment. However, Mr. Diefenbaker temporized. Finally on Monday, February 4, 1963, an exasperated Harkness resigned as Minister of Defence. George Hees and Pierre Sévigny followed, and soon the Conservative caucus was in open revolt.

In the House of Commons, Mr. Harkness explained the difference between himself and Mr. Diefenbaker:

> I differ from the Prime Minister in this way, that I believe we should have obtained nuclear warheads for our weapon carriers as soon as the latter were ready. I thought throughout that by remaining in the Cabinet I could better achieve this purpose than by taking the easier course of resigning. I resigned on a matter of principle. The point was finally reached when I considered that my honour and integrity required that I take this step. . . .

Diefenbaker had enunciated his own point of view a few weeks before. This was based on his assessment of the Kennedy-Macmillan talks in Nassau in December 1962. Diefenbaker insisted that it had become quite apparent that 'more and more the nuclear deterrent is becoming of such a nature that more nuclear arms will add nothing material to our defence'. For his part, Mr. Harkness believed that Canada's defence policy and her international agreements since 1957 made imperative the Canadian acquisition of nuclear war-heads as quickly as possible. This interpretation was essentially supported by General Norstad, the retired NATO Supreme Commander, in a press conference on January 2, 1963, and by the American government, which did not hesitate to issue press releases attacking the Diefenbaker position.

The government was not able to withstand the onslaught of Harkness's resignation and the palace revolution that followed. On February 6, 1963, Mr. Diefenbaker was defeated in the House. He asked for a dissolution and called for a general election on April 8, 1963.

The issue in this election essentially revolved around the

From *Toronto Daily Star Cartoons*, by Duncan Macpherson.

question of leadership and decision-making. Mr. Pearson, who had changed the nuclear policy of the Liberal party by insisting that Canada's international commitments demanded nuclear weapons, promised 'Sixty Days of Decision', and went on to attack the vaccillations and delays of the Diefenbaker administration. On polling-day, Canadians appeared unable to make up their own minds. Mr. Pearson's party obtained 129 seats, while the Conservatives elected 95, Social Credit 24, and the N.D.P. 17.

Most pundits agreed that John Diefenbaker had really defeated himself. His indecision over defence, the disappearance of the 'Vision of the North', his anti-American pronouncements, his inability – or unwillingness – to speak to and to understand French Canada: all of these contributed to *la déroute*. Peter Newman in his book *Renegade in Power*, published in 1963, explained:

> By the time he had been forced into the 1963 election, Diefenbaker's indecision and mismanagement had been publicly revealed by his inability to reach a sensible defence policy and by the disintegration of his cabinet. He had compromised so many convictions during six years of power that he no longer seemed to have any clear idea himself of the kind of future he was offering his followers. Sensing this, even some of his most loyal disciples began to regard him as a man to be cherished for his symbolic value, rather than for his capabilities as prime minister.

Very few were prepared to question this assessment.

If Diefenbaker contributed to the decline of federal prestige, Lester B. Pearson and his Liberal party have not emerged as the means to refloat federal fortunes. By June 1963, the famous 'Sixty Days of Decision' had become days of indecision and fumbling. The budget presented by the Minister of Finance, Walter Gordon, on June 13 proved to be the beginning of the Liberals' difficulties. Mr. Gordon, who in the 1950s had presided over an important royal commission on the economic prospects of Canada, was determined to revive Joseph Israel Tarte's conception of 'Le Canada pour les Canadiens'. His first budget withdrew many sales-tax exemptions and laid down measures to prevent the persistent American take-over of Canadian industries. Many viewed these policies as a curtailment of the expansion of the economy, and the business community cried for vengeance. The fact that Mr. Gordon had had the assistance of 'three special consultants who joined the Department of Finance on a temporary basis shortly after the government took office', all of whom had contributed to the drafting of the Liberal platform, added to the furor. In the face of the tumult, the Prime Minister, refusing to accept Mr. Gordon's resignation, decided to fight. The result was that on July 8 Mr. Gordon presented a new budget which seemed to pacify almost everybody but retained few of his original propositions.

During the following two years of his prime-ministership, Mr. Pearson's government went from one catastrophe to another. Two of his ministers were accused of having bought furniture on extremely generous credit terms. One of his ministers without portfolio had to resign after it was alleged that he had accepted a bribe of $10,000 to facilitate the obtaining of a racetrack permit for his constituency. And in the fall of 1964 it was divulged in the House of Commons that the Executive Assistant to the Minister of Citizenship and Immigration had offered a bribe of $20,000 to a Montreal lawyer to allow bail in the case of Lucien Rivard, a narcotic smuggler. A considerable sum of money was also to be deposited in the coffers of the Liberal party, and the Minister of Justice was accused of being delinquent in the pursuit of his duties since he failed to inform the Prime Minister and to refer the matter to his law officers. The Opposition saw the Rivard affair as an immense conspiracy, since most of the people involved were supporters of the Liberal party.

With characteristic indecision, the government did nothing until it was finally forced to name a royal commission of inquiry. In the summer of 1965, the Royal Commissioner, Chief Justice Frédéric Dorion of the Superior Court for the Province of Quebec, presented his report, in which he severely censured the Minister of Justice and insisted 'that there is certainly "prima facie" evidence of an offence under the Criminal Code'. Faced with such a rebuke, the Minister of Justice, Guy Favreau, resigned to become President of the Privy Council.

These scandals merely intensified the feeling of frustration that had been a part of federal politics for quite some time. They also seemed to have sapped the vitality of the Liberal party, with the result that many Liberals feared the outcome of a possible election. And to add to its problems, the Liberal government seemed unable to recover from the demise of its first budget, and the bitterness of the long and protracted debate on the new Canadian flag.

The early sixties saw the resurgence of two smaller political parties which added to the confusion in federal politics. The

"What Happened to My Strawberries?"

From *Toronto Daily Star Cartoons*, by Duncan Macpherson.

first was the New Party Movement, which ended in the creation of the New Democratic Party. Growing out of proposals made in the Winnipeg Declaration of 1958 which had attempted to re-direct labour politics, the party was officially founded between July 31 and August 4, 1961, after three years of active discussion. Its program, which rejected thoroughgoing socialism and nationalization, was dedicated to full employment, effective economic planning, a national investment board, job retraining and relocation, public and co-operative ownership of utilities and national resources, more effective control of the Canadian economy through the curtailment and supervision of foreign ownership, free education, and a national labour code. Its defence and foreign policies tended to support the United Nations and its various activities, and to reject NATO and NORAD since these military alliances depended on nuclear weapons, which the New Democratic Party rejected. On matters of national unity, the New Democratic Party went further than any other federal party, aside from the Créditistes, to adapt itself to Quebec's quiet revolution. It had no hesitation in accepting the theme of the two 'nations' and in adjusting its federal policies to meet Quebec's demands for greater autonomy. Although unsuccessful in Quebec, the New Democratic Party made impressive gains elsewhere in the various federal elections in the early years of the sixties. By the middle of the sixties, it had become a political force that could – in time – lead a movement to the left.

Social Credit was the phenomenon of the 1962 federal election. In that year the party, under the co-leadership of Robert Thompson and Réal Caouette, managed to win 30 seats, 26 of them in Quebec. Pundits have been at a loss to explain this development. In simplest terms, it may be stated that many French Canadians, disappointed in the failure of 'old' parties to cope with the plight of those living in areas where unemployment was rife and economic conditions poor, seized upon Réal Caouette's claim that they had nothing to lose and voted accordingly. In the 1963 election, although its strength was decreased by six seats in Quebec, it still remained a considerable force. Caouette, a fiery leader with an unusual knack of being able to communicate, managed to retain his popularity in spite of the attempts by the Liberals to ridicule him through the rhetoric of Yvon Dupuis and the economic lectures of Eric Kierans, then President of the Montreal Stock Exchange.

After the election, however, Mr. Caouette terminated his *entente* with Robert Thompson. He had accepted the Associate State theory for Quebec and had even courted separatist support during the elections. His views on foreign and defence policy resembled more those of the N.D.P. than those of Mr. Thompson, and it is an open secret that Mr. Thompson believes more in the spirit than in the letter of Social Credit economic policies, a heresy that Mr. Caouette cannot easily forgive. The party therefore split between the Social Credit party headed by Mr. Thompson, and the Créditistes, led by Mr. Caouette. In addition to the four parties represented in Parliament after the election of 1962, federal politics were now further confused by the vociferous presence of a fifth.

In the face of all these developments and weaknesses, it was relatively easy for the provincial leaders to assert their will and effect what has been called the 'processes of decentralization', or, to use a more colloquial phrase, 'the ganging up' of the provinces against Ottawa. Increasingly, the provinces – much more than the federal government – appeared the best vehicles for Canada's economic and social development.

In a way, the federal government itself assisted in this process of decentralization. The sixties confirmed a trend in this direction that had become apparent in the 1950s. Mr. Diefenbaker had done much to begin it, not only by the better financial terms he granted to the provinces, but also by his solution of the vexatious problem of grants to universities.

Although there had been much discussion over the years of federal assistance to education, the federal government had never embarked on what was essentially a by-passing of the provincial authorities through a system of direct subsidies to provincial institutions, scholars, and students. It was not until the beginning of the 1950s that the federal government created a system of federal grants to be paid directly to Canadian universities and colleges in order to assist them to meet their operating costs and capital investment. Propelled by the Report of the Royal Commission on National Development in the Arts, Letters and Sciences (the Massey Commission of 1951), the federal government provided for a per-capita subsidy of 50 cents in aid of university education. In 1957, this was raised to one dollar, and every province except Quebec availed itself of federal moneys. By 1960, the Canadian University Foundation, which had replaced the National Conference of Canadian Universities, held in trust some $25 million for Quebec.

To remedy this situation, the federal Minister of Finance proposed an amendment to the federal-provincial tax-sharing agreements to give an additional abatement of 1% in the rate of corporation tax in the province to any province that did not wish to accept federal grants to universities. Thus was the opting-out formula with full fiscal compensation introduced into Canada's already complex constitutional framework.

As the sixties progressed, the crisis within Canadian Confederation demanded some reassessment of the relations of Ottawa with the provincial governments. All the provinces asked for such a reassessment and every province participated in the process of decentralization. Provincial dissatisfaction with Ottawa was general over the questions of the Canada Pension Plan, Medicare, the development of health facilities, and the division of revenues.

However, the attention of Canadian public opinion was focused on the Province of Quebec, for only that province availed itself of the negative formula called 'opting out'. By this method any Canadian province may withdraw from a joint program (that is, a program conducted jointly by the federal and provincial governments) and receive its cash equivalent, to be spent within the province, without federal supervision. Since only Quebec has used the opting-out formula, and since Quebec has also declared its intention to withdraw from all the joint programs, the result has been that many mistakenly believe that the federal government is making important concessions to that province and that the French Canadians are dictating to the rest of the country. But because these joint programs arise out of concurrent jurisdiction, in truth no concessions are being made to Quebec. The impression created by the opting-out formula has certainly injured Canadian unity.

The Pearson government liked to use the phrase 'co-operative federalism' to describe federal-provincial relations. By co-operative federalism was understood a gentlemen's agreement that both levels of government would facilitate the other's task, would not attempt to force one level to accept the views of the other, and would undertake to have their legislative bodies pass the necessary legislation embodying the agreements reached at federal-provincial conferences. Over the years, this agreement has been severely tested. For example, at the March-April federal-provincial conference of 1964, two different communiqués were issued, one by Prime Minister Pearson in the name of the federal government and the nine English-speaking provinces, and one by Mr. Lesage in the name of the Province of Quebec. Although a solution was found, it met only the need of the moment. Co-operative federalism was not established on a sound and permanent basis. In January 1966 it was further placed in jeopardy by the provincial government of Quebec. Like the other Premiers of Canada, Mr. Lesage had originally agreed to the Fulton-Favreau Formula for amending the Canadian constitution and had accepted the responsibility of presenting the necessary resolutions in the legislature of his province. While the Premiers of the other provinces presented such resolutions and gained their endorsement (with difficulty in some cases), a re-evaluation of the Fulton-Favreau Formula was going on in Quebec. Many felt that the acceptance of the Fulton-Favreau Formula would mean in the long run placing the constitutional evolution of Quebec in a strait jacket. After months of indecision and vacillation, the Prime Minister of Quebec wrote to Mr. Pearson to withdraw his endorsement of the formula. The gentlemen's agreement which demanded that the provinces should adhere to collective agreements was broken. This was a heavy blow to 'co-operative federalism'.

In operation, that principle led to a considerable increase in the number of federal-provincial conferences held. So frequent were these conferences, so far-reaching their conclusions, and so disturbing the secrecy of the negotiations, that many wondered if the legislative responsibilities of this country had not passed from Parliament and the provincial legislatures to the conference. In fact, the conferences began to develop a quasi-constitutional status. Members of the elected bodies began to feel that they were required to pass almost automatically the decisions that had already been agreed on. The speed and secrecy that surrounded some of these meetings, the hurried plane trips at night, the last-minute summoning of assistants, fascinated some editorial writers, who predicted the eventual impotence of the legislatures and of Parliament. However, in spite of this, as the sixties continued, the elected legislative bodies not only survived but managed to initiate new social welfare measures.

II

The federal government – sometimes helped and at other times hindered by the provinces – laid down the foundation of significant social legislation. For instance, through the Agricultural Rehabilitation and Development Act (ARDA), the most important achievement of the Diefenbaker regime, the war on rural poverty, was begun in June 1961. Its basis was a general recognition that one of Canada's top priorities was to improve the economic opportunities and living standards of the country's rural areas. Through better land use, regrouping of farms, and the introduction of a more diversified economy, it was hoped that this goal would be attained. By 1970, the federal government will have spent close to $125,000,000 in co-operation with the provinces on this project.

Furthermore, the Conservative government passed the Technical and Vocational Assistance Act in 1960. This Act provides federal assistance for the building and equipping of vocational training facilities, the training of technicians, vocational teachers, and students in technological training programs, and the training or re-training of many categories of Canadian citizens. By the end of the fiscal year of 1964, the federal and provincial governments had accepted projects valued at more than $583,400,000 to provide 292 new schools and 159,417 new places for students.

For their part, the Liberals contributed the Canada Assistance Plan to help the provinces in the constant fight against misery and destitution, and following in the footsteps of the Conservatives they have encouraged the expansion of technical education and the mobility of the labour force. However, at the time this article was written, no legislation had as yet been presented on manpower development and allied services, though the federal government had begun to attack the problem through the moving and re-training of the unemployed and unskilled. Finally, with the official announcement in 1965 of a Canadian 'war on poverty' and the establishment of a Company of Young Canadians, Ottawa showed that it intended to launch a major offensive against the worst problems in Canadian society.

It was also in the sixties that Canadians acquired the beginning of a universal and portable pension plan to ensure dignity and security after retirement. On July 18, 1963, the then Minister of Health and Welfare, Miss Judy LaMarsh, introduced the pension measure in the House of Commons. The plan was to be entirely self-financing with the exception of the flat-rate pension of $65 a month ($75 by 1964) at the age of seventy. Employers and employees were to share the payment of the 2 per cent contribution to the first $4,000 of annual earnings. A procedure was established to calculate the eventual increases in wage standards.

Unfortunately, the plan was unacceptable to the two largest provinces, Ontario and Quebec. The provinces were well served in their arguments, since it was generally conceded that they had prior constitutional rights in matters of social welfare. The controversy became more acute and bitter as the months progressed, and it was not until April 1964 that a solution was finally found. By then, relations between Quebec and Ottawa had become so bad as to endanger the course of Confederation. Yet, by the end of 1964, almost every Canadian was assured of a more secure old age and of a fund of $4 billion which would become available within the space of ten years for various provincial developments. In order to meet Quebec's insistence that social welfare was a provincial responsibility, the Canada Pension Plan provided for the establishment of provincial pension plans with 'comparable benefits' to its own. Quebec is the only province so far to have made use of this formula, although there are some indications that Ontario may wish to do the same in some not too distant future.

During the early years of the sixties, medicare was also uppermost in everyone's mind, and it was hoped that by the time Canada celebrated its first centenary, a universal medical care plan would be in existence, although this now appears an unrealizable goal. However, the same problem over constitutional jurisdiction has already arisen, since many provinces have already established medical care programs of their own, while others have signified their intention of doing so.

Such legislative action suggests that at long last the era when social welfare meant government handouts to indigents and misfits has ended, and that a new era of social justice has begun. This new awareness is essentially due to the intensive growth of urbanization and industrialization since the end of the Second World War. The census of 1961 showed that almost 70 per cent of Canada's population lived in urban centres, while only 12 per cent of her population lived on farms or in rural areas of less than 1,000 population. In fact, 53 per cent of Canadians lived in or on the fringes of urban centres that had a population of 30,000 or more.

These developments increased the individual's feeling of insecurity. More and more the state became the only instrument capable of providing him with services that could minimize this vulnerability. There thus emerged a consensus that a democratic society must take the necessary steps to alleviate poverty, eradicate disease, and guarantee the equality of all its citizens by providing them with equal opportunities. There is no doubt that during the early sixties Canada made a considerable advance in the realization of that noble ideal.

III

After the débâcle in international relations of Diefenbaker's regime, a new feeling of international responsibility emerged when Lester B. Pearson took office. In fact, if in the fifties Canadians had taken a new interest in world affairs, in the sixties their views became more sophisticated and more independent of American pressures as they became more and more involved in international politics. The 'fireproof house' theory had indeed become obsolete. Much of the credit for this belongs to Mr. Pearson himself, for as Peyton V. Lyon remarked: 'The Prime Minister himself had more success dealing with world affairs than with Canadians.'

During the years after 1963, Canada continued its support of American involvement in Viet Nam, although the Canadian government and particularly Mr. Pearson advocated a quick and peaceful settlement. The Prime Minister even risked his good relations with Lyndon B. Johnson by suggesting, on American soil, important changes in the United States' policy towards Viet Nam and China. Mr. Pearson was no doubt encouraged by the fact that more and more Canadians were becoming disenchanted with the American position and Canada's tacit support of it. Protest marches, sit-ins, and demonstrations outside American consulates in Canada often expressed this Canadian dissent.

In other areas of international involvement Canada attempted to regain its former status as the disinterested middleman. Canadians kept up their peace-keeping missions in Kashmir, Indo-China, the Gaza strip, Cyprus, and the Congo, and also in the corridors of the U.N. and in NATO. At the U.N. the Canadian delegates continued their attempts to solve the financial impasse and to press for disarmament; while in Geneva they tried, with little success, to break the deadlock between the great powers. Disarmament also became a fashionable conference topic at private meetings of industrialists and professional groups, perhaps a further sign that Canadians in the sixties were more interested in the international scene.

In Commonwealth meetings Canadians were more successful in fulfilling their almost traditional role of middleman. Both Mr. Diefenbaker and Mr. Pearson tried to prevent the Commonwealth from dividing along racial lines over the issue of South African and Rhodesian racial policies, first in London in 1961, and then in Lagos in 1965. At Lagos, where the attempt to reconcile the cautious Britons and the militant Africans over Rhodesia seemed almost impossible, it was finally agreed to wait and see what effect the British policy of economic sanctions would have on the Smith regime. Later when Rhodesia cut off Zambia's oil supplies Canadian aircraft helped to fly in oil. Although Britain welcomed Canadian support, and even Canadian initiative, at these times, she was embarrassed by Canada's insistence on Commonwealth trade protection during the difficult talks preceding her attempts to enter the European Common Market in 1961-2. The growing and increasingly complex problems of the Commonwealth caused the Afro-Asian nations to propose the creation of a permanent secretariat. Canada's traditional opposition to such proposals was abandoned – perhaps yet another sign of a new approach to international affairs – and a senior Canadian diplomat, Arnold Smith, became the first Commonwealth Secretary-General.

As always Canada's relations with the United States were the most controversial and demanding area of international relations. Canadian-American relations, already strained by differences between President Johnson and the Prime Minister, were not improved by diverging attitudes towards France and General de Gaulle. Mr. Pearson and the Secretary for External Affairs, Paul Martin, were determined to resist any measures that might give the French grounds for pulling out of either NATO or the U.N. Canada remained sympathetic as de Gaulle attempted to return to France's traditional European policy of the balance of power even if it meant closer ties with Russia. For this reason the U.S. proposal that NATO acquire its own nuclear force received little support in Ottawa. Canadian policy towards South Viet Nam, France, Cuba, Russia, and the Congo was certainly influenced by her military agreements with the United States as well as by an instinctive sympathy for her most vital North American neighbour.

The extension of U.S. control over Canadian industry alarmed many Canadians, who complained that no other nation allowed another power so much influence and profit within its borders. Their concern was accentuated by the constant shifts in government policy as both Conservatives and Liberals at times favoured a large and growing U.S. investment in Canada and at other times criticized our economic dependence. This erratic behaviour was particularly apparent in the dismissal of James Coyne as Governor of the Bank of Canada during a quarrel with the government over his support of a nationalistic economic policy.

The sections of Walter Gordon's 1963 budget designed to limit U.S. control disappeared in an unprecedented barrage of criticism and dissension in the government, the House, and the press. Yet the government still enacted legislation to protect Canadian banks against foreign ownership and pointedly issued guide-lines to shape the behaviour of U.S. companies as good Canadian citizens. Wheat sales to Communist-bloc countries, particularly to Red China, ran counter to both the Canadian policy of not recognizing Peking and the wishes of the U.S. State Department. George Hees, as Minister of Trade and Commerce, exuberantly welcomed the possibility of an increase in Canadian sales to Cuba, leaving other members of the government to reassure an aroused Washington that the trade would not involve military equipment. Canada's exports to Cuba then declined in dollar value until 1964, when they rose again and at $60 million were almost as high as those to Venezuela. Far from appreciating the benefits of U.S. investments, it seemed that Canadians could not even make up their minds what they wanted from their own trade or from U.S. investment in Canada. To some it was a disaster, the sale of our birth-right. To others, equally qualified to judge, it was an unquestionable good.

The same ambivalence appeared in Canada's attitude towards the management of resources. The long negotiations with the United States on the use of the Columbia River resulted in the signing of a treaty that was quickly rejected by Premier Bennett of British Columbia. Ottawa and Victoria proved no easier to reconcile than Ottawa and Washington, and further negotiations were necessary before a solution agreeable to all parties could be found. The public's sudden awareness of their fundamental resources, highlighted by a growing knowledge of the effects of water and air pollution, produced instant disagreement over how to use these resources. Certain Americans referred to 'continental water resources', and Canadians replied that they had never before heard the Mesabi iron range or the Butte copper deposits described as 'continental'. Further advanced than Canada, and pressed for resources, especially water, Americans were impatient with Canadian ignorance of their problem and the benefits of a mutual solution. The emotionalism of the water resources discussion was a compound of ignorance, old quarrels over continentalism, and strongly nationalistic press reports. Here again, the Canadian ambivalence appeared. The possibility of a sale of Canadian water, highly hypothetical, provoked lively comment, while the existing ownership and exploitation of Canadian forest, iron, and oil resources by Americans was not seriously disputed by anyone. Even the critical negotiations over the auto parts agreement raised relatively little discussion. Yet this agreement, signed in 1965, provided, for the first time in North American history, virtually free trade in a single manufacturing industry. It was designed by the government as a major step in reducing Canada's balance-of-payments problem with the United States, and by 1966 it had already begun to function as expected, although it caused severe hardship to many Canadian auto workers. As Canadian wheat sales continued to increase, and as wheat prices began to rise, Canada's old imbalance-of-payments problem was lessened, if not actually solved.

By the end of their first century, Canadians expected more skilful and effective diplomacy than they had had in the past. While they had tolerated the wavering, often ineffectual idealism of the Diefenbaker era, they approved of Lester Pearson's more productive, if less high-minded, policies. By the mid sixties, although Canadians were still often troubled, if not divided, by the conflicting loyalties that had been so apparent during Suez and even the Cuban crisis, some identifiable 'policy' towards international relations was emerging. The trade and resources agreements, the peace-keeping missions, and the positions taken at NATO and at the U.N. – none of them really new approaches – were all part of this 'policy'. Gradually some Canadians came to think of their country as having a foreign policy, not merely isolated reactions to the problems of others. Essentially, although some Canadians tended to sound pretty pious about the benevolent role of their country in international forums, this policy was based on intelligent self-interest, as a realistic foreign policy inevitably must be.

IV

In the search for greater equality among the citizens of Canada, the provincial governments have had to provide strong leadership, since on their shoulders rests most of the responsibility. Yet, for the most part, provincial action has been limited to the expansion of already available services, in spite of a booming economy and a wave of popular enthusiasm for reform on which the provinces could have capitalized to reassess and adapt their welfare and educational services.

There were, of course, notable exceptions. In Newfoundland, the Premier established free university education with a living allowance for all university students. Newfoundland was thus a pioneer in recognizing an essential element in the battle for social equality. In New Brunswick the government of Louis Robichaud has undertaken long-overdue reforms. Fighting their own war on poverty, the people of New Brunswick have launched a threefold attack against the poverty and backwardness that have plagued their province for so long. Through a Youth Assistance Act and various educational reforms, through economic planning, and through a complete overhaul of municipal power and responsibility, the province can look to better days ahead.

And there was, of course, the Medical Care Act of the Province of Saskatchewan, making it the first province to provide complete medical insurance. Unfortunately, its beginnings were marred by a conflict between the government and the doctors, who objected in principle to a universal, state-operated medical care program on the grounds that such a scheme would disturb the sacred doctor-patient relationship and would transform them into civil servants. Having staffed emergency hospital services in 31 hospitals (out of 147) with some 240 doctors, between 400 and 500 physicians went on strike on July 1, 1962. After three anxious weeks during which the government saw to it that the irresponsibility of the doctors did not endanger human life, an agreement was reached with the medical profession which appears relatively satisfactory, at least sufficiently so for the Liberal Opposition, who opposed the legislation violently when it was passed, to leave it intact when they gained power a few years later.

Medicare appeared to be only one of the symptoms of the provinces' growing pains. In fact, provincial governments reflected more closely the needs and desires of the Canadian people. The growth of urbanization affects the provinces more than Ottawa, since they are primarily responsible for urban renewal, municipal affairs, and social security. Provincial expenses for most services surpassed federal expenditures, and many observers felt it not too far-fetched to suggest in the early sixties that unharnessed provincial economic power could well destroy the federal government's ability to direct the Canadian economy and to maintain a proper balance between the have and have-not provinces.

The danger of provincial exclusiveness – or a tendency to consider the part more important than the whole – is best demonstrated by the startling and disturbing 'renewal' that took place in the Province of Quebec. As was suggested above, the sixties have above all focused on the emergence of a new Quebec, and on Canada's adjustment to that fact. Quebec's 'renewal' was startling because it appeared to be so sudden. And it was disturbing because Quebec in the process of her reassessment put an end to many Canadian myths.

Yet, many conditions made Quebec's renewal in the sixties almost imperative. Since the Second World War, Quebec's population has increased by over 8 per cent and by the middle of the sixties more than four million of its citizens live in urban centres. One can easily imagine what this has meant in terms of industrialization and urbanization, expanded facilities and opportunities, and the conflict with older values. As Michael Oliver has remarked, Quebec's social revolution, greatly aided by the development of mass communications, especially television, has 'led to a transformation in the image of the good life and the good society which most French Canadians hold'. The old concept of a Quebec of large families grouped and protected by their parish has become untenable. The urban concept, with its mobility, more sophisticated services and opportunities, its broader vision, and the constant and needed intervention of the state, has replaced it, and French Canadians are now entering into the mainstream of North American society.

The seeds of this social revolution were planted in the 1950s. That they did not come to fruition until the sixties was essentially due to the presence of Quebec's benevolent despot, Maurice Duplessis, who governed the province with a firm hand from 1944 until his death in 1959. Duplessis's conservatism would not allow the transformation of structures and traditional institutions to meet the demands of the new era, and so the social revolution grew in the catacombs. No sooner had Duplessis died than his successor, Paul Sauvé, acknowledged its presence. When Jean Lesage came to power in 1960 on a platform of social reconstruction, Quebec was already prepared to receive his message.

If one looks for a simple way to explain what has been taking place in Quebec in the sixties, one can say that 'the days of Maria Chapdelaine are over'. Even in the sixties,

Canadians have been accustomed to consider the following passage from Louis Hémon's novel as the basic philosophy of Quebec:

> C'est pourquoi il faut rester dans la province où nos pères sont restés, et vivre comme ils ont vécu, pour obéir au commandement inexprimé qui s'est formé dans leurs coeurs, qui a passé dans les nôtres et que nous devrons transmettre à notre tour à de nombreux enfants: Au pays du Québec rien ne doit mourir et rien ne doit changer.

From this philosophy, the image of an agricultural, clerically controlled, monolithic, and politically unconcerned Quebec society emerged. Yet Quebec has changed, and is changing. A refusal to grasp this fact is an essential reason for what has become the 'crisis of Canadian national unity'.

Many people suggest that French Canadians are merely attempting to catch up with the rest of Canada. But what is going on in Quebec in the sixties is not 'catching up'. It is the collective effort of hundreds of thousands of individuals to reassess completely their individual and collective values, their institutions, their ways of thinking, their way of life, and even the relationship that binds them to their Creator. Such profound soul-searching means a massive program of adaptation, a careful assessment of priorities, and a constant effort to maintain the momentum of reform.

Since the government of Jean Lesage came to power in Quebec in June 1960, the province has been experiencing an upheaval, *la révolution tranquille.* The fundamental goals of this revolution are a radical reconstruction in education; the improvement of living standards, especially in rural areas; the creation of a viable economy in which public and private ownership can both flourish; a sharp break with the patronage-plagued political morality of the past; the development of a managerial class which is French-speaking and which takes its place in the business community of Canada and of the world; a complete re-appraisal of the relations between Church and State; the elaboration of a coherent social welfare program; increased assistance to those French-speaking Canadians who live beyond the borders of Quebec; the emergence of a new type of French-speaking politician in Ottawa (on whom rests most of the responsibility for creating a truly bilingual and bicultural Canada); the nourishing of French culture by closer association with the French-speaking community of the world; and ultimately the realization of the dream that French-speaking Canadians can play an equal role within Confederation.

Since 1960, much has been done to implement this program. Because education is at the root of Quebec's *révolution tranquille,* the first reforms were to begin to equip Quebec with an educational system based on the realities of the present. To change the obsolete system which had been conceived almost a century before and which was dedicated to the maintenance of a clerical and professional élite, the Lesage government appointed a royal commission to suggest extensive reforms. The task of the Parent Commission was to devise a way to move Quebec's educational system out of the nineteenth century and into the twenty-first, ignoring the fact that in education Quebec has really missed the twentieth century.

In 1963 the Commission presented its first report, which dealt with the administrative structure of the educational system in Quebec. The Commission recommended the creation of a Ministry of Education to govern and co-ordinate every aspect of education in the province. At the same time it advised the establishment of a Superior Council of Education, a non-confessional and bilingual body, to serve as the watchdog of the Ministry. The Council was to be aided in this task by a Catholic Committee, a Protestant Committee, and several commissions which would look into primary, secondary, and university education.

This first report met with severe opposition. Many of the privileged groups who had for years been free to manipulate the educational facilities of Quebec objected violently to this threat to their power. They managed to delay, and almost succeeded in preventing, the establishment of the new Ministry in spite of the support of many groups and the work of the then Minister of Youth (who was slated to become the first Minister of Education), Paul Gérin-Lajoie, who exhausted himself barnstorming the province in favour of the new Ministry. Although he succeeded in selling the people on the necessity of a Ministry of Education, Gérin-Lajoie was forced to compromise with the objections of the episcopacy, the Fédération des Collèges Classiques, and other groups (French and English) who opposed the whole idea. The result was that the legislation that created the new Ministry (the much publicized Bill 60) appeared to many to be a retreat on the part of the government, although the Minister's co-ordinating powers remained intact.

The Commission's second report, presented in 1965, dealt with the pedagogical structure of the educational system and a possible program of study. In 800 pages, the Commission made more than 300 recommendations on nursery schools and kindergartens, the duration of primary and secondary and university education, the novel idea of establishing institutes as a sort of midway point between high school and university, and a complete overhaul of all programs of study and curriculum with definite suggestions as to methods of teaching.

The government accepted most of the recommendations of the Commission and undertook to change the school system at every level. Quebec's public schools are still all either Catholic or Protestant, and those who do not belong to either of these two religious denominations simply have to find a place in one of the systems.* Nor did the Liberal government find a satisfactory solution to the presence of a privileged private-school system (*collèges classiques*), which has for years blocked the progress of public-school graduates into university. Unless solutions are found to these important problems, many doubt that the educational reforms now undertaken will have real influence.

The Lesage government also recognized that the key to

* Before its defeat in 1966 the Liberal government had not tackled the problem of confessionality, and the policy of the new Union Nationale government, while not yet clear, appears less favourable to change than that of the Liberals.

Quebec's future lies in its economic development. The vigorous program aimed at what René Lévesque called 'la reconquête de notre économie', will undoubtedly continue through the sixties. More and more Quebec universities are producing the economists, engineers, and other professionals needed in industrial administration – areas traditionally dominated by English-speaking Canadians – and the proposed reforms in the educational system will further increase the supply. New organizations such as the General Finance Corporation and the Quebec Council of Economic Reorientation are encouraging French Canadians, traditionally cautious with their money, to invest in the economic future of their province.

The process of 'economic emancipation' has also been carried out through the nationalization of the private power companies, the establishment of a steel complex largely owned and financed by the state, immense hydro-electric developments such as the one on the Manicouagan River, the creation of an Industrial Research Council, and the curtailment of the powers and privileges of private companies that exploit Quebec's natural resources. The population on the whole seems to agree with the government that only by such careful economic planning can French-speaking Canadians realize the Liberal slogan *maîtres chez nous,* and they appear determined that political and constitutional barriers will not stand in the way.

With the move of René Lévesque and Eric Kierans into the ministries of Social Welfare and Health in 1965, the province shifted some of its strength to the battle against social inequality. It is still too early to speak of specific legislation, but it appears that Quebec's antiquated social welfare structure fragmented by racial and religious divisions and dominated by out-dated concepts of what constitutes 'charity' will soon disappear.

Fully realizing that the French-speaking Canadians of North America want to be sustained by close cultural ties with the French-speaking community of the world, the Quebec government in 1965 signed a cultural *entente* with

France. This international agreement dealt largely with the exchange of professors, students, and educational experts, and the establishment of a joint Permanent Commission of Franco-Quebec Co-operation. Later another agreement was signed dealing with other cultural exchanges, and it is hoped that in time similar arrangements will be made with other French-speaking countries involving not only culture and education but also technical aid and economic and industrial co-operation.

During the sixties, organizations like the Institut Canadien des Affaires Publiques and the Mouvement Laïque de Langue Française, reviews like *Cité Libre*, *Parti-Pris*, and the Dominican *Maintenant* have greatly influenced the re-evaluation of Quebec's traditional institutions, especially the legacy of clerical paternalism. Often with great foresight, they have highlighted the need for revolutionary changes and today there are few French-speaking Canadians in Quebec who are willing to let any traditional institution or constitutional limitation interfere with their *révalorization*.

Because part of this *révolution tranquille* involved relations with the federal government or with the English-speaking community at so many points, it was only natural that French-speaking Quebeckers should reassess the links that bind them to an entity called Canada. And although most French Canadians would look upon a separation of Quebec from the rest of Canada as an extreme solution to their problem of *l'épanouissement du fait canadien-français* in North America, nevertheless there were few of them who would not agree with the sentiments expressed in Raymond Barbeau's *J'ai choisi l'indépendance* and Marcel Chaput's *Pourquoi je suis séparatiste*. These two books, written at the beginning of the 1960s demonstrated the deep dissatisfaction of the French-speaking Canadian population.

The foundation of this dissatisfaction lies in the fact that the six million French-speaking Canadians of Canada form *une nation*; they are a people who share a common heritage, speak the same language, have their own political and social institutions, live in a geographical unit that by the will of both English-speaking and French-speaking Canadians has become a sort of reserve for French-speaking Canadians, and above all, possess *un vouloir vivre collectif* – a will to live as a distinct people in North America.

V

The question then arises, can Confederation as established in 1867, or as possibly reformed by 1967, satisfy the legitimate ambitions and claims of the French-speaking Canadians? The over-all answer seems to be no. Economically the French Canadians still count for little. English-speaking Canadians and Americans exercise a decisive influence on the everyday existence and standard of living of the French-Canadian people. Furthermore, many have accused the federal government of using the immense economic powers granted to it by the British North America Act of 1867 for the benefit of the English-speaking majority at the expense of the French-speaking minority.

Although a great number of French Canadians share these sentiments, they constitute an oversimplification of the economic situation. A study of Quebec's economic development shows that it has also been hindered by geographical considerations, by the fact that its natural resources have only recently been considered valuable, and by the neglect of Quebec's politicians, who were for years cajoled or bribed into selling these resources for a song. It is also true that Quebec's educational system has not been geared to the modern industrial and technological age.

Socially many French-speaking Canadians feel that they are considered second-class citizens. They live in what a separatist has called a 'ghetto confédératif', with the federal government (that is *les Anglais*) offering only token gestures such as bilingual cheques and sermons on national unity. French Canadians see further demonstrations of this discrimination in the fact that they are expected to be bilingual while their English-speaking compatriots need not be. The fundamental criterion of whether a French Canadian is competent is whether he is bilingual. This is true even though Quebec is the world's largest French-speaking area outside of France and Montreal is the world's second-largest French-speaking city. In the face of what amounts to racial and/or linguistic discrimination, it is not surprising that many French Canadians doubt that Confederation can provide them with the atmosphere they need for complete *épanouissement*.

Many French Canadians also see Confederation as a threat to French Canada's cultural evolution. Radio, television, movies, billboards, and even textbooks impose cultural values that originate outside Quebec. Moreover, the French Canadian must earn his living by using not only the English language but also 'English' methods, approaches, and know-how. Many fear that the end result of this avalanche of foreign influence will be assimilation for the French-speaking Canadian.

Surrounded as it is on an English-speaking continent, Quebec has a problem of cultural development that should be faced not only by the French Canadians but by all Canadians – for their country is supposed to be a bilingual and bicultural one. Yet the cultural needs of the French linguistic minority have been largely overlooked ever since Confederation. In the eyes of many Quebeckers it is imperative for Quebec to step in where Ottawa has failed and to link the province to the French-speaking community of the world. Quebec, in the sixties, has become French Canada's international voice.

The established structure of the national political parties is another matter about which the French Canadians have been increasingly concerned in the sixties. Some feel that the only positive action French-speaking Canadians can perform in Ottawa is to delay the inevitable day when the majority will have its way. This interpretation of French-Canadian power in Ottawa is no doubt an oversimplification, since it refuses to recognize that, in the past, Quebec has not been well served by its politicians. Inept and in many instances the dupes and supporters of clerical control of Quebec's political life and that of other vested interests, French-Canadian federal leaders have wasted their time and the little talent they had.

Yet, French-Canadian politicians at Ottawa have had to contend with the fact that although Confederation acknowledged the dual nature of the Canadian heritage, it did not enforce the recognition of equality between the two cultures across Canada. French was abolished as an official language in the west; there were angry quarrels over separate schools for Roman Catholics (and by virtue of this for French Canadians) in New Brunswick, Ontario, and Manitoba, and in the newer provinces of Alberta and Saskatchewan; the Métis leader Louis Riel was hanged; Canadians quarrelled about troops for the Boer War and about conscription in the two world wars. In all these incidents the limitations of French-Canadian political power at the federal level was apparent. And the story was still the same even when the Prime Minister was himself a French Canadian. In the light of this experience, it is difficult to conclude that Confederation ever meant there was to be a French-speaking Canada parallel to an English-speaking Canada. It only permitted Quebec to be a province *pas comme les autres*. Today the refusal of the English-speaking provinces to make constitutional or administrative arrangements to meet the linguistic, cultural, and educational needs of their French-speaking populations suggests to many that the pattern of the past is to be continued. And this means that to the majority of English-speaking Canadians French Canada is to be understood only in terms of the Province of Quebec. If this is true, Quebec City and not Ottawa is and must remain the pivot of French-Canadian life.

This anxiety about Ottawa's role in the daily life of the French Canadians was amply demonstrated by the important divisions in the Quebec wing of the federal Liberal party which characterized that party during the 1960s. On the one hand there was a group of politicians, known as the Old Guard, who seemed to be quite content to carry out Quebec's traditional political role in Ottawa. This meant accepting as inevitable French-Canadian minority status, being satisfied with minor cabinet portfolios, plus one prestigious but often powerless position, and presenting their party as the best guardian of French-Canadian 'survival'. International, economic, or broad social questions did not concern the Old Guard particularly. They preferred to immerse themselves in the routine decisions of party politics and to supervise the distribution of patronage.

On the other hand, the New Guard, made up of dynamic and active young men, rejected this traditional concept of the French-Canadian role in Ottawa. They saw the French Canadians as equal partners in the federal sphere with a vital and real role to play in the administration of the affairs of the country. Equal partnership to them meant that Canada is the product of an association between those Canadians whose language of expression is English and those Canadians whose language of expression is French. In practical terms, as Maurice Sauvé has demonstrated, this meant an equal division of at least the important economic cabinet portfolios between French-speaking and English-speaking Canadians. This was not the case during any of the federal administrations that succeeded each other in the sixties. French-speaking Canadians continued to be excluded from those portfolios that traditionally have been associated with the greatest amount of influence and power.

To explain Ottawa's inability to draw the new type of Quebecker in any significant number, two reasons may be given. First, it would appear that the standards of competence applied to French-speaking Canadians are rather different from those applied to English-speaking Canadians. Many French-speaking Canadians are at a great disadvantage in Ottawa if their command of English is limited. On the other hand many English-speaking members and ministers have absolutely no knowledge of French, and yet they get ahead successfully in government. Secondly, the delay in making Ottawa a truly bilingual capital with adequate educational and cultural facilities for French Canadians has deterred many able French Canadians from moving there.

If French Canadians are being told, in effect, to stay in Quebec, can they be denied the right to transform their province into an autonomous country? Many have asked themselves this question, and some have answered with militant nationalism. On February 23, 1963, this nationalism exploded into terrorism for the first time. At first through the Réseau de Résistance and then through the Front de Libération Québécois, commonly called the F.L.Q., bombs were planted in radio stations, military establishments in Montreal, the R.C.M.P. barracks, the Legion Hall in St. Johns, Quebec, Montreal's central Post Office building, and ten mail-boxes in residential Westmount; attacks were made on several national monuments; F.L.Q. slogans were painted on prominent buildings and on the home of the Lieutenant-Governor in Quebec City; and an attempt was made to derail a train carrying the Prime Minister. The first victim of these terrorist activities was a sixty-five-year-old veteran, W. V. O'Neill, who was killed instantly on April 20, 1963. On May 17 of that year Sergeant Major Walter Leja was seriously and permanently injured while dismantling a bomb that had been placed in a Westmount mail-box.

The purpose of these terrorists, who were in time arrested and sent to jail, was to destroy what they saw as the symbols of colonial control, such as the Royal Canadian Mounted Police and the armed forces; to eliminate the English-speaking communications network; and to sabotage any commercial or industrial establishment that did not use French as its main language or practised discrimination against French-Canadian employees. French-Canadian collaborators were also to be attacked by the F.L.Q. Although there have been other bombings since 1963, no large-scale terrorist activity has taken place. The militant nationalists have been concentrating on demonstrations and marches.

The climax of this more pacific type of nationalism was apparently reached during the visit of Her Majesty Queen Elizabeth II to Quebec City in the fall of 1964. Expressions of anxiety about the Queen's safety made by Raymond Barbeau and Marcel Chaput, two discredited members of the separatist movement, were taken seriously in English-speaking Canada, with the result that some believed that the

Queen might be attacked in the old city of Champlain. The federal government, which unwisely insisted on the visit, took intense security precautions. In fact, Quebec became an armed camp for her visit. Terrifying riots marred the Queen's visit, largely caused by panicking Quebec Provincial Police. The Quebec population, fearful of the thousands of police, preferred to watch on their television sets the lonely rides of the Queen through the streets of the city lined with troops and yellow barricades.

Le samedi de la matraque, as October 10, 1964, is called, with its spectacle of charging police and swinging clubs in the midst of demonstrators, accentuated French-Canadian resentment against those responsible for the visit. As for English-speaking Canadians, served by a sensational press which presented to its horror-struck readers photos of riots and empty streets, many decided that this 'French-Canadian nonsense' had lasted long enough. The visit that was to be productive of so much 'national unity' became instead a national nightmare which six million French Canadians would not soon forget.

VI

In the face of the vast transformation of Quebec that has taken place since the beginning of the 1960s, and the varied incidents and frustration the *révolution tranquille* has caused, a reassessment of Canadian federalism became inevitable in this decade. Since 1960, many solutions have been suggested and many steps taken in order to effect such an adjustment. In order to recommend 'what steps should be taken to develop the Canadian Confederation on the basis of an equal partnership between the two founding races', the federal government appointed a Royal Commission on Bilingualism and Biculturalism on July 9, 1963. The Commission, made up of an equal number of French-speaking and English-speaking Canadians, spent over thirty months travelling across Canada ascertaining the views of every sector of the Canadian community. At the same time, the Commission carried out a vast research program on bilingualism and biculturalism, or cultural diversity, in Canada.

In its preliminary report issued on February 1, 1965, the Commission concluded that 'Canada, without being fully conscious of the fact, is passing through the greatest crisis in its history.' The Commissioners believed that the source of this crisis lay in Quebec, and that the crisis itself had arisen because for the first time since 1867 the French Canadians of Quebec were seriously questioning the constitutional and political arrangements made in that year. Unfortunately this recognition of a state of crisis was not endorsed by important elements within the English-speaking community. Many instead tended to view French Canada's dissatisfaction as the expression of a lunatic fringe, as an exercise in emotionalism, or as the opinion of pessimists and radicals.

And yet no one appeared able to find a solution to resolve the crisis. The formulae of co-operative federalism and federal-provincial conferences only seemed to intensify the dissatisfaction of the French Canadians and the frustration of the English-speaking Canadians. Many longed to find the answers to two questions: What could reconcile Quebec, and what constitutional formulae would best meet her needs? Many solutions were put forward, but at the time this article was written none had been adopted and the entire discussion had degenerated into wordy debate.

The first and most clear-cut solution has been separatism. The complete separation of Quebec from the rest of Canada is a feasible remedy, not only because of the dissatisfaction of many French Canadians, but also because since the Second World War less developed and poorer nations than Quebec have achieved independence. The majority of French Canadians are separatists at heart, finding solace in the thought of *un état canadien-français* where they could really be *chez nous*. But most view it as the last possible solution.

Another solution that has been suggested is the maintenance of the existing constitutional *status quo*, but with a greater emphasis on provincial autonomy. However, this solution was no longer acceptable in the sixties. To satisfy the economic and social demands of the French Canadians and to carry out the projects that have already been proposed by the provincial government, it has been necessary (and will continue to be necessary) for Quebec to encroach seriously on the powers of the central authority.

Realizing that Ottawa will not allow any usurpation of its prerogatives and responsibilities, the government of Quebec has begun to talk officially of a particular status for that province. Particular status means many things to many people. For some, it implies the transformation of Quebec from a province of Canada into an associate state in Canada. This would probably mean that all legislative, executive, and judicial power would be vested in the Province of Quebec. After having negotiated an international agreement, Quebec would then delegate certain fields of jurisdiction to the central authority (Ottawa) and provide the sums of money necessary to administer them. It would be difficult for these delegated powers to be exercised through a democratic Parliament, and thus Quebec would have to send delegates to a Central Council. Others tend to modify this extreme position and suggest that the federal government and Quebec should arrive at a definite division of power with full autonomy for each in carrying these out. In this context, Quebec could still elect representatives to a central Parliament and thus maintain the over-all benefits of Confederation.

In this way, also, Quebec would not lose the free-trade area and the attraction of foreign capital that Confederation provides. Moreover, no one would need to suffer from a dislocation of Quebec's economy or an exodus of English-speaking business from Quebec. In return for these constitutional arrangements, Quebec would forgo independence, co-operate fully in the projects of the central authority, maintain the bilingual character of the province, and guarantee the educational rights of the English-speaking minority.

The sixties, however, showed that the solution of associate state was unacceptable to the majority of English-speaking Canadians, since it would mean revolutionary constitutional changes. Furthermore, many felt that it would deprive Canada of the powerful centralized authority needed to maintain a proper equilibrium between the component parts of the country and to enact measures to equalize Canada's vast economic and social differences.

As the debate continued, it gradually became apparent that what most informed people understood by 'particular status' was a constitutional affirmation of the distinctness of Quebec. Because of its very generality and lack of definition, it is considered the most useful formula for Quebec. Already Quebec is not constitutionally *une province comme les autres*. It has among other differences a Legislative Council and its own civil law, and the affairs of its government are conducted in both languages. Any new Canadian constitution will have to emphasize this peculiar character of Quebec.

The constitutional recognition of Quebec's particular position within Confederation would no doubt put an end to the anxiety that Quebec's constant opting-out has generated among English-speaking Canadians. Such a document would also recognize that Quebec fulfils its role best within Confederation through the full use of its constitutional powers, that it must be in complete command of them, and that it can either delegate them or accept intervention only in times of national emergency. Then no one need worry about concessions to Quebec or the dictatorship of the French Canadians.

Hand in hand with this type of particular status there would have to be accepted two suggestions that were frequently made during the sixties. When the quarrel over Quebec's off-shore mineral rights occurred in the summer of 1965, Mr. Lesage rejected the federal government's offer that the Supreme Court of Canada should decide what level of government owns the right to exploit the wealth that may lie off the Canadian coastlines. Since, in his mind, the Supreme Court was the 'creature' of the federal government (which alone names its judges), it could not serve as the final court for constitutional questions. Consequently, he espoused the view that Canada should be provided with a constitutional tribunal made up of judges named by both the federal and the provincial governments. How this court would function has never been made very clear, but one can assume that it would become a sort of arbitration board.

The second suggestion recognizes that Quebec and the other provincial governments do not live in a vacuum. Governmental action at any level is bound to overlap and the provinces often cannot carry out their responsibilities without Ottawa's co-operation. For these reasons it was suggested many times during the sixties that the provinces should be officially consulted before the elaboration of the federal government's policies in many fields of jurisdiction. This idea has provoked no great trauma. It is already part of the Canadian way of doing things.

VII

Throughout the early sixties, French-speaking Canadians asked themselves if Confederation could continue to serve their purposes, while their English-speaking counterparts wondered what Quebec wanted. Unable to obtain satisfactory answers to either question, both groups were for the most part anxious about the direction in which the debate was leading them. Few Canadians, however, felt that the dialogue had lasted long enough or that the time had come to reach satisfactory conclusions.

So far none have been reached. A persistent sense of injury still permeates French-Canadian thinking on the subject, and exaggeration and distortion still accompany the *phrases ronflantes* of the most militant nationalists. Quebec politicians continue to reassess the agreements they have reached with English-speaking Canada and to insist that in certain areas they must retain exclusive jurisdiction. Many of their people are thus encouraged to view Quebec as an isolated spot in the universe and not as part of a universal order with varied cultural elements under one constitutional roof. In fact in the sixties one became aware that most of Quebec's spokesmen no longer had either the desire or the will to develop a close relationship with English-speaking Canada.

On the other hand, the majority of English-speaking Canada spent little time in the sixties trying to understand what equal partnership meant, let alone doing anything about it. Many, of course, sympathized with Quebec's aspirations to reform the province and its institutions. There was not much difficulty there, for many people outside Quebec felt that Quebec was 'catching up' with them. The trouble occurred when Quebec challenged Ottawa's traditional role in Canadian affairs and at the same time began to look seriously at the plight of those French-speaking citizens who lived outside the frontiers of the province. Few people in English-speaking Canada wanted to hear anything about particular status for Quebec, and fewer still seriously thought of changing their provincial constitutions to provide schools and other facilities for the French-speaking population of their province. Such changes were not even made in New Brunswick, where 49 per cent of the population is now French-speaking. In fact, in that province the population has also split along linguistic lines over the government's bold plans to fight poverty. In Saskatoon, French-Canadian parents organized a strike to force the Roman Catholic School Board of that city to grant a few hours during which the language of instruction would be French, but for the moment at least it has not been successful. Elsewhere the story was the same, although Ontario announced a sort of cultural exchange program with Quebec in 1966.

So popular was anti-Quebec feeling in western Canada that Mr. Diefenbaker did not hesitate during the election of 1965 to capitalize on it to recover his political fortune. One wonders also if Mr. Pearson's inability to obtain a majority in this same election was not due to an anti-French backlash as much as to his own failures of leadership.

Yet through the uproar of the bigots and the fears expressed by moderates, some sane voices were still heard in the sixties. There were some in Quebec who believed that French Canada could not limit itself to the banks of the St. Lawrence, for the glory of New France was that a few men had opened a continent and made possible a country stretching from sea to sea. There were also some in English-speaking Canada who worked tirelessly to convince their people that a Canada that did not take into account the duality of its heritage, and adjust to it, would not long endure.

In the early sixties Canadians gave themselves a flag which is their own, and prepared for a World's Fair which is a monument to their past and a promise of their future. In 1967 they will celebrate not only the beginning of a constitutional reality called Canada, but above all their willingness to live and build together. This will demand a degree of generosity of spirit that was often lacking in the first half of this most critical decade.

INDEX